Convents and Nuns
in Eighteenth-Century French
Politics and Culture

CONVENTS AND NUNS
IN EIGHTEENTH-CENTURY FRENCH
POLITICS AND CULTURE

Mita Choudhury

CORNELL UNIVERSITY PRESS
Ithaca and London

First published 2004 by Cornell University Press

Printed in the United States of America

Library of Congress Cataloging-in-Publication Data

Choudhury, Mita, 1964–
    Convents and nuns in eighteenth-century French politics and culture / Mita Choudhury.
        p. cm.
    Includes bibliographical references and index.
    ISBN 0-8014-4110-2 (hardcover : alk. paper)
    1. Monasticism and religious orders for women—France—History—18th century. 2. France—Church history—18th century. I. Title.
    BX4220.F8C485   2004
    271'.90044'09033—dc22
                2004005009

Cornell University Press strives to use environmentally responsible suppliers and materials to the fullest extent possible in the publishing of its books. Such materials include vegetable-based, low-VOC inks and acid-free papers that are recycled, totally chlorine-free, or partly composed of nonwood fibers. For further information, visit our website at www.cornellpress.cornell.edu.

Cloth printing   10 9 8 7 6 5 4 3 2 1

CONTENTS

ACKNOWLEDGMENTS

No undertaking of this nature could have been possible without the financial, intellectual, and moral support of various institutions and individuals. A fellowship from Northwestern University contributed to my research trip in France. Thanks to a summer grant from the National Endowment for the Humanities and the Edouard Morot-Sir fellowship from the Institut Français de Washington, I returned to Paris in 1998 and finished the research that enabled me to complete the book. The Research Committee at Vassar College provided generous funding for editing and illustrations.

The investigation of such a wide range of literature owes much to the patience of librarians and archivists. I would like to thank the staffs at the Bibliothèque Nationale de France, the Bibliothèque de l'Histoire de la Ville de Paris, the Bibliothèque de l'Arsenal, and the Archives Nationales. I am especially grateful to Valérie Guittienne-Mürger and Fabien Vandermarq as well as the late Odette Barenne of the Bibliothèque de Port-Royal. They went above and beyond my requests and provided me with access to a variety of treasures. In the United States, I received the assistance of librarians at Northwestern University, especially in Special Collections, the Newberry Library, and the Rare Book Room at Princeton University. I am indebted to the resourceful interlibrary loan staff of Vassar College for procuring a variety of materials difficult to obtain.

I could not have completed this project without the encouragement of a great many people. From the book's inception through its final stages, Sarah Maza has been the ideal mentor, generously sharing her time and her vast knowledge of eighteenth-century France. With humanity and humor, she has helped me evolve as a scholar, and her friendship has meant a great deal. Bernadette Fort and Tessie Liu engaged me intellectually, forcing me to think carefully about eighteenth-century literature and about the complex nature of gender analysis. For over a decade, Lynn Mollenauer and I have exchanged ideas about early modern France, and she has been a generous listener and reader. Special thanks goes to Sharmistha Roy Chowdhury, who graciously read the entire manuscript and provided excellent advice as a content editor. I would also like to extend my appreciation to Lloyd Kramer, Doris Bergen, and Michaela

Hönicke-Moore, who have been intellectual inspirations during my brief years at Chapel Hill and afterward. At different times and in different ways, they have taught me the importance of raising large and sometimes unanswerable questions.

Over the past several years, scholars in the field of French history have been important to the evolution of this book. There are no limits to the generosity of Thomas Kaiser, whose enthusiasm has sustained me since I was a graduate student; during my summers researching in Paris, I could count on him to listen intently to my findings and provide yet another possible source. I am grateful to him for reading an entire early draft and offering his incisive comments. Jeffrey Merrick and Jeffrey Ravel have read sizable portions of the manuscript and have been supportive of my efforts. I would also like to thank Elizabeth Rapley for her lengthy feedback on Jansenist nuns. Discussions with Dale Van Kley and David Bell greatly sharpened my thinking about Jansenism and eighteenth-century political culture. Over the years, conversations with Jennifer Jones, Janine Lanza, Sara Chapman, Leslie Tuttle, and Megan Armstrong provided food for thought at various points, and I am glad to have an opportunity to thank them. Comments on conference papers by James Collins, Alexander Sedgwick, Sarah Hanley, and Elaine Kruse further contributed to my thinking on nuns and eighteenth-century politics.

This project metamorphosed into a book at Vassar College, where I have found a dynamic intellectual community. One could not ask for more encouraging and enthusiastic colleagues than the denizens of Swift Hall. James Merrell and Nancy Bisaha weighed in with their valuable comments at a critical moment, while David Schalk provided unwavering support and insight. Lydia Murdoch patiently listened to my ideas over our weekly lunches, and she kindly read portions of the manuscript. I would like to thank the programs of Medieval Renaissance Studies and Women's Studies for giving me opportunities to present my work. At various stages, Karen Robertson listened and commented on aspects of the project. I am also deeply grateful to Laurie Nussdorfer at Wesleyan University for taking time from her leave to read my work with such great care and interest. Rebecca Edwards, Mark Seidl, Susan Zlotnick, Susan Hiner, and Lise Schreier have all been good friends and contributed to the fruition of this manuscript in different ways.

I would like to extend my thanks to the staff at Cornell University Press for helping bring this project to completion. John Ackerman's enthusiasm helped push the manuscript quickly through the pipeline. Catherine Rice showed much patience in shepherding me throughout. I am indebted to the anonymous readers whose extraordinarily careful and lengthy comments sharpened my thinking and added polish to the manuscript.

I owe even more gratitude to my family. There are no sufficient words to express my thanks to my parents, Suhas and Dolly Choudhury. Without their financial generosity and moral support, I could not have completed the book. Through their influence, I came to love learning and was exposed to the diversity of the world. Joe and Linda Schwartz were there at a critical point in the process; with care, humor, and good food, they enabled me to complete this project.

Cornell's acceptance of this manuscript coincided with the birth of my daughter Sophie Malika, who has opened up a new world full of endless delight. While I was holed up in my study, Sophie's laughter and chatter often reached me and were constant reminders of what is truly important. From her, I continue to learn the virtues of patience and serenity.

Of all those to whom I am indebted, one person stands above all others: my husband, John Reisbord. Since my first year as a graduate student at Northwestern, he has been my partner in all things. I have nothing but love and respect for his endless consideration and powerful intellect and for being a wonderful father. Without his insightful comments, his love, and his confidence in me, I could not have written this book. I dedicate this book to John with heartfelt thanks and admiration.

Convents and Nuns
in Eighteenth-Century French
Politics and Culture

INTRODUCTION

AT THE ONSET OF THE FRENCH REVOLUTION, THE FRENCH READING public was inundated by anticlerical pamphlets, many of which called for the abolition of convents and monasteries. Less interested in laying out concrete plans for such a venture than in scoring polemical points, pamphleteers launched an unrelenting tirade against monasticism and its nefarious impact on French society. In *De la nécessité de supprimer les monastères* an anonymous author took a respite from his diatribe against male monasteries—those "licentious retreats, known under the improper name of religious houses"—and turned his attention to "the impenetrable retreat of nuns." Unlike monks who preyed upon an unsuspecting laity, women religious were "innocent victims . . . made for the charm and happiness of man." They had been sacrificed to increase their brothers' inheritance and to prevent them from forming *mésalliances* by marrying for love as opposed to wealth and status. Their vows were not founded on any personal inclination for religious life but on "caprice and paternal despotism." The author exhorted the National Assembly to "deign to cast your eyes on female convents; those are the Bastilles one should fight; those are the prisoners that one should deliver." It was the responsibility of the National Assembly to reinstate nuns within the nation, to restore them to that universal right guaranteed by the Revolution—liberty, "the first and most gentle of the rights of man!"[1] The pamphlet's characterization of convents

and nuns carried with it all the vehemence and loathing associated with
Enlightenment anticlericalism, but the reference to the Bastille also revealed a political dimension to the critique of the convent. Moreover, this
rhetoric was not just the result of an imagination inflamed by the events of
the Revolution. The author drew from a rich reservoir of images and arguments made by eighteenth-century writers and their audiences, who
conceived of the female convent not just as a religious institution but as a
political one, emblematic of all the disorders associated with the larger
body politic.

In this book I investigate the place of convents and nuns within the
volatile political culture of eighteenth-century France. I examine the varied and often contradictory images associated with nuns between 1730
and 1794: nuns as victims, despots, intriguers, religious fanatics, saintly figures, and sexual creatures. Those outside of the cloister saw nuns as both
fearful and fantastical, powerless and powerful, virginal and debauched,
surveilled constantly yet nonetheless autonomous. In the public's imagination the nun was simultaneously the heroine of Jean La Harpe's 1770
play *Mélanie*, the promiscuous Sainte Nitouche from the 1745 erotic novel
Histoire de la tourière des carmélites, and the malevolent mother superior in
Denis Diderot's *La Religieuse.*

What was it about nuns that made them such a compelling and relevant
topic to the eighteenth-century reading public? For many modern readers, a preoccupation with nuns is mystifying. Twentieth-century Holly-
wood productions like *Sister Act* and wind-up toys labeled "Nun-zilla" illustrate how nuns today are symbols of the ridiculous and the irrelevant, out
of step with modern (let alone postmodern) morals and social relations.
While novels, plays, and pornography from the eighteenth century contained similar stock "nun" characters, these images had wider cultural and
political connotations. After all, women religious were not just creatures
of fantasy; they had very real ties to the core institutions of the body
politic, the clergy, the monarchy, and the family.[2] They were drawn from
across the social spectrum: from noble, bourgeois, and working families.
Even members of the royal family—such as the daughter of the duc d'Orléans, Marie-Adélaïde, and the daughter of Louis XV, Louise—took vows.
Although the cloister by definition denoted isolation from societies, convents, like the Abbaye-aux-Bois or Val-de-Grâce, were often located in
towns and cities. Moreover, women religious often fulfilled important social functions as teachers and caregivers. If asked, people of the eighteenth century would have probably have been able to differentiate between the contemplative Carmelites and the teaching Ursulines.
Nevertheless, the eighteenth-century public also maintained a general-
ized image of nuns. Neither Father Michel-Ange Marin, the author of *La
Parfaite Religieuse* and a venerator of women religious, nor the anonymous

author of the racy *Vie voluptueuse des capucins et nonnes* saw fine distinctions between the different religious orders. This complicated relationship with the outside world, defined by both the sacred and the sexual, made the nun a rich topic, ripe with symbolic potential in an early modern world that recognized neither the separation of church and state nor that of public and private. In that world, gender and religion, the defining qualities of the nun, also characterized the absolute monarchy, the central source of power in Old Regime France.

Over the course of the sixteenth and seventeenth centuries, the French monarchy had embraced the ideology of divine-right kingship, which justified its all-embracing authority as a sign of God's will, as a religious truth even when it was not a political reality.[3] All other authority, personal or private, derived its legitimacy from the monarchy and, therefore, could also be interpreted as divinely ordained.[4] Within this framework, a mutually dependent relationship developed between the early modern church and the monarchy, one in which "kings, lords, patrons and ecclesiastics . . . all represented themselves as fathers and as the representatives of God."[5] However, in the decades after Louis XIV's death in 1715, the sacred nature of the king's authority eroded as the church's own hold on French society weakened. During the eighteenth century, the crown, the parlements, and the clergy came to blows over Jansenism, an Augustinian movement within Catholicism. The explosive combination of these political battles, the doctrinal and institutional divisions within the church, and the church's loosening grip on the French population gradually undermined the church's preeminence in French society.[6] Such a decline was further compounded by the voices of Voltaire, Diderot, and other Enlightenment philosophes whose anticlerical harangues gained momentum and popularity over the course of the eighteenth century.

The monarchy's sacral image further suffered from the declining personal reputation of the monarchs as masculine figures. Whereas the various liaisons of Louis XIV (1643–1715) signified his virility, the amorous associations of Louis XV (1715–74) were interpreted by contemporaries as signs of a weak and self-indulgent character.[7] The personal life of the *Bien Aimé* spawned volumes of political pornography that attacked the social origins of his mistresses Madame de Pompadour and Madame du Barry, depicting them as monsters feeding off of the king's power and the country's coffers. A decade after Louis XV's death, Marie-Antoinette, queen of Louis XVI, became the target of similar calumny once reserved for Louis XV and his courtesans.[8] The perceived power of royal mistresses and an Austrian queen, as well as the influence of Enlightenment *salonnières* and actresses, troubled many eighteenth-century commentators, who argued that the presence of women in public, particularly within the realm of politics, had an emasculating impact. Social commentary and political pornography presented the public with images of gender confusion at the top. Women had become manly and men feminine, signifying a destabilized state governed by an inadequate patriarchal power.[9]

In this political and cultural climate where the religious and gendered pillars of patriarchal authority had begun to crack perceptibly, the representations of nuns assumed power and urgency. Between 1730 and 1789, lawyers, religious pamphleteers, and men of letters used women religious and the convent to oppose political, religious, and social authority on a variety of fronts. The theologian Jean-Baptiste Gaultier made a career of denouncing the Jesuits and other orthodox clergy by defending Jansenist nuns. Similarly, the dramatist Baculard d'Arnaud, author of numerous weepy *drames bourgeois*, used the story of the *vocation forcée*, or forced vow, to denounce authoritarian parents who had coerced unwilling daughters into the cloister. And despite their subordinate position, women religious confounded expectations because they did not always accept their fate passively, choosing instead to antagonize the very powers that supported them. In 1748 the confessor at the priory of Torcy informed the sisters that the archbishop of Paris had ordered their disbandment. According to the Jansenist *Nouvelles ecclésiastiques* the nuns of Torcy vehemently responded that "they neither could nor would accept [this order]," and would "would never consent to the destruction of the monastery."[10] At the same time, their cloistered status and their position as women meant that nuns often had to channel their voices through mediators such as lawyers and men of letters who used the convent to advance their own agendas in writings ranging from political pamphlets to private letters, from legal briefs to novels, and from Enlightenment pedagogical treatises to pornography. These sources chronicled the conflicts between nuns, between nuns and the male clergy, and between nuns and their families. Out of the vast array of discussions and representations of convents and nuns, certain themes came to the surface, such as despotism, citizenship, female education, and sexuality.

For almost all the participants in these debates, anxieties about disorderly women and feminized men served as the link connecting the convent to larger political and social concerns. In the Jansenist controversies of the 1750s ultramontane bishops regarded Jansenist nuns as infected by heresy, a disorder often associated with women in the early modern period. In turn, Jansenist theologians and lawyers demonized these prelates, such as Poncet de la Rivière bishop of Troyes, as despots who used their authority in "feminine" ways, willfully and capriciously. Such charges also extended to mother superiors like Madame de Rossignol, prioress of Bon Secours, who admitted a novice in 1759 despite the majority of votes rejecting the candidate.[11] These attacks on mother superiors were compounded by accusations of being aristocratic. Such charges placed superiors in the same category as aristocratic women who were harshly denounced for abandoning their homes to pursue luxury and power. From the 1760s onward, *gens de lettres* further criticized these women by positing an ideal of affective and biological motherhood. They also called into question religious vows of celibacy. All nuns appeared as deviant women unable to fulfill their "natural" vocation as wives and mothers. But no matter how writers characterized feminine disorderliness, they all believed that the solution to the problem lay in the intervention of a legitimate and *masculine* authority figure, whether it was a magistrate, a lawyer, or a husband.

Between 1730 and 1770 these gendered anxieties all converged on the same fundamental question: Who should control the female convent and women religious? This basic query yielded subsidiary questions regarding authority. What limits were there, if any, on the authority of bishops and mother superiors over convents? Were church elites bound by institutional constitutions, and what recourse did nuns have if they believed such constitutions had been violated? Did nuns have rights as French citizens that superseded their vows of obedience? The pressing nature of these questions became apparent in conflicts such as those involving the Commission de Secours, a royal agency created in 1727 to assist the numerous convents suffering from John Law's failed fiscal reforms. The Commission simultaneously represented the interests of these communities, the crown, and private families whose daughters and sisters resided in those communities: "Because families have a great interest that persons engaged in the religious profession do not return to their charge, this is the justification for a public policy to assist poor monasteries by uniting them with those that are comfortable, or by suppressing them gradually by prohibiting them from receiving novices."[12] This statement exposed the overlapping nature of authority in the Old Regime and the blurred divisions between public and private. Thus, a straightforward question of administration and regulation could lead to conflicts between nuns and other institutions and among the institutions themselves. In 1745 the nuns from the Abbey of Malnoue defied the king and their superior Madame de Rossignol by opposing efforts to unite their community with the priory of Bon Secours. Their lawyers argued that each nun had the right to vote on this decision.[13] In such cases, all participants employed images and accusations of female disorder in their efforts to win support for their positions.

As I will argue, such debates over the convent underwent a significant transition during the eighteenth century. Beginning in the 1760s, the question of who would control the convent shifted to larger issues concerning the purpose and utility of the convent. Unlike lawyers and magistrates who praised nuns as the personification of virtuous Christian women, *gens de lettres* evaluated nuns according to more secular norms in which the moral woman was the "natural" woman devoted to being a wife and mother. These conclusions were derived from a more systemic interpretation that focused on the convent's structure and not specific individuals. Furthermore, the questions about authority within the convent became increasingly irrelevant to men and women of letters who viewed nuns as both victims of the cloister and perpetrators of its pernicious influence. The convent then had no purpose in society, except as a reminder of the problems inherent in the Old Regime. Worse than that, the convent turned potentially productive and useful citizens into disorderly women, an obstacle to the creation of a strong, rational, masculine social and political order.

Within these different perceptions of the convent's function and powers, the cloister became a symbol of despotism, the equivalent of the Sultan's seraglio or the King's Bastille. All three, the convent, the seraglio, and the Bastille, were hidden spaces, prisons whose shadows protected the powerful while leaving its victims entirely defenseless. The seraglio was an imaginary world where the inhabitants were tangled in a web of eroticism and power which, as Montesquieu's *Persian Letters* demonstrated, continually threatened to destabilize the body politic. The Bastille represented the more reprehensible practices of the state, a place where critics like Voltaire were summarily incarcerated; families also had unruly individuals sequestered in the Bastille. The convent fused the attributes associated with both. Like the seraglio, the convent was a highly charged erotic space, one where the oversexed and the impotent coexisted in an uneasy fashion, ready to explode at the slightest provocation. And like the Bastille, the convent served as a dumping ground for the state and the family to dispense with undesirable individuals whose presence jeopardized social order.

I would argue, however, that the convent and the nun were more compelling metaphors for tyranny and social disorder than either the seraglio or the Bastille. Both the seraglio and the Bastille were fluid symbols, changing as French political culture itself transformed. Nonetheless, the seraglio was a fictional construct, a reified "other." And, although very real, the Bastille remained static, a prison of the Old Regime. But the convent was an institution whose internal makeup and place in the larger society continued to evolve. Over the course of the eighteenth century, administrators, such as those who headed the Commission des Secours or the Commission des Réguliers, tackled issues of reform pertaining to finances or to the age at which novices took their vows. Moreover, as the eighteenth-century debates on female education and lengthy treatises like the *Moyen de rendre nos religieuses utiles* demonstrate, some men and women of letters envisioned a convent adapting to a more secular vision of society. Throughout this period, the convent's inhabitants continually made their presence felt as religious dissenters, litigants, educators, and nurses. Thus, the special symbolic resonance of the convent lay in the relationship between the institution's own changing structure and purpose and the seismic political and cultural shifts taking place in eighteenth-century France.

༺ ༺ ༺

In arguing that convents and nuns were powerful political symbols as well as participants in the turbulent politics of this period, I am building on the recent trend in French historiography that places political culture at the center of inquiry into the Old Regime and the French Revolution.[14] This research has resulted in a dramatic reconstitution of the political. In Lisa Graham's words, "the political . . . [has] expanded to encompass cultural practices, social configurations, forms of representation and communication, as well as theoretical forays into gender studies and cultural criticism."[15] As a result, the world of theater, art, and festivals has offered insights to historians, proving how various cultural forms, both high and low, were invested with political meaning. These findings have broadened awareness of the ways in which elites and non-elites absorbed and appropriated ideas such as sovereignty, citizenship, and sociability.[16] Many of these studies have returned agency to individuals and communities who, although removed from positions of authority, nonetheless formulated their political concerns in dynamic ways.[17] A cultural history of women religious demonstrates how different writers of the Old Regime integrated disparate assumptions regarding convents and nuns into their political thought and expression, turning them into vehicles for scrutinizing and challenging the Old Regime.

My exploration of the multiple representations of nuns is indebted to two pathbreaking insights that have rejuvenated the political history of the Old Regime, namely, that oppositional politics had a strong religious foundation and that political rhetoric and thought were gendered. During the last two decades, Dale Van Kley and other scholars have shown how religious conflicts surrounding Jansenism played a critical role in the erosion of Bourbon absolutism.[18] By persistently evoking the language of constitutionalism and conscience, parlementary magistrates and lawyers did more to undermine the prestige and authority of the clergy and monarchy than the philosophes and their vitriolic anticlericalism.[19]

My understanding of both absolutist ideology as well the opposition to the monarchy has also benefited from the emergence of gender history. Since the late 1980s, "gender has moved from the margins to the center of the historian's project," raising questions about the symbiotic relationship between early modern familial and monarchical power.[20] In examining the language of sexual difference and hierarchy, historians of the early modern period have uncovered not only how gender and power operated within the private realm but also how they shaped public authority, underscoring the porous boundaries between private and public, between the personal and the political. Feminist scholars have drawn attention to a critical turning point in the eighteenth century when men of letters, most notably Jean-Jacques Rousseau, became intent on clearly demarcating public and private in gendered terms. Joan Landes has argued that the emergence of the modern public sphere was predicated on the notion that this public sphere was inherently masculine and that the private arena was gendered female.[21] In positing a purely masculine authority in the public realm, men of letters criticized the monarchy and other institutions of power for allowing women—actresses, *salonnières*, royal mistresses—to interfere in the world of politics. Moreover, critics of the Old Regime characterized many of the traditional uses of power, such as the *lettre de cachet*, as secretive and authoritarian, in effect, "feminized" authority.

My focus on the meaning of convents and the multiple images of nuns within certain political and social debates uncovers the interplay between the religious controversies of the Old Regime and the evolution of gendered public and private spheres. I thus offer a sharper picture of eighteenth-century political culture, one that demonstrates how two apparently unrelated strains of opposition to the Old Regime were, in fact, intrinsically connected. Jansenist polemicists and *parlementaires* welcomed efforts by women religious to assert their conscience as yet another blow against clerical despotism. According to the author chronicling the trials of the nuns of St. Charles and St. Loup in Orléans, the nuns' gender enhanced their cause because it pleased God "to chose those who are the most feeble to confound those who were the strongest."[22] In contrast, men of letters considered religious vocations to be antithetical to feminine nature since all women, according to Voltaire, "were born for propagation; and not for reciting Latin that they do not comprehend."[23] These contrasting views of women religious not only underscore the gendered nature of religious conflict but reveal how gender categories of the period were themselves contested ground.

Although in this book I pursue an analysis of the representations and discourse surrounding nuns, I remain sensitive to the fact that at the center of this study is a population of women who were both agents and objects within the French public sphere. Current studies of French convents and nuns have revealed much about the internal dynamics of convent life as well as about the connections of the cloister to the outside world. They remind us of the nuns' own sense of corporate identity and distinction, even when their lay contemporaries were careless of or indifferent to the genuineness of their vows and the unique nature of each community's constitutions and regulations. By the same token, these investigations have mostly remained a subset of women's history and have had little bearing on our understanding of eighteenth-century French political life.[24]

While drawing on the fruits of this important research on convent life, I seek to bridge this gap by engaging in the debate over the place of eighteenth-century women in the public sphere. Joan Landes's work has promoted further investigation of this topic and prompted feminist scholars such as Dena Goodman to put Landes's argument to the test. Although Goodman does not question Landes's overall assertion regarding the eventual expulsion of women from the public arena, she challenges the notion that the public and private could have been so exclusively gendered in the eighteenth century, given that the distinction between the two was so fluid and ambiguous.[25] In their examinations of salons, law courts, guilds, and print culture, Goodman and others have found that although eighteenth-century women could not escape the patriarchal domination of Old Regime corporate institutions, they could find a public voice that was both legitimate and subversive.[26]

Likewise, nuns were not always passive entities, mere objects to be shaped by the political needs of others. They made repeated use of the Old Regime's legal system in quarrels with the crown, the church, their families, and each other. Their efforts remind us that the world of politics beyond the court was not just a series of discursive exercises. The lives of real people were at stake, and often these people strove against the odds to establish a space of action and autonomy. However steadfast their convictions, women religious knew that they were in treacherous waters. The public, although generally sympathetic, did not look kindly upon women who rocked the boat. Sworn statements, letters to lawyers, and appeals to the king and state institutions offer a glimpse of how nuns who presented themselves in public carefully maintained the dignity and modesty associated with their religious status. Moreover, because nuns often relied on men to make their voices heard, the place of women religious in the public sphere was a complex one based on negotiations between female action and male subjectivity, a projection of the goals and ambitions of male writers.

The connection between experience and discourse, between agency and representation, informs my examination of convents and nuns. No such investigation can be comprehensive in its treatment, of course; here I pursue lines of inquiry pertaining to women religious in the political culture of the period, demonstrating how lawyers, polemicists, and men of letters attached issues of despotism and authority to the female convent. In exploring this phenomenon I have relied on a broad range of printed sources that also shed light on how different authors attempted to reach their readers and to influence public opinion.[27] Pamphlets, trial briefs, novels, and plays were some of the means through which writers gained the attention and support of their audiences. Archival materials such as letters and police reports not only reveal the process by which women religious were constructed as objects of public scrutiny, but also unveil how nuns placed themselves within public debate. The intricate exchanges between nuns, theologians, lawyers, polemicists, and men of letters reflected the multifaceted, unpredictable nature of eighteenth-century political culture.

In subsequent chapters I investigate the conflicts and debates over Jansenism, female authority, the forced vow, and female education and sexuality. Certain themes reappear in the different chapters, thus giving the overall discussion a certain synchronic element. Nevertheless, the chapters also follow a chronological sequence that highlights a shift toward a more thoroughgoing structural assessment of the convent itself. In the 1750s and 1760s lawyers and magistrates still respected the convent and blamed disorders on figures such as the archbishop of Paris or mother superiors such as Madame de Lantilhac; indeed, their suggestions for reform revealed an abiding belief in the convent. But by the 1770s, men of letters embraced a more systemic critique in which they concluded that because of its isolation and emphasis on celibacy, the cloister was beyond recall and was in fact, a dangerous institution. Both the changing nature of this overall critique and the protean image of nuns are reflected in the arguments made within each chapter. Moreover, the depictions of nuns, even by the same authors, was not without contradictions. Indeed, the treatment accorded to nuns during the French Revolution reflects the tensions and inconsistencies that emerged from the political culture of the Old Regime.

In chapter 1, I examine how the interests of the church, state, and family were intertwined in the history of the convent. Social elites, the church, and the state strove to control the activities of women religious; but they were not always successful, as nuns sought institutional and spiritual independence. Moreover, while sharing anxieties about female autonomy and sexuality, the different groups sometimes came into conflict. The tangled issues over authority that defined the cloister also made it a lightning rod for eighteenth-century political and cultural anxieties. The eighteenth-century's most famous treatise on nuns, Denis Diderot's *La Religieuse*, exemplifies how criticism of the convent represented a political diatribe against despotism in which gender was a key component.

In chapter 2 I consider the issues of despotism and citizenship in the resistance of Jansenist nuns to the 1713 papal bull *Unigenitus*, which provoked Jansenists and many non-Jansenists to oppose the ultramontane clergy and the monarchy. Considering the bull as illegitimate, many Jansenist women religious followed their consciences and articulated their opposition through correspondence, memoirs, and sworn statements. Male Jansenist polemicists took the lead in showcasing their dissidence before the public. They feminized Jansenist spirituality by making women religious the embodiment of Jansenist principles. After examining the cause célèbre involving Sister Perpétue and the Parisian convent of Sainte-Agathe (1752–53), I go on to argue that Jansenist lawyers and magistrates politicized these traits, forging nuns into political weapons against ultramontane clerics such as the archbishop of Paris. Whereas nuns represented the virtuous Christian woman, bishops acted as despots, wielding authority in disorderly, "feminine" ways. Magistrates put forth an image of themselves as temperate and reasonable judges, idealized masculine figures who protected helpless citizens like nuns.

But as I demonstrate in chapter 3, male ecclesiastics such as bishops and confessors were not the only problematic figures associated with the convent. In trials such as those involving the Abbey of Beaumont in Clermont-Ferrand (1764) and the Hôtel-Dieu in Pontoise (1769), lawyers sought to circumscribe legitimate female authority by evoking contemporary notions of feminine virtue and vice, and their trial briefs were eagerly received by a public already hostile to female power. In both cases lawyers argued that despotic mother superiors were vice-ridden aristocrats who had violated their subordinates' rights as citizens. Instead of taking the superiors to task for failing to be good Christian models, lawyers chided superiors for not living up to secular standards of motherhood. Lawyers offered two solutions: reigning in unruly individuals and reforming the convent's structure.

While Jansenist controversies and trials involving mother superiors attracted attention, what haunted the public's imagination was the vocation forcée narrative, of which Diderot's *La Religieuse* was but one example. Chapter 4 begins with an analysis of two court cases and then moves on to compare legal and fictive narratives. Plays and novels such as *Sophie, ou la vocation forcée* and *La Religieuse malgré elle*, as well as the legal briefs from the vocation forcée trials of Lusignan (1752) and Delamarre (1758), all demonstrate how eighteenth-century writers grafted political fears of despotism on to the private sphere of the family. I argue that the central struggle in the vocation forcée narrative was between the individual's rights and the family's prerogatives. The effectiveness of this message was partially derived from the different ways in which the narrative circulated in Old Regime society. Indeed, the themes of the vocation forcée and its diffuse presence made it a cultural phenomenon, a fully realized symbol of despotism.

This reappraisal of the convent appeared in another forum, the debate on female education that took place between 1740 and 1789 and is the subject of chapter 5. Men and women of letters no longer considered questions of who had legitimate control over the convent. Instead, they assessed the convent's function as a pedagogical institution, and not as a religious establishment. Critiques of convent education could be found in novels such as Choderlos Laclos's *Les Liaisons dangereuses,* treatises such as Madame de Miremont's seven-volume *Traité de l'éducation des femmes,* and pornography such as *Les Plaisirs du cloître, comédie en trois actes.* Pornographers and social commentators alike, I contend, stripped the convent of any social utility or moral superiority, demanding instead that women religious become just women.

The final chapter examines how during the early years of the French Revolution, officials and polemicists availed themselves of these complex images of nuns. In those years, polemicists and politicians continued to use women religious to denounce despotism and celibacy. In turn, individual nuns and entire monastic orders worked tirelessly to preserve their communities on the grounds that they too were useful French citizens. When the Revolution began to radicalize in 1791, however, tensions between revolutionary officials and nuns erupted. Entire religious communities began defying the secularizing policies of the government. Thus by 1794, when religious orders legally ceased to exist, nuns who were once revered citizens now became transformed into "enemies of the people." They no longer had a place in a political world whose logos was secular and male-centered. This dramatic shift in the public perception of nuns would have an enduring legacy. For nineteenth-century moderates and radicals, the steadfast commitment that women religious professed for the church was seen as a continuation of the counterrevolution, a threat to the very image of citizenship nuns had come to represent in the decades before the French Revolution.

1

Authority in the
Eighteenth-Century Convent

FROM THE EARLY DAYS OF CHRISTIANITY, MALE CLERICS AND THE
laity were caught between two opposing visions of nuns as either excep-
tional holy women or intrinsically sexual creatures, figures of virtue or
figures of vice, that needed to be sequestered. The church fathers, ranging from Paul to Jerome, configured women in terms of their sexuality
and women's sexuality in terms of pollution and corruption. Operating
within this patristic tradition, the church's policies dictated that the only
way women could transcend their nature and pursue the path to spiritual perfection was through sexual renunciation.[1] In other words, God
considered women to be holy only when they had ceased to be women.
At the same time, male clerical authorities continued to prescribe a
nun's religious status within the parameters of her femaleness; although
Carolingian hagiographies of female saints endowed women with traits
associated with male sanctity, such as asceticism, they also portrayed
these women within a nurturing familial context.[2] This ambiguity
helped engender a dualistic image of nuns as both saintly women and
sexual creatures. The solution clerical authorities arrived at was to push
women religious into enclosure, thus, in theory at least, ensuring female
purity while maintaining *male* clerical supremacy. But the efforts to marginalize nuns were only partially successful. Although regarded as a
sanctuary separate from society, the convent was in fact, defined by the

interests of different groups, each of whom sought to influence this female enclave.

The first section of this chapter briefly follows the development of the convent in France from early Christianity until the eighteenth century, examining the dialectic between the attempts by nuns to express their religious convictions and the efforts of both secular and ecclesiastical authorities to keep such expressions in check. Instead of cataloguing the different orders and well-known personalities, the discussion will take a broader approach, analyzing the convent's relationship with the church and secular society. Throughout the Middle Ages and into the early modern period, convents forged tight connections with the bastions of authority—the church, the crown, and the family—even as they fought to maintain their autonomy. And although the church, the state, and the family were united in their efforts to keep women religious enclosed, they also came into conflict with one another. This examination of the convent thus exposes the degree to which the church, the state, and the family were themselves contested entities, much like the convent.

The second section of this chapter serves as a starting point for the rest of this book. Here I offer an analysis of how eighteenth-century writers regarded the convents' relationship with the larger world and its very structure as symptomatic of the political and social disorders corrupting the Old Regime. Specifically, I discuss Denis Diderot's *La Religieuse* and his investigation of despotism, focusing on the novel not as an anticlerical polemic but as a political document. For eighteenth-century critics of the Old Regime, the story of the vocation forcée raised troubling questions about the helplessness of the individual before the clergy, the family, and ultimately the state itself. Notions of individual freedom, and emerging expectations of family life and motherhood, struck at the foundations of these traditional sources of power. Moreover, Diderot's critique of the cloister indicates the importance of gender in the eighteenth-century construction of despotism. In the end, his exposé of convent life indicts not any single person or gender but an institutional structure devised by a society that consistently denied an individual his or her inherent rights.

❦ ❦ ❦

The history of the convent in France reflected the efforts of ecclesiastical and secular authorities to monitor female religious expression even while embracing it. In the sixth century the clergy advanced Christianity's status in Frankish society by tying the church's interests to those of the nobility. Frankish noblewomen played a key role by converting their families and taking monastic vows. Furthermore, the clergy encouraged aristocratic families to build monasteries for their female kin.[3] During the "Golden

Age" of female monasticism from the mid-seventh century to the early eighth century, powerful women, including queens and noblewomen, built monasteries such as the Abbey of Remiremont. Recognizing the importance of these women to the advancement of Christianity in Frankland, seventh-century church leaders, such as Columban, considered religious women to be spiritual equals and acknowledged their abilities to lead others.

Such female influence began to wane, however, with the ascendancy of the Carolingian dynasty, an event that also marked the beginning of a symbiotic relationship between French bishops and kings. The Carolingians secured much of their legitimacy by linking themselves to the Catholic Church, a development facilitated by Frankish bishops. To demonstrate their gratitude, French monarchs assisted the episcopate in expanding and solidifying the latter's jurisdiction over other clerical institutions, including control over monasteries in which both men and women often acted independently of the church hierarchy.[4] In addition, royal capitularies and church regulations now restricted the powers of abbesses. For example, they prohibited abbesses from attending ecclesiastical assemblies in which their male counterparts participated. While nunneries in earlier centuries had maintained a level of learning comparable to male monasteries, more rigid enclosure now limited nuns' access to new scholarship. Where nuns once had been active elements in Frankish society and government, they became more peripheral and inconsequential.

Claustration became the most effective means of curtailing female participation and leadership in public religious affairs.[5] During the late Merovingian period, abbesses who presided over double monasteries could function in a clerical capacity by hearing confession and giving absolution and benediction.[6] But twelfth-century Gregorian reforms, as well as other papal edicts, strove to enhance the prestige of the male clergy by separating the laity from the clergy and increasing the distance between male and female religious. Now, only male clerics could be ordained and administer the sacraments.[7] The crowning act in these efforts to limit female religious activity was Boniface VIII's bull *Periculoso* (1293), mandating that nuns of all orders submit to perpetual closure; indeed, during the early modern period, this bull justified the church's insistence that women religious be cloistered.[8] As a result, the status of nuns essentially became analogous to that of the laity, since both depended on male clerics to perform masses and administer the sacraments.[9] Convents were further marginalized because they were financially more vulnerable. Nuns could not go out and raise money for the community; instead, they had to depend on outside help from male clerics and members of the laity. Thus, "the church from the time of the Gregorian reform *was* the clergy, and the clergy was male."[10]

   Despite these efforts to marginalize women, the church could not always repress the intense outpouring of female piety. In fact, the gap between the reality of such devotion and canonic and papal decrees dimin-
ished only in the early thirteenth century.[11] Medieval female piety often
defied the authority of the male clergy, and women found modes of devotional expression beyond the cloister. The most significant attempt to lead
an active religious life or *vita apostolica* was the beguine movement which
sprung up in Flanders, Italy, Germany, and northern France during the
thirteenth century.[12] Living in communities without male supervision, the
beguines evaded the venues normally available to women—marriage or
the monastery. Their lives revolved around pious acts assisting the poor
and sick, especially in urban areas. Without actually denying the authority
of priests, the beguines' form of devotion and their lifestyle circumvented
the traditional dependency of women on clerics. Whereas the dominant
clerical forms of spirituality were grounded in knowledge of liturgy and
canonic literature, female worship in the later Middle Ages acquired a distinctly mystical quality, accentuating the individual's direct relation to
God.[13] Initially, the church tolerated the mysticism of the beguines, but
the need to uphold the authority of the ordained clergy prevailed, and in
1311 the church denounced the beguines as heretics. Within this context,
"*Periculoso* seems to have been an attempt to cordon off nuns (the most
traditional and generally the most well-born women religious) from that
growing welter of groups, sects, and individuals."[14] In the wake of the beguines' suppression until the advent of the Reformation, convents in
France witnessed a period of spiritual degeneration and material decay,
particularly during the French Wars of Religion at the end of the sixteenth
century. Under Henry IV (1589–1610), convents such as Maubuisson and
Longchamp became extensions of the court itself![15]
   In spite of such decline, the Catholic Reformation in the seventeenth
century was a watershed for the early modern convent, ushering in an era
of heightened female devotion. Although France never formally adopted
the decrees of the Council of Trent, the reforming spirit of change pervaded the clerical hierarchy and made its way into female convents.[16] By
the middle of the seventeenth century, forty-seven new religious foundations were established within Paris and in outlying areas.[17] In many instances, young abbesses, such as Marie de Beauvilliers of Montmartre,
took the initiative to improve the spiritual condition of their convents, an
act supported by proponents of ecclesiastical reform.[18] Devout lay individuals also promoted religious orders. For example, in 1604 Barbe Acarie
invited the contemplative order of the Discalced Carmelites, founded by
Saint Teresa of Avila, to establish itself in France. Indeed, 80 percent of
the convents founded in Paris between 1604 and 1632 were contemplative.[19]

Ursuline de la Congrégation de Paris.

.38

An Ursuline from the Congregation in Paris. The costume was most likely from the late seventeenth century. Cliché Bibliothèque Nationale de France, Paris.

What is perhaps more remarkable was the emergence of orders, most notably the Ursulines, who sought to provide a more apostolic life for religious women in the form of teaching and charity work. Unlike nuns who belonged to contemplative orders, the Italian Ursulines, who appeared in Brescia in the 1530s, initially took simple vows that did not include mandatory enclosure. The company consequently enjoyed an autonomy and flexibility that helped them fight Protestant heresy through the education of young women. At the turn of the seventeenth century, the Ursulines expanded their operations beyond Italy and took up residence in France, a move that would reshape the order. Financial straits forced the Ursulines to look beyond teaching daughters of the bourgeoisie and artisans and to appeal to generous patrons among the nobility. Although the French nobility responded positively to the Ursulines' pedagogic aims, it was uneasy about the respectability of an order comprised of *uncloistered* women religious. In the case of the Paris Ursulines, their female patron, Madeleine de Sainte-Beuve, urged enclosure, believing "that incorporation as an order, with enclosure and formal vows, represented the highest and most perfect form of religious life."[20] As a result of these attitudes and the church's own disquiet regarding uncloistered women religious, the Ursulines in France had to submit to claustration in 1610, and their efforts as educators were confined within cloister walls.[21]

Despite such regulations, there were limits to the vigilance either the state or the church could exert over convents. In her study of sixteenth- and seventeenth-century religious houses in Paris, Barbara Diefendorf has asserted that "the Catholic Reformation was less structured, less closely supervised, and more open to individual initiative—for better or for worse—than we usually imagine as the inheritance of Trent."[22] Diefendorf has also demonstrated that patrons of communities claimed certain rights over a convent and insisted on exercising visiting privileges, a fact that underscored the close ties of the convent with secular society. And male clerics, occupied with other matters, were sometimes unaware of financial problems and other irregularities within the cloister. Such inconsistent supervision suggests that under certain conditions, women religious could achieve a certain degree of independence.

Ironically, the inability to isolate nuns completely or make them pliant also reflected the mutually dependent relationship between the convent and the secular world. Many female monastic communities relied on the temporal world, especially elite social groups who provided them with prestige, donations, and protection.[23] Convents had to be resourceful in order to be financially viable by exacting dowries from novices, admitting boarders, manufacturing luxury items, and most notably teaching.[24] Even communities that were not oriented toward teaching, like Port-Royal, began to accept pupils. Educating girls not only represented a dependable financial resource but could potentially allure new members. While reliant on elite families, convents also served these families in a variety of ways. Religious sentiment motivated devout parents to send their daughters to the cloister: the consecration of a daughter to religious life was a means to salvation.[25] The convent also provided more worldly assistance by enabling elites to dispose of daughters or female kin, who added to family expenses. Other families sought to consolidate one child's inheritance by placing siblings in monastic institutions. Conversely, a daughter who belonged to a well-known religious community could also enhance a family's prestige in the secular world. On a more sinister note, some convents such as La Madeleine or La Visitation, both located in Paris, served as prisons for recalcitrant daughters or wives.[26] Convents thus supplied a means of social control by removing unwanted or unnecessary members of elite society, preserving familial resources, and educating women.[27]

Despite the reciprocity, clashes were inevitable, and elite families did not hesitate to bring in secular authorities when convents did not comply with their needs and wishes. Responding to the laity's complaints about the high dowries required for entering a convent, Louis XIV issued an edict in 1693 placing limits on these dowries. The edict forbade all superiors from requiring "anything, directly and indirectly, in view and consideration of the reception [of postulants], the taking of the habit, or the profession."[28] At the same time, such restrictions protected convents. Parents and families were prohibited from donating enormous endowments in order to assert their influence over a community.[29] By demarcating the relationship between convents and families, the king of France acted as "the 'protector' and the 'conservator' of families," exercising his prerogatives as the ultimate paternal figure in the Gallican church.[30]

The most immediate patriarchal presence, however, was the male clergy, a critical factor that would play a role in eighteenth-century politics when the sovereign courts fought to curb ecclesiastical authority. By the end of the seventeenth century, all female monasteries in France were under episcopal jurisdiction, unlike male orders, such as the Jesuits, which were exempt from episcopal supervision. According to the edict of April 1695, each diocesan bishop was required to visit all the convents under his jurisdiction in order to confirm that, among other things, "monastic discipline, the use and administration of the sacraments, [and] the closure of female monasteries" were being carried out.[31] Episcopal authorities appointed a community's spiritual director as well as a cleric to say mass and hear confessions. Bishops also became involved in certain special events pertaining to convent life. For example, the convent had to notify the bishop if it was planning to accept a new member.[32] And a woman seeking holy orders had to submit to separate interrogations by her superior and a male cleric, something her male counterpart did not undergo. These regulations illustrate how the convent, in effect, had two superiors, one male and one female.

Although the mother superior remained subservient to such male authority, she was the central figure of power within the convent. The mother superior was both a spiritual mentor and an administrative leader, responsible for the souls of her subordinates as well as the convent's financial well-being. The government of abbeys and convents also included a set of "officers" who worked with the superior to maintain order and discipline. Each individual nun had a specific task that contributed to the proper operation of the community as a whole. These women religious fell into two distinct and separate groups: sisters of the choir and converses; the latter enjoyed a more exalted status and were often exempt from laborious physical tasks.[33] Further down the ranks were novices and postulants, who had very little communication with professed nuns except for the mistress of novices and the mother superior. *Pensionnaires,* or boarders, were also kept separate, and convents sometimes made financial distinctions between those who paid fees and those who received a free education.[34] Thus, while the convent operated as a single body governed by a superior, everyone within was clearly ranked, in keeping with the principles of hierarchy and authority that formed the backbone of early modern French society. The convent, then, was a microcosm of French society, a corporate structure in which its members played by specific rules and enjoyed certain unequal privileges.

In general, the population of convents was drawn from the elite section of society. The most prominent women religious came from the upper nobility and took their vows at prestigious abbeys such as the Abbayé-aux-Bois or the Abbayé de Penthémont. These royal abbeys essentially functioned as aristocratic enclaves, dominated by women of high rank including members of the royal family. Abbesses were generally appointed by the king, who often used abbeys as "benefices" to reward noble families. Since the Middle Ages, many abbesses were, in fact, large landholders whose feudal rights included receiving homage from the nearby population.[35] Abbesses' lifestyles sometimes matched their social status, and inhabitants of these abbeys lived in a state of luxury comparable to that of their worldly peers, a lifestyle that welcomed guests from court and high society.[36] Nuns belonging to a less prestigious convent often selected a leader from among themselves, a woman who came from the less exalted local nobility. These convents recruited choir nuns from local elite families, which encompassed both the nobility and the bourgeoisie. In his study of religious communities in central France, Dominique Dinet has concluded that by the end of the Old Regime, most women religious belonged to the roturier or non-noble landholding class. Converses, the second tier of nuns responsible for manual labor in the convent, came from the more modest artisanal and peasant classes, and their numbers also increased over the course of the eighteenth century.[37] By replicating the social hierarchy of the outside world, the convent contradicted the egalitarian ethos on which it was founded: all nuns are equal before God.

Despite the various social and institutional checks placed on them, nuns were not always passive and acquiescent before the various figures of authority. For instance, the nuns of the Abbey of Longchamp tenaciously continued to elect a superior while the king continued to nominate abbesses up until 1789.[38] In the seventeenth century the abbeys of Saint-Andoche and Saint Jean in Autun defied episcopal authority by declaring that they were answerable only to the pope.[39] Moreover, nuns sometimes disregarded familial authority. Although contemporary writers, much like present-day scholars, focused on forced vows, there were also instances of women entering the convent despite their parents' wishes, a striking example being Louis XV's own daughter, Princess Louise, who became a Carmelite in 1771.[40] Perhaps the most frequent conflicts were between women religious and their mother superiors, often precipitated by a superior's irregular use of power.

Nuns aired their grievances by bringing their superiors before ecclesiastical and secular courts. Individuals could launch their complaints before the diocese's *officialité*, the office of the ecclesiastical judge, usually appointed by the bishop. But they could also go through the judicial process known as the *appel comme d'abus*. This appeal enabled an injured party to bring an ecclesiastical superior or a clerical judgment before a secular court such as the Grande Chambre of the parlements, thereby obviating papal or episcopal authority by going to the lay courts.[41] Nuns used the *appel* to counter charges of Jansenism, to challenge superiors, to contest claustral elections, the acceptance of novices, and to annul vows. Such actions not only flouted ecclesiastical control but potentially sparked tensions between the latter and secular powers about the location and uses of authority with respect to the convent. Trials involving the *appel comme d'abus* raised inflammatory questions about who had the right to decide on the spiritual health of convents: nuns as a community or their leaders? ecclesiastical powers or the realm's secular bodies?

The difficulties eighteenth-century writers had in answering these questions draw attention to the complex inheritance the convent represented. When they turned their attention to the convent, authors did not find an empty imaginary vessel but an institution whose internal makeup and relationship with the outside world made it a powerful political and cultural metaphor for authority. As a female institution in a patriarchal society, the convent naturally prompted elites and state and clerical officials to regulate its structure and activities. Not surprisingly, the interests of so many individuals, including nuns themselves, created the possibility for conflict. Moreover, in the eighteenth century, the very structures of patriarchy were being scrutinized and criticized. The cloister and the lives of women religious naturally dovetailed with the incendiary issues of power and sexuality that dominated eighteenth-century political culture. Thus, a variety of writers connected the convent to the major source of political anxiety: despotism. And, by the middle of the century, the literary public had come to associate the vocation forcée in particular with despotism, and the convent with the vocation forcée.

The best-known eighteenth-century work on the vocation forcée remains Denis Diderot's novel *La Religieuse,* a graphic and compelling assessment of power in the convent. While literary scholars have attempted to unpack the authenticity of Suzanne's voice, by analyzing *La Religieuse* through historicist, feminist, or psychoanalytic approaches, the following reading examines the novel as a political and social pamphlet.[42] It is neither a comprehensive nor a close literary analysis of the novel but considers its major themes as enmeshed in the prevalent issues of the day, especially despotism. Diderot's treatment of the convent does not limit itself to a catalogue of all the convent's shortcomings but assesses the institution as a kind of government, a microcosm of the larger polity. His investigation also reveals the importance of gender in the eighteenth-century critique of despotism, one that depicted the uses of power as feminine and therefore illegitimate. Gender issues also inform Diderot's systemic examination of the convent's physiological and emotional impact on nuns. His protagonist, Suzanne Simonin, is a victim because she is a helpless woman before an entire social and political structure that fails to protect the individual.[43] My investigation follows the structure of Diderot's own evaluation of eighteenth-century society and politics. The novel essentially begins outside of the walls of the convent, steps into the cloister itself, and then delves into the hearts of its inhabitants. Diderot ends the novel by following Suzanne as she leaves the convent and discovers that her troubles follow her into the larger society.

In this gothic novel Suzanne Simonin vividly recounts her plight as a nun whose family has coerced her into taking monastic vows despite her deep aversion to cloistered life. Suzanne's problems stem from her illegitimacy, the result of an indiscretion on the part of her mother, and Suzanne must pay for her mother's sins by removing herself from the world. Once locked away in the Abbey of Longchamp, she endures a series of horrific trials at the hands of a vindictive mother superior, Sister Sainte-Christine. The tyrannical superior and her coterie torture Suzanne, accusing her of Jansenism and demonic possession. When Suzanne attempts to nullify her vows, the sovereign courts rule against her, leaving her trapped within the monastic life she detests. However, Suzanne gains a transfer to another convent, Sainte-Eutrope in Arpajon, where she hopes to live out her life in peace. There, however, she becomes subject to the whims of yet another superior, who attempts to seduce her. When Suzanne rebuffs her, the once vivacious superior loses her mind and dies in mental and physical agony. Some of her peers in the convent blame Suzanne for the superior's horrible death and for the general malaise now hovering over Sainte-Eutrope. The novel concludes with Suzanne's flight from the convent in the company of her confessor, who transforms from a sympathetic confidante to a brutal seducer. Suzanne escapes from his clutches but finds that instead of gaining her freedom, she has become a fugitive, fearful of discovery and living a desperate life as a laundress.

Suzanne's sorrows stem in large measure from her authoritarian family, whose ambitions make them the antithesis of a closely knit loving family bonded by mutual affection. The relationships within the Simonin family are measured in terms of worldly interests and ambition. Indeed, Suzanne characterizes M. Simonin's aversion to her in financial terms: "He [Suzanne's father] had more than enough money to settle all three comfortably, but that supposed at any rate an equal share of love for them, and that is the last thing I can give him credit for."[44] Financial considerations and ambition direct the choices Suzanne's parents make when deciding their daughter's fate. When Suzanne enters her first convent, her mother's confessor informs her that, contrary to Suzanne's expectations, her parents have spent her marriage dowry in order to enhance her sisters' marriage portions. For Madame Simonin, it is imperative that Suzanne be a nun in order to atone for her own adultery, but even such moral arguments are driven by financial motives: "Apparently my mother was afraid that one day I should come back to the subject of the sharing of property and demand my legal share, thus associating a natural child with legitimate ones" (35). When Suzanne suggests that someone might be willing to marry her without a dowry, her mother rejects this possibility because of the scandal such a marriage would bring to the Simonins. The convent seals her family's triumph: "This is the place where ambition and ostentation sacrifice one part of a family to secure a more comfortable life for the remainder. . . . How many mothers like mine expiate one secret crime with another!" (104). In essence, the family in *La Religieuse* behaves like a corporate entity, fiercely protecting itself and the prerogatives of those who are at its head, all at the expense of an individual like Suzanne.

La Religieuse offers a counterweight to this despotic, corporate family by putting forth the notion that families should be tied by stronger ties of love and respect. Although Suzanne ostensibly agrees that her parents should treat her differently than her sisters because of her illegitimacy, she does not fully accept it. Her responses to her parents are visceral and come out of her biological attachment to her mother and the absence of any such bond with Monsieur Simonin: "I felt as though I had two hearts.

I could not think of my mother without emotion and wanting to cry, but that was far from the case with Monsieur Simonin" (43). She reminds her mother of these ties: "I am still your child, you have carried me in your womb, and I hope that you will not forget that" (39).[45] But Suzanne fails to move her mother, and Madame Simonin's rejection of her daughter marks her as an unnatural mother and woman. Thus, Suzanne finds herself orphaned because of this absence of affection: "Alas, I have no father or mother, I am a poor, wretched creature they detest and want to bury alive in this place" (23).

What enables Suzanne's parents to pursue their heartless course is the complicity of French society, in which institutional and legal structures buttress parental authority. As Diderot suggests, it is not just the Simonins who are interested in placing Suzanne in a convent, but a myriad of people who make the family's private affair their own business. Suzanne itemizes the different people involved: "I saw the Bishop of Aleppo, I had to argue with certain pious women who concerned themselves with my business without my knowing who they were. There were continual discussions with monks and priests, my father came, my sisters wrote and last of all my mother appeared" (30). In the end, however, the law itself enables the Simonins to behave as tyrants by stripping Suzanne of any rights. When Suzanne swears that she will not attempt to reclaim her financial portion, Madame Simonin informs her that even this is not possible because parents alone can disinherit a child. Nor, as Suzanne's lawyer Monsieur Manouri argues, does the judicial system assist those who challenge their parents, no matter how just the cause. According to Manouri, a politician is afraid to assist nuns in leaving the convent "for he feels in his heart of hearts that if the prison gates were once allowed to be thrown down in favour of one unhappy woman, the whole mob would hurl itself against them and try to force them" (101). Manouri's remarks emphasize eighteenth-century fears of social disorder and familial upheaval, but they also cast doubts on that very society by identifying it as a "mob."

Through Monsieur Manouri's criticism of the judicial system, Diderot transforms *La Religieuse* into a larger political critique of the Old Regime. In the judicial brief at the heart of the novel, Monsieur Manouri directly connects the state to the convent: "in a properly governed state it should be the opposite: difficult to enter into religion but easy to come out. . . . Are convents so essential to the constitution of the state?" (102). Manouri makes his case for why convents are not vital by outlining a natural order in which procreation and individual freedom are its underlying principles. According to Manouri, "a vow of chastity means promising God continual breaking of the wisest and most important of His laws, a vow of obedience means giving up man's inalienable prerogative, freedom. If one observes these vows one is a criminal, if not one is a perjurer" (103).

Within Manouri's arguments, social order stems from the respect and protection of universal individual rights. In this manner, Diderot faults the state for two reasons. First, the government allows the convent to exist despite the fact that it inherently goes against nature and individual rights. Second, the state makes it possible for the Simonins to incarcerate Suzanne with very little opposition. Diderot thus implies that such a government is, in effect, misusing its own authority and casts doubts on its legitimacy.

La Religieuse further denounces this illegitimate government in its investigation and condemnation of claustral governance. In the novel, the mother superior, the head of the convent, represents a gendered embodiment of despotism that highlights unruly passions. Diderot demonstrates that the character and whims of an individual mother superior influence daily life within the convent. To accentuate his arguments, Diderot locates Suzanne's terrible suffering at the hands of Sister Sainte-Christine in the context of the eighteenth-century conflicts surrounding Jansenism. But if one considers *La Religieuse* in connection with Diderot's short essay "Sur les femmes" (1772), one may conclude that the novel also challenges the idea that any female can rule at all, given their physical makeup.

In *La Religieuse* the mother superior is the embodiment of the cloister's various dysfunctions, an inherently problematic figure of power whose reign over others is based on private, unrestrained proclivities. When Madame Moni, Suzanne's protector at Longchamp, dies, her successor Sister Sainte-Christine seeks to eradicate any remaining influence of the deceased mother superior, restructuring the convent to suit her own preferences. The convent transforms into a faction-ridden court where the fortunes of each individual depend entirely on whom she backs. According to Suzanne, the new superior "took a dislike to all the favourites of her predecessor, and in a moment the house was full of dissensions, hatred, back-biting, accusations, calumnies and persecution" (55). Similarly, the atmosphere of Sainte-Eutrope reflects the volatility of its superior: "And so order and disorder succeed each other in the convent: there were days when everything was sixes and sevens, boarders mixed up with novices, novices with nuns . . . and then in the middle of this tumult the Superior's face would suddenly change, the bell tolled, everyone shut herself up and retired, and the deepest silence followed the din . . . you would have thought everything had suddenly died" (122). Because the mother superior exercises such far-reaching control, the convent mirrors her personality, and individuals who defy her authority do so at their own peril.

Eighteenth-century readers would have encountered numerous examples of such capricious leadership in the Jansenist controversies of the mid-century, and some of these instances made their way into *La Religieuse*.[46] According to Suzanne, "Sister Sainte-Christine . . . went in for modern ideas and had discussions with Sulpicians and Jesuits . . . and in a moment the house was full of dissension. . . . [W]e had to argue about questions of theology" (55, 57). Determined that all must adopt her anti-Jansenist beliefs, the superior takes an aggressive approach that estranges Suzanne and others in the community. Suzanne adopts a Jansenist position of resistance that incurs the ill will of Sister Sainte-Christine and her followers. She adamantly announces that she will not accept "the name of Jansenist or Molinist," echoing the response of many Jansenists who rejected the term "Jansenist" that hostile observers used for them (57). Like many Jansenist nuns of the period, she guards the dictates of her conscience ferociously and does not accept the authority of her superior or the ultramontane clerics who are technically in charge of her soul. When clerics question Suzanne as to whether she recognizes the bull *Unigenitus*, she avoids a direct response and answers that she accepts the Gospels, thus placing her conscience above papal edicts. There are, however, costs for such declarations of independence. Suzanne endures endless interrogations, spies who search her room, and physical and psychological torture, the same trials experienced by the nuns of Port-Royal, for example.

Like those nuns, Suzanne personifies the Jansenist defiance of authority, which combines obedience and resistance. On the one hand, Suzanne memorizes every rule and regulation of the community. On the other hand, she refuses to go beyond those regulations and thereby subverts her vows of obedience. Indeed, obedience shades into defiance, as Suzanne herself remarks: "I hastened to make my position worse by actions you will call imprudent or steadfast according to the way you look at them" (55). For a brief moment, Suzanne acknowledges that she herself has created upheaval in the cloister by refusing to adapt to a standard of religious uniformity. However, she legitimates her position by declaring that "I was always on the side of rules and against despotism" (56), a statement that echoes the ones the parlements made when defending the rights of religious communities and individuals in their stance against *Unigenitus*.

Diderot's brief incursion into Jansenist politics reflected the complicated place of early modern women in French Catholicism. Like many Jansenists, Diderot appears to support individual conscience, a notion consistent with his plea for universal individual rights. Nonetheless, both Suzanne and Sister Soeur-Christine adopt fanatical positions. Indeed, for Diderot, such fanaticism is inevitable because they are women, and as he argues in the essay "Sur les femmes," "love, jealousy, superstition, anger" are pronounced in women because of their sexuality.[47] But in the case of the superior, such impassioned zealotry was the price of disorderly feminine rule.

Diderot's portrayal of impassioned female rulers is magnified by the sharp contrasts he draws between male and female religious. Whereas the mother superiors act in an uncontrolled manner, their male counterparts appear more reasonable. Suzanne describes the vicar-general who comes to investigate the affairs at Longchamp as "a man of age and experience, sharp of tongue but just and wise" (87). At Sainte-Eutrope, it is Father Lemoine, known for his austerity, who identifies for Suzanne the "crimes" of the mother superior. Indeed, it is the men, like Monsieur Manouri, who recognize the problems within the convent, and they are the ones who have the power to rectify the situation because they are rational and fair. In comparison to them, the female superiors are destined to fail because they are not men, and because they are women. In "Sur les femmes" Diderot contends that a "woman caries within herself an organ susceptible to terrible spasms, commanding her, and arousing in her imagination all kinds of phantoms."[48] This comment suggests that the gender distinctions Diderot makes in *La Religieuse*, which are grounded in biological determinism, are an attack not just on feminized rule but on female rule.

Diderot expands on this gendered argument against female monastic rule by identifying the failure of mother superiors as a failure to nurture and love—a failure, in effect, to be mothers. In *La Religieuse* the ideal of motherhood is a secular one based in nature, divorced from the hierarchical world of the corporate structure. Madame de Moni, the first superior at Longchamp, represents the ideal mother superior who understands the filial relationships that hold a convent together: "She was a sensible woman who understood the human heart, she was indulgent, though nobody needed to exercise it less, for we were all her children" (46). Suzanne's subsequent superiors fall short and, much like Suzanne's own mother, they behave irresponsibly toward their children. Their choice of favorites creates divisions within the monastic family. They demand unconditional obedience without reciprocating with maternal warmth, which makes them failed women as well as unsuccessful superiors. Thus, the superiors are caught in an impossible gender construct, one that requires them to be both men and women and also expects them to be neither. It is a gendered conundrum that fundamentally negates legitimate power since a convent must have a female superior.

In the final analysis, Diderot attributes this disorderly feminine rule to the convent itself, "a place of servitude and despotism" (103). Isolated from the world, the convent fosters passions that fester and corrupt others. Neither Sister Sainte-Christine nor the superior of Sainte-Eutrope can separate her personal feelings from her public functions. Both abuse their power and create disarray in the convent. For example, Suzanne suggests that perhaps Sister Sainte-Christine confided in a young priest for reasons that were other than spiritual. Suzanne's knowledge and indiscretion spurs the superior's hatred and persecution of her. Hidden from public view, the convent allows such passions to run rampant and enables people in positions of authority to rule according to those passions. The convent symbolizes an arbitrary government where regulations have no meaning because there are no restraints.

Diderot's political critique of the superiors and the convent shades into a more systemic psychological critique of the convent as an "unnatural" social space which potentially triggers hysteria, a condition to which all women are susceptible.[49] According to Anne Vila, "the observations of convent life presented in *La Religieuse* are consequently predicated on the assumption that the best means of determining the soundness or salubrity of a social institution like the convent is to analyze, through painstaking observation and decoding, how it acts upon the sensibilities of the individual bodies who dwell within it."[50] Diderot thus employs the methodology of sensationalism, which emphasizes how external conditions shape individuals, as opposed to the more traditional models of disorder that implicate individuals as the source of political and social malaise. Diderot regards seclusion as aberrant because it suppresses a fundamental human characteristic, sociability, and transforms individuals into either monsters or emotional cripples incapable of behaving normally in or out of the convent.

For Diderot, the cloister's isolation from familial relations and friendships represents the antithesis of a vision of human nature and society founded on social exchange.[51] In his legal brief Monsieur Manouri argues that the inherent sociability of humanity makes monastic vows abhorrent: "Can these vows, which run counter to our natural inclinations, ever be properly observed except by a few abnormal creatures in whom the seeds of passion are dried up, and whom we should rightly classify as freaks of nature" (102). Through Suzanne's eyes, we see multiple examples of such freaks. Her first glimpse of the convent's nefarious impact is a young woman whose insanity is inscribed on her body: "She was all disheveled and half naked, she was dragging iron chains, wild-eyed, tearing her hair and beating her breast, rushing along and shrieking" (27). Even when confinement does not result in madness, it is nonetheless unhealthy because the convent produces "that fathomless boredom, that pallor, that emaciation which are all symptoms of wasting and self-consuming nature" (102). During her period of torment at Longchamp, Suzanne shows similar signs of physical depravity and emotional collapse. The convent becomes a "prison" in which she contemplates ending her life, much like those who "rend their garments and tear their hair . . . [or] look for a deep well, high windows, a rope to hang themselves, and sometimes find what they want" (78–79, 177). Suzanne's desire to end her life flies in the face of her "natural" instincts, that of survival and sociability.

By constructing sociability within physical parameters, Diderot concludes that the convent's unnatural structure generates other abnormalities, particularly sexual "deviance." Diderot defined feminine existence in sexual terms, and he regarded female celibacy as an aberration. Within this framework, lesbianism is a pathology or "illness" to which women like the mother superior of Sainte-Eutrope succumb when placed in unnatural conditions.[52] Dom Morel describes the woes of this superior as a process of degeneration: "She was not cut out for her way of life, and this is what happens sooner or later when you go against the universal law of nature: this constraint deflects it into monstrous affections which are all the more violent because they have no firm foundation. She is a sort of maniac" (176). These episodes involving the superior at Sainte-Eutrope and other incidents expose the convent not as a sanctuary of virtue but as a den of vice. That which the church sees as sacred and moral, Diderot reconfigures as unholy and unnatural. And in that context, even the innocence and purity symbolized by Suzanne can be corrupted.

Indeed, Suzanne's own innocence is tested in her retelling of the sexual episodes she witnesses in the convent.[53] How can Suzanne describe what takes place and still maintain her unblemished virtue? She does so by insisting on her own lack of knowledge and understanding.[54] Accordingly, she observes that "these women must be very corrupt of heart—anyway they [other nuns] know that you can commit indecent acts alone, which I don't know, and so I have never quite understood what they accused me of, and they expressed themselves in such veiled terms that I never knew how to answer them" (86). Within the Lockean psychology Diderot adopted, the physical experiences such as those Suzanne has with the superior of Sainte-Eutrope should naturally lead to knowledge, to sexual awareness. Thus, we can never trust Suzanne's disingenuous disclaimers because seduction has the potential to transform the innocent victim into an enlightened creature. Suzanne appears to erase traces of such knowledge because it undermines her efforts to arouse compassion.

Suzanne's story represents a last-ditch attempt to gain the sympathy and indignation of a potential savior, the marquis de Croisemare. Indeed, one may argue that Suzanne's efforts to gain the confidence and trust of the marquis are a form of seduction. The persuasive nature of *La Religieuse* may, in part, be attributed to the impetus for the novel involving the real marquis de Croisemare. Originally, the novel was part of a plan to persuade Croisemare to leave his estates in Normandy and return to Paris where his circle of friends, including Diderot, dearly missed him. Knowing that Croisemare had taken an interest in the efforts of Marguerite Delamarre, who had attempted to annul her vows in 1758, Diderot and his friends set up an elaborate ruse in which another young nun, also seeking to leave the convent, would plead for Croisemare's help. During the course of the 1760s, Diderot perfected the story of this fictitious nun; it was published in the *Correspondance littéraire* in 1783 and then for the larger public in 1796. Although more polished, his novel retained the urgency of a narrator who had a mission to accomplish: to win her readers'

pity and support. Weaving together the voices of Suzanne and her lawyer
Monsieur Manouri, the complex narrative of *La Religieuse* blends the epistolary with the forensic in order to garner the compassion and approval of
the marquis, the judges, and ultimately the anonymous reader.[55] The idealized marquis, "well born, enlightened, intelligent and witty, [who] is
fond of the arts and above all has an original mind" (23), epitomized the
larger reading public Suzanne hoped to sway.

For historians, Suzanne's narrative voice sheds light on the difficulties
an eighteenth-century woman faced when appearing in the public lime-
light, regardless of how legitimate her case or how sympathetic the public
was to her plight.[56] A woman who made her voice heard potentially threatened the traditional gender hierarchy on which the social order was predicated. It was therefore imperative that the act of going public be accompanied by feminine protestations against that very act. Throughout the
novel, Suzanne insists on her reluctance to reveal herself to the public.
Her account begins with this assertion: "I have made up my mind to overcome my pride and reluctance and embark on these recollections in
which I shall describe part of my misfortunes without talent or artifice,
with the ingenuousness of a girl of my age and with my natural candour"
(21). She maintains that she does not desire to impugn her parents, her
sisters, or even convent life: "I spared no pains to persuade them that my
action was not promoted by self-interest or passion" (74). By averring her
innocence, Suzanne seeks to conform to gender expectations in which
virtuous women do not compromise their families or social norms.

While these appeals suggest an effort to manipulate readers, they also
reveal that Suzanne is trapped by the constraints of her gender outside the
cloister as well as within it. Suzanne's last words indicate that she walks a
fine line between eliciting sympathy for her feminine modesty and manipulating her reader through her personal and equally feminine qualities: "I am a woman, and perhaps a bit coquettish, who can tell? But it is a
result of our nature, and not of artifice on my part" (189). In this statement she advances a notion of femininity that denies women reason and
the ability to act out of volition. Even "good" women such as Suzanne cannot be expected to behave in a rational manner that rises above gender
and sexuality. Suzanne therefore is helpless, not because she is an unwilling nun and an orphaned daughter, but simply because she is a woman.
Speaking to Croisemare, she plaintively declares: "I am a woman, and
weak in spirit like others of my sex. God may abandon men, and I don't
feel I have the strength or courage to bear much longer what I have
borne" (99). Just as her superiors are guilty because they are women, so
Suzanne is innocent because she is a woman. But that same quality traps
her in the end.

Suzanne's desperation raises certain questions regarding Diderot's critique of the Old Regime. On the one hand, he challenges the ways in

DENIS DIDEROT

De l'Académie des Sciences de Berlin

A Paris chez le Bas Graveur Pensionnaire du Roi, et Conseiller en son Académie de Peinture, Sculpt. et Gravure rue de la Harpe.

Denis Diderot (1713–84), philosophe and novelist. Cliché Bibliothèque Nationale de France, Paris.

which corporate institutions work together at the expense of the individual, suppressing his or her universal rights such as freedom and sociability. On the other hand, Diderot does not deviate from the normative gender categories that in effect, deny women these universal rights.

Despite these contradictions, Diderot's *La Religieuse* remains one of the most eloquent and stinging attacks not just on the female convent but on the Old Regime itself. Diderot's discussion of convents and nuns indicates the ways in which the family, the state, and the church formed an axis of power within the Old Regime. His analysis illustrates the intrinsic connection between authority and gender in the eighteenth century, especially the configuration of despotism as feminine. In providing a structural critique of power and the convent, Diderot denounces the convent as an unnatural space in which seclusion and celibacy produce unhealthy beings fit for neither the cloister nor society. While Diderot's narrative arguably remains the most exemplary work on how nuns were a nexus for eighteenth-century political and cultural concerns, it was not an isolated one. The following chapters will illustrate how lawyers, religious polemicists, and men of letters invested the convent with larger political and cultural significance as they tackled Jansenist causes célèbres, various court cases, the vocation forcée, and female education.

Martyrs into Citizens

Nuns and the Resistance to Unigenitus, *1730–1753*

IN APRIL 1747 SISTER SAINT-BASILE, A BENEDICTINE FROM NOTRE-Dame-du Val-de-Gif made the following declaration: "There is a time to keep silent and a time when one must speak up. . . . Today silence is no longer permitted. The Constitution wishes to reign over all and makes itself adored. No asylum, no solitude, no monastery is protected from its violent pursuits. It [the Constitution] troubles all, ravages all, disperses all. One must necessarily opt for one or the other of the two parties."[1] The "Constitution" in this case referred to the papal bull *Unigenitus* which condemned many of the Augustinian beliefs of Jansenism. Proponents of *Unigenitus* strove to compel all Catholics to accept the bull, and followers of Jansenism stood firm in their opposition to the papal edict. Thus, *Unigenitus* sparked a conflict between obedience to the church and adherence to individual conscience, a conflict so widespread that it disrupted the sacred peace within convents throughout France.

As the Old Regime's police records from the 1730s through the early 1750s indicate, a large number of nuns representing the Carmelites, the Ursulines, the Benedictines, the Franciscans, and other orders shared Sister Saint-Basile's convictions. Sister Sainte-Geneviève of Notre-Dame of Rouen wrote to the bishop of Rouen that she had wished "for a long time to join my feeble voice to those of a great number of pious virgins who . . . have entreated in favor of the truths outlawed by the bull *Unigenitus;* and had sufficient courage even to join together publicly."[2] Other women religious retracted previous statements made in favor of *Unigenitus*, declarations they now condemned as a "crime" committed under pressure from ultramontane clerics.[3] These statements reveal that scores of women religious deliberately defied their superiors in order to follow their consciences. Jansenist nuns assumed the role of martyrs, willing to suffer public and spiritual censure because of their opposition to the edict.

Ironically, the creation of the papal bull was the result of Louis XIV's efforts to ensure religious conformity necessary to his absolutist vision of state and society.[4] In 1713, yielding to unrelenting pressure from Louis XIV, Pope Clement XI issued the bull, which condemned the translation and commentary on the New Testament by the Jansenist Pasquier Quesnel.[5] Written in 1671, Quesnel's *Réflexions morales*, as this work came to be known, went well beyond embracing Augustinian notions of efficacious grace and humility before God. Quesnel advocated a broader definition of the church, one that essentially denied the hierarchical relationships between upper and lower clergy and between the laity and the clergy. For a monarch whose reign was a never ending display of patriarchy, such notions (and the discovery of Quesnel's leading role in what amounted to an international Jansenist conspiracy) represented a direct challenge to Louis XIV's authority. *Unigenitus* then was designed to crush such threats once and for all.

From the beginning, however, *Unigenitus* unleashed a series of interlocking religious and political conflicts.[6] When the Sun King sought the French bishopric's support for *Unigenitus*, he encountered resistance from those who felt that by not consulting the French bishops, the papacy was infringing on episcopal rights within the Gallican church. Although Louis XIV would manage to get the majority of bishops to accept the papal edict, some more willingly than others, he also faced the opposition of the parlements. The sovereign courts regarded monarchical attempts to railroad *Unigenitus* into law as a threat to Gallican rights, an opinion echoed in the Faculty of Theology at the University of Paris. The king's efforts to gain episcopal support by reinforcing the bishops' power within the church also alienated a growing number of the lower clergy who believed that their spiritual authority was equal to that of the bishops. Thus, contrary to Louis XIV's intentions, *Unigenitus* gave a foundering Jansenist movement new life. The bull attracted new sympathizers and provided a common cause for the clergy and the parlements, both of which saw opposition to *Unigenitus* as a battle against the overreaching authority of the papacy, the monarchy, and the episcopacy in the Gallican church.

From the start, Jansenist nuns featured in the ranks of those who refused to accept the papal bull. Indeed, since the early seventeenth century, the history of Jansenism had been tied inextricably to such female religious activism, most notably associated with Port-Royal-des-Champs.

Moreover, the antagonism of nuns to *Unigenitus* was brought to the public's attention mainly through the efforts of their male supporters who neither suppressed nor muted the resistance and distress of nuns. In this chapter I focus on how women religious figured in Jansenist polemics between 1730 and 1753, when Jansenist nuns faced the greatest persecution, and on how they were politicized during the crisis of religious and monarchical authority in the early 1750s.

The importance Jansenist theologians and lawyers assigned to nuns lay in figurism, which, as Catherine Maire has convincingly demonstrated, was the cornerstone of Jansenist thought during the eighteenth century. Figurism suggested a cyclical history in which events in the Old Testament "prefigured" or prophesied the history of the church both in the past and in the immediate present. For adherents of figurism, events and individuals (such as circumstances involving nuns) were neither random nor trivial; both informed each other within the larger history of the church. Given that every event and object counted within the figurist worldview, the symbolic importance of nuns was not incidental but fundamental.

Maire's study establishes the importance of figurism to Jansenist ideology and activity, but falls short of addressing the critical issue of gender, as does much of the study on eighteenth-century Jansenism. Women were unquestionably important figures in the Jansenist movement. Maire and Robert Kreiser have noted the dominance of women in the convulsionary scandals, while Shanti Singham has uncovered the important role Jansenist women played during the Maupeou crisis of the early 1770s.[7] The following discussion goes further and addresses the question put forth by Dale Van Kley: "In place of a Jansenist feminism, should one rather speak of a feminine Jansenism?"[8] Van Kley answers in the affirmative, noting how beginning with Pasquier Quesnel, Jansenists valorized female simplicity and innocence over the complex casuistry of their opponents, assigning these attributes not just to women but to others who suffered for the Jansenist cause during the course of the eighteenth century.

In this chapter I closely examine the gendered nature of eighteenth-century Jansenist polemics and politics. Through a study of nuns, I seek to uncover, within the figurist reading of events, how competing images of feminine behavior captured Jansenist ideals and critiqued the hierarchy of the Gallican church. Male Jansenist theologians and polemicists made nuns the embodiment of eighteenth-century Jansenism, heroic symbols of female virtue and religious martyrdom. These writers praised nuns for their submissiveness. They also portrayed these nuns as morally superior to clerics who insisted that they receive *Unigenitus*, clerics they repeatedly defied and disobeyed. This gendered inversion of the clerical hierarchy continued to be relevant in the crisis over the refusal of sacraments in the early 1750s. I would take Van Kley's assertion of a "feminine Jansenism" further and extend it to the realm of politics. Jansenist lawyers and magistrates used the passive figure of the nun to highlight the despotism of ultramontane bishops, despotism which carried with it the connotations of impassioned and unruly behavior—feminine conduct that contrasted with the virtuous Christian femininity of nuns.

This investigation into how Jansenists forged female religious dissent into religious and political weapons falls into three parts. The first section uncovers how between the 1730s and early 1750s Jansenist nuns, such as Sister Marie-Thérèse of Lectoure and the Franciscans of Beauvais, constructed their resistance to *Unigenitus* as obedience to their vows, whereas their ecclesiastical superiors and the king regarded their defiance as insubordination. The second section examines how during the same period, male Jansenist theologians and polemicists, like the figurist Jean-Baptiste Gaultier and the periodical the *Nouvelles ecclésiastiques*, vigilantly reported these incidents to the reading public, configuring nuns as models of suffering and spiritual resistance. As the final section of this chapter demonstrates, during the early 1750s Jansenist lawyers and magistrates replaced theologians as the principal champions of nuns. In their debates and remonstrances they deployed nuns to censure episcopal despotism. This standoff between women religious and their opponents transformed female convents throughout France into battlefields in the larger war between Jansenists and ultramontane clerics, between those clerics and the parlements, and ultimately, between the parlements and Louis XV.

Jansenist religious writers and lawyers exploited the symbolic potential of women religious by tapping into the history of female religious dissension that had characterized Jansenism from the beginning. During the second half of the seventeenth century, the nuns of Port-Royal took an unequivocal (and what many deemed uncompromising) stance against Louis XIV's efforts to make them accept papal decrees denouncing the writings of the Augustinian theologian Cornelius Jansenius. The Port-Royal nuns and the theologians who advised them placed conscience at the center of their faith, situating it above and beyond the authority of their superiors. In keeping with this legacy many women religious repudiated *Unigenitus* for the sake of their consciences. They assumed the mantle of martyrdom, enduring spiritual and sometimes physical trials designed to wear down their defiance. Significantly, although these nuns attempted to construct a passive opposition emphasizing spiritual interiority, their words and actions suggest that the boundaries between passive and active were fluid.

This balancing act between martyrdom and rebelliousness was a response to Louis XIV's persecution of Jansenism when the nuns of Port-Royal adopted a position that blended defiance and acquiescent suffering. These characteristics had defined the convent as early as 1609 when Mère Angélique Arnauld, the former Jacqueline Arnaud, refused her family entrance into the abbey, an incident that became known as the "journée du guichet."[9] Mère Angélique ushered a new contemplative spirit into Port-Royal, which Alexander Sedgwick has described as a *mépris du monde*, or contempt for worldly affairs, an attitude that drew the nuns to the Augustinian principles of the abbé Saint-Cyran later in the 1630s. This austere piety also attracted powerful members of elite society to the convent, but was antithetical to the baroque Catholicism espoused by the royal courts. Both the monarchy and the papacy regarded Port-Royal's focus on individual devotion and its renunciation of worldly matters as schismatic and seditious.[10] As a result, by the mid-seventeenth century, Mère Angélique and her followers were caught in a conundrum as to how best to act, "whether to suffer persecution in silence as a gesture of humility or to engage one's enemies in a public debate in order to have the truth prevail within the Catholic community."[11]

In the defense of their beliefs, the nuns used different strategies in the face of persecution. Mère Angélique regarded persecution and suffering as signs of God's grace as she wrote to her mother: "I entreat you to believe, dear Mother, that the recent occasion that we have to suffer enables us to attach ourselves more firmly to God by submitting to his holy will and having confidence in his mercy."[12] But where Mère Angélique advocated silence, other nuns such as Jacqueline Pascal were more active in their resistance, and they refused to accept papal condemnation of Jansenius's teachings.[13] In a recent study, Daniella Kostroun has argued that the Port-Royal nuns offered a political challenge to Louis XIV. When the Sun King appointed an abbess of his choice to keep the uncompliant nuns under surveillance, the latter devoted themselves to updating and publishing their constitutions, which advocated elections for that office.[14] Thus, despite their withdrawal from the world, the nuns of Port-Royal did not hesitate to act in very public ways, using their writings as well as legal venues to protect their community and their faith. As Linda Timmermans has noted, within the masculine church of the post-Tridentine era, women religious were expected to be the embodiment of "modesty, humility, simplicity, and piety," characteristics that were derived from their femininity more than their religious vocation.[15] Whatever form of resistance they chose—silence, theological disputation, or legal recourse—Jansenist nuns rejected the notion of blind submission that was expected of all Catholics, but especially of women and even more so of women religious.[16]

Nevertheless, these displays of female religious activism received the support of many male advocates, who also influenced the spiritual legacy of obedience and defiance. In a letter to the Port-Royal nuns written shortly after the community's dispersal in 1709, Pasquier Quesnel transformed their plight into a quintessentially Augustinian experience of the faithful, one infused with suffering and humility, the stamp of righteousness. Quesnel cast the nuns in the role of martyrs: "It is true that like good Nuns you can say that the world crucifies you, that is to say, its maxims, its morals, its crimes, that its spirits and even its false virtues are insupportable to you."[17] As "victims of their [enemies'] furor," the nuns had to suffer their enemies' attempts to seduce or to threaten them, and to endure the "tribulations" of being called "disobedient and rebellious." Moreover, such "afflictions" were to be embraced by the brides of Christ. If the nuns were willing to bear "these crosses of thorns and blood" with humility, then, he reminded the nuns, "your Spouse will carry them with you."[18]

Despite his emphasis on such "spousal" duties with its connotations of acquiescence and subservience, Quesnel condoned defiance toward ecclesiastical authority. The theologian urged the nuns to oppose "tyrannical" behavior because "it is not Lucifer's pride to resist injustice, but rather it is to imitate the holy angels who stayed firm in Heaven because they did not obey Lucifer who was above them." According to Quesnel, these oppressors were "those persons who would wish to take advantage of their authority which the quality of priest and Confessor gives them in order to weaken you; *you should no longer listen to them nor respond to them.*"[19] Quesnel thus merged devotional steadfastness with insubordination, in effect advocating a challenge to ecclesiastical authority. However, Quesnel also suggested that female rebelliousness affirmed mainstream ideals of feminine behavior: "it is even an entirely holy humility to resist men in order to stay perfectly submissive before God."[20] Quesnel's characterization of appropriate feminine behavior was derived from his religious position. His emphasis on humility reflected the larger cultural expectations of female compliance, but it also revealed how Jansenists considered it imperative that true believers not betray their consciences. Moreover, the theologian endowed female steadfastness with a sanctity that clearly placed them above their male superiors. Much like his mentor the great Antoine Arnauld, Quesnel opened a channel for independent female spirituality that undermined the jurisdiction of the male clergy.[21] Two Jansenist nuns, Jacqueline Pascal and Christine Briquet, went further in their challenges to the male clerical hierarchy by debating theological issues, activities absolutely forbidden to women.[22] These contradictory notions of obedience and the different examples of defiance contained the blueprint for eighteenth-century Jansenist nuns who opposed *Unigenitus*.

Between the 1730s and 1750s, when ultramontane clerics actively sought to compel Jansenist women religious to accept *Unigenitus*, nuns carefully constructed a form of resistance within a discourse of obedience, one that attempted (not always successfully!) to negotiate between social expectations of female submissiveness and their personal need for action. Even by the late 1720s, they felt the burden of their choices as tensions over *Unigenitus* escalated as a result of two factors. First, starting in the late 1720s the young Louis XV's cardinal minister, André-Hercule de Fleury, began replacing bishops opposed to *Unigenitus* with those who supported the bull. Second, in an attempt to consolidate these gains, Fleury orchestrated the declaration of March 24, 1730, stating that *Unigenitus* was "a law of church and state" and that all members of the clergy must accept it.[23] Overzealous prelates, backed by the Fleury ministry, began a campaign to extirpate Jansenism from the realm, including from the inner sanctum of the cloister. From the perspective of the ultramontane clergy and monarchy, nuns who refused to accept *Unigenitus* presented a threat to theological and political order.[24] Thus in Paris, Troyes, Orléans and throughout the rest of France, many women religious found themselves accused of heresy and, as a result, had to endure exile, the refusal of the sacraments, and constant harangues from spiritual directors and other nuns who demanded that they yield to the bull. For example, the Benedictines of Saumur were persecuted in a manner similar to Port-Royal: the members of the community were exiled all over the realm, and the convent itself was destroyed in 1747.[25] As Sister Sainte-Basile and Diderot's Suzanne demonstrate, Jansenist nuns were equal to the ultramontane offensive, refusing to succumb to seductive reasoning or to threats.

The approach Jansenist nuns took blended the various models of resistance offered by Mère Angélique, Arnauld, Quesnel, and nuns like Jacqueline Pascal. At the request of a fellow nun, Sister Marie-Thérèse, a Carmelite from Lectoure, wrote a thirty-three-page chronicle of her trials and tribulations while in exile at the Carmelite convent of Montauban and at the Visitations of Montpellier during the 1730s.[26] Her *relation* is a rare firsthand account of how a Jansenist nun articulated her spiritual position while under pressure.

Sister Marie-Thérèse's narrative indicates an awareness of how the credibility of her story depended on her conforming to a model of female religious behavior. When Sister Marie-Thérèse arrived at Montauban, the nuns of that community commented on the "scandal" that she had created for her convent at Lectoure, for the Carmelite order, and for the church as a whole.[27] But as Sister Marie-Thérèse noted, they were also struck by her modest behavior. The nuns of Montauban found her to be "an incomprehensible mystery" because she had "a natural gentleness of spirit" and "at the same time a spirit of bronze, a heart of stone."[28] By showcasing these comments, Sister Marie-Thérèse maintained the appearance of a modest woman. Indeed, toward the end of her letter, Sister

Marie-Thérèse begged her reader not to pass her story on to others because she feared the consequences, including further damage to her reputation.

At the same time, Sister Marie-Thérèse could not always sustain this timid front, and she continued to voice unwavering opposition to *Unigenitus*, her "supposed crime of resistance." When some of the nuns refer to the appellants against the bull as "heretics," Sister Marie-Thérèse claimed that "I could not keep quiet without wounding my conscience." She then tried to correct the nuns who "spoke from ignorance."[29] Perhaps more telling were her descriptions of disputes with spiritual directors. In one interaction with a confessor, Sister Marie-Thérèse showed herself to be so conversant in certain theological matters that the confessor was forced to terminate the conversation and further research the subject.[30] Her failure to remain silent in these instances betrayed her self-portrait as a modest female, and instead revealed a spirit of independence and self-righteousness grounded in faith.

Using a similar rhetorical strategy, other Jansenist nuns went a step further and placed their consciences above the institutional authority of both church and state. Moreover, they were not very scrupulous in hiding their words and actions from the public, as indicated by the coverage they received in the *Nouvelles ecclésiastiques*.[31] During the late 1740s, the *Nouvelles* devoted three issues to the conflict between the bishop of Beauvais, Potier de Gesvres, and the Franciscan nuns whom he denounced as "rebels of the Church."[32] Responding to the bishop's undisguised animosity, the mother superior of Saint-François in Beauvais declared that "she has submitted to all the *decisions of the Church*, but that she rejected *Unigenitus* because she did not regard it as such."[33] In retaliation the bishop used a *lettre de cachet* to exile the mother superior and other officers, installing in their place women religious specifically chosen by him. However, many of the other nuns refused to recognize these appointed officers. When the intendant of Paris informed them that it was the "will of the King" that the nuns comply, one member of the community countered that they had sworn to uphold the convent's constitution, that straying from its requirements would be a crime, and that "*the King is not above God . . .* and the power of the King does not extend over our souls."[34] Like Sister Marie-Thérèse, this nun as well as her mother superior, had stepped over the line with respect to the expectations of her sex.[35] Their decision to stake a claim based on personal belief effectively repudiated the intercessory nature of priests and the king, both of whom had worked for centuries to delimit female spirituality.

Some Jansenist nuns further defied clerics and the king by enlisting the aid of the parlements, an act that turned their spiritual resistance into a political challenge. In 1738 Cardinal Fleury succeeded in getting Pope

Clement XII to issue an edict against the Filles du Calvaire in the Marais who harbored strong Jansenist beliefs. When the papal brief placed the order directly under the jurisdiction of the archbishop of Paris, the archbishop, Charles-Gaspard-Guillaume Vintimille du Luc, took the opportunity to make sure that the officers elected in the community subscribed to the brief as well as to *Unigenitus.* The Filles du Calvaire may have depicted themselves as timorous souls caught between "the fear of offending God and of displeasing their Prince," but they did not hesitate to challenge the authority of the archbishop.[36] They objected by writing to the king and to Fleury and finally engaged in public acts of opposition; between 1739 and 1742 they had each act, letter, and trial brief printed and circulated.[37] While it is unclear if the Filles du Calvaire composed the published letters, it remains significant that the nuns placed themselves directly before the public, using the *appel comme d'abus* to bring their grievances before the Parlement of Paris.

The Filles du Calvaire consciously entered into the larger political quarrel between secular and ecclesiastic authority precipitated by *Unigenitus.* They argued that without letters patent registered by the parlement, the archbishop's claims had no weight, especially because his jurisdiction was not laid out in the constitutions and laws to which they had sworn obedience.[38] With the help of barristers, the order placed serious limits on the archbishop's authority. In response to charges that they had rebelled against the king by appealing to the parlement, the nuns reminded the king "that it is only your authority that is exercised in all the tribunals . . . and that your wisdom and that of the kings, your august predecessors, dictated that laws, which restrict all those that come from Rome, are by necessity verified by the parlements, depositories of your authority."[39] The nuns thus put forth an image of the Gallican church that gave the parlement a powerful role at the expense of the papacy and the monarchy itself. Their arguments were supported by lawyers who in a legal brief for the Filles du Calvaire described the papal *bref* as "the exercise of an arbitrary and infinite power." Consequently, the legal brief declared that if this was the case then the nuns' refusal to acquiesce to it was "no longer an act of disobedience, a scandal, a revolt; but a legitimate defense, an indispensable duty."[40] The story of the Filles de Calvaire demonstrates how women religious could be political players, and it underscores how gender expectations on women took a backseat to the power struggles involving the Gallican church.

Sister Marie-Thérèse, the Franciscans of Beauvais, and the Filles du Calvaire were just some examples of the many Jansenist nuns who decided for themselves what constituted legitimate church doctrine. All women religious had to contend with social expectations of female submissiveness, but for Jansenist nuns these expectations became difficult to heed when

their principles of personal conscience conflicted with the dictates of institutional and doctrinal authority. Although we can only infer what
Jansenist nuns were thinking during these episodes, I would argue that
they understood their own resistance in terms of a larger struggle and not
as an assertion of individuality or personal fulfillment. During the controversy over the Grand Carmel in Paris, one Sister Joubert refused to submit
to *Unigenitus*, writing that "by the grace of Jesus Christ, I am prepared to
shed my blood in order to support to the death the cause to which I have
had the happiness to be attached."[41] As we shall see, male Jansenist
polemicists and lawyers also regarded Jansenist nuns as crucial figures
within that larger cause.

Despite the ferocity of their opposition, it remains difficult to gauge how
many nuns were actually persecuted. In their study of the index of the
Jansenist *Nouvelles ecclésiastiques*, roughly covering the years 1728 to 1760,
Madeleine Foisil, Françoise de Noirfontaine, and Isabelle Flandrois have
demonstrated that the actual number of known Jansenist nuns was relatively small: 129 nuns out of 8,668 were known appellants against *Unigenitus*. However, nuns represented 44 percent of the 293 women.[42] Although
these numbers alone indicate that it would be easy to dismiss nuns, they
also reflect how women were almost systematically underreported in the
public arena. Moreover, the numbers are not always consistent in what
they tell us. For example, 69 percent of the nuns mentioned in the *Nouvelles* were favorable toward Jansenism as opposed to 42 percent of the
male regular clergy, 54 percent of priests, and 50 percent of canons and
curés.[43] As Foisil and her colleagues acknowledge, the numbers remain in-
conclusive because they are impersonal and do not convey the passion and
meaning that the authors of the *Nouvelles ecclésiastiques* attached to nuns.[44]
The early-twentieth-century Jansenist historian Augustin Gazier opens a
window into this eighteenth-century Jansenist mental world in his characterization of Jansenist nuns troubled by *Unigenitus*. Using the *Nouvelles* and
Gabriel Nicolas Nivelle's *La Constitution Unigenitus déférée à l'église uni-
verselle, ou recueil général des actes d'appel interjetés au concile générale de cette
constitution* (1757), Gazier declared that "thousands" of Jansenist nuns
openly flouted the dictates of ecclesiastical and *secular* authorities.[45] Although not borne out by the numerical evidence, Gazier's statement signals the symbolic weight of nuns within eighteenth-century Jansenism.

The stories of Sister Marie-Thérèse of Lectoure, the Filles du Calvaire,
and others were often publicized by their supporters, especially the authors of the indefatigable periodical *Nouvelles ecclésiastiques* (the weekly
journal founded in 1728 by two brothers Jean-Baptiste and Marc-Antoine

Desessart, both deacons who had strong ties to Saint-Magloire).[46] The authors of the *Nouvelles* acted as Jansenist watchdogs, unearthing any incident that showcased the sufferings of true believers and the treachery of
the ultramontane clergy. Moreover, they were quick to pick up any relevant publications, such as the *Apologie sommaire des carmélites du fauxbourg S.
Jacques* (1749) and the *Relations des refus de sacremens sous lesquels religieuses,
des monastères de S. Charles d'Orléans gémissent depuis 23 ans* (1756).[47] The
papers of the lawyer Louis-Adrien Le Paige in the Bibliothèque de Port-
Royal also suggest that many nuns kept in contact with the outside world,
informing selected individuals of their affairs.[48] Did the painstaking
chronicles of the trials endured by individual communities represent just
a series of obsessive recitals, an itemization of grievances? Not at all, as we
shall see in the following section. For Jansenist theologians and their audience, the persecution that Jansenist convents and nuns faced came to em-
body the plight of all Jansenists.
    The centrality of nuns in eighteenth-century Jansenism also exposes
the complicated place of women within Jansenism and the Catholic
Church itself. Just like women religious themselves, supporters of
Jansenist nuns had to negotiate between polar images of women. On the
one side was the "theological" woman who, despite her inherent ignorance, interfered in religious matters that she was mentally and emotionally incapable of understanding. On the other side was the virtuous Christian female, passive and submissive. By the 1730s, this latter feminine
image, exemplified by the timid and long-suffering nun, received greater
attention. This figure was a gendered ideal because women religious
never ceased to be women. For theologians and their supporters, the inherent feminine passivity of the nuns, enhanced by a voluntary withdrawal from the world, encapsulated the Jansenists' willingness to suffer
completely for *la Vérité,* or "Truth," which "was generally understood
among Jansenists to mean the doctrine of efficacious grace."[49] At the same
time, Jansenists did not necessarily reject the image of the "theological
woman." Time and again, they applauded nuns who refused to yield to
threats, and verbally fought back opponents. Indeed, the suffering of
nuns symbolized a continuation, indeed, a restaging, of the history of
Port-Royal.
    Catherine Maire has demonstrated how the concerted efforts of the-
ologians and polemicists preserved the memory of Port-Royal-des-Champs
at the heart of eighteenth-century Jansenist thought.[50] Accounts of the
convent's struggles with the crown not only provided readers with models
of religiosity but portrayed the dramatic events surrounding Port-Royal as
a defining moment in the history of the church itself. Writing to Mademoiselle Joncoux, a tireless warrior for the Jansenist cause, Quesnel remarked in 1706 that "despite their enemies, posterity will regard them

[the Port-Royal nuns] as saints, and for neither today's papacy nor the current reign, will it be a commendable event to have ruined a monastery, perhaps the holiest that ever was in the Church."[51] The histories that appeared in the first decades of the eighteenth century were not just a compilation of hagiographies. They assumed a more militant tone, focusing on the stand the nuns took against their persecutors. In the process, Port-Royal was transformed: "a community of holy examples destined for the faith, the monastery was elevated to the supernatural rank as an instrument of the divine plan."[52]

As Maire has shown, this shift stemmed in large measure from the theological ferment that took place at the Oratorian seminary of Saint-Magloire in Paris during the first two decades of the century. Under the leadership of Jacques-Joseph Duguet and his disciple the abbé Jean-Baptiste Le Sesne des Ménilles d'Etemare, the theologians of Saint-Magloire advanced a figurist system of exegesis that regarded the Bible in a prophetic lens.[53] "In part a hermeneutics of biblical prophecy, figurism, as this theology was known, held that Holy Scripture had foretold this period of *Unigenitus*-engendered apostasy."[54] Thus, the Saint-Magloire exegetical method embraced *contemporary* events in its history. The thread running through this figurist approach was that church history revolved around the persecution of a small group of "true" believers, a select group stalwartly bearing witness to the truth of Christ in their struggle against those who had strayed from God. For these theologians, Port-Royal was the figure of Rebecca. "She carried in her own heart two different peoples who tore each other apart: Esau and Jacob, Saint Augustine and Pelage, Jansenius and Molina." Port-Royal's own nemesis were the Jesuits, the masterminds behind the convent's destruction and the infamous *Unigenitus*.[55]

Images of this manichaean struggle dominated Jansenist works on Port-Royal as the conflict over the bull intensified.[56] By publishing materials such as the convent's constitutions, various hagiographies, and narratives of martyrdom, figurist clerics strove to attract followers to the cause of Port-Royal and the fight against *Unigenitus*. In conferences and didactic publications, the seminarians of Saint-Magloire instructed both laity and clergy on how to use figurism to interpret contemporary events in the light of this larger struggle.[57] According to Duguet and his followers, because contemporary events represented a continuation or even a repetition of Biblical episodes, they merited careful scrutiny. While all supporters of Jansenism were not figurists, it is unquestionable that the most prolific Jansenist writers in this period were in some way or another connected to the figurist movement. Through the efforts of these figurist theologians, like-minded polemicists, and the *Nouvelles*, Port-Royal-des-Champs came to symbolize a critical moment not just in the Jansenist saga but within the larger history of the church itself, its memory belonging to the public.[58]

Figurist authors also recounted the similar plight of other convents, an indication that many Jansenists regarded *all* female religious who struggled against *Unigenitus* as perfect martyrs, archetypal followers of *la Vérité*.[59] The anonymous author of the 1753 *Lettres édifiantes, écrites pour la consolation de deux religieuses persécutées en France,* claimed that "all sorts of people . . . will find in it [the collection of letters] luminous principles and sure rules of conduct for a time when one cannot be too enlightened or too fortified against the spirit of seduction which prevails over all."[60] Like Quesnel, the author praised the way nuns accepted their fate while withstanding their enemies. He advised his readers that "if you had put all your attention into conforming to this divine model, through patience and suffering, through a sincere and thorough renunciation of yourself, you would be strong today, and you would find in yourself the vigor and courage which would make you superior to all the attacks of the enemy."[61]

Other Jansenist polemicists strengthened this notion of nuns serving as universal models of martyrdom by applying figurist interpretations to specific episodes. Figurism permeated the *Lettres apologétiques pour les carmélites du fauxbourg S. Jacques de Paris,* a lengthy account of the scandal surrounding the Carmel de l'Annonciation or the Grand Carmel.[62] In 1747 the bishop of Béthléem, Dom La Taste, a sworn enemy of the Jansenists since the convulsionary movement two decades earlier, arrived at the Grand Carmel with a royal commission to investigate and ultimately extirpate entrenched Jansenist influences.[63] La Taste's emissary was Mère Cathérine-Dorothée de la Croix, from the Carmelite convent of Saint-Denis, whose report to La Taste disclosed a series of irregularities in the Grand Carmel.[64] Mère Cathérine found badly maintained records as well as the sale of valuable church items, all indications of financial disarray. The community exhibited alarming signs of spiritual disorder: members were erratic in partaking in the sacraments, inconsistent in their observation of enclosure, and unobservant of periods of required silence.[65] Mère Catherine also reported that many of the nuns not only disdained *Unigenitus* openly but showed distinct disrespect for the Virgin Mary, the saints, and the clergy. These transgressions ultimately resulted in the dispersal of many Jansenist nuns to other Carmelite convents in France, thus cleansing the Grand Carmel of Jansenism by the late 1750s.

In contrast to Mère Catherine's hostile account, the Jansenist *Lettres apologétiques* contained nothing but unreserved praise for the Carmelites and unveiled contempt for their persecutors. It also received the support of the irrepressible *Nouvelles ecclésiastiques,* which printed large excerpts during 1748 and 1749, thus keeping the public abreast of the Grand

Veuë de l'Eglise des Carmelites du Faubourg Saint Iacques.
Israel siluestre delin.et sculp. *Israel ex.cum priuil.Reg.*

View of the Church of the Carmelites of the Faubourg Saint-Jacques. Courtesy of Bibliothèque de Port-Royal, Paris.

Carmel affair with a distinctly Jansenist slant.[66] The *Lettres apologétiques* provided a lesson in figurism, a testament to the theological training of its author, the abbé Jean-Baptiste Gaultier. Educated at Saint-Magloire, Gaultier belonged to the "A-team" of the abbé Jean-Baptiste d'Etemare, the figurist theologian. He earned his reputation by actively supporting Jansenist clerics and the Parlement of Paris as well as tirelessly campaigning against the Jesuits.[67]

As a trained figurist, Gaultier linked the trials of the Carmelites to Port-Royal's struggles and to the battle between good and evil within the church. In the *Lettres apologétiques* the theologian interpreted the histories of the two convents as one: "with respect to the nuns of Port-Royal, their history is the history of the Carmelites and other persecuted nuns, the same hate for their sentiments, the same artifices to seduce them."[68] Gaultier endowed the Carmelites' ordeals with weightier significance by situating them well beyond the immediate conflict of the eighteenth-century Gallican church. The nuns' history, according to Gaultier, combined the stories of the Maccabees, Susanna and the elders, and the early Christians; conversely, La Taste belonged to the ranks of false priests, "a priest from the race of Aaron."[69] The most striking parallel Gaultier drew was between Christ and the Carmelites. He stated that "to declare war on these irreproachable Carmelites in their faith and their morals . . . is to persecute Jesus Christ in their person."[70] Through these comparisons, the figurist abbé seamlessly placed the sorrows of the Carmelites in both the sacred, timeless history of the Bible and the profane current history of the Jansenist struggles. The Carmelite nuns, like many of the communities in Orléans, Troyes, Riom, and other towns, reminded readers that the turmoil and anguish of Port-Royal continued.

The spiritual importance that Gaultier, the *Nouvelles ecclésiastiques,* and other Jansenist sympathizers assigned nuns like the Carmelites contrasts sharply with the criticisms that opponents aimed against Jansenist women, attacks that attempted to discredit the sect as a whole. By the mid-seventeenth century, women, such as the Port-Royal nuns and powerful patrons like the *frondeuse* duchesse de Longueville, were leading figures in the sect. Linda Timmermans has noted that "according to the detractors of Port-Royal, the Jansenists not only made women believe that were capable of knowing all, they also gave the illusion that they *were* savants."[71] The culmination of the Jansenist openness toward women was exemplified by Quesnel in the *Réflexions morales,* which stated that "the abuse of the Scriptures, and heresy, come not from the simplicity of women but from the arrogant science of men."[72] In essence, women had as much right to engage in reading the Bible, and perhaps their unscholarly minds could come closer to the Truth than the obscure pedantry of male scholars.

Decades later, the visibility of both elite and non-elite women in the sordid convulsionary movement of the 1720s and 1730s would add to the critics' fodder.[73] The movement which began in 1727 centered around the tomb of the Parisian deacon François de Pâris, who had been famous for his piety and austere lifestyle. Many of the pilgrims who paid the deacon homage at the cemetery of Saint-Médard began to experience convulsions, to speak in tongues, and to claim miracle cures. The cult drew such large crowds that Cardinal Fleury shut the cemetery down in January 1732. Women featured heavily in the convulsionary movement, and anti-Jansenist polemicists quickly denounced them, arguing that women should not have the temerity to engage in theological issues. The anonymous play *La Femme docteur* reproached women who, once seduced by Jansenism, ignored the well-being of their families and thus their duties as good Christian women.[74] Another piece, the *Entretiens de Madame la Comtesse *** au sujet des affaires présentes,* written by the Jesuit Jacques-Philippe Lallement, described how Jansenism had contaminated the cloister. In the *Entretiens,* a non-Jansenist converse reveals that certain members of the community "no longer know any saint except M. Pâris . . .

they have, I don't know how many, little pieces of wood from his bed, and bits of earth from his Tomb, with which they pretend to make miracles."[75] Nor did Jansenist women always refute these accusations. Pamphlets, such as *Lettres des dames de la paroisse de saint Louis dans l'Isle au R. P. le Fevre Jésuite* and the *Troisième lettre des cent-une dames* argued for the right of women to speak on doctrinal issues.[76] Beyond engaging in theological debates, women displayed their devotion to Pâris in more dramatic, physical ways that included self-flagellation and visions.[77] In effect, they epitomized an unrestrained and disorderly femininity, a danger to society. Lindsay Wilson has noted that, like their opponents, the more traditional Jansenists were appalled by such displays, which diverged considerably from the tenets of chastity and humility associated with the prevailing model of female religiosity.

During the height of the Catholic Reformation, seventeenth-century clerics and other writers obsessed about how best to produce this virtuous Christian female. Steeped in a long tradition of misogyny, theologians, priests, and others believed that it was necessary to conquer inherent feminine weaknesses such as ignorance, curiosity, frivolity, and a tendency toward excess, which could lead to heresy and apostasy. Women had to be chaperoned through Christian thought and practices by male confessors and spiritual directors. The standards for female religious comportment were inseparable from this paradigm of femininity imparted to all women. Linda Timmermans has noted that in the seventeenth century the understanding was that "the woman who obeys her lord and master will obey God; the nun who remembers the subordination of her sex will do the same. Thus, that which contributes to feminine submission contributes to religious submission."[78] The prerequisites of modesty and humility embraced not only how nuns talked and prayed but how they carried themselves. In *The Perfect Nun*, Father Michel-Ange Marin of the Minim order required that a nun who appeared in the parlor carry herself in a controlled manner: "There, she should keep a severe demeanor, serious, and a countenance totally religious. She should avoid bursts of laughter and repress the unsteadiness of the senses, especially the eyes, by the restraint of an exact modesty."[79] As Marin's words indicate, piety went hand in hand with female modesty and social order.

Jansenist writers of the mid-eighteenth century embraced this moderate image of the virtuous Christian female, projecting all her worthwhile attributes onto the nun and transforming her into a religious icon. According to Timmermans, in the seventeenth century blind submission was considered to be "the premier virtue" of the Christian. Given that submissiveness was considered to be a "natural" feminine virtue, all lay Christians were expected to assume a "feminine" attitude toward the church—one of complete deference.[80] Such notions fell in line with the Augustinian view that human nature had fallen and was now corrupt. Therefore, the ideal path for the true believer, male or female, was to withdraw from this world and to contemplate one's weakness before God. Early modern women religious were the perfect vehicle because they were complicated figures, women who retained their femininity even as they renounced all that it implied. As a result of "their sex and their state," women religious came to exemplify the Augustinian true believer, the embodiment of Jansenist spirituality.[81] Jansenist theologians accentuated the nun's gender and vocation to highlight key Jansenist ideals such as the rejection of worldly pleasure and humility before God. At the same time as they advocated a believer's submission before God, they rejected capitulation before the church. They extolled the moral resoluteness of nuns in the face of various tribulations, which led them repeatedly to subvert certain gender norms as well as the church hierarchy itself.

Jansenist pamphleteers praised women religious for their renunciation of the world, which made them "admirable examples of humble and religious constancy."[82] In a battle with Voltaire regarding the utility of enclosure, one anonymous pamphleteer argued in 1751 that the convent served "as an asylum for Christian women who would have the courage to embrace virginity."[83] Other writers reminded readers of the sacrifices a nun made when taking religious vows: "an entire renunciation of her friends, her parents, her home, and of herself."[84] The repudiation of the world consisted not only of renouncing property, maintaining enclosure, obeying superiors, and being assiduous with certain exercises, "but meant continual penitence for the corruption of the world." A monastic view was equal to a "death to the world and to themselves."[85] The acceptance of claustration was all the more courageous because it was at variance with "natural" feminine frailty. In his epic on the Carmelites, the abbé Gaultier observed that "[the nuns'] sex, their feebleness, their enclosure . . . all demand that one should have more sentiments of compassion for them than for all the others [who suffer because of *Unigenitus*]."[86] A nun's decision to take vows meant that she not only sacrificed herself to a life of unending suffering but transcended the inherent flaws of her sex to devote herself to God.

The champions of Jansenist nuns revered the fragility of women because it signaled one's complete humility before God. Although meekness before God was a universal expectation that applied to all believers of *la Vérité*, it was exemplified by the submissiveness, the inherent female weakness, and the female "modesty" of the Port-Royal nuns and those who emulated them.[87] As a result of their gender and their vocation, nuns personified the powerlessness of humanity before God, the core principle of Augustinian thought. Gary Kates has shown how the Chevalier d'Eon believed that the ideal nun followed the "doctrine of Saint Augustine." "A nun, he [d'Eon] believed, had to demonstrate modesty and humility in order to live for God alone."[88] And, in his *Mémoire historique et chronologique sur l'abbaye Port-Royal*, the abbé Pierre Guilbert spoke passionately about the ways in which enemies like the Jesuits had victimized nuns by taking advantage of the "feebleness of their sex."[89] Part of what defined "their sex," others claimed, was "natural timidity," a "simplicity" that also removed women from the intrigues surrounding contemporary theological disputes.[90]

The term "simplicity" was heavily gendered, denoting a certain kind of Christian virtue that did not engage in theological disputation. Simplicity signified a lack of curiosity and of intellectual learning, an unaffected and almost intuitive approach to faith.[91] The *Nouvelles ecclésiastiques* repeatedly described scenarios in which "simple" nuns confounded male clerics with straightforward questions that exposed the latter's erroneous defense of *Unigenitus*. For example, in 1729, the ultramontane abbé Savalette visited the Jansenist Carmelites of Troyes and interrogated the nuns about their position regarding the bull. The prioress responded "that she was a daughter of the church, submitting to all its decisions, but not to the new bull because she did not regard it as a decision of the Church," an argument that clearly echoed those given by other appellants against the bull. The prioress then explained that her decision was based on her conscience and the catechism she learned when taking her vows. Exultant over her refusal to yield to Savalette, the *Nouvelles* noted that "the Truth preaches more effectively than he [Savalette] does in the hearts of those who listen."[92] The contrast between the Carmelite's candor and the sophistry of ultramontane clerics was highlighted in the lengthy poem "Quatrième remonstrance des fidèles du diocèse de Troïes . . . au sujet des religieuses." After inveighing against the efforts of Savalette and his predecessor Lallement to gain the "blind submission" of the nuns, the poem lauded the nuns for responding "with insight and firmness" to the "new sophistry" of the clerics, who left defeated, "speechless and not knowing what to say."[93] Thus, the hardships of the cloister and the simplicity of faith gave nuns a righteousness that not only allowed them to resist their tempters and survive persecution but also placed them above their male superiors.

This image of nuns, a composite figure of suffering and resistance, functioned on two fronts in the eighteenth-century Jansenist world. First, Jansenist authors constructed an answer to their critics who decried female interference in theological affairs. They offered a counterimage to the disorderly woman: the "perfect" nun who had retreated from the confusion of the world and had chosen instead to dedicate herself solely to God. The author of the *Lettres édifiantes* applauded the vulnerability and the resoluteness of the nun: "her heart firmly attached to God will suffer the rudest of things; and in a fragile body, despite her natural timidity, she will be the most heroic person."[94] Second, this same model of feminine virtue, the nun with unwavering faith, also served as an ideal for the followers of *la Vérité*, an ideal that was perhaps more palatable than the visionaries of the convulsionary movement. Femininity and a religious vocation, fused together, transformed the nun into a compelling martyr and the epitome of the eighteenth-century Jansenist, humble before God but resolute against His enemies.

Nonetheless, Jansenist polemicists did not jettison the "theological" woman in favor of this feminine icon of humility; instead, they fused the two together. As we have seen, the attributes of "simplicity," such as ignorance and naïve candor, legitimated unyielding defiance so long as it was seen as spontaneous and intuitive. That Jansenist writers clung to these qualities derives in part from the inner contradictions of Jansenism. However much Jansenists called for a retreat from the corrupt world, "for Jansenists, a reformed Christian was an informed Christian."[95] As a result, Jansenist polemicists did not go so far as to portray nuns as blindly compliant, crumbling before the ultramontane clerics who were pressuring them to accept *Unigenitus*. For Jansenists, a feminine devotion that emphasized both obedience and resistance was not a contradiction but a necessity in the face of religious persecution.

The behavior that Jansenist writers extolled was not restricted to nuns or to women, although I would maintain that nuns remained the definitive model. Jean-Pierre Chantin has shown the importance of the eighteenth-century curé in both urban and rural areas. Educated in Jansenist seminaries or influenced by the flood of literature following the promulgation of *Unigenitus*, the curé was a powerful figure who could shape the spiritual tone of his parish by establishing an austere and well-ordered administration, preaching sermons, educating the young, and, of course, leading a righteous life.[96] Like nuns, male monastics such as the Oratorians garnered praise from the *Nouvelles ecclésiastiques* and other Jansenist polemicists for their stand against *Unigenitus*. Moreover, many male monastic orders, like their female counterparts, required that entrants take vows of enclosure. However, monks were not as strictly confined to the cloister; mendicant orders such as the Capuchins and other Franciscans moved within the larger society. Furthermore, monks could be ordained, thus having the power to administer the sacraments. Curés had a higher status than in the church and, for most of the laity, acted in a mentor position. And both monks and curés could move up the ranks of the church hierarchy. Nuns could not claim to have the same influence as the secular clergy or the male regular clergy, if only because of their limited mobility. Nevertheless, nuns held a place of honor in Jansenism. For all Jansenists, Port-Royal remained the icon of the movement, the heart of Jansenist history, not easily dislodged. The destruction of Port-Royal and the persecution of the nuns continued to be a preoccupation. Given that eighteenth-century Jansenism extolled martyrdom and suffering, what better model than a figure who was unable to help herself? Their marginal position within the church, ironically, made nuns more universal figures within Jansenist rhetoric.

By pushing a feminine model of faith, Jansenist theologians also advanced a gendered criticism of the existing church. For the early modern church, gender was an organizing principle, one that advocated a patriarchal model with papacy and priesthood as core institutions. Responding to Luther's and Calvin's emphasis on a familial patriarch, the church of the Catholic Reformation reasserted its masculine authority. As a result, church authorities were determined to enforce strict closure and to maintain control over these female enclaves.[97] Nonetheless, this gender hierarchy was never stable. Caroline Bynum has shown how late medieval male writers often embraced feminine imagery in their construction of spirituality because "'to become woman' was an obvious image of renunciation and conversion." Meekness and frailty, qualities that were gendered female, were signs of one's utter dependence on God and an inversion of existing structures of authority.[98] Eighteenth-century Jansenists adopted the more "feminine" aspects of Catholic culture and history, espousing the Augustinian emphasis on humanity's servility before God and regarding submissiveness as a sign of God's grace and as a natural state for all true believers. By advancing a model determined by closure and feminine nature, Jansenist polemicists undermined the masculine hierarchy of the post-Tridentine church. For example, Gaultier, the figurist author of the *Lettres apologétiques*, provocatively engaged in semantic redefinitions in his defense of the Grand Carmel: "that which he [La Taste] calls the nuns' 'revolt,' we will call firmness, courage, generosity. With respect to his conduct . . . is it too much to call it violence, oppression, tyranny?"[99] Nuns became martyrs because within this unstable gendered space, they held the moral high ground, that of true Christians who humbled themselves before God while embracing their own suffering.

To what degree did Jansenist nuns see their own actions as subversive, and how did they interpret their own resistance to male clerics? Although it remains unclear as to whether or not Jansenist clerics imparted figurist thinking to women religious, it would not be inconceivable that nuns were exposed to it, especially given the intermittent access they had to the *Nouvelles*.[100] They certainly looked to each other as models of resistance. For example, in 1756 Marie-Thérèse Thébault de Boisgnorel, or Sister Saint-Louis (of the Religieuses Hospitalières of Paris), observed in a letter to the Jansenist magistrate André Le Febvre de Saint-Hilaire that "I have actually read the relation on the three convents of Orléans. The conduct of these nuns inspires me with respect and admiration."[101] Hostile contemporaries also interpreted the behavior of Jansenist communities as imitative of Port-Royal. Indeed, the abbé Lallement accused the Carmelites of Troyes of wishing to make their community "*a second* Port-Royal."[102]

After Port-Royal, women religious such as these Carmelites and the Filles du Calvaire gave substance to Jansenism's public image of fierce martyrdom and defiance. To further their own cause, these women religious often elicited and received the support of Jansenist writers. In turn, the latter carefully constructed and repackaged female resistance for the consumption of supporters and opponents alike. During the 1750s, the willingness to confront their enemies in public made Jansenist women religious a potential flash point for political controversy and intrigue. Indeed, the words of the Franciscan nun from Beauvais who declared that the king had no jurisdiction over her soul foreshadowed the ways in which Jansenist lawyers and *parlementaires* would politicize the resistance of nuns to *Unigenitus* in the 1750s.

Although Jansenist theologians and polemicists continued to defend Jansenist nuns before the public, starting in 1749 Jansenist magistrates and lawyers assumed the lead in the effort to win public support. Historians such as Dale Van Kley, David Bell, and Peter Campbell have shown how the participation of judges and lawyers in a series of causes célèbres surrounding *Unigenitus* undermined both the clergy and the monarchy.[103] For *parlementaires* and certain members of the clergy, *Unigenitus* represented a conspiracy to establish papal supremacy over the Gallican church and to subjugate the French monarchy.[104] Over the next few decades, the magistrates of the Parlement of Paris took it upon themselves to protect the Gallican church and intervened in numerous cases of clerical abuse.[105] These parlementary activities pitted secular institutions against clerical ones as each side sought the upper hand. The potent question central to this bitter conflict revolved around authority. Who had legitimate control over the Gallican church: the clergy or the sovereign courts?

Magistrates and lawyers often asserted their jurisdictional claims within the church through the *appel comme d'abus*. The *appel* had always been politically charged, creating tensions not only between the parlements and the church but also between the king and his sovereign courts as each sought to impose its vision of the Gallican church. In the interest of configuring Gallicanism strictly within the parameters of royal absolutism, Louis XIV's edict of 1695 called for the parlements to moderate their use of the *appel*.[106] Responding to Cardinal Fleury's decree of 1730 forbidding its use, however, the Parlement of Paris advanced arguments stressing the appeal's importance. In a remonstrance issued to Louis XV in September 1731 the magistrates defended the *appel*: "It is these appeals of abuse, brought before your parlement, which have been so useful to your predecessors and have so many times been regarded as an invincible rampart for stopping the usurpation by the ecclesiastic power of the legitimate and immutable rights of royal authority."[107] Monique Cottret has noted that by the middle of the eighteenth century "the *appel comme d'abus* before the parlement transformed the latter into a champion of the Gallican cause, the cause of the state and that of the public well-being against the excesses of the clergy."[108] Such clerical abuses included the refusal of the sacraments, which generated a political crisis between 1749 and 1754.

This crisis opened a new chapter in the acrimonious conflict between magistrates and lawyers, on the one hand, and the ultramontane clergy and the king on the other. By the late 1740s Louis XV had more or less emptied the bishoprics of Jansenist sympathizers, replacing them with zealous prelates eager to rid the kingdom of heresy. In turn, these ultramontane bishops ensured that the confessionals and pulpits were occupied by priests who shared their anti-Jansenist sentiments. These priests began their onslaught against Jansenists by demanding that those seeking the last rites produce a *billet de confession,* or written statement, swearing that they had received confession from an approved (non-Jansenist) priest. Subsequently, many clerics and lay individuals died without receiving the Eucharist and extreme unction. The controversy over the refusal of sacraments, "which dominated—even constituted—French domestic politics throughout the 1750s," began in Paris in the parish of Saint-Etienne-du-Mont.[109] There a determined opponent to *Unigenitus,* Charles Coffin, a rector at the University of Paris, was denied the last rites by the curé Bouëttin. Such incidents fostered public anxiety, and in response the parlement began to act more forcefully. In April 1752 it issued a decree that forbade clerics from refusing the sacraments to those in need of the last rites. However, many ultramontane clerics persisted in denying suspected Jansenists of the sacraments, including nuns who found themselves deprived of the last rites at their deathbed.

Although nuns featured more in the partisan *Nouvelles ecclésiastiques* than they did in parlementary debates, they nevertheless afforded the Parlement of Paris with an opportunity to condemn ultramontane activities. The following discussion centers on a controversy surrounding Sister Perpétue and the Parisian convent of Sainte-Agathe that arose in December 1752. An examination of the discourse pertaining to nuns reveals how Jansenist lawyers and magistrates used gendered images to articulate their opposition to the episcopal and monarchical policy. Jansenist *parlementaires* exploited different images of femininity and masculinity to undermine the position of the ultramontane episcopacy while shoring up the parlement's own position as mediator between the king and his subjects. Adopting a figurist approach, many of these men used the same elements that had made women religious such compelling symbols of Jansenist spirituality and formed nuns into political emblems of citizenship.

In December 1752 a scandal involving the convent of Saint-Agathe brought the plight of nuns to the attention of the public, who were mesmerized by the extreme and sometimes unexpected behavior of nuns, magistrates, bishops, and kings. The Cistercian convent of Sainte-Agathe, established in 1697 and located in the Jansenist parish of Saint-Médard, had a mixed reputation. In his diary the lawyer Edmond Barbier described Sainte-Agathe as an institution that "educated boarders perfectly well, but which, for a long time, has been suspected of Jansenism."[110] The community, in fact, merited these suspicions. Sainte-Agathe sometimes served as an "office" for the clandestine *Nouvelles* and had close ties to the figurist school and the convulsionary movement.[111] Police records indicate that the authorities regarded this convent as a danger to the parish. One handwritten *mémoire* from 1742 categorically stated that "one should regard this community as one of the most corrupt ones in all of Paris. Its girls [nuns] have been educated by the famous abbé Duguet of the party, they are Jansenist by principle . . . And as for the parish of Saint-Médard, this single house is capable of annihilating all that one will endeavor to teach."[112] These accusations were written by the ultramontane curé of Saint-Médard, Pierre Hardy de Lavaré, who also claimed that the nuns read Quesnel and were openly devoted to François de Pâris. To add insult to injury, they outmaneuvered Hardy de Lavaré's efforts to confess, or more accurately, to deny confession and the last rites to a sickly nun.[113] The noncooperation of the Sainte-Agathe nuns reflected the larger resistance of the parish of Saint-Médard, whose worthies refused to go along with Hardy de Lavaré's attempts to eradicate Jansenism.[114] Thus, for both the police and the ultramontane clergy, closing down Sainte-Agathe would help destroy the Jansenist elements in the parish that had been the nucleus of the convulsionary movement.[115]

The dispersal of the closely watched Sainte-Agathe community occurred ten years later, but unlike other confrontations between nuns and male clerics, it triggered a constitutional crisis involving the archbishop of Paris, the Parlement of Paris, and Louis XV. On December 12, 1752, the parlement learned that Pierre Hardy de Lavaré had refused the last rites to two elderly nuns of Sainte-Agathe, Sister Thècle, seventy-three, and Sister Perpétue, seventy-five.[116] The parish of Saint-Médard complained vociferously against Hardy-Lavaré's demand that individuals produce *billets de confession*, and it presented a signed protest before the parlement.[117] With Sister Thècle dead and Sister Perpétue hovering near death, the parlement formally denounced the curé.[118] But when Hardy-Lavaré refused to obey the sovereign courts' order to administer the sacraments, the parlement redirected its energies against his superior, Christophe de Beaumont, the archbishop of Paris. The parlement delivered an *arrêt* requesting Christophe de Beaumont "to stop this scandal and to make provisions for the administration of sacraments to the sick woman."[119] In response, Beaumont defended the curé, ironically using Jansenist-like arguments emphasizing how Hardy-Lavaré was following his conscience and that, in spiritual matters, the curé received his orders from God alone. As for himself, Beaumont declared that he was answerable to the king alone, a statement that flatly invalidated parlementary authority in ecclesiastical affairs.[120] When Beaumont refused to relent despite parlementary threats, the sovereign courts decided to convoke the peers of France in order to try the archbishop in his capacity as duc de Saint-Cloud. The diaries of both Barbier and the marquis d'Argenson indicate that the escalating confrontation between convent, bishop, and the parlement aroused widespread public curiosity and anxiety, which intensified when Louis XV intervened in the affair.[121]

The king angrily responded to his parlement by forbidding the peers from meeting and by prohibiting the discussion of any such assembly. The conflict thus expanded to include the king's prerogative, on the one hand, and the rights of the parlement and the princes of the blood on the other. At this juncture, the magistrates' attention was momentarily deflected from Sainte-Agathe, in part because Sister Perpétue had sent a notarized statement declining the courts' assistance. But then on December 23, the crown's own actions unexpectedly shifted focus back to the convent. To terminate the affair, the king issued a *lettre de cachet* to have Sister Perpétue removed from Sainte-Agathe, an act carried out by four men late at night.[122] The *Gazette d'Utrecht* provided dramatic details of this incident, describing how "such an unforeseen incident had caused her [Sister Perpétue] to faint. When she came to, she was transported by carriage, and she was conducted to Port-Royal."[123] Six days later at the instigation of Christophe de Beaumont, the king ordered the *pensionnaires* of Sainte-Agathe to return home to their families, an episode the *Gazette* embellished with a dramatic account of a sick woman being carried out of the convent on a mattress.[124] The king and the archbishop subsequently had the remaining nuns exiled, thereby achieving their ultimate goal, the destruction of Sainte-Agathe.[125] The conclusion of this affair with respect to the Parlement of Paris was equally spectacular. After issuing the "Great Remonstrances" on April 9, 1753, twenty thousand copies of which sold almost immediately, the magistrates were exiled by Louis XV in May, not to be recalled until September 1754.[126]

How did the initial conflict between the nuns of Sainte-Agathe and the ultramontane Pierre Hardy de Lavaré—a conflict that, at least initially, resembled other such quarrels—precipitate one of the defining moments in eighteenth-century French political history? The answer lies in the conjunction of volatile developments that would trigger political strife for nearly a decade.[127] The first of these involved the king's appointment in the late 1740s of ultramontane prelates determined to stamp out Jansenism once and for all. One of these newly appointed prelates, Christophe de Beaumont, almost single-handedly perpetuated the animosity between the Parisian archbishopric and the parlement for the next three decades. A man of unwavering zeal and obstinacy, Beaumont waived aside all political caution from the moment he assumed his seat in August 1746.[128] The second development was the rejuvenation of a somewhat torpid Parlement of Paris, the result of Beaumont's policies and Louis XV's efforts to impose new taxes during the War of Austrian Success. A popular verse satirically noted that the parlement owed Beaumont a debt of gratitude for its resuscitation: "The Parlement is an ingrate / It owes its life to the Archbishop / Because Beaumont by a brilliant act / Pulled it out of its Lethargy."[129] The hard-line ultramontane policies and the revitalization of the sovereign courts, combined with a crown desperate for fiscal solutions, created an unstable and combustible political atmosphere that transformed the convent of Sainte-Agathe from a community devoted to *la Vérité* into a minefield.

This dramatic metamorphosis was possible because of the continuing importance of figurism to Jansenist thinking in the early 1750s. According to Catherine Maire, the divide between the "religious" Jansenism of the seventeenth century and a "political" Jansenism of the eighteenth century was a superficial one. She has argued instead for the ongoing importance of a theological Jansenism, claiming that the thread of continuity may, in fact, be located in figurism, which provided "a model of resistance that animated the magistrates of the opposition."[130] At the time of the Sainte-Agathe affair, key "Jansenist" magistrates, or at least those who may be classified as having pronounced antipathy toward *Unigenitus*, included Robert de Saint-Vincent, Clément de Feuillet, and Guillaume Lambert. The first of these three would play an eloquent role in the debates on Sainte-Agathe that took place in the Chambres des Enquêtes in December 1752 as well as in the drafting of the Great Remonstrances.[131] However, David Bell's study of the Parisian Order of Barristers indicates that "while the Jansenist magistrates remained a small group in the lower and middle ranks of the court who guided and manipulated their colleagues rather than commanding them, Jansenists dominated the Order."[132] A satirical tune from the period went so far as to advise people to consult their lawyer instead of their bishop on matters of conscience.[133] Spearheading the opposition to Beaumont and the ultramontane upper clergy was the prolific and indefatigable troika of legal minds, comprised of Louis-Adrien Le Paige, Gabriel-Nicolas Maultrot, and Claude Mey.

An avid Jansenist, Le Paige, more than the other two, bridged the gap between "religious" and "political" Jansenism. Maire has noted that "he perfectly integrated the great principles spread by figurist literature: the call to readers' conscience, the will to convince, to gain compliance through argument and the knowledge of the facts, above all, the need to speak in the name of public opinion."[134] Le Paige's interest in women religious persecuted by ultramontane prelates was not political opportunism but was grounded in his unshakable faith. Indeed, he had flirted with Jansenism's seamier activities, namely, the convulsionary movement, and unlike many of his contemporaries, he defended and admired convulsionary women. Praising the convulsionary Sister Sainte-Bazile of the Hôtel-Dieu, Le Paige linked her demeanor to more respected Jansenist icons: "She was nevertheless extremely lively, but she kept a close watch over herself in order to moderate this natural vivacity; she admired the nuns of Port-Royal, and concerned herself with walking in their footsteps."[135]

For Le Paige, as for the Saint-Magloire theologians, the plight of all Jansenist women religious embodied the ongoing struggles of the adherents of *la Vérité*, and he worked tirelessly on their behalf. In a letter congratulating Le Paige on the successful conclusion of the affair of the Religieuses Hospitalières in 1758, the magistrate Le Febvre de Saint-Hilaire applauded Le Paige's efforts in figurist terms: "I am overjoyed to bear witness before you to the innocence of the oppressed. Saint-Loup, Saint-Charles, the Filles du Calvaire, the Religieuses Hospitalières, the curé of Ronchère . . . after ten and twenty years of oppression, what incentives of courage and confidence in the defense of the truth! Is it not the image of that great day of judgment when the persecuted innocence will finally be made known and crowned."[136] These words underscore how Le Paige and Le Febvre de Saint-Hilaire did not distinguish between the sacred and profane, and they alert us to how the convent could be politically charged precisely because of its religious nature. A close examination of the Great Remonstrances as well as the parlementary debates surrounding Sainte-Agathe suggests that many of the same gendered and religious qualities Jansenists revered in nuns helped magistrates and lawyers denounce the despotism of the church and the king.

By the mid-eighteenth century, critics of the Old Regime applied the term "despotism" to signal abuses of power that stemmed from personal whim and excess. Since the late seventeenth century, when Fénelon had criticized Louis XIV's absolutist agenda in *Télémaque*, despotism had received attention from a variety of writers, most notably the philosophe and *parlementaire* Montesquieu.[137] As Lisa Graham's work has demonstrated, ordinary men and women also voiced concerns about despotism.[138] One of the arenas in which despotism provoked great concern was the juncture between the public and private. The relationship between Louis XV and his mistresses aroused deep anxiety because many viewed these women as having usurped the king's power for private purposes.[139] The marquis d'Argenson summed up the consensus regarding the problems of women and power: "All women, and above all this one [the marquise de Pompadour], are vindictive, dominated by their passions and limited intelligence and honesty."[140] D'Argenson's comment reveal how for eighteenth-century observers, "despotism . . . corresponded to the rule of passion, the lack of restraint, arbitrary and selfish authority, stereotypically female characteristics."[141]

This gendered rhetoric of despotism was not limited to the monarch and his courtesans but also encompassed clerics, even someone as notably pious as Christophe de Beaumont. The archbishop's first clash with the Parlement of Paris began in 1749 over the appointment of a new mother superior at the Hôpital général, Paris's premier poor relief institution. From the beginning of his appointment as archbishop in 1746, Beaumont was determined that the Hôpital's officers, reputed Jansenists, would accept *Unigenitus*.[142] When the incumbent mother superior fled the scene, Beaumont installed his own candidate, Louise-Urbine de Moysan, the unknown widow of one Hébert de Moysan.[143] After nineteen of the twenty-two administrators of the Hôpital resigned in protest, the marquis d'Argenson declared that "the archbishop of Paris has seized for himself the administration of the Hôpital général with a despotism that revolts everyone."[144] For historians, this controversy is noteworthy because it precipitated the nearly decade-long confrontation between the archbishop and his sovereign courts, of which the Sainte-Agathe affair was another chapter. But in the short term, what drew public attention was a full-scale Jansenist offensive against the central figure of this conflict, the new superior Madame de Moysan.

From the onset, opponents of the archbishop, including Adrien Le Paige, assailed Moysan in terms reminiscent of those used to characterize the king's mistress, namely, as a woman who had seized power through sexual means. In a satirical poem dedicated to Madame de Moysan, the Jansenist pamphleteer Nicolas Jouin portrays Moysan declaring to her subordinates, "Here [in the Hôpital général] all recognize my empire and my laws."[145] Thus, Moysan personified feminine rule by defining power in terms of her personal wishes. The critics of the archbishop seized the opportunity to smear his reputation, referring to the prelate and his protégé as "La Moisan and her pimp."[146] Their insistent reference to the new superior as "*his* Madame de Moysan" or "*his* widow" (my italics) almost created a doppelganger: Moysan symbolized Beaumont's feminine double. The archbishop's opponents thus sought to tarnish his reputation by linking him closely to feminine rule and through insinuations that Moysan's

Christophe de Beaumont du Repaire, 1703–81, archbishop of Paris and duke and peer of France. Courtesy of Bibliothèque de Port-Royal, Paris.

appointment had been motivated by an intimate association between him and the new superior.

Gendered elements continued to influence how Jansenist magistrates and lawyers portrayed nuns, prelates, and the parlement during the Sainte-Agathe affair and in the Great Remonstrances. I am not suggesting that nuns were the central figures of the lengthy remonstrances nor the sole motivation for their composition. Nevertheless, they are a window into how the rhetoric of gender could inform religious and political debates. The Parisian public had already been bombarded with images of the perfect nun, the submissive female who epitomized Christian virtue, and it would undoubtedly have been familiar with scandals such as the Hôpital général affair. More to the point, I would argue that the public would have picked up the magistrates' derogatory characterizations of the archbishop of Paris and ultramontane prelates as disorderly, feminized figures. These opposing images of feminine behavior also helped shape a masculine image for the parlement, one that stressed its reasonable behavior and adherence to law. This complicated gendered configuration was made apparent through the comparisons magistrates drew between bishops and themselves, between bishops and curés, and of course, between bishops and nuns.

The debates surrounding Sainte-Agathe established the archbishop of Paris as an illegitimate authority and the parlement as a legitimate one, a position that was underscored by gendered imagery that contrasted "feminine" arbitrariness and "masculine" justice. During the discussions regarding the Sainte-Agathe affair, magistrates cast Christophe de Beaumont in a feminized light to accentuate the ways in which he had exceeded his authority. The magistrate Frémont de Mazy described the archbishop as having "established an intolerable despotism." What characterized this despotism was the illogical nature of Beaumont's behavior: "he makes the administration of the sacraments depend on his caprice and fantasy; he makes such arbitrary rules that he judges apropos regarding these matters."[147] Words such as "caprice," "fantasy," and "arbitrary" were, of course, frequently used to critique feminine rule. Although Beaumont was not an explicitly "feminized" figure in this context, the implication was that he did not behave like a man who uses reason to moderate his behavior.

The magistrates did not hesitate to contrast their own, more rational behavior with that of the unreasonable activities of the archbishop. Beaumont's "arbitrary" behavior and his use of subterfuge and threats became even more pronounced when compared to that of the sovereign courts. In a meeting held on December 13 during which the magistrates heard about Beaumont's refusal to back down, Lefèvre d'Ormesson argued that there was "a contrast between the parlement's conduct, full of moderation and reverence, and the inflexible and obstinate conduct of Monsieur the archbishop of Paris." Ormesson then went on to describe the actions of the archbishop as "ruses and detours," behavior clearly beneath the parlement. In contrast, the *Nouvelles ecclésiastiques* depicted the courts as a serious and conscientious debating body seeking to correct the wrongs done by the archbishop, issuing *arrêts* that were legal and forthright. The writers of the *Nouvelles* argued that unlike the apparently self-serving prelate, the magistrates only sought "to use all their efforts to procure such a great good [the last rites]."[148] Thus, within a broad gendered political discourse, the parlement was an upstanding masculine body committed to the rational and open venue of the courts. Whereas the magistrates acted like responsible men and served others, the archbishop and his cohorts were, in effect, attempting to co-opt the power of others, especially the king, to satisfy their own ambitions.

Part of feminine rule included the desire to impose one's will on others, and the authors of the Great Remonstrances argued that ultramontane bishops sought to dominate both the monarchy and the clergy. The magistrates contended that ultramontane bishops were potential usurpers, harboring worldly aspirations to be "the arbiters of your subjects, the judges of magistrates, the sovereigns of sovereigns themselves."[149] These bishops also hoped to extend their control over the lower clergy. Addressing Louis XV, the authors of the remonstrances described how in many dioceses "bishops, more zealous about their domination than your authority, sire, have abused your confidence by making trouble in their churches and by making their inferiors submit to rigorous laws."[150]

The apprehensiveness of the lower clergy reflected the concerns of one of the key contributors to the remonstrances, the lawyer and canonist Claude Mey. Influenced by the seventeenth-century syndic of the Sorbonne, Edmond Richer, the lawyer espoused Richerism, the notion of a primitive church whose spiritual authority was derived from councils that had greater authority than bishops or the papacy. Mey and the abbé Gabriel-Nicolas Maultrot had elucidated their Richerist ideas in *Apologie de tous les jugemens rendus par les tribunaux séculiers* in 1752. In addition to justifying the right of the parlements to intervene in the refusal of the sacraments, the two-volume treatise argued that curés ruled dioceses *with* bishops and not *under* them. The authors of the Great Remonstrances voiced such Richerist principles when they placed simple priests on a par with bishops. The arrogance and high-handedness of ultramontane bishops was accentuated by the description the remonstrances offered of "the many curés faithful to their responsibilities" who had been removed from their parishes "by the false zeal of bishops."[151] Like the sovereign courts, the "good" curé described in the remonstrances possessed certain positive masculine attributes, such as a sense of responsibility and moderation.

And the resistance of Jansenist curés was shown as righteous behavior, confined within the parameters of their obligations, unlike the defiance of ultramontane bishops who exceeded their authority. Thus, a Richerist vision of the Gallican church acquired a gendered dimension through the contrasting behavior of Jansenist clerics and ultramontane prelates.

How did magistrates position nuns within this highly inflammatory political rhetoric? Did nuns feature in this "gendered" Richerism? Yes, just as the contrast between bishops and curés opposed feminine disorder to masculine order, so the polarity between bishops and nuns opposed femi-

Engraving of the parlements' magistrates presenting their remonstrances to Louis XV, 1753. The image in the lower right corner depicts Soeur Perpétue of Sainte-Agathe being denied the last rites. Courtesy of Bibliothèque de Port-Royal, Paris.

nine despotism to female virtue. The paragraph immediately following the discourse on curés provided a description of women religious that, with its overblown rhetoric and heart-wrenching imagery, verged on melodrama. While noting how numerous priests had suffered, the authors of the remonstrances maintained that an "infinite multitude of nuns [had been] snatched from these sacred asylums which they had vowed to God never to leave." Their numbers and their suffering presented the most "grievous spectacle afflicting Religion."[152] The exaggerated terms "infinite" and "multitude" gave the impression that nuns were the group most singled out by bishops because of their helplessness. "Despite their [the Jansenist nuns'] entire submission to the church and the innocence of their morals," bishops treated these women religious scandalously by denying them "all forms of spiritual support, even those that are not refused to criminals before their death."[153] The references to the obedience of nuns, their sacrifices, and their afflictions were strongly reminiscent of the image of the model nun, the female figure so popular in Jansenist literature.

I would suggest that the same principles that made nuns icons in Jansenist rhetoric were at play in the Great Remonstrances.[154] The remonstrances exalted nuns whose vows and gender made them worthy of sympathy. The authors of the remonstrances emphasized that unlike priests who were assigned to their parishes, nuns had ties to their convent that reflected a personal choice and their bond with God. By ejecting nuns from a place both removed from the world and closer to God, ultramontane bishops, in effect, defiled their vows, the cornerstone of monastic life. Aging or dying nuns, whose vows tended to be less elastic, were even more helpless than male monastics.

The authors of the Great Remonstrances used these images of the submissive and sequestered nun to highlight the despotic intentions of the ultramontane bishops. In January 1753 the parlement became preoccupied with the Orléans communities of Saint Loup, Saint-Charles, and the Filles du Calvaire, where women religious had not received the sacraments for more than twenty years.[155] It had long fought the bishop of Orléans, Nicolas-Joseph de Pâris who had recently refused the last rites to a dying nun deprived of the sacraments during this period. According to the remonstrances, although the nun had not accepted *Unigenitus,* she had made "the most authentic and the least equivocal declaration of her submission to all the decisions of the Church."[156] But, as had been the case for the martyred Port-Royal nuns, sacrifice and obedience, the hallmarks of monastic vows, were rewarded with unjust slurs, such as being labeled "a rebel child of the Church."[157] The authors of the remonstrances argued that the real villain in this instance was the bishop who denied the sacraments to her, arrogantly declaring himself "the author of this schismatic act." Furthermore, the remonstrances suggested that the prelate wanted nothing less than to undermine the king's authority, and by extension that of the parlement because he "wishes to cover your Majesty's absolute power with this open schism."[158] The difference between bishops and nuns was not so much an opposition between masculine and feminine as that between unruly femininity overreaching itself and virtuous femininity accepting its place. Unlike Jansenist pamphlets, parlementary debates and remonstrances did not place this female model of spirituality at the center of their arguments. Nonetheless, by extolling the former, parlementary rhetoric negated the subordination of nuns to bishops. Women religious may have ranked lowest within the clerical hierarchy, but their actions as believers possessed a moral superiority over those who attempted to coerce and command.

Parlementary discourse surrounding nuns also implicated the king as a despot. As we have seen, public opinion, fed on stories of Louis XV's voracious sexual appetite and his mistresses' equally voracious thirst for power, regarded Louis XV as an unmanned king who, ruled by women, failed to rule justly.[159] The king's decision to use a *lettre de cachet* to remove Sister Perpétue from Sainte-Agathe was a sign of this weakness, and it did not go unnoticed or uncontested. The remonstrances implicitly took the king to task. The authors described how Sister Perpétue was "kidnapped suddenly during the night by a severe order, without any regard for her age or infirmities." Arbitrary uses of the *lettres de cachet* damaged the relationship between sovereign and subjects since "the French, in whom love is the principle and gage of their loyalty, become alarmed and troubled when they have to fear their sovereign."[160] The implications of this statement were apparent. A good monarch was a paternal figure, one whom subjects could trust as children would their father. Louis XV had undoubtedly lost that trust. The public, or at least the Parisian public, took to heart the events of December 1752 to May 1753. Indeed, a pamphlet appeared later in May 1753 entitled *Lettre de cachet du public au Roy, en réponse de celles de sa Majesté adressées aux officiers de Parlement de Paris la nuit du 8 ou 9 Mai 1753.*[161] Although this polemic was not a direct response to Sister Perpétue's abduction, it does indicate that the public would have interpreted Louis XV's actions in the Sainte-Agathe affair as high-handed and arbitrary and not the legitimate actions of a just king.

In the parlementary debates that took place in December 1752, the magistrates added the public to the cast of characters implicated in the Sainte-Agathe scandal. From the beginning of the affair, those associated with the sovereign courts argued that the predicament of the ailing Sister Perpétue alarmed "the public" as a whole. The magistrate Frémont du Mazy described Sister Perpétue's trials as a "public calamity," a time when "the state, public tranquillity and the safety of citizens is being attacked."[162] Further debates indicate that the magistrates strengthened the link between Sister Perpétue's situation and this larger public in the days following the nun's forced removal from the convent of Saint-Agathe. Speaking on December 29, Robert de Saint-Vincent noted that "the public, which is paying close attention to these nocturnal and violent kidnappings, sees in it [their] connection with the vexations that this sick woman previously endured." Given the royal use of *lettres de cachets* and late-night kidnappings, "what citizen must not be terrified?"[163] The citizen in question was the larger public.

In tying the fears of citizens at large with Sister Perpétue, Robert de Saint Vincent transformed, in effect, the nun into a secular symbol, one whose fate inspired terror in French citizens, who now considered themselves to be at the mercy of a scheming clergy and unjust king. For Jansenists, Sister Perpétue represented one of the many martyrs to *la Vérité*, but for magistrates interested in gaining public support, she now personified the vulnerable citizen. Women religious were not the only ecclesiastical figures configured as citizens within the Great Remonstrances, but unlike other monastics, nuns and the laity shared the same reliance on ecclesiastics. Without them, neither could take communion, confess, or, most abhorrent of all, receive the last rites. Thus, women religious, more than any other clerical person, resembled the laity insofar as they depended on male clerics to legitimate their membership within the French polity and society. The magistrates also claimed to protect the *independence* of the same citizens. Thus, the construction of nuns as citizens was also linked to matters of conscience at the core of the struggle between Jansenist nuns and the ultramontane clergy.

During the refusal of sacraments crisis, Jansenist *parlementaires* and polemicists suggested an approach to citizenship that was founded on individual conscience. In their clashes with the ultramontane clergy they repeatedly demanded that bishops desist from interfering in the personal consciences of women religious. Their mandate strained the fundamental link between the Gallican church and citizenship. As two of the more controversial legacies of Louis XIV's reign, the Edict of Fontainebleau and *Unigenitus*, indicate, catholicity was intrinsic to the early modern definition of citizenship. Jeffrey Merrick has noted that the state "compelled subjects to attest births, marriages, and death through participation in the baptismal, matrimonial, and mortuary rites of the national faith."[164] Thus, the Gallican church determined civil existence within the French state, and each of these rites necessitated the presence of a male cleric, the ordained mediator between God and the laity. Now, however, Jansenist *parlementaires* argued that internal conscience was a private matter that neither temporal *nor ecclesiastical* authority could disturb.[165] Moreover, nuns became one of the vehicles through which magistrates and lawyers sought

to delimit ecclesiastical activity. Indeed, Jansenist nuns themselves politicized their spiritual independence and regarded it as a right. For example,
in 1738 the ultra-Jansenist Filles du Calvaire of Paris declared that they
were "French before being nuns" and therefore could not be denied the
sacraments.[166] Although hardly an assertion of citizenship, this statement
essentially privileged membership within a secular body rather than commitment to the church. Moreover, the right to private conscience without
any interference from the clergy increasingly sounded like secularized
civic autonomy.

In an examination of the recent historiography on citizens in the Old Regime, Gail Bossenga has noted that modern citizenship "called for the formation of a new kind of state based on the principles of equality, freedom,
secularization, and national determination."[167] While the year 1789 con-
tinues to be the definitive moment when such notions were fully articulated and institutionalized, some historians have argued that the foundation was laid in the previous decades. For example, Keith Baker and David
Bien have suggested that the principles of the Declaration of Rights are located not in Enlightenment political thought alone but also in the traditional institutions and practices of the Old Regime.[168] Dale Van Kley and
David Bell have argued that religious developments and rhetoric lay the
groundwork for the French Revolution and modern notions of nation-
hood.[169] The association of Sister Perpétue with French citizens points to
the increasingly fluid and unstable definition of citizenship in the eighteenth century, one which prefigured modern understandings of citizenship while remaining rooted in early modern institutions.

Bell has claimed that Jansenists tolerated female voices like the Filles
du Calvaire because of their views regarding the private nature of religious belief.[170] For Jansenist *parlementaires* and polemicists, conscience was
a private arena of religious faith, immune from scrutiny, that negated the
public functions of the Gallican church within the state. The support of
Jansenist nuns certainly did not mean that male authors embraced female
agency and autonomy. Whereas Jansenist theologians and polemicists acknowledged female resistance to *Unigenitus*, Jansenist magistrates and
lawyers, speaking to a larger and more diffuse public, muted such opposition. The authors of the remonstrances were not about to include Sister
Perpétue's sarcastic comment about *Unigenitus* being "a fine document"
or her refusal to condemn Quesnel.[171] Instead, in a conversation with
Louis XV, René-Charles de Maupeou remarked on the "weakness of her
sex" when referring to Sister Perpétue and her removal from Sainte-
Agathe.[172] The citizen constructed within such rhetoric, while a legitimate

public figure, continued to be a passive one. Jeffrey Merrick has noted that "the *parlementaires* did not infantilize citizens by describing them, like subjects, as the children of the royal father, but neither did they transform them into adults endowed with political initiative and equal rights."[173] Citizenship then did not denote popular sovereignty, but reflected the citizen's subordinate and submissive position with respect to the king. Thus, Maupeou's characterization of Sister Perpétue helps explain why Jansenist nuns could sometimes exemplify citizens in the volatile 1750s and into the 1760s.

But as the place of women religious in Jansenist rhetoric suggests, the exclusion of women from the public sphere and citizenry did not follow a straight course with an apparent end. At the height of the refusal of sacraments crisis, religious interiority was itself a contested space. Jansenists may have been attempting to shut out clerics from the realm of conscience. Nevertheless, Jansenist *parlementaires* themselves repeatedly entered into the mysterious world of the cloister, taking their public with them. And although nuns were hardly making a determined stance against the patriarchal nature of the church, they were certainly willing to go to great lengths to assert their beliefs, risking their reputations as virtuous women. Therefore, gender was not always automatic grounds for exclusion from the political arena, particularly in a patriarchal system that was becoming increasingly unsteady and unsure. Within the fluctuating understanding of authority and citizenship, Jansenist nuns came to be one of the most dramatic examples of the besieged citizen, whose defenselessness was underscored by her feminine weakness and institutional marginality.

These same characteristics enabled the magistrates to forge a certain political identity for themselves. As Merrick has observed, the Parlement of Paris "did not hesitate to speak out, on behalf of the subjects who could not speak for themselves, against injustices of various sorts."[174] It appropriated the conflict between women religious and prelates in order to appear as the protectors of "the liberty of faithful subjects" threatened by "the arbitrary will of certain ecclesiastics."[175] Thus, the images of passive and beleaguered nuns, which represented the vulnerability of the laity as a whole, were important in shaping a heroic and masculine identity. Without such helpless figures to justify their actions and rhetoric, to mute their own defiance of the crown and church, *parlementaires* would come across as rebellious and self-serving. Indeed, the efforts of Jansenist lawyers to limit episcopal authority within the convent continued into the 1780s. Examples include the controversies surrounding the Religieuses Hospitalières of the Rue Mouffetard, the Ursulines of Saint-Cloud, the Hôtel-Dieu of Paris, and the Ursulines of Mans.[176] Lawyers became involved in sorting out the constitutions of these communities and defending the rights of

Engraving praising the magistrates of the parlements as defenders of French laws against the "scourge of France." The female figure bearing the cross draws attention to the masculine identities of the *parlementaires.* Courtesy of Bibliothèque de Port-Royal, Paris.

nuns to elect superiors and to admit novices. The convent became a forum for translating political abstractions into concrete reality. Over and over, lawyers depicted nuns as citizens with rights, rights that could not be trammeled even by those who had legitimate authority over nuns, such as mother superiors.

3

DESPOTIC HABITS

The Critique of Feminine Power in the Cloister, 1740–1770

DURING THE 1750S, JANSENISTS, SUCH AS THE FIGURIST THEOLGIAN Jean-Baptiste Gaultier and the lawyer Louis-Adrien Le Paige, raised the alarm about clerical despotism and the dangers it presented throughout French society, including the convent. They argued that ultramontane bishops and other like-minded clerics introduced confusion into the cloister by interfering with the laws and constitutions of female religious communities. Polemicists, lawyers, and *parlementaires* publicly denounced such clerics as abusing their authority in order to maintain an illegitimate presence in the convent. In 1777 the *Nouvelles ecclésiastiques* ominously remarked that in many convents, "since the violence committed in favor of the bull *Unigenitus,* one has seen abbesses imitating zealous bishops, pretending to reign in the most absolute and most arbitrary manner . . . requiring the most blind obedience."[1]

Despite such hostility, the powers and influence of the mother superior were, in fact, legitimate under law as well as custom. Whether she was selected by her peers through an election process or appointed by the king, the mother superior exercised authority as the head of a corporate entity

An earlier version of this chapter was published as "Despotic Habits: The Critique of Power and Its Abuses in an Eighteenth-Century Convent," *French Historical Studies* 23, no. 1 (2000): 33–66.

with legal privileges. On one level, the superior resembled other women who possessed genuine powers, for example, an absent nobleman's wife who acted as *seigneur* in his place or the widow of a master printer who assumed the responsibilities of the print shop.[2] But unlike these women, who often acquired authority by default, the mother superior held an irreplaceable position, since the cloister had to be governed by women. She possessed institutional, spiritual, and social power guaranteed by the rules and constitutions of that community. A *mémoire judiciaire* written in 1769 outlined the full scope of the mother superior's authority: "Canon law gives them [mother superiors] the title of spiritual mother, in the same sense that abbots have the quality of father. They [mother superiors] are in charge of souls . . . their jurisdiction is spiritual like abbots, they have the same right to order, punish, correct matters that concern monastic disciple." With respect to the rest of the nuns in the community, they must "obey them, and like a mother, and like a superior invested with the episcopacy."[3] As this statement suggests, the power of the mother superior brought together the authority of parents, monarchy, and upper clergy, asserting a "paternal" presence in the all-female environment of the cloister.[4] In effect, the superior's authority derived its legitimacy from its links to the masculine power of fathers, priests, and kings. A good mother superior overcame the weaknesses of her sex and assumed the characteristics of a rational masculine figure able to command the willing obedience of her subordinates.

But as the *Nouvelles*'s ominous remarks suggest, eighteenth-century readers distrusted this apparently unassailable authority figure, who had transformed into a figure of despotism by the 1770s. Three factors contributed to the growing suspicion of the mother superior: the anxieties about female power, the hostility toward monasticism, and the readiness of nuns to oppose their superiors publicly. As the previous chapter demonstrated, despotism, whether clerical or temporal, came to have a distinctly feminine cast, and female figures of power such as Madame de Pompadour and Marie-Antoinette became the focus of vitriolic attacks.[5] While the polemical literature of the early modern period indicates that fear of feminine power was constant, this antifeminine rhetoric coincided with the emergence of a "model of the egalitarian public sphere, which rested on the bourgeois family and the cult of domesticity."[6] At the center of this ideal was the mother who devoted herself to her duties as parent and wife, thus eschewing the world of the salons and the court. This normative vision of maternity functioned as a critique against elite women, such as mother superiors, who wielded what contemporaries regarded as unlimited influence and power.

In the mid-eighteenth century, mother superiors were vulnerable to charges of despotism not only because they were women but because they were a part of the regular clergy. The antagonism leveled at monastics emanated from two factions who were hardly allies: the Jansenists and the philosophes. Although Jansenist lawyers and magistrates praised the virtues of Jansenist female religious communities, they had firmly and irrevocably linked despotism to religious orders through their unwavering and highly publicized campaign against the Jesuits. According to one magistrate, " 'all Jesuits without distinction are subjected and bound to the absolute and arbitrary will of the General alone, by all the fetters which it is possible to imagine.' "[7] While Jansenist *parlementaires* spoke out against a specific monastic order, Enlightenment philosophes espoused a more far-reaching anticlericalism that condemned the monastic system. In 1765 d'Alembert celebrated the Jesuits' banishment by publishing *Sur la destruction des jésuites en France, par un auteur désinteressé,* which declared that the "monastic spirit is the scourge of all states."[8] In this antagonistic climate, the mother superior combined what had come to be twin evils: clerical authority and female power.

What made the superior an easy target for those outside the convent were those who lived with her in the cloister. As the scandals involving Sainte-Agathe or the Franciscans of Beauvais suggest, female religious had distinct ideas about who had authority over their consciences, their constitutions, and their communities. Mother superiors were not exempt from the rules and regulations that governed the convent. The same rules that gave superiors prerogatives also governed them. When a mother superior acted in ways that apparently denied these rules, nuns did not hesitate to go over her head to ecclesiastical and secular courts for justice and order. During the 1760s such trials acquired larger political meaning, as the despotism of a mother superior added to the pool of public discourse that inveighed against authority figures who overreached themselves.

This chapter examines two such conflicts between superiors and nuns in which lawyers attacked the legitimate authority of the mother superior and proposed reforms for female monastic communities. The first case, involving the royal Benedictine abbey of Saint-Pierre de Beaumont near Clermont-Ferrand, took place in 1764, and the second, concerning the *hôtel-dieu* (or hospital) of Saint-Nicolas in Pontoise, occurred five years later. Although replete with details worthy of a scandalous novel, the internal contestations that tore apart the abbey of Beaumont and priory of Saint-Nicolas were not unique events. Indeed, both trials belong to a cluster of similar cases tried between 1750 and 1775 in which nuns charged their superior with abusing his or her authority.[9] For example, one of the legal briefs in the Beaumont trial cited the ongoing saga involving the Ursulines of Saint-Cloud and the archbishop of Paris.[10] And at the same time that the Saint-Nicolas affair was attracting attention, the nuns of Bon Secours were challenging the appointment of their new prioress Madame de Saillant.

For the lawyers defending the nuns, the quarrels between superiors and nuns amounted to more than internecine bickering; it represented a struggle between feminine despotism, embodied by the mother superior, and feminine virtue, personified by the nuns who opposed her. In the Beaumont affair, analyzed in the first half of the chapter, two lawyers for the nuns, Duclosel and the Parisian barrister Pierre-Daniel-Jean Le Roy de Fontenelle, focused on the transgressions of the abbess Madame de Lantilhac and her sister, Madame de Sedières, two aristocratic women who abused their status for power. The lawyers argued that the abbess's depraved reign was the source of conflict and disorder in the convent, and that peace would be restored if the Madame de Lantilhac did her duty as a mother. As the second half of this chapter demonstrates, the lawyer Jean-Baptiste Faré attacked the Saint-Nicolas prioress in a similar fashion, criticizing her aristocratic pretensions and her lack of "maternal" feeling. For the lawyers of the Beaumont affair, the solution was to keep Madame de Lantilhac in check, but Faré went further and concluded that the cloister was an inherently bad structure of government needing reform. Although in neither trial did the lawyers challenge the position of the mother superior, their arguments weakened the authority of the superior by casting her as a woman unable to rule because of her sex and unfulfilled because of her vocation.

Speaking before the Grande Chambre of the Parlement of Paris on July 21, 1764, the *procureur-général* Joly de Fleury warned his audience "you are going to see war kindled and discord reigning among girls consecrated to the service of God who should only be occupied with the practice of virtue."[11] This cloistered "war" referred specifically to the sensational case that pitted fifteen nuns from the Benedictine abbey, Saint-Pierre-de-Beaumont in Auvergne, against their abbess, Marie-Thérèse de Lantilhac. At the center of this trial was the nuns' accusation that the superior had introduced a regime of disorder into the cloister. The abbess had grossly mismanaged the affairs of the abbey, behaved abusively toward her subordinates, and conducted herself in an indecent manner. According to the nuns, immediately after her appointment as abbess in 1757, Madame de Lantilhac and her sister Madame de Sedières, also a nun at the abbey, began pursuing a life of luxury and excess.[12] The abbey witnessed the constant traffic of male clerics and laity who were entertained at sumptuous fetes serving the choicest delicacies and finest wines; these parties also sponsored activities in which participants engaged in dancing and even cross-dressing. In the meantime, maintained the nuns, the abbess and her sister starved the sisters who were outside their inner circle, depriving them of basic nourishment, visiting privileges, and even the sacraments.

In May 1763 rumors of this disorder reached the ears of the bishop of Clermont, the convent's male superior, who intervened on two occasions. He exhorted the nuns to obey their superior and reprimanded the abbess for distancing herself from the community.[13] Despite these efforts, relations within the abbey continued to deteriorate. In September of that year three of the nuns, Albanel, Brunel, and Gaschier, used the *appel comme d'abus* and brought criminal charges against the abbess before the lieutenant general of the *sénéchaussée*. When the provincial secular courts ruled against her, Madame de Lantilhac rejected their decrees and proceeded to bring charges against her three opponents before the *officialité*, the diocesan ecclesiastical courts which were, her lawyer argued, "their [all monastics'] natural judge[s]."[14] Claiming that she could no longer gain any justice in Auvergne, Madame de Lantilhac and her lawyers then took the case before the Parlement of Paris. The sovereign courts finally terminated this sordid scandal with a fifteen-page *arrêt* to be posted throughout Paris.[15] Although the *arrêt* afforded the abbess satisfaction in that it, more or less, declared her innocence, it also complied with her opponents' wishes that an accountant from the outside be appointed to supervise her administration.

This *arrêt* indicates how by 1764, the very year the Jesuits were expelled from France, the Parlement of Paris had come to assume a powerful, albeit contested, role within the Gallican church. Not only did the sovereign courts act as arbitrators in appeals cases lodged against ecclesiastics, but as the earlier Jansenist controversies indicate, the parlements increasingly policed ecclesiastical institutions, always on the lookout for clerical abuses of power. However, the Beaumont affair was not a Jansenist one. Unlike the scandal involving Sainte-Agathe, this trial did not result from theological conflicts over *Unigenitus*, as is clearly indicated by its absence from the pages of the Jansenist *Nouvelles ecclésiastiques* or the papers of the Jansenist mastermind Le Paige.[16] There is nonetheless evidence of some Jansenist influence. The principal barrister representing the Beaumont nuns before the Parlement of Paris was Jean-Baptiste Le Gouvé, who had close ties to Le Paige and had earned his reputation by working on behalf of the creditor Jean Lioncy against the Jesuits in 1761.[17] It remains difficult to ascertain Le Gouvé's role in shaping the public images of the Beaumont affair, since he did not sign any of the relevant printed *mémoires judiciaires* or legal briefs; one may only conjecture that he had a hand in Le Roy de Fontenelle's *Mémoire aux chambres assemblées*, written and circulated while the parlement was hearing the case. What remains unquestionable is the pervasive influence of Jansenist anticlericalism, if not in motivation then certainly in rhetoric and argument.

The lawyers Duclosel and Le Roy de Fontenelle appear to have followed the blueprint created by their Jansenist colleagues, portraying the conflict as one between proper and improper expressions of feminine nature. They depicted their clients as the embodiment of the virtuous Christian female, passive victims forced to violate the silence imposed on them by their monastic vows. In contrast, the lawyers portrayed the abbess Madame de Lantilhac and her sister Madame de Sedières as female monsters, despots who abused their power and aristocratic status to satiate their libertine proclivities. Moreover, whereas her opponents were seen through the prism of a seventeenth-century ideal that fused Christian morality and feminine virtue, the superior was measured by a new secular standard of femininity, one that was rooted in physiology and newer understandings of familial bonds. Duclosel and Le Roy de Fontenelle attributed disorder in the convent to the abbess's inability to meet competing expectations of masculine rationality and maternal love.

While the anticlerical comments of Duclosel and Le Roy de Fontenelle about the abbess and her sister reflected those found in the political controversies previously discussed, the more sordid images of the abbey derived from seventeenth- and eighteenth-century fiction. The literary public would have been familiar with seventeenth-century titles such as *Les Lettres portuguaises* and *La Religieuse malgré elle,* and perhaps pornographic pieces such as *Vénus dans le cloître*.[18] Some convents, such as the Abbey of Longchamp, had an element of notoriety.[19] And given that the laity's actual access to the cloister was intermittent and erratic, how was the reading public to differentiate between the daily lives of women religious and the fictive fantasies of love, sorrow, and bitterness raging in this closed female space? We must imagine that when Duclosel and Le Roy de Fontenelle faithfully recorded their clients' stories about scandalous behavior in the cloister, they were, in effect, fulfilling the readers' expectations. Drawing from the political discourse on clerical despotism and the fictional images of the libertine convent, the lawyers could argue that feminine aristocratic authority engendered chaos not just in the cloister but in the larger society.

In their attack on the abbess Madame de Lantilhac, Duclosel and Le Roy de Fontenelle attributed the abbey's disorder to the ways in which the abbess and her sister clung to their aristocratic rank. By the 1750s a stereotype of the degenerate aristocrat had gained currency among nobles and non-nobles alike. Enjoying legal privileges and unearned wealth, the stereotypical aristocrat embodied a decadent way of life devoted to luxury and libertine pursuits.[20] The men and women who indulged in this opulent lifestyle filled with gambling, extravagant fashion, and sumptuous surroundings were easy targets in an environment where utility, citizenship, and concern for public welfare were increasingly the reigning virtues. Similarly, the accusation against Lantilhac of maintaining aristocratic habits comprised a host of faults including arrogance, excess, gender disorder, and despotism.

A pamphlet titled *A monsieur le lieutenant-général,* issued in Auvergne on behalf of the nuns of Beaumont, constructed an image of the abbess that fell in line with this stereotype of the debauched aristocrat. It was the first public volley against Madame de Lantilhac and set the standard for subsequent arguments made by Duclosel and Le Roy de Fontenelle. The anonymous author condemned Madame de Lantilhac and her sister Madame de Sedières for their refusal to shed their worldly status: "There are in all communities these haughty nuns; believing they have honored the convent in which they have professed, [they] imagine that their birth precedes their duties and [claustral] regularity."[21] These references to the two sisters' social origins were not a reflection of "class conflict." Indeed, the legal briefs omitted any reference to the ranks of the Beaumont nuns, thereby avoiding any comparison of social status.[22] For the lawyers it was not the sisters' birth per se that was at issue. Rather, it was the manipulation of their status for their own purposes that was reprehensible, especially in an arena that purportedly renounced social distinctions.

Madame de Lantilhac and Madame de Sedières used the privilege of their rank to live a life of self-indulgence and idleness in a manner reminiscent of the caricature of the aristocrat. *A monsieur le lieutenant-général* and the two *mémoires judiciaires* for the nuns read like a veritable catalogue of aristocratic depravity, citing numerous examples of libertinism and luxury that violated two tenets of monastic vows, poverty and chastity.[23] As mentioned earlier, the abbess had used the community's income to throw lavish fetes to entertain male ecclesiastics and laity. These extravaganzas not only allowed the abbess's followers and friends "to share her luxury and her pleasures" but also enabled young novices and boarders to socialize freely with men.[24] The charges of indulging in luxury were hardly offhand remarks, given that "in eighteenth-century France it [the concept of luxury] brought together such different concerns as the state of Christian values, worries about aristocratic profligacy, the effects of commerce and consumerism on society, and the condition of the countryside; in sum, it was a convenient code for all of society's perceived problems."[25] For many social theorists, the aristocratic devotion to pleasure led to an overall weakening of the body politic. Lantilhac's excesses damaged the foundation of the cloister, the preserve of female chastity whose sanctity depended on the renunciation of men and of worldly activity. Le Roy de Fontenelle provided a graphic description of festivities in which "one danced the Sauteuse to the voice of a novice, which often exposed [the novices] to falling, and each fall was punished by a monkish embrace."[26] Moreover, the abbess herself had taken this interaction between men and women a step further. According to Le Roy de Fontenelle, "Madame de Lantilhac put on a monk's habit, permitted all the monks to wear her ab-batial breast cross one after the other, [and] one of them to adopt her de-shabille."[27] Duclosel declared that the abbess had converted her apart-ments into a "theater of fetes and pleasures" and the convent itself into a "theater of licentiousness," so that it was "no more than a House of Plea-sure."[28]

These charges of theatricality and gender disorder possessed added meaning in the context of contemporary criticisms aimed against two groups of very visible women: elite women and actresses. In the *Lettre à M. d'Alembert sur son article "Genève"* (1758), Jean-Jacques Rousseau censured the visibility and dominance of the Parisian *salonnière*. Rousseau argued that in addition to displaying themselves in an unseemly fashion, these women stifled men by dominating them. As a result, men were "going to learn from women what they [men] should take care to teach them." Ac-cording to Rousseau, this relationship represented a "reversal of natural relationships."[29] Actresses, he claimed, similarly contributed to this gen-der disorder by flaunting themselves and by performing in plays which clearly gave them the upper hand over male protagonists.[30] This gender disorder, or perhaps more accurately this emasculation, and the ensuing reversal of power relations, resulted in the decay of French society. Thus, by introducing gender confusion, the abbess threatened not only the chaste serenity of the cloister but the natural order of the sexes. She had brought to life what readers encountered in fiction: the convent turned into a brothel, which led to further disorder, namely, women turned into men. In fact, Lantilhac and Sedières's insistence on rank inverted the world of the convent, transforming it from a refuge of devotion and chastity to a stage for libertinism. Moreover, as Sarah Maza has argued, Rousseau's critique of the theater represented a political critique: "the theater equals high society equals the court equals absolute monarchical government, or *despotisme*. Each term in the succession of equivalences is a feminized world of display and deceit, and in each the power of the fe-male principle dictates the weakening of the male."[31]

The insinuations of sexual depravity and theatricality easily shaded into accusations of despotism as the lawyers for the Beaumont nuns linked the lavish worldly activities to the corruption of power. Le Roy de Fontenelle pinpointed disorderliness in the abbey to a particular vice: the abbess's ad-diction to alcohol.[32] The lawyer described how "wine consumed her, it nearly deprived her of her existence"; according to Duclosel, wine re-duced the superior to a state of "total inertia."[33] The effects of this

la Religieuse   *Page 219.*

Une autre avoit pris ma place sur le bord
du lit de la supérieure,

"Another had taken my place at the edge of the superior's bed." Frontispiece from a 1798 copy of Diderot's *La Religieuse*. The engraving features the "court" of the mother superior of Sainte-Eutrope, indicating how contemporaries regarded superiors. Cliché Bibliothèque Nationale de France, Paris.

predilection had been twofold. First, the abbess's penchant for wine added to the financial hardship of the community; Duclosel claimed that in three weeks Lantilhac and her sister had consumed 133 livres' worth of fine wines.[34] But even more devastating than the resulting penury was the abbess's transference of the convent's government to her sister, who ruled with a "rod of iron."[35]

In their legal briefs both Duclosel and Le Roy de Fontenelle implied that Madame de Sedières had seized power, thus recalling the popular eighteenth-century metaphor of the oriental despot, a lord of the realm who is so immersed in the pleasures of the harem that he neglects his duties.[36] According to this narrative of despotism, in the absence of true leadership the lord's minister assumes control, wields power with unrestrained brutality, and becomes a feared and hated figure throughout the realm. France under the Bourbons had more than its share of hated ministers, most notably Richelieu and Mazarin in the seventeenth century, and later, in the 1770s and 1780s, Maupeou and Calonne. But for the public of the early 1760s, the person who best fit the role of the despotic minister was not a man but a mistress: Jeanne-Antoinette Poisson, the marquise de Pompadour. The marquis d'Argenson bitingly described her as a woman "who assumes complete power as a cardinal prime minister might have done. She regards the king's ministers as hers." Critics contended that in order to maintain her usurped power, Pompadour corrupted the French court by converting it into a pleasure palace, or in d'Argenson's words "the interior of a seraglio."[37] Arguably, such images of Pompadour helped shape the depiction of Madame de Sedières in the Beaumont controversy.[38]

Both the pamphlet *A monsieur le lieutenant-général* and Duclosel's *Requête présentée à monsieur l'official* catalogued Madame de Sedières's misdeeds, transgressions that closely paralleled those associated with despotic ministers and mistresses. They included the appropriation of legitimate power, the misuse of that power, and the subversion of legal procedure. Just as Pompadour had debased the sacred nature of the monarchy, so had Madame de Sedières converted the convent from a sacred space of prayer and contemplation to a den of hedonistic pleasures. She was the antithesis of a nun, "not very content with not practicing any kind of [monastic] rule, replacing the duties and austerities of her state with a voluptuous life."[39] Moreover, the unflattering dissimilarities between Sedières and her fellow nuns only fueled the former's rancor against her claustral peers. The nuns described Sedières as continually punishing them because "their crime is loving their state, their crime is contrasting an edifying conduct with her own excessive taste for pleasure, their crime finally, and it is an unpardonable crime in her eyes, was daring to complain."[40] In his *Requête* Duclosel argued that Madame de Sedières was able to extract her revenge by employing "the power of her sister so as to fulfill her ever renewed projects of hatred and vengeance."[41]

The lawyer also contended that Sedières had dared to subvert the law itself. Although he never provided his audience with specific details, Duclosel charged Sedières with attempting to stop the trial by seducing the lieutenant general of the *sénéchaussée*.[42] When that failed, Duclosel suggested, Madame de Sedières made her supporters submit false deposi-

tions by having them copy statements written by others.[43] Thus, she had
not only engaged in despotic activities to punish her enemies but manipulated and corrupted those loyal to her. In this manner, Sedières had per-
verted her usurped authority in particularly "feminine" ways—through
unruly passions and illicit means, all for the purposes of her own pleasure
and ambition.

Duclosel and Le Roy de Fontenelle went on to challenge *legitimate* feminine authority, namely the abbess herself. The acquisition of her position
through royal decree may have distinguished Madame de Lantilhac from
her sister, but her misuse of power effectively rendered the superior's authority illegitimate. The lawyers for the Beaumont nuns set out to prove
that Lantilhac had upset the natural relationship existing between a
mother superior and her subordinates, a relationship defined by "filial"
bonds. Duvert d'Emalleville, the lawyer for the opposition, argued that
the abbess, as a "mother," rightly denied the nuns visits with relatives on
the basis that the ensuing effect would be to "agitate spirits, [and] corrupt
hearts." Le Roy de Fontenelle countered this assertion by vehemently declaring that "this is not the act of a mother, this is despotism."[44] The accusation that she had deprived the nuns of food also illustrated Madame de
Lantilhac's lack of maternal love. From the beginning, the nuns maintained that the abbess had provided them only with a basic allowance of
bread at the same time as she lavishly entertained visitors.[45] As the trial
progressed, these charges became more exaggerated. Le Roy de
Fontenelle vividly depicted the nuns as being "reduced to soothing their
young [charges] through that [food] which animals would refuse."[46] Regardless of the fact that in the eighteenth century only lower-class women
actually supplied and cooked food for their families, these accusations
against the abbess would have resonated for readers exposed to the diverse writings emphasizing motherhood and parental affection.[47]

The readers of the *mémoires judiciaires* would have encountered appeals
to parental affectivity in contemporary political rhetoric and the emerging ideal of the family. Early modern French political theory espoused a
patriarchal model where the king was the father of his people. By the beginning of Louis XV's reign, however, this patriarchal ideal had become
muted, more paternal.[48] Parlementary remonstrances repeatedly appealed directly to the king's benevolent paternalism and his love for his
subjects.[49] Nor were these appeals limited to the king. Jeffrey Merrick has
noted how the "*parlementaires* complained that the clergy, who were supposed to serve their flocks like 'fathers,' behaved instead like 'masters' of
the souls of French men and women."[50] Indeed, in 1756 the barrister Antoine-Gabriel Gravière du Rauloy had directed exactly such a charge
against the archbishop of Paris when he excommunicated the Jansenist
Religieuses Hospitalières for electing a new superior despite his objec-

tions. According to Gravière du Rauloy, the archbishop had failed to be a "gentle and moderate father adjusting the crime to the punishment."[51] In effect, magistrates and lawyers used these familial expectations to inhibit the abuse of power by figures of authority.

Such rhetoric was bolstered by new ideas of the family based on emotional bonds, ideas that featured the maternal figure. Throughout the eighteenth century, the authors of innumerable novels, pedagogical works, and social treatises crafted a prescriptive definition of motherhood closely linked to the biological functions of a woman. They maintained that the "natural" relationship between a mother and child stood at the moral center of domestic life. The nurturing qualities of a mother's love superseded the more traditional emphasis on a child's obedience to his or her parents.[52] A woman's virtue derived from her ability to love her children and husband and to create an ideal domestic space for them. The appeal to a superior to have motherly virtues, like the notion of the Mother Church, was certainly not new. However, until the eighteenth century, motherly virtues were inseparable from Christian virtues. The newer model of maternity was secular, emphasizing a woman's capacity to fulfill her biological functions and not her Christian behavior.

While the lawyers for the Beaumont nuns explicitly attacked the "feminized" abuse of power, they also cast doubts on female power by accentuating how superiors were "mothers." The argument could be made that similar restrictions encompassed male as well as female superiors. For example, a *mémoire judiciaire* written for a vocation forcée case involving the Abbey of Sainte-Geneviève stated that "the authority of monastic superiors is an image of paternal authority, but if he is a father, he should therefore love his children, protect them, be a support for their weakness, provide for their needs, encourage their virtues, repress their vices."[53] Nevertheless, this rhetoric should not obscure the fact that the eighteenth-century public understood the roles of fathers and mothers differently. The expectation was that both parents would demonstrate affection, but the father remained the head of the household, a far more active figure both in the public and private world. In contrast, the increasingly pervasive image of the ideal mother tied her to the domestic arena, which was considered her "natural" destination. As we shall see in chapter 5, within this normative vision a woman was a deviant when she resided anywhere else, no matter how legitimate her position and her powers. Moreover, the emphasis on nature raised doubts about the mother superior's ability to wield "paternal" as well as maternal authority. Le Roy de Fontenelle's and Duclosel's insinuations against Madame de Lantilhac essentially reconstituted what it meant to be a mother superior. The position of a mother superior was no longer defined by religion and power but increasingly by maternal sensibility.

But bad mothering did not just poison the family within the cloister. Duclosel and Le Roy de Fontenelle further demonstrated that malevolent motherhood in conjunction with female debauchery had ramifications for the world outside the cloister walls. Just as an ideal maternal figure was the source of civic virtue, the unnatural mother could be the source of civic disorder. The lawyers argued that in persecuting the Beaumont nuns, Madame de Lantilhac endangered certain rights guaranteed to all subjects. She also threatened the well-being of citizens by challenging the authority of their protectors, the magistrates of the sovereign courts.

One of the abbess's alleged crimes against citizens was bound to excite parlementary and public rancor: the refusal of the sacraments. According to the Beaumont nuns, the abbess had denied them the right of confession and communion by stipulating that the nuns could use no other cleric but one of her choosing.[54] During the crisis over the *billets de confessions*, lawyers and magistrates reconstrued the sacraments, regarding them as "property" and therefore, rights the clergy could not deny citizens in the name of *Unigenitus*.[55] Lantilhac had done so not out of any doctrinal rancor but in order to isolate her opponents further. But Duclosel cast her actions as a "crime" by employing the arguments *parlementaires* used in Jansenist cases involving the refusal of sacraments.[56] The lawyer defended the right of the secular courts to intervene on behalf of the nuns and all other monastics because when "a monastic left the tumult of the world he did not leave the bosom of his country; he abandoned his possessions, but he did not shed his citizenship."[57] By using the language of citizenship, Duclosel's and Le Roy de Fontenelle's arguments signaled that the concerns of the cloister were closely tied to the concerns of the nation.

These assertions had three implications, all of which positioned the Beaumont affair squarely in the conflict between the parlements and the clergy. First, the claims regarding a monastic's citizenship threatened to dissolve the boundaries defining the monastic state. Not only did solemn vows demand that a nun turn her back on society, but French law declared her to be dead within civil society, renouncing all worldly claims such as inheritance rights.[58] Duclosel essentially negated the religious ideal of renunciation through the term "citizen," which placed the nun within the nation and endowed her with certain rights. His contentions implicitly moved women religious out of the church's jurisdiction. Second, the charges that Madame de Lantilhac had denied the nuns the sacraments firmly planted her in the camp of France's enemies, namely those ecclesiastics who acted against individual citizens.[59] Third, the lawyers legitimized the secular courts' intervention in the affair by arguing that "if the days of Citizens are in danger, the Magistrate cannot exempt himself from remedying abuses so pressing."[60] As a result, the courts' authority superseded that of the abbess, whose crimes made her an enemy of the Gallican church as it was being defined within parlementary discourse.

In the trial's last brief, Le Roy de Fontenelle's aggressive *Mémoire aux chambres assemblées*, it became clear that the Beaumont affair was no longer a battle between Madame de Lantilhac and the nuns, but one between the abbess and the sovereign courts. When she had refused to submit to decisions made by the provincial courts, Madame de Lantilhac had thrown down the gauntlet. The abbess's actions and the words of her barristers disputed the legitimacy of the sovereign courts and by extension that of the lawyers themselves. Her lawyer Duvert d'Emalleville had derided the secular courts' supposed respect for ecclesiastical jurisdiction, making the following accusation: "You usurp it [ecclesiastical authority], you destroy it by new decrees." In response Le Roy de Fontenelle addressed the abbess directly with pointed remarks such as "Our Judges are suspect to you? He [one of the magistrates] works for *our* existence."[61] This statement clearly identified Lantilhac as an outsider, separate from the amorphous entity of the nation on whose behalf the parlements claimed to speak.

In taking up the cause of the parlements Le Roy de Fontenelle and Duclosel pitted legitimate power against illegitimate, a contest coded in gendered terms. Le Roy de Fontenelle attributed "feminine malice" as the impetus behind the acts of the abbess and her coterie of favorites. Feminine power within these legal briefs was configured as distinctly self-serving and dangerously irrational. It was the kind of spiteful behavior the public had come to associate with clerics during the Jansenist controversies. Moreover, like the ultramontane clergy, Madame de Lantilhac's vicious spirit subverted the law. For example, Le Roy de Fontenelle proclaimed that "we [the lawyers and the courts] do not run from enlightenment, we require it; and you, through your own hand, you extinguish the flame of truth."[62] Not only did the abbess force the nuns opposing her to submit to her caprices, but she sought to impinge on their right to use the *appel comme d'abus*.[63] The *appel* was, of course, a right granted by secular authority, and more important, it was the means through which the courts entered into the convent's disputes.

The judges embodied a masculine authority that the lawyers portrayed as unselfish, rational, and working within the detached world of law and contract. Although the lawyers did not explicitly define the parlements' authority as masculine, they implied that the magistrates' protection of the weak was the proper fulfillment of the parlements' paternal or at least fraternal role.[64] According to Duclosel, all who appeared before the secular courts were equal, and therefore the weak as well as the powerful were assured justice. After all, unlike the abbess, who had transformed the convent into a "theater of licentiousness," parlementary magistrates maintained a "sanctuary of justice [which] is a sanctuary of truth."[65] Moreover, the magistrates derived their authority from "the first principles of the social contract that all people necessarily form with their sovereign."[66] The *parlementaires,* then, represented everything that was fair and impartial, especially when compared to the irrational femininity of the abbess.

In order to emphasize Madame de Lantilhac's various failures as superior and mother, the lawyers praised the positive images of femininity embodied by nuns. Although neither of the *mémoires judiciaires* written for the nuns included an abstract on femininity, they depicted the Beaumont nuns as virtuous Christian women and model nuns. Duclosel and Le Roy de Fontenelle adopted the same manichaean structure used in Jansenist polemics. While Madame de Lantilhac and Madame de Sedières behaved in a manner antithetical to religious vows, their opponents personified those vows. In contrast to the two sisters, the nuns in question "hoped to live their days under the law of Jesus Christ. [They] had consecrated themselves to retreat so as to sever themselves from the contagious attractions of the pleasures of the world."[67] Such selflessness distinguished them from their selfish mother superior who, so Le Roy de Fontenelle suggested, used the abbey's resources for her own aristocratic family's benefit.[68] Like Jansenist nuns, the Beaumont nuns did not cease to be women once they had taken claustral vows. Instead, their merits were intertwined with their devotion, as suggested by Joly de Fleury's reference to the "natural delicacy of their sex and their state."[69]

What these statements reveal is that the Beaumont nuns were being held to a different standard than the abbess. As we have seen, Duclosel and Le Roy de Fontenelle faulted Madame de Lantilhac for being a bad "mother," one who did not adhere to emerging *secular* notions of maternity. They censured her for failing to observe claustral rules, but at no point did the lawyers condemn the superior for not setting a spiritual example. In other words, their criticism was directed not against a religious figure but against a figure of authority. Her opponents, however, were very much religious characters, women who had dedicated their lives to Christ. They adhered to a traditional model of feminine behavior that emphasized Christian piety and morals. The lawyers' choice of this model of femininity suggests that the domestic icon of feminine virtue was still not in place; after all, Jean-Jacques Rousseau's *La Nouvelle Héloïse* (1761) and *Emile* (1762), the canonical texts for the new domesticity, had only just appeared. Thus, the representation of nuns, as indicated the Beaumont affair, were caught in the different currents of debate on female virtue.

Both religious and secular paradigms expected women to be reticent about putting themselves forward. Accordingly, their lawyers placed the Beaumont nuns in a position of triple subordination: nuns subordinate to their superior, "daughters" subordinate to their "mother," and women subordinate to men. Appropriately, the opening pages of Duclosel's *Requête présentée à monsieur l'official* and Le Roy de Fontenelle's *Mémoire aux chambres assemblées* described the Beaumont nuns as "victims of despotism" and "innocent victims."[70] Their natural feminine meekness transformed the nuns into victims, which, in turn, minimized their challenges to their abbess's authority. But what rendered the nuns' sufferings more poignant and compelling was their ostensible reluctance to disclose their woes before the secular judges and the public. Despite their distress, the nuns insisted that they had difficulty speaking out "against an abbess to whom they had sworn a just tribute of love and obedience." It was "religion [and] the filial respect that suppressed their voice."[71] Statements such as these underscored the Beaumont nuns' voluntary espousal of their subordinate positions and their devotion to duty. Their understanding of those duties also provided a loophole for action, much like the appeal to conscience justified the opposition of Jansenist nuns to *Unigenitus.* After all, subordination did not mean total subservience. What made these women religious speak out was a greater loyalty, one that took precedence over their obedience to their "mother" superior. Their loyalty to the claustral family and their vows outweighed their subordination because "such were their vows that the conservation of their abbey forces them [the nuns] to address the court."[72] Le Roy de Fontenelle declared that "as for the nuns, would their voice, timid and confined to the walls of the grill, have loosened if their unhappiness were not extreme?"[73] Significantly, the nuns were not acting as individuals. Rather they were forced to work on behalf of the community in order to save it from ruin.

In offering these images of their clients, Duclosel and Le Roy de Fontenelle followed a pattern Nadine Bérenguier that has identified, one in which lawyers highlighted their female clients' diffidence in presenting their troubles before the public. As Bérenguier has rightly argued, the defense of women who brought cases before the parlements was a delicate one. Referring to trials pitting mothers and daughters against husbands and fathers, she has suggested that "in such cases women were breaking the mold of ideal womanhood which prescribed modesty, acceptance of a life led in obscurity, obedience, submission, and self-control as the most acceptable forms of female behavior." According to Bérenguier, lawyers developed a strategy within their *mémoires judiciaires* that portrayed their clients as women who went before the public unwillingly and only out of a desperate need to preserve the family. Lawyers employed this strategy to obscure female agency, which could potentially undermine masculine authority.[74]

But the resemblance between the Beaumont nuns and the women of Bérenguier's study stops here. I would like to suggest that on a certain

level, Le Roy de Fontenelle and Duclosel did not just construct their
clients as passive victims of clerical despotism but indeed acknowledged
them as legitimate actors on a public stage beyond the cloister. As we have
seen, the lawyers stressed that nuns were citizens, which meant that they
had a right to *act* as citizens, including the right to appeal their case before the secular courts. In recognition of these rights, Le Roy de
Fontenelle allowed the nuns to speak for themselves, allowed their voices
to be heard by the public. In an extensive note covering two pages, the
lawyer included excerpts of the exact testimony given by the fifteen nuns
whom he named in bold letters.[75] Even more strikingly, his legal brief included a letter from Sisters Albanel, Brunel, and Gaschier to Le Roy de
Fontenelle, dated May 20, 1764, which he presented without any prefatory
remarks. Unlike the printed *A monsieur le lieutenant-général* circulated eight
months earlier, this letter refrained from making any references to legal
precedence or procedure. Rather, its declarations were purely emotional,
focusing on the plight of the nuns.[76] The issue of authorship remains ambiguous. However, it is not as significant as the possible strategy that
prompted Le Roy de Fontenelle to expose the female voices with such de-
liberate openness. The contents indicate that the letter served two purposes: to reiterate previous arguments made on behalf of the nuns and to
highlight the important role played by the lawyers themselves.

    The preface to Le Roy de Fontenelle's *Mémoire aux chambres assemblées*,
in conjunction with this letter, suggests that the identity of the lawyer was
both a legal and a masculine one.[77] The *mémoire judiciaire* began with a
dramatic preface in which the author apologized for his vehement and
passionate tone. As he explained to his readers, "this is not the nuns
speaking . . . This is a lawyer, *vir probus*."[78] In this statement, the lawyer was
invoking a statement made by the Roman orator Cato the Elder: "Vir
bonus, dicendi peritus" [a good man skilled in speaking].[79] Embedded
within this expression was the belief that a good speaker was in essence a
man of moral fortitude.[80] Since the sixteenth century, this phrase had
profound significance for the French legal world, which, as David Bell has
argued, described itself in masculine terms derived from classical republicanism. Specifically, it was an austere republicanism, one in which men
like Cato asserted their moral authority in an appropriately somber fashion.[81] Thus, Le Roy de Fontenelle legitimated his own voice by locating
himself within this masculine tradition of the French legal world; indeed,
he augmented his position by substituting the fiercer *probus*, or "upright,"
for the tamer *bonus*. Le Roy de Fontenelle also enhanced his image as a
crusader by referring to the words of a former *avocat-général* of the Parlement of Paris, Antoine Portail, who had declared in 1707 that "it is permitted for them [lawyers] to employ all the most proper terms to fight in-

iquity. There is a noble vehemence and a sacred fearlessness that is a part of their ministry."[82]

But this preface also indicates that this combative and distinctly masculine self-portrayal depended on Le Roy de Fontenelle's relationship with the Beaumont nuns. The lawyer described himself as "convinced of the vexation they [the nuns] have experienced and *armed* [italics added] with pieces that provide evident proof" of his clients' innocence and their adversary's guilt. In contrast to this martial self-image of the "upright man," he evoked the timidity of the nuns, whose "gentle voices did not match the excess of their unhappiness."[83] Some fifty-five pages later, the nuns' letter strengthened the lawyer's own claims of passion, dedication, and masculine agency with its declaration that "we have the greatest confidence in your zeal in protecting the oppressed."[84] In this manner "weak" feminine voices validated the lawyer as a masculine protector. Working together, the nuns and their lawyers presented a united front against their enemy, Madame de Lantilhac, the epitome of feminine despotism, whose vices underscored their own gendered virtues.

The charges of despotism against Madame de Lantilhac were powerful because she embodied a feminine *and* ecclesiastical strength emerging from its cloistered world and seeking to overthrow the masculine world of law. But did this depiction of the abbess categorically reject the mother superior as the head of a convent? On the surface, no. Neither Duclosel nor Le Roy de Fontenelle appear to have belonged to the radical anticlerical camp of the philosophes. Indeed, in 1790 when arguing for his daughter's right to enter the Abbey of Montmartre, Duclosel praised its abbess, Marie-Louise de Montmorency-Laval, for having imbued Montmartre with "peace, unity, and above all this spirit of equality in other respects so rare in abbeys."[85] No doubt Duclosel felt that he spoke from experience! The arguments made by Duclosel and Le Roy de Fontenelle contested neither the basic corporate framework of the convent nor the superior as an essential authority within that structure. Rather, their arguments emphasized how Lantilhac and her sister had brought corruption into the convent and therefore needed to be rehabilitated by the parlement. But the solution Duclosel and Le Roy Fontenelle brought to the problem of claustral despotism was not the only one in circulation.

During the 1760s, some lawyers began to consider the question of who was responsible for abuses within the cloister from a different angle, a more systemic examination that shed light on how the convent's government configured power. An analysis of the Saint-Nicolas affair in Pontoise, which took place in 1769, demonstrates how lawyers had begun to focus on the *structure* of the convent, increasingly regarding the institution itself and not the individual, as the source of corruption. Enclosure, which had once given the convent its revered status, now became the convent's most suspect feature. As the arguments made in the Saint-Nicolas case indicate, lawyers offered a more radical solution: reorganizing the convent itself.

In January 1768 Marie-Anne Le Coq, the daughter of a Parisian merchant, became a novice at the convent of Saint-Nicolas, which as an *hôtel-dieu*, also functioned as a charitable hospital. She entered the convent only a year after the prince de Conti had appointed Françoise-Julie de Sesmaisons prioress of Saint-Nicolas.[86] Unlike the new mother superior, Le Coq was no stranger to the convent where she had prepared for her first communion. A great favorite with the nuns, Le Coq earned their praise for her devotion and relentless hard work in the hospital. Despite Le Coq's piety and exertions, Madame de Sesmaisons declared the novice to be unfit for religious life. Subsequently, in the summer of 1768 the mother superior returned the novice home to her astounded parents. Le Coq's outraged father brought the case before the Parlement of Paris in 1769 with the intention of having his daughter reinstalled in the convent. He accused Sesmaisons of not only injuring *his* daughter but of mistreating the other nuns in the convent. This case became doubly charged because it had a Jansenist component. In a separate case the nuns of the *hôtel-dieu* claimed that the mother superior had, in fact, broken the 1754 Law of Silence forbidding any discussion of *Unigenitus* or related subjects. The affair ended in May 1769 when the sovereign courts ruled in favor of Le Coq and the nuns, and the novice returned to the convent.[87]

Le Coq's triumphant reinstatement to Saint-Nicolas may, in large part, be the result of her lawyer Jean-Baptiste Faré, whose legal briefs placed his personal crusade within a universal campaign for monastic reform. Far more than Le Roy de Fontenelle, Faré resembled the *avocat sensible* who would become the professional ideal by the 1780s.[88] Instead of taking a detached tone, he assumed personal responsibility for bringing the case before the Parlement of Paris: "I must, with the sacred ability of my ministry, make the truth be heard. I must tear away the veil that has hidden the internal troubles of the monastery."[89] Much like Duclosel and Le Roy de Fontenelle, Faré attributed the problems to Sesmaisons's personality and background, but he also made it clear that the Sesmaisons case had consequences not just for the *hôtel-dieu* but for all monastic institutions, baldly declaring that "this cause is that of all religious communities." According to the lawyer, he and his readers were living in a time when "all superiors seek to make themselves absolute, when they are accused of instituting their caprices and passions as well as laws, of putting their wishes in place of rules." Thus, Faré interpreted the Pontoise controversy as symptomatic of an endemic crisis of despotism in the monastic world. But he went further and analyzed how the shadowy environment of the convent itself exacerbated the situation by enabling superiors to behave tyrannically. Faré did not demand Madame de Sesmaisons's departure, but he did call for a substantial renewal of convents, which was possible only through the intercession of secular powers like the parlements.[90]

For Faré, as for Duclosel and Le Roy de Fontenelle, the crisis in Saint-Nicolas could be ascribed to the new superior's aristocratic tendencies. In the first *mémoire judiciaire* for Marie-Anne Le Coq, Faré chose to refer to Sesmaisons not as "prioress" but as "abbess," alluding to her previous status as abbess of Bival. The insinuations behind Faré's reference become clearer when read in conjunction with a pamphlet defending the Saint-Nicolas *hospitalières*. The polemic described how Sesmaisons separated herself from her fellow nuns. Residing in apartments isolated from the rest of the community, she behaved like "a lady of the first rank," creating "a kind of court."[91] The pamphlet's author claimed, "she lived like an abbess [*en abbesse*], although she was a simple prioress of a hospital, and without any income except that of the poor and the nuns."[92] Ideally, a superior's rank meant responsibility and not privilege. However, as Faré's characterization of Sesmaisons suggested, some individuals treated their religious rank as an extension of their social status in order to enhance their personal prestige and power, thus implicitly violating the monastic vows which made nuns equal before God. Thus, Faré's use of "abbess" was itself an accusation that the aristocratic Sesmaisons was almost destined to create disorder.

Although a conflict between an aristocrat and a bourgeoise was not the central drama of the Pontoise affair, the differences in social status between Sesmaisons and Le Coq underscored differences in character. While Sesmaisons's background was never explicitly outlined, it is probable, given her selection by the Prince de Conti, that she came from a noble family. The prioress's own lawyer, Henri Racine, suggested as much when he questioned whether Marie-Anne Le Coq, "alone and without quality," had the right to bring charges against Sesmaisons.[93] In Faré's briefs, Sesmaisons's social rank was manifest in her excessive pride and vice. The prioress, he argued, represented one of those women so "acutely attached to a society they miss that they busy themselves only with bringing in luxury and pleasures into the convent."[94]

The superior's flaws became magnified when compared to the virtues of Le Coq and her merchant family. According to Faré, "her [Le Coq's] parents are not puffed up by wealth and birth; they pride themselves on their attachment to their duties, and their love for their religion and virtue." Their daughter replicated these virtues when fulfilling her claustral duties, demonstrating that she had a marked penchant for seclusion

and hard work. But where Le Coq's upbringing exhibited itself in obedience and piety, Sesmaisons's background revealed an unsteady character
that made her regime unpredictable. Faré's client was "a timid and virtuous novice," whereas the superior was "impassioned."[95]

As a result of these unruly emotions, Sesmaisons, her opponents contended, did not behave as a good mother. According to the *Nouvelles ecclésiastiques*, while the prioress was railing against the supposed disobedience of the community, "they [the nuns] for their part said not a word,
and continued to fulfill their duties with new fervor. They prayed to God
to open the eyes of the Mother, so that she recognized them for her true
daughters."[96] Faré also drew attention to Sesmaisons as a bad mother by
offering a positive image of motherhood: Marie-Anne Le Coq's own
mother. According to Faré, when Le Coq's parents heard the distressing
news of their daughter's eviction from Saint-Nicolas, Madame Le Coq
acted impulsively with all the instincts of an exemplary mother. Despite
being seven months pregnant, Madame Le Coq traveled from Paris to the
Pontoise convent to learn more about her daughter's fate. Her encounters
with Sesmaisons and the nuns of Saint-Nicolas so upset Madame Le Coq
that she gave birth before term, nearly dying in the process.[97] The contrast
between the two "mothers" made it clear who was the dysfunctional one.
Instead of being motivated by selfless maternal sentiment, Sesmaisons
ruled in a capricious and disorderly fashion. Her character led her to
despotism, the scourge of political and social order.

The politicization of the Saint-Nicolas affair took place in a period of
political ferment during which political theorists laid out their theories regarding the fundamental laws and constitutions of the realm. As Keith
Baker and Dale Van Kley have demonstrated, individuals such as Louis-
Adrien Le Paige and Gabriel Bonnot de Mably delved into historical investigations that produced an "ideological arsenal," one that supported
the claims of the sovereign courts to speak on behalf of the king and for
the nation. Treatises such as Le Paige's *Lettres historiques sur les fonctions essentielles du parlement* made historical claims about France's "fundamental
laws" and its ancient constitutions.[98] The parlements acted as a vigilant
custodian protecting these constitutions, opposing "like an iron wall
everything that might weaken or [interrupt] the tradition of the [funda-
mental] laws," which included the efforts of the king and the clergy to impose their will arbitrarily.[99] In this spirit the parlements fought for "the legitimate liberty of subjects" against any such infractions.[100] For Le Paige,
the parlements had responsibility to protect the constitutions of religious
communities, and the lawyer fought against ultramontane clerics who
tampered with the constitutions of the Religieuses Hospitalières of the
Rue Mouffetard or the Paris Hôtel-Dieu. Le Paige's figurist bent of mind

would suggest that he interpreted claustral constitutions as an extension of the kingdom's constitutions, a viable reading given that a convent's constitution did, in fact, have to be approved by the king.

But the constitutions of religious communities like the Religieuses Hospitalières were not the only ones that occupied Le Paige. During the early part of the 1760s, Le Paige and other Jansenist lawyers obsessed about the "secret" constitutions of their nemesis, the Jesuits. According to the Jansenists, the Jesuits' constitution essentially denied the rights of its members while placing supreme authority in the hands of a superior general who could change the constitution to suit his personal wishes.[101] In the *Histoire général de la naissance et des progrès de la compagnie de Jésus en France,* Le Paige and his coauthor, Christophe Coudrette, contrasted this practice with those of other religious orders whose constitutions required decisions to be made "capitularly" or democratically, usually through a plurality of votes.[102] Thus, by 1769, lawyers and other political writers had essentially theorized two kinds of constitutions, one that was sacrosanct and another, an anti-constitution, that was inherently illegitimate.

The arguments surrounding these two constitutions came together in the trial of Sesmaisons and Le Coq. From the start, Sesmaisons was fair game for Jansenist attacks because she was the great-niece of a seventeenth-century Jesuit, a fact the *Nouvelles ecclésiastiques* gleefully exploited. At the end of its first article on the conflicts in Saint-Nicolas, the periodical delivered a brief tirade against the Jesuits. Despite the Jesuits' banishment from France, the authors of the article declared that "the spirit of the Jesuits is preserved" through individuals like Sesmaisons. The superior had harassed the entire community over Jansenist books such as Quesnel's *Prières Chrétiennes* and had denounced the nuns and novices as heretics.[103] The *Nouvelles*'s authors accused the superior of assuming "nearly sovereign independence and power," so much so that "it was nearly impossible to push despotism and fanaticism any further."[104] Faré made similar allegations, noting that Sesmaisons's claims of heresy were derived from "secret enemies, who without a doubt wished to deal fatal blows to the convent of Saint-Nicolas, through her hands."[105] In other words, Sesmaisons was part of a Jesuit conspiracy. She committed the same infractions "for which one reproached, with good reason, the Institutes of those famous monks."[106] The prioress interfered with "the most natural rights, those of remonstrance and representation," accusations that clearly echoed parlementary remonstrances from the 1750s.

Faré also argued that Sesmaisons had shown contempt for the constitution of the *hôtel-dieu,* which gave the sisters a voice in their own governance. He repeatedly noted that "the form of admission to the novitiate or the profession is fixed by the Constitutions; both can only take place through a capitulary deliberation." Such laws were in place to prevent superiors from straying from their duties. When Sesmaisons had dismissed Le Coq without consulting the community, she had disregarded the rights of both Le Coq and the nuns as guaranteed by the convent's constitution. "Although the demoiselle Le Cocq had been admitted capitularly, she [Sesmaisons] opportunely judged that she [Le Coq] could be removed . . . based on her own authority." In this manner, the prioress ran an "arbitrary government" by rewriting monastic law, because "such was her will."[107]

The lawyer's accusations against Sesmaisons also encompassed a more systemic analysis of "monastic governments."[108] The second, more vitriolic brief, *Plaidoyer pour le sieur Lecoq,* a response to Sesmaisons's own *mémoire judiciaire,* devoted considerable space to a sometimes convoluted discussion of this government, one that appears to have incorporated elements from Le Paige's *Lettres historiques* and Montesquieu's *L'Esprit des Lois.* In his *plaidoyer,* or brief for the defense, Faré constructed a history of monasticism that followed a narrative of disintegration and renewal. Because of an absence of effective laws, early monastic governments had often degenerated into "absolute monarchies" or despotic regimes. Fortunately, secular and ecclesiastic authorities had joined forces and given monastic governments "a democratic and aristocratic form all at the same time."[109] According to Faré, the convent's constitution made it a "democratic institution" by stipulating that all important decisions be made through a plurality of votes. However, since a mother superior took charge of minor day-to-day affairs, the convent had an "aristocratic" structure. But even as he conceded such authority to the superior, Faré warned that "the Prioress is not absolute; her will, by itself, is powerless."[110]

Despite the checks and balances guaranteed by monastic constitutions, scandals such as those involving the Pontoise *hôtel-dieu* indicated that something had gone very wrong in the cloister. The fusion of aristocratic and democratic government had collapsed, and the convent had disintegrated into despotism. In his diagnosis Faré attributed the problems of the convent to its cloistered structure. Unlike even "the most absolute civil governments" in which "public opinion" stayed certain brutal acts, the cloister had no parallel means of hindering abuses of power. Why? Because "it is in the shadows that they [superiors] exercise their power, that they find the hope of immunity; it is with the sacred arms that they execute their blows . . . the screams barely pierce through the enclosure, where they are stifled and powerless."[111] Within the closed world of the cloister, superiors justified their rule by responding with "I want it," a "revolting maxim that was the devise of the absolute monarchs of unhappy countries in the Orient."[112]

As we saw with the Lantilhac affair, eighteenth-century political theorists and their public easily made a link between oriental despotism and the convent. Superficially, the convent closely resembled the seraglio, the feminized space central to the metaphor of oriental despotism. Like the seraglio, the convent was populated by celibate men and women who were secluded from the world. Like the seraglio, the convent's inhabitants were often at the mercy of their passions and fears. But most significantly, like the seraglio, the convent was a hidden space. Despite the safeguards contained in its constitutions, the same elements that made the convent a sacred space, namely, its enclosed spaces, also nourished a despotic climate that enabled and indeed encouraged superiors to misuse their authority.

According to Faré, the solution was parlementary intervention. The lawyer made the magistrates the guardians of monastic constitutions as well as the "constitution" of France itself. The resolution Faré suggested resembled those associated with parlementary constitutionalism. It was essentially the role of the parlement to make Sesmaisons understand that the *hôtel-dieu*'s constitution had as much authority over her as it did over the other nuns. The courts had to teach this truth not only to Sesmaisons but to all superiors "who would be tempted to disregard it."[113] Faré appealed to the magistrates to reform the cloisters: "Fix, Messieurs, fix the authority of Superiors with precision; curb the despotism of their regime."[114] Although Faré failed to provide any concrete solutions, he clearly understood that the problems of the convent reflected its institutional makeup as much as it did personalities.

Through his references to the parlement and his allusions to the harem, Faré essentially coded legitimate power against illegitimate power, tyranny against justice, in gendered terms. Faré did not necessarily negate the superior's authority because she was a woman, but because she used her power in "feminine" ways. Like his legal counterparts, Faré invalidated Sesmaisons's rule while justifying the parlement's authority by contrasting "feminine" arbitrariness with "masculine" justice. According to Faré, Sesmaisons disregarded the laws of the convent, and preferred to establish her own regime based on her whims and passions, which exceeded the powers prescribed by Saint-Nicolas's constitutions. However, the magistrates of the parlements were very much masculine emblems of authority, their masculinity emphasized by their role as reasonable moderators who upheld the law and operated openly with the public's interests in mind. They operated in a world of transparency that contrasted sharply with the secrecy of the cloister. Indeed, Faré asserted his own masculine legitimacy by repeatedly claiming to unveil Sesmaisons's abuses before the magistrates and the public and to dispel the shadows of the convent: "I must explain to you with candor the obscure and hidden motives [of Sesmaisons]."[115] Thus, Faré's characterization of the prioress on the one side, and of the magistrates and himself on the other, were given meaning in the context of a cultural balance sheet that understood power in gendered terms. Sesmaisons represented "feminine" power, impassioned, secretive, selfish, and therefore inherently illegitimate. The lawyer and the magistrates embodied "masculine" authority, reasonable, law abiding, selfless, and transparent, all that was legitimate in government.

Despite these arguments regarding monastic governments and the possible solutions to their problems, Faré did not repudiate the convent and call for its destruction. The lawyer's attitude toward Le Coq and her allies in the *hôtel-dieu* clearly reveal his respect for sincere vocations and his belief that the convent had a place in the Old Regime. Indeed, Faré began the *Plaidoyer pour le sieur Lecoq* by noting how Marie-Anne Le Coq differed from her peers who "did not blush to nurture public malignancy by their indiscreet endeavors, and even more by the recital of their scandalous disorders."[116] But by emphasizing the convent's political structure as opposed to its religious dimensions, Faré undermined the sacred nature of the convent, making it indistinguishable from other institutions of the Old Regime. Just as the dissection of monarchical authority would contribute to the structural erosion of absolutism, so would such systemic analyses of the convent undermine its legitimacy.

Did such an unflattering appraisal of the convent have implications for the larger body politic beyond the monastic world? Did it contribute to the gradual erosion of absolutist authority, to its "desacralization"? Yes and no. In a literal sense, at no point did Faré take a rhetorical leap and demand that his readers compare monastic government with the French state. Yet the possibility existed. In his first *mémoire judiciaire* Faré declared that "one can say that claustral Associations are, in miniature, that which policed Nations are on a larger scale."[117] Through this direct analogy, he also intimated that the secular state contained many of the flaws associated with a monastic regime. Contemporaries increasingly spoke out against the covert nature of governmental machinations, symbolized in institutions such as the detested *lettre de cachet* that had become "glaring symbols of the crown's despotic tendencies."[118]

The convent was also evolving into a metaphor for all that was arbitrary and highhanded in the society of the Old Regime. As we have seen, Faré repeatedly endeavored to unveil Sesmaisons's abuses before the magistrates and the public, to dispel the shadows of the convent, and to expose the mother superior.[119] I would suggest that this insistence on transparency was necessitated by the ever increasing presence of the "public." If public opinion was going to hold sway, and eighteenth-century lawyers were determined that it would, then government needed to be public in the most literal sense of the word. It would have to be visible to all. Only then would government's authority and legitimacy be guaranteed.

᪥ ᪥ ᪥

The trials involving the Beaumont abbey in Clermont-Ferrand and the *hôtel-dieu* of Saint-Nicolas in Pontoise are examples of how lawyers cast the mother superior as an untrustworthy figure embodying many of the evils of the Old Regime. The lawyers who challenged the authority of Madame de Lantilhac and Madame de Sesmaisons considered these women despotic rulers who threatened not just the convent but society at large. As these two trials suggest, mother superiors presented an excellent illustration of feminine uses of power within an institution that was, in many ways, a microcosm of the Old Regime. In the face of growing criticisms against superiors, both male and female, public opinion called for secular authority to step in and initiate reform, thus imposing order in the cloister.

Such calls for reform became pressing after the disclosures made about the Jesuits before the Parlement of Paris in the early 1760s. In 1766, at the behest of reform-minded prelates, Louis XV established the Commission des Réguliers, designed to reform male monastic communities—a commission that, it should be noted, was beyond the purview of the parlements. For women religious, this commission had little meaning except for an 1768 edict that raised the minimum age of religious profession from sixteen to eighteen.[120] According to Suzanne Lemaire, women religious were excluded from the more sweeping reforms that closed or reorganized male communities, because women religious were untainted by the corruption of the age and deserved only great praise.[121] However, the reasons for the absence of female religious communities were probably more prosaic. In 1727 after the John Law debacle, the crown already had created the Commission des Secours to help destitute communities, and it was not dissolved until 1788.[122]

While the king's commission and the Assembly of the Clergy may have felt that female convents were under control in the 1760s, public perception was the opposite. Indeed, in a letter dated August 6, 1764, Joly de Fleury exhorted the Beaumont nuns to be loyal to their abbess and to work at maintaining peace in the abbey in the hope that "your union will be the edification of your province, as your disunion had cast the disfavor of public opinion on your community."[123] Joly de Fleury's apprehensions of public disgrace were borne out. At the outbreak of the French Revolution, an eight-page pamphlet entitled *La Chemise levée* began its diatribe against monasticism by recounting the 1764 scandal surrounding the Abbey of Beaumont. According to the anonymous author, "all citizens, in learning of the profane and despotic conduct of the principal nuns [Lantilhac and Sedières], were justifiably indignant in seeing the holiest of institutions, enveloped in the shadow of mysteries, degenerate into a very reprehensible abuse."[124] His warnings corresponded with the images of disorder and despotism found in histories of Port-Royal that had appeared in earlier decades.[125] Images of terror embodied in the rampaging mother superior appeared in prerevolutionary plays such as Dubois de Fontanelle's *Ericie, ou la vestale* (1768) and would appear in revolutionary works such as Boutet de Monvel's *Victimes cloîtrées* (1792) and Marie-Joseph Chenier's *Fénélon, ou les religieuses de Cambrai* (1793). And even as late as 1786 Louis XVI exiled the ultramontane abbess of Maubuisson, Gabrielle-Cesarine de Baynac, because she had abused her authority and ruined the abbey.[126]

Both the literature and the *mémoires judiciaires* written for the Beaumont and Saint-Nicolas trials indicate that eighteenth-century notions of clerical despotism were not just developed in the realm of high politics, but were refined in a wide range of contexts, including the internal "politics" of the female convent. These cases and others like them served as a bridge between the politico-religious controversies examined by Dale Van Kley and David Bell and the "domestic dramas" documented in Sarah Maza's study of prerevolutionary causes célèbres and in Jeffrey Merrick's work on the desacralization of the French monarchy. On the one hand, as we have seen, the lawyers in both trials linked the cases inextricably to larger political themes. On the other hand, they opened a window onto an arena that, if not "private," was at least theoretically hidden from public scrutiny.[127] Moreover, certain themes that Duclosel, Le Roy de Fontenelle, and Faré used in their arguments suggest an overlapping of the public and private. By virtue of their appointments as the heads of established institutions, Madame de Lantilhac and Madame de Sesmaisons were, in fact, public figures possessing legitimate authority. But they were also judged and condemned because they failed to exhibit the love and nurturing of a "good mother," a claim grounded in the notion of a separate private sphere.

In the *Plaidoyer pour le sieur Lecoq* Jean-Baptiste Faré also illustrates that the anxieties regarding the misuse of power encompassed the family itself. At one point, Faré came close to admonishing the judges for their fears that favoring Marie-Anne Le Coq would undermine the authority of superiors in general. If the influence superiors had over their subordinates was comparable to the "sacred authority of fathers over their children and of husbands over their wives," then the parlement had to take measures, since with respect to parents "every day you punish their abuses, every day you deal severely against paternal or maternal despotism."[128] Faré's statement signals how even as barristers used familial metaphors in their critiques of the clergy and the monarchy, parental authority itself, which the sovereign courts once had supported unquestioningly, now became problematic. As the next chapter will demonstrate, lawyers and men of letters began to expose familial despotism through the most dominant image of the convent: the vocation forcée scenario, in which the convent became a resource for abusive parents, a space where they could hide their victims and their own misdemeanors. However, men of letters did not concern themselves with the questions of who was a good nun or a bad nun. They no longer asked who should control the convent. Rather, they asked what the convent's function was, whether a nun was a legitimate figure, and if the convent was a sustainable space.

4

THE VOCATION FORCÉE IN FRENCH POLITICAL AND LITERARY CULTURE, 1740–1789

IN HIS EFFORTS TO REINSTATE MARIE-ANNE LE COQ AS A NOVICE IN Saint-Nicolas, Jean-Baptiste Faré began his *plaidoyer* by accentuating the sincerity of his client's vows. According to Faré, Marie-Anne Le Coq stood apart from many of those "impudent monastics who dare to invoke the assistance of the law in order to escape the austerity of the Cloister."[1] The lawyer's remarks indicate that he took Le Coq's vows seriously and, indeed, regarded them as a point in her favor. They also suggest that he was aware of how the eighteenth-century public sometimes doubted the authenticity of these vows and automatically associated the convent with the vocation forcée narrative.

The vocation forcée story is the tragic tale of a young woman whose family forces her into the convent. Throughout her girlhood she finds herself marginalized within her family, often because a parent or both parents devote their energies to another child. As a result, the girl is sent to a convent as a teen, and there she eventually learns that her parents have destined her for a religious life. The convent's superior promotes this enterprise, softening monastic rules to lure the daughter into accepting convent life. Despite her efforts to resist this course of action, the young woman ends up pronouncing her vows, her final protest expressed in a loss of consciousness at the altar. She finds her new life intolerable, and her despair is so extreme that she contemplates throwing herself into a well. However, reprieve becomes a possibility upon the death of one or both of the parents who are the source of her unhappiness. The woman attempts to renounce her vows legally, claiming that she was the victim of parental coercion. It is at this juncture that the young woman's private sufferings become a public cause célèbre.

Readers may assume that this story is another summary of Denis Diderot's *La Religieuse,* since it contains similar elements: unfeeling parents, a conniving mother superior, misery in the cloister, and a desperate attempt to escape the monastic prison. However, this particular vocation forcée tale was not taken from the pages of fiction but from the *mémoires judiciaires* written in 1752 for Marie-Michelle de Couhé de Lusignan.[2] The lurid details of her story and that of Marguerite Delamarre, the model for Diderot's novel, were not confined to the pages of legal briefs. Although *La Religieuse* was not published until 1796, earlier titles—*La Religieuse malgré elle; Rosalie, ou la vocation forcée; Sophie, ou la vocation forcée*—had already embellished and recycled the vocation forcée narrative to a receptive and eager public.[3] Even works in which the convent was secondary managed to include a forced vow subplot, as did Marivaux's *Marianne* or Madame de Genlis's *Adèle et Théodore.* Actual incidents and rumors of women religious who lacked a vocation also commanded attention. In July 1764 *Le Courrier du mardi* reported a fire purportedly started by an unhappy nun at the Abbey of Mouchy-le-Perreux in Compiègne.[4] The insidious nature of the vocation forcée story not only attested to its staying power but to the porous boundaries between fact and fiction, between public and private. While Jansenist controversies or tales of despotic mother superiors surfaced in a variety of media, neither of these stories cropped up as insistently as did the tale of the vocation forcée. Perhaps more than any other description of nuns in the eighteenth century, the myth of the unwilling nun imprisoned in the convent had a "life" of its own.

Despite gossip and the volumes of vocation forcée literature, the records of the *officialité* of Paris tell a very different story. Between 1731 and 1789 only two nuns, Marie-Michelle Couhé de Lusignan and Marguerite Delamarre, appeared before the *officialité* to renounce their vows.[5] After 1730, the number of abjurations made by men greatly exceeded that of women. This scarcity of female efforts to renege vows in the eighteenth century reflected certain trends of the last two centuries. Both Barbara Diefendorf and Elizabeth Rapley have shown that in the wake of the Catholic Reformation, sixteenth- and seventeenth-century women gladly embraced religious life.[6] Nor did a woman's fellow nuns necessarily conspire against her. In her account of the heart-wrenching story of Mademoiselle de Rastignac taking the veil, Hélène Massalska, princesse de Ligne, described how the headmistress Madame de Rochechouart of the Abbaye-aux-Bois was opposed to forced vows. When asked if Rastignac took her vows unwillingly, Rochechouart replied that "if she thought she [Rasti-gnac] was being made to embrace a monastic life against her will she would not give her vote."[7] Furthermore, the process through which a woman entered the convent was designed to prevent families from exert-ing force over daughters and sisters. Fictional tales often ignored the fact that novices faced a series of examinations conducted by male superiors to determine if their vows were genuine. Were contemporaries aware of this discrepancy between perception and facts? To some degree, yes. The playwright Louis-Sébastien Mercier, no friend to the clergy, acknowledged in his *Tableau de Paris* that there were, indeed, very few forced female vows.[8] But as the ubiquitousness of the vocation forcée narrative indicates, knowledge of this fact did not stop writers from presenting the experience of a few women religious as the story of *all* women religious. At the end of the day, the vocation forcée signaled the nun incarcerated in the convent, not the monk in the monastery.

Why then, despite actual evidence to the contrary, did the story of the forced vow become the story of the convent? On the surface, the intensi-fying anticlericalism of the eighteenth century provides a simple response to this question. The vocation forcée story was another example of the hypocrisy of a church that was uninterested in sincere vocation but was in-tent on securing the dowry required for entry. For anticlerical polemi-cists, priests and mother superiors represented a fanaticism and ignorance that ruined the lives of young girls.

However, I would suggest an alternative explanation as to why the vo-cation forcée story was so compelling. The eighteenth-century public's obsession with the vocation forcée dovetailed with the anxieties about au-thority. English Showalter has argued that the mid-century's great novel-ists such as Rousseau and Diderot condemned the ways in which families employed public institutions such as the police or the church to maintain their authority.[9] Indeed, as Diderot's *La Religieuse* illustrates, the archetyp-ical forced vow story revealed an array of authoritarian figures associated with the convent. And whereas the Jansenist conflicts and the scandals in-volving mother superiors exposed the conflicts between the family, the state, and the church, the vocation forcée portrayed the Old Regime's triad of power apparently working in concert.

The works of Sarah Maza, Jeffrey Merrick, and Lynn Hunt have effec-tively shown how French barristers and men of letters critically examined the authoritarian dynamics that sometimes characterized the relation-ships between parents and children, between husbands and wives, and even between the king and his subjects.[10] Their critique was grounded in a larger redefinition of the familial entity in which "the synchronic family of love had displaced the diachronic family of bloodlines."[11] Philosophes and other writers promoted the notion of marriage based on love and mutual respect, and they spoke out against unions in which women, in particular, were sacrificed for the sake of familial ambition. Social critics, such as the pamphleteer Cerfvol, spoke in favor of divorce, which gave women more status and power within marriage.[12] The widespread concern over families misusing their authority pervaded the political arena, in which lawyers and magistrates repeatedly used familial metaphors to critique abuses of power, emphasizing the paternal over the patriarchal. Lawyers held mother superiors to a standard of natural motherhood that accented nurturing over discipline. The ideal of the family, then, was reconstituted around displays of affection and not power within the private arena. Moreover, while principles of hierarchy never disappeared in this new familial model, they were muted. Parents were expected to be responsive to individual family members.

The fascination with the vocation forcée narrative was located in these challenges to traditional ideals of familial authority and the reconfiguration of the family as more tolerant and loving. Although the eighteenth-century practice of incarcerating wives in convents was more prevalent, the fate of daughters who were made to pronounce vows pervaded the pages of fiction and nonfiction.[13] Many readers were either unwilling or unable to take seriously a woman claiming to have a sincere vocation. Lawyers and the very few writers who sided with the families may have regarded nuns who sought to leave the convent as disorderly women, but an increasing majority saw them as victims of familial misrule. An examination of both legal and fictive discussions together demonstrate that by the end of the Old Regime, the vocation forcée narrative encompassed a series of relentless indictments of the family, the convent, and more implicitly a society that would uphold or, at the very least, turn a blind eye to these victims.

Legal briefs and fictional works condemned the practice of the vocation forcée, not simply by substituting one monolithic image of the family for another, but rather by employing a variety of familial models that focused on different dysfunctions, both social and political. Out of these shifting images a new model of the family emerged, a family in which individuals were reconciled, tied together not by lineage but by love. At the center was the model of the "natural" woman, a creature whose virtues were biologically defined. But if the family was reconsecrated in this new configuration, the convent was not. In the more prevalent images of the vocation forcée the convent became fully realized as a symbol of disorder, the institution in which religious, political, and social dysfunction manifested itself most completely.

In the first half of this chapter I consider the vocation forcée cases of Lusignan and Delamarre, focusing on the *mémoires judiciaires* written for the families as well as those for the nuns. Lawyers in both trials projected polar images of the nun: the nun as an impassioned and unruly individual, and the nun as a victim of parental abuse. At the same time, both sides appealed to different definitions of the family. In the second half of the chapter, I analyze the Lusignan and Delamarre cases in their larger context, the cultural phenomenon of vocation forcée. Here we see that public opinion embraced the image of the victimized nun in large measure because the proliferation of fictional vocation forcée material eclipsed other images of nuns. I argue that the intertextual nature of the forced vow story in part explains its power.

By examining the vocation forcée as an unstable narrative, I am seeking to bridge the gap between two disciplinary approaches to forced vows. On the one hand, literary scholars analyzing *La Religieuse* tend to focus on the intricacies of Diderot's text and pay scant attention to the connection between the novel and the wider political and literary culture of the eighteenth century. On the other hand, historians investigating the social history of the convent uncover important statistics but do not fully account for the discrepancy between the numbers of forced vow cases and eighteenth-century views of nuns. As a narrative, the vocation forcée sustained its hold over the public because it circulated in a variety of written and oral sources. Indeed, the lawyers in the Lusignan and Delamarre trials were forced to deal with the larger cultural story in their arguments as well as with the facts of the case. In the end, both for lawyers and for most men of letters, the reality of convent life was less important than authorial ideologies and commitments.

Ironically enough, the eighteenth-century clarion call against forced vows had its antecedents, not in novels and other forms of fictions, but in clerical denunciations of such practices. Many eighteenth-century authors and their readers considered the vocation forcée to be the perfidy of a united front of the church, the state, and the family. But in fact the opposite was often true. Monastic vows were a flash point for conflict between the state and the family on the one hand and the church on the other. Religious vows raised the incendiary question of who had the authority to determine who should enter the cloister and under what conditions.[14] In the late sixteenth century Tridentine decrees attempted to shield children from parental coercion regarding both marriage arrangements and monastic vows. With respect to the latter, the Council of Trent raised the minimum age for female vows from sixteen to eighteen, a proposal accepted by the French clergy but rejected by the crown until the royal edict of 1768. And in the late seventeenth and early eighteenth century, the most stinging criticism against the vocation forcée came from clerics, some of whom delivered sermons aimed at elites they regarded as the main culprits in this matter. At the funeral of Anna of Gonzagua in 1685 Jacques Bossuet, bishop of Meaux, publicly censured certain parents for "immolating" young girls in convents "for the sake of familial interests," that is, for social and economic ambition.[15] In his study of Diderot's *La Religieuse* Georges May has argued that some of Diderot's arguments echoed the words of Bossuet, Massillon, and other seventeenth-century clerics.[16]

However influential the seventeenth-century clerical position on monastic vows might have been, it was at out of step with the political and social trends of the period. The prevailing ideology was vociferously patriarchal, privileging the authority of the monarch and the family. Indeed, Bossuet's denunciation of forced vows was somewhat at odds with his own treatises in support of patriarchal authority and with the convictions of his patron, Louis XIV, who was directing the state's energies into expanding paternal power through legislation and royal edicts.[17] In her study of early modern law and courts, Sarah Hanley has interpreted this symbiotic relationship between the monarchy and fathers as an alliance, a "family-state compact" that shored up the patriarchal powers within private and public affairs.[18] Over the course of the early modern period, the French legal system evolved to support parental authority, in order to secure the social and political order. Early modern jurists and state officials equated parental dominance with social harmony, as they did monarchical authority with political stability. In certain instances, as in the case of clandestine marriages, both crown and family strove to push the church out and thereby place family matters directly under royal jurisdiction.[19] But according Julie Hardwick, there were limits to this family-state alliance, and "women and subjects had considerable room to maneuver."[20] Monastic vows provided such opportunities for children and sometimes became a point of contention between children and their families, but not in the way clerics described. Indeed, parents often tried to prevent their children from taking monastic vows.[21] Thus, claustral vows triggered conflicts between the church and the family, and between children and their parents, revealing the vulnerability of the ties between church, the state, and the family.

The vocation forcée trials of Marie-Michelle de Couhé de Lusignan and Marguerite Delamarre indicate that while monastic vows in the eighteenth century continued to spark tensions between this triad, a realignment had taken place. The previous chapters have shown how eighteenth-century conflicts involving women religious often placed the parlements in opposition to the crown and the church. In the vocation forcée cases, the parlement now stood against the family as well as the church. A new question emerged involving the sovereign courts: Should the parlements protect the family as a whole, or should they throw their weight behind the

solitary nun who could disrupt familial relations? For lawyers and *parlementaires* who were not necessarily interested in precipitating a social revolution, a vocation forcée case presented a challenge. The defense of individual conscience, articulated in Jansenist scandals, was in line with a
certain strand of early modern religious thought emphasizing the individual's direct relation to God. But the protection of an individual's legal
rights went against the ideological principles underlying the Old Regime,
principles that emphasized authority, hierarchy, and corporate identity.
Magistrates had to preserve the familial institution at the same time as
they were under increasing pressure to temper and, indeed, directly oppose parental despotism.

The Parlement of Paris faced these issues in two vocation forcée cases
during the 1750s, at the height of the clashes between the parlements, the
crown, and the ultramontane clergy. The first of these involved the
younger daughter of a provincial noble family, Marie-Michelle de Couhé
de Lusignan. According to her lawyer, Claude-Thévenot d'Essaule, Marie-
Michelle's story began in 1714 when, at the age of five, she lost her father.[22] She, her elder sister Elisabeth, and her two brothers were left in the
care of their mother who, Lusignan's lawyer would later claim, had a decided preference for Elisabeth. As a result, Madame de Couhé placed
Lusignan and her younger brother, Barthélemy, in monasteries with the
intention that they would eventually take vows, thereby enlarging Elisabeth's inheritance. Ignoring her daughter's protests, Madame de Couhé
entered Marie-Michelle in the convent of Saint-François in Poitiers in
1725, where the young girl pronounced her vows three years later.

When Madame de Couhé passed away in 1744, the path was clear for
Lusignan to revoke her vows.[23] Going before the *officialité* of Poitiers in
1748, she stated that her vows were illegitimate on two counts. First, they
had been pronounced because she feared violent retaliation on her
mother's part, and second, there was no actual record of her novitiate.
When the Poitiers *officialité* rejected her claim on December 15, 1750,
Marie-Michelle filed an *appel comme d'abus* before the Parlement of Paris
against them, against the convent of Saint-François, and against her elder
sister, now Madame Elisabeth de Saint-Georges, who fought to prevent
Marie-Michelle from leaving the convent.[24] According to Madame de
Saint-Georges's lawyer, Pierre-Jean-Georges Caillère de l'Estang, Mademoiselle de Lusignan's suit was invalid because she had failed to reclaim
her vows within five years after taking them.[25] Madame de Saint-Georges
also produced a letter in which Lusignan had affirmed her vocation.[26] In
response Lusignan's lawyers contended that monastics still maintained the
right to reclaim their vows within five years *after* the death of the parent or
parents, given the risks of acting while the parents were still alive. At the
end of the day, Lusignan's claims apparently held greater weight. After

nearly two years of wrangling in the courts, the parlement overturned the *officialité*'s verdict and restored her civil rights, including her inheritance.[27]

The verdict was otherwise for Marguerite Delamarre who began her efforts to leave religious life in 1752, the same year Lusignan won her case. Delamarre started her monastic life at the age of three when her parents, goldsmiths by trade, placed her in a series of convents because of the professional constraints placed on their time.[28] Delamarre went on to pronounce her vows in 1736 at the royal abbey of Longchamp in Paris, where she had once been a *pensionnaire*. During this period, Delamarre held the office of precentor, porter, and turnkey, positions of responsibility that on the surface did not suggest any dislike of monastic life. Furthermore, letters to her mother indicate that there were no signs of discord between mother and daughter.[29]

This apparently cordial relationship between mother and daughter was shattered when Marguerite brought her suit before the *officialité* of Paris on September 2, 1752.[30] In addition to accusing her deceased father, Claude Delamarre, of intimidating her into becoming a nun, Delamarre contended that in 1731 her parents had prevented her marriage with a Monsieur Gennes. She also claimed that her mother had abandoned her, passing her off as the illegitimate daughter of the duchesse de Berry. Her parents' cruelty also extended to her siblings who, she hinted, had all died mysteriously. As for herself, once in the convent, she had to endure the surveillance of "spies" employed by her mother. For her part, Madame Delamarre denied these accusations and declared that if anything, her daughter had shown a marked preference for religious life, even renewing her vows once. After the *officialité* ruled against her on August 28, 1756, Delamarre filed an *appel comme d'abus* against the *officialité* and took her case to the Grande Chambre of the Parlement of Paris, an act that now embroiled the other heirs of Claude Delamarre. The affair had caught the attention of the Paris public—for as the *procureur-général* Joly de Fleury observed in his notes, "the causes that involve the state of men, in effect, attract the attention of the Public."[31] In the end, however, the parlement backed the ruling of the *officialité* and ordered Marguerite Delamarre back to Longchamp on March 17, 1758. Although for some, this verdict was just, others, such as the periodical *Le Courrier d'Avignon*, took a negative view, noting that the "famous trial of the nun from Longchamp" had ended with the nun being "*condemned* to stay in the convent."[32]

These impressions were no doubt fueled by the efforts of lawyers who promoted their clients' interests by linking the cases to larger political and social issues. The arguments the lawyers made in the two vocation forcée trials reflected the growing tension between a more traditional view of society, in which power was located in corporate institutions, and a newer vision emphasizing the individual citizen. But unlike the refusal of sacraments and the trials involving monastic superiors, the vocation forcée cases opened up a more sensitive topic for debate, namely, the acceptable parameters of parental authority. The lawyers for the nuns characterized the mothers as despotic and uncontrollable women whose malevolent treatment of their helpless daughters was a threat to social stability. Their opponents argued that the nuns were unruly women seeking to be independent. For us today, these cases shed light on the ways in which the eighteenth-century French public was coming to terms with new understandings of the family as they played out in juridical as well as social and political terms.

Although Lusignan and Delamarre undoubtedly garnered public support from people who assumed the veracity of any vocation forcée story, their lawyers still needed to legitimate their clients' efforts to come forth publicly with their family quarrels. The arguments of Lusignan's lawyer, Thévenot d'Essaule, were far more expansive; he composed two *mémoires judiciaires,* whereas Delamarre's barrister Louis Doulcet wrote only a seventeen-page *Mémoire pour la demoiselle Delamarre.* We can only surmise that perhaps Doulcet was so confident about public support that he presented the narrative of the victimized nun and the unnatural parents as a self-evident truth for which the public did not need substantial documentation.[33] Despite these differences, the two lawyers presented similar arguments that also replicated certain points found in concurrent Jansenist writings on nuns. For example, Thévenot d'Essaule and Doulcet showcased the vocation forcée cases in a recognizable manichaean battle between victim and oppressor. Moreover, both lawyers politicized their cases by using the language of citizenship, rights, and despotism, in which the reading public were becoming well versed. This political rhetoric also advocated the sentimental ideal of the family. However, the lawyers did not stop there. Thévenot d'Essaule and Doulcet constructed a vision of the family that guaranteed individual citizen's liberties against the more "corporate" interest of the family.

In their efforts to overcome suspicions about their clients, who, after all, had apparently rebelled against their parents, the lawyers cast them as victims. This defenselessness derived directly from their femininity, a point underscored by contrasting the plight of men and women.[34] Thévenot d'Essaule argued that an adult male, such as one of Lusignan's brothers, had options, since he could "support himself in another state with his talents and works" by taking "refuge in the army."[35] But innate feminine traits hampered Lusignan: "One believes more willingly that a daughter is constrained in her vows, whether it be the result of natural timidity or the feebleness of her sex."[36] Thus even "the bravest daughter" found herself caught between Scylla and Charybdis. She had to choose either the convent she hated or return home, an alternative fraught with problems for Lusignan and Delamarre because the "home of [their] mother[s]" was the original site of their afflictions.[37] Thévenot d'Essaule stripped Lusignan of agency, portraying her as incapable of controlling her own fate. Furthermore, he implied that women were passive both by nature and circumstances, victims who had no choice but to accept the dictates of their parents and to suffer without hope.

The importance of the vocation forcée victim as a gendered character becomes even more apparent when compared to a forced vow trial of a male monastic. In 1764 René Le Lievre attempted to reclaim his vows at the Abbey of Sainte-Geneviève. Although Le Lievre's lawyer, Claude-Christophe Courtin, did not explicitly gender the monk female, he portrayed Le Lievre as a passive figure incapable of reason. According to Courtin, "one sees a character of naiveté, simplicity and of foolishness, which betrays the most feeble, the least reflective mind, one that is bordering on infancy."[38] This description did not necessarily "feminize" Le Lievre, but it certainly unmanned him. In the case of Lusignan and Delamarre, being painted as passive victims suggested that they were virtuous and modest women, compelled to speak out by external forces and not by any willfulness on their part. Thus, Thévenot d'Essaule argued that Lusignan "was forced . . . to accuse in some way the memory of her mother."[39]

To enhance the portrayal of their clients, both Thévenot d'Essaule and Doulcet characterized their mothers as "bad" mothers who physically and emotionally abused their children. According to Thévenot d'Essaule, Madame de Couhé forced Lusignan to live like a servant in her own home "locked up for months at a time in a room in which she was forced [to eat and drink] bread and water." When she became aware of Lusignan's reluctance to become a nun, she threatened her daughter with death, declaring that "if I learn that you have left the convent, you will have no other executioner than me."[40] Similarly, Madame Delamarre treated "her daughter with such severity and inhumanity" that at one point, the nuns in the convent where Delamarre was boarding had to separate the mother from her daughter. Delamarre's father also appeared as a tyrannical figure. After terminating the marriage negotiations with the sieur Gennes abruptly, he behaved brutally. According to Doulcet, "Mademoiselle Delamarre was overcome by blows, and locked in a bedroom with grilled windows," and Monsieur Delamarre "even rose at night to mistreat his daughter."[41] This brief description indicates that there were no substantive differences in terms of how lawyers portrayed mothers and fathers. In general, we see a pattern similar to the one found in the "Great Remonstrances" and the accusations against mother superiors: feminized behavior emanating from unrestrained and irrational passions.

Nevertheless, mothers, even more than fathers, were held up to the standards of affection and nurturing, standards derived from "nature." Indeed, Madame de Couhé's lack of maternal affection was the centerpiece of Thévenot d'Essaule's *Mémoire pour demoiselle Marie-Michelle de Couhé de Lusignan*. After cataloguing her numerous transgressions, the lawyer cast serious doubts on Madame de Couhé's maternal feeling: "Is this then the kind of care a tender mother provides in such a case? A mother who would have loved her daughter, who would not have forced her vocation, who instead would have been distressed to see her dead to the world, to her family and to herself."[42] These rhetorical questions implied that Madame de Couhé had failed to meet a normative ideal of motherhood, one infused with love and concern for children. Instead, Madame de Couhé expressed herself in a "maternal furor," spurred by her "blind love" for Lusignan's sister Elisabeth and "maternal hatred" for Lusignan and her brothers.[43] Doulcet also began his *mémoire* by noting that parents "after having given natural life to their children . . . should not be the masters of their abandonment to civil death [*la mort civile*]." Such allusions of tender emotion and affection placed a domestic model of familial relationships at the center of the vocation forcée story, thus conveying to the magistrates and the public that these were the standards by which the case should be judged. As Doulcet observed, "the renunciation [of vows] is a veritable accusation" indicting parents who did not adhere to beliefs of intimacy and domestic harmony.[44]

Thévenot d'Essaule and Doulcet also exploited current political anxieties by linking the vocation forcée trials to debates on citizenship and despotism. In the *Mémoire pour demoiselle Marie-Michelle de Couhé de Lusignan* Thévenot d'Essaule transformed Lusignan from "a sacrificed child" to a "Citizen thus sacrificed." The barrister forcibly employed the language of rights, noting "that at the same time as she was sacrificing her daughter to the cloister, Madame de Couhé was only thinking of stripping her of her rights," namely, her right to inherit. These actions held larger consequences because "public order, humanity, and Religion were all compromised." Countering the arguments that emphasized "le repos des familles," or family tranquillity, Thévenot d'Essaule stated that it was the responsibility of the magistrates "to maintain a golden mean between *family tranquility* in general, and that of *each Citizen* in particular."[45]

The lawyer's assertions had far-reaching implications for both the world of the convent and that of the family. First, like his Jansenist cohorts, the lawyer legitimated his client's claims by bringing the concerns of the political world into the sacred space of the convent. In the process, Thévenot d'Essaule's arguments weakened the convent's spiritual authority by making its affairs the purview of secular magistrates who were called to protect the interests not of the community but of an individual seeking to separate herself from it. Second, by emphasizing Lusignan's rights as an heir, Thévenot d'Essaule repudiated the notion of *mort civile*, the monastic renunciation of worldly goods and status when pronouncing vows. The lawyer's arguments suggested that a monastic did, in fact, retain concrete civil rights. Therefore, the monastic state had, at best, a tenuous claim on him or her. Third, the lawyer's arguments about parental abuse voided Madame de Couhé's claims of authority based on her role as mother. Thévenot d'Essaule had placed Lusignan's status as a citizen above her position as a daughter. He not only rejected her mother's authority but gave her an identity independent of her family and the church. The lawyer's emphasis on Lusignan's "citizenship" suggested a new kind of political subjectivity based not necessarily on action and participation but apparently on inalienable rights. Moreover, this political identity did not make the distinction between religious and nonreligious status or, at least on the surface, between men and women. And it was the responsibility of the magistrates to preserve this status because they were "intrepid Protectors of the oppressed citizen."[46]

In a similar manner, Doulcet's *Mémoire pour la demoiselle Delamarre* petitioned the magistrates to end "despotism," a word that by the mid-1750s had come to denote the worst crime possible. Doulcet's appeal opened with politically charged expressions that would resonate with readers. After urging the magistrates to rule in favor of his client because "it was essential [for society] not to surrender an *arbitrary* and *despotic* authority to parents," he went on to demonstrate how Delamarre had to suffer under an "empire of unjust tyranny" of a mother who gave her the option between prison and the cloister and, therefore, no choice at all.[47] Once Delamarre had chosen her place of incarceration, she had to endure "the veritable despotism" of nuns her mother had paid to spy on her and prevent her from contacting the outside world.[48]

Although Thévenot d'Essaule had provided detailed descriptions of Madame de Couhé's infamy, he did not use expressions comparable to Doulcet's "arbitrary" and "despotic." What this difference reflects is the changed political climate in which Doulcet wrote his legal brief. By the mid-1750s, thus, "associated with images of degradation and misery, *despotism* consequently had become one of those words, terrible and convenient," that produced "an instinctive horror."[49] A year earlier, in 1757, Damiens had attempted to assassinate Louis XV, an act that the Jansenist segment of the parlement blamed on the "despotic" Jesuits. In addition Claude-Adrien Helvétius's *De l'Esprit* had appeared, strongly condemning despotism. By explicitly evoking despotism within this agitated political atmosphere, Doulcet's *mémoire judiciaire* made the abuse of parental authority a matter of public concern.

Did Doulcet's references to "despotism," as well as Thévenot d'Essaule's discussion of citizenship, suggest a radical political and social agenda, nothing less than the repudiation of parental authority? Emphatically, no. After all, as suggested in the *Mémoire pour demoiselle Marie-Michelle de Couhé de Lusignan*, Thévenot d'Essaule concluded that the magistrates had to strike a balance between the family and the individual citizen, a statement which also affirmed the importance of stability within the larger world.[50] Moreover, evoking the model of an affective family was not enough for either Thévenot d'Essaule or Doulcet when arguing for the legal rights of their clients. They configured the family within juridical parameters. As noted earlier, under Louis XIV, the state had acted as the bulwark of parental authority, promoting a patriarchal ideology that was widely supported by the parlement.[51] However, Thévenot d'Essaule and Doulcet argued for a realignment of parlementary loyalties. In defending Lusignan's and Delamarre's rights as citizens and calling for the restoration of their inheritance rights, Thévenot d'Essaule and Doulcet complicated familial relationships by placing the individual's legal rights on par with the family's prerogatives, a shift that struck at the principles defining the society and politics of the Old Regime. Their rhetoric of citizenship and despotism necessitated a family model that adjusted legally to individual rights and autonomy.

But as the arguments defending the prerogatives of the families demonstrate, the early modern association of social order and parental authority still carried weight in the eighteenth century. The lawyers who worked on behalf of Madame de Saint-Georges and Madame Delamarre never proffered an explicit definition of the family that outlined its incontestable rights, no doubt because they were aware of the growing sentiment against any high-handed parental behavior. The lawyers nonetheless evoked an image of the family as the bedrock of order, and of the nuns in question as a menace to that order. Both Pierre-Jean-Georges Caillère de l'Estang, Madame de Saint-Georges's lawyer, and Odot Briquet de Mercy, Madame Delamarre's attorney, repeatedly stressed that if Lusignan and Delamarre succeeded in leaving the convent, their departure jeopardized "public tranquility" and "public surety."[52] These phrases indicate that the private affairs of families were anything but that. It was assumed that children would obey their parents and that family members would overcome their individual desires and act to preserve the family as a whole.

Both Caillère de l'Estang and Briquet de Mercy stressed how the laws of the land were designed to give families security. The lawyers acknowledged that cases of *vocation forcée* did indeed exist, and that in such instances individuals should be guaranteed the restitution of their freedom and rights. But there were also laws "that did not permit listening to a religious person who did not make his petition within the prescribed time," referring specifically to the five-year limit for annulling vows.[53] According to Caillère de l'Estang, painstaking and time-consuming regulations, such as a bishop's examination of a female novice, existed to ensure a family's peace of mind and of course, a sincere vocation.[54] Madame Delamarre's barrister, Briquet de Mercy, went further by privileging these laws over Delamarre's natural rights, which supposedly had been violated. In effect, Briquet de Mercy turned the notion of "natural rights" on its head. Instead of respecting a law that "puts boundaries on all actions by the force of prescription, which reprimands enterprises contrary to good order," Delamarre evoked rights based on "Nature," which, because it is "by itself ineffectual" and "defective," is "insufficient to police the Universe." Thus, exclaimed Briquet de Mercy, "Without the wisdom of laws that check the unsteadiness and inconstancy of cloistered people, what trouble in Religion! what disorder in the families! what upheaval in society!"[55] These professions clearly presented laws, which buttressed and legitimated familial authority, as the safeguards of order against individual inconstancy.

Both Caillère de l'Estang and Briquet de Mercy sought to demonstrate that the mothers of Lusignan and Delamarre also deserved the court's sympathy because they were caring parents using their influence in judicious ways. Although the two lawyers clearly sought to defend a traditional model of the family, one that placed parental authority at the forefront, they did not necessarily adhere to a static set of values. The feelings of good mothers also needed to be broadcast, so that readers would respond sympathetically to their clients and see the depth of their opponents' transgressions. The lawyers drew upon a cultural vocabulary that would be familiar to their readers. Caillère de l'Estang and Briquet de Mercy tempered the image of parental authority with idealized notions of a nobility and a bourgeoisie grounded in values of hard work and virtue.[56] This depiction of the parents contrasted sharply with the images of the haughty aristocrat drawn to luxury that were used to characterize Lusignan and Delamarre. Moreover, the vocabulary attached to the hardworking noblewoman, the industrious bourgeoise, and the willful nun all carried with them certain gendered values. The portrayals of both Lusignan's and Delamarre's mothers fell in line with notions of virtuous feminine behavior, while their daughters were exposed as disorderly women.

In the *Mémoire pour dame Elizabeth de Couhé* Caillère de l'Estang employed parallel dichotomies between urban and rural, aristocracy and nobility, and corruption and vice to praise Madame de Couhé's maternal character. The lawyer described the Couhé family as leading "the life of Nobility retired in the country in the remote provinces," far removed from the gilded and debauched existence of the Parisian aristocracy. Such nobility manifested itself "in an active life, in modesty, in proper simplicity, in the decency of their actions, and in the natural graces which solely announce the true character of the nobility in its origin." "The young provincial women" understood that real nobility did not consist of "clothing and fatuous ornaments." In dressing Lusignan simply, Madame de

Couhé had provided an "example and model for her daughters, whom she had raised, wisely, to work as she herself did and to shun . . . luxury and indolence."[57] Anticipating scenes from Rousseau's *La Nouvelle Héloïse*, these comments evoked the critique of the aristocracy found in current discussions of luxury. Caillère de l'Estang concluded that Lusignan's complaints about how her mother had deprived her of a lifestyle suitable to her rank merely reflected her own "indocile and arrogant humor." The nun misinterpreted and deliberately misrepresented her mother's efforts to discipline "a headstrong child, under the greatest of all the gentle laws of maternal law."[58] Lusignan's defiance of a virtuous mother betrayed an ideal of nobility that was as much about character as it was about lineage.

Briquet de Mercy similarly located his critique of Marguerite Delamarre in a social context by praising the hardworking bourgeois Delamarre family. He applauded Madame Delamarre's appreciation of the values attached to their social status and the dangers that came with social ambition. The barrister insisted that ever since their daughter's early childhood, "one saw them [her parents] occupying themselves with the project of establishing her in the world."[59] The Delamarres placed Marguerite and her brothers into convents as *pensionnaires* so as "procure for their children the privilege of the Nobility."[60] But unlike Delamarre's father who sought to climb the social ladder by arranging an advantageous marriage for Marguerite, Madame Delamarre "desired that her daughter remain in her sphere to spare her the mortification almost always attached to such unequal alliances."[61] But maternal affection overruled cautious wisdom, and Madame Delamarre's generosity of spirit failed to curb her daughter's worldly habits and tastes. According to Briquet de Mercy, his client's affections made her too permissive: "Did she [Madame Delamarre] not leave her daughter the liberty to do everything she judged appropriate?" Even when Delamarre launched her case before the *officialité*, her mother "was content to suffer from the mistakes of a daughter who was always dear to her."[62] Thus, both Madame Delamarre and Madame de Couhé embodied feminine virtue: they understood the value of staying within one's social station and, like good mothers, they tried to transmit such virtues to their daughters.

Caillère de l'Estang and Briquet de Mercy argued that Lusignan and Delamarre, despite their mothers' best efforts and intentions, failed as daughters because they espoused a false notion of aristocracy, one that privileged a prestigious name and lineage over domestic family values. Instead of accepting the names they were given, both nuns literally attempted to rename themselves. Lusignan used the name "Lusignan" instead of "Couhé," claiming that her parents had added it to their title after getting married.[63] According to Caillère de l'Estang, Lusignan's claims to this "illustrious name" were "gross lies" concocted to demonstrate the extent to which she had been deprived of living "nobly in the world." The lawyer declared that "the soeur de Couhé should blush for the outrageous exaggerations she made regarding the fortune of her father and mother, for the injurious attacks she made against the memory of her mother."[64] Briquet de Mercy portrayed Delamarre in a similar light, although the details of her story were more lurid. According to the lawyer, the nun maintained that the real Marguerite Delamarre had died while she had been put out to nurse, and the wet nurse had substituted another child in her place. Delamarre had intimated to her fellow sisters in Longchamp that she was in reality the illegitimate daughter of the duchesse de Berry, daughter of the Prince Regent.

Not only did Briquet de Mercy refute Delamarre's claims by presenting baptismal records, he also set out to prove how her pretensions followed from Delamarre's flawed character. In the *Mémoire pour les héritiers* he asserted "that Sister de la Marre, in order to assume superiority over the other nuns, gave herself illustrious origins within the convent."[65] Delamarre arrogantly flouted the convent's renunciation of the world by adopting the social values of that world in order to put herself at an advantage over her peers. The superficial nature of Delamarre's so-called nobility was further illustrated in her penchant for luxury, which contrasted sharply with her mother's frugality.[66] In order to satisfy "all her excesses," Delamarre committed "outrageous injuries . . . against the memory of her father" and disregarded the gentle admonishments of a well-intentioned mother.[67] Through her claims to social superiority, Delamarre not only betrayed her own family and the convent but also the ideal of the emotionally bonded family. Thus, the accusations Briquet de Mercy and Caillère de l'Estang made against Delamarre and Lusignan fused more recent ideals of domestic life with older notions of familial privilege.

By disassociating themselves from their families, Lusignan and Delamarre sought to act as independent agents. Through their newly chosen names, the two women tried to redefine themselves and suggest that they ranked above their families. In the early modern world, where identity was shaped by family and community, such an act of individual self-assertion was regarded as inherently deviant.[68] Whereas their mothers looked out for their daughters' interests and those of the larger family, Lusignan and Delamarre could not look beyond their personal desires, which were defined by "fickleness and inconstancy."[69] The terms "caprice" and "passion" indicated that neither Lusignan nor Delamarre operated on the basis of reason, which then made them vulnerable to those with stronger wills.[70] Both women were susceptible to bad influences which undermined the legitimate authority of their parents. Caillère de l'Estang noted how "the dangerous spirits in whom she [Lusignan] had the misfortune of putting her blind confidence . . . lent her the tricks, gross lies, and speech," which originated in "the corruption of their heart."[71] As for Delamarre, Briquet de Mercy argued that she had fallen under the spell of a "man known for the celebrity of his talent" who had "found the secret of introducing himself into the interior of the Convent" and led Delamarre down her current path.[72] As a result, the families were threatened by malevolent persons who exploited the character flaws of their daughters, thereby weakening the influence of well-meaning mothers.

The lawyers for Madame Delamarre and Madame de Saint-Georges also had to contend with an amorphous public that by 1752 had become "judges" along with the magistrates. Pleading for Lusignan, the lawyer Thévenot d'Essaule stated that "everything seems to converge to increase the Judge's attention and to excite that of the Public."[73] During this same period, the years of the refusal of sacraments crisis, the magistrates similarly appealed to public opinion, which for them remained an abstraction that was "free from interference by any actual, tangible members of the political audience they [the magistrates] claimed to represent."[74] At the same time, the magistrates and other educated writers feared "popular" opinion, the sentiment of a disorganized mass of readers and onlookers who could not be trusted.

The *mémoires judiciaires* for Madame de Saint-Georges appeared in 1751, precisely at this transitional moment, and they echoed the uneasiness about public opinion. According to Caillère de l'Estang, repeated rumors had been transformed into "a public voice which could deservedly be called *vox diaboli*."[75] To some degree, the lawyer's portrayal of public opinion resembled his own characterization of Lusignan: both were manipulating and being manipulated. These remarks remind us that the notion of a rational and stable "political opinion" was not yet fully realized. As a result, lawyers like Caillère de l'Estang challenged the authority of public opinion by linking it to the fickle and feared *peuple,* with its connotation of an irrational mob.[76] In the end, it may not have been a wise strategy for the lawyer, for he lost his case, perhaps because he failed to take into account the public sympathy that the pervasive vocation forcée theme had aroused. Writing in 1758, Madame Delamarre's lawyer Briquet de Mercy, more savvy than Caillère de l'Estang, avoided any mention of public opinion, only noting that Delamarre was sure to find "partisans disposed to credit her complaints"; such persons "bemoan her fate without knowing her; they depict her, without any investigation, as a victim sacrificed to the ambition and greed of her parents."[77] What Briquet de Mercy understood was that the "tribunal of public opinion" used more than the facts of the case: it availed itself of a diffuse cultural arsenal that regarded the vocation forcée as a certainty.[78]

In large measure, the different connotations of "public opinion," as well as the shuttling between different familial models, reflected the changing political climate of the mid-eighteenth century. As we have seen in the previous chapters, the parlement never repudiated the monarchy but insisted that the king show a more benevolent and paternal face, a petition that only served to make the monarchy more "politically dysfunctional."[79] Similarly, when adjudicating a vocation forcée case, the sovereign courts now faced a dilemma with respect to the family. Although the family continued to be a microcosm for French society and government, the magistrates had to accommodate a family model that stressed the importance of each individual and not just the parents. Just as *parlementaires* were wresting control of the convent from ultramontane prelates and the crown itself, they were regulating the kind of influence family members could have over daughters and sisters in the convent. As the Delamarre affair or the case of the monk René Le Lievre indicate, the sovereign courts did not always rule in favor of individuals. Nevertheless, the widespread discourse on the vocation forcée as well as the parlements' own rhetoric about assisting citizens, signaled a challenge to the traditional family.

By addressing larger social and political issues the lawyers on both sides of these cases tailored their arguments for a public already conversant with the vocation forcée as a "social drama."[80] Significantly, that familiarity did not stem from the public's witnessing a barrage of forced vow legal trials. Indeed, Lusignan and Delamarre, the only two women religious in Paris who attempted to revoke their vows legally, would appear to be anomalies. However, the remarks by a contemporary journalist indicate how enmeshed the vocation forcée was in the public imagination. In a vitriolic review of Jean-François La Harpe's *Mélanie* the anti-philosophe Elie Fréron derided La Harpe for writing a play about a young woman whose family forces her to take vows, a subject Fréron described as "most common, worn out, repetitive; one has discussed it a hundred times in prose, in verse, in the novel, in plays, etc."[81] As Fréron rightly pointed out, the vocation forcée motif was ubiquitous in the eighteenth century, in hearsay and rumor, and in novels and plays. In the following section I investigate this phenomenon in two stages. First, from a methodological standpoint the image of the nun was an intertextual one, shaped not only by the issues writers attached to it but by the very way in which this image circulated. Thus, the vocation forcée narrative was powerful because contemporaries encountered this story in a variety of forms that reinforced one another. An understanding of the relationship between these different sources leads to a broader, more diffuse analysis in the second half of this section, where I examine the larger discourse on the vocation forcée as it pertained to the family.

Sensational rumors and diverse literary works, as well as the lively interest of contemporaries, all demonstrate that the vocation forcée narrative in eighteenth-century French culture was itself a cultural phenomenon, one of the recurrent "stories in history." It was what Victor Turner has termed a social drama, that is, an "experiential matrix from which the many genres of cultural performance, beginning with redressive ritual and juridical procedures and eventually including oral and literary narrative, have been generated."[82] During certain periods of history, these narratives persistently appear in a variety of media, indicating a resonance that goes well beyond the plot. In an essay exploring this trend Sarah Maza has laid out how historians have come to understand these stories as "performative rather than simply expressive."[83] In other words, these stories did not just reflect a certain "reality" but themselves influenced and shaped cultural attitudes and expression.[84] The various forms in which a theme manifested itself, the relation of different texts to one another and to a more "real" social experience were a part of these "stories." As Gabrielle Spiegel has noted, an intertextual study of such a phenomenon may also shed light on how "texts both mirror *and* generate social realities, are constituted by *and* constitute social and discursive formations, which they may sustain, resist, context, or seek to transform depending on the individual case."[85]

The overwhelming fascination with the vocation forcée indicates that on a certain level it was, in fact, "real" for contemporaries, a cultural and intellectual experience in which they participated and helped perpetuate. But the isolated trials of Lusignan and Delamarre also indicate that the narratives were not necessarily reflective of the lives of most eighteenth-century women religious. Nonetheless, many contemporaries believed that the vocation forcée epitomized claustral existence. The eighteenth-century public sustained the vocation forcée drama by listening to and disseminating rumors and speculation; it devoured novels, attended plays, many of which became causes célèbres in their own right. Trial briefs were not separate from the other discourses on the vocation forcée but were intrinsically woven together in the imagination of the French literary public of the eighteenth century. The voyeurism and curiosity of the public was itself a part of the forced vow story.

The intertextuality of the vocation forcée literature shaped how contemporaries viewed the forced vow and indeed the convent itself. An analysis of the vocation forcée narrative probing the varying relationship between texts also addresses issues of production, consumption, and reception. Such an inquiry, of course, applies not just to the forced vow story but also to the Jansenist controversies involving nuns as well as the scandals regarding mother superiors. However, the story of forced vows overshadowed other representations of nuns, even though actual nuns played a negligible role in it. The number and variety of sources gave it greater weight and influence. A nun may have been cloistered from the world, but if she tried to annul her vows or flee the convent, her story was broadcast in the salons, newspapers, *nouvelles à la main* or newsletters, the stage, and the pages of novels. Textual accounts claimed veracity because they were based on verbal reports while the latter gained legitimacy when it made its way into print. This phenomenon indicates that the porous boundaries between different cultural texts—rumor, fiction, theater, and legal brief—made distinctions between genres somewhat artificial. Within this context, eighteenth-century authors and audiences could not but help believe that the vocation forcée was a true story, especially in an anticlerical climate where monasticism was becoming synonymous with despotism and libertinism. An intertextual study of the vocation forcée reveals the way in which this narrative reflected and produced a certain social phenomenon pertaining not just to nuns and their vows but to the larger political and social anxieties about families and despotism.

The life of the notorious *salonnière* Claudine-Alexandrine Tencin, known by her detractors as "la religieuse Tencin," demonstrates how even a profligate nun could thrive in the heart of elite society as a *salonnière* and political intriguer. Coerced by her parents into becoming a nun, Tencin, who would one day be the mother of the philosophe d'Alembert, repudiated her vows in 1712. According to the duc de Saint-Simon, the acerbic chronicler of Louis XIV in his later years, "the habit of a nun, the shadow of regularity . . . a cloister . . . was an insupportable constraint for someone who wished to swim in deep waters, and who felt she had talents for intrigue."[86] Convents also provided the backdrop for Tencin's novels such as *Mémoires du comte de Comminge*. But Tencin's successful exit from the convent and her high-profile life remain an exception. Most victims of the vocation forcée did not participate in shaping public opinion. Instead, it was lawyers like Thévenot d'Essaule and Doulcet, as well as the men and women of the Republic of Letters and their responsive reading audience, who continually brought the tragic image of the unwilling nun to the public's attention.

The question of authorship would suggest that the public "entered" the world of the convent purely through the written text, an assumption that ignores the "semi-orality" of the public sphere. According to Hans-Jürgen Lüsebrink, "semi-orality thus concerns a particular phenomenon like gossip and rumors reported and noted in writing, public reading, transcribed songs, anecdotes and stories circulating orally and then recorded, phenomena constitutive of literary and cultural genres such as the ballad, vaudeville, catechism and certain theatrical forms."[87] The *mémoires judiciaires* for Lusignan and Delamarre attest to the circulation of the vocation forcée theme in this "semi-oral" space. Thévenot d'Essaule argued that

Madame de Couhé had attracted bad press because Lusignan's profession "had not made less noise in the Town [Poitiers] and surrounding areas, where the Madame de Couhé's violent acts had achieved a kind of public notoriety."[88] Similarly, Delamarre's trial caught the attention of people in the salon world, individuals like Diderot and Grimm. Given that the vocation forcée narrative was disseminated orally in the salons, did similar episodes elicit interest in the world of "popular culture"? An examination of the diary of the glazier Jacques-Louis Ménétra provides no corroborative evidence. On the other hand, the final paragraphs of *La Religieuse* depict Suzanne Simonin working as a laundress among people who have heard her story and readily condemn the renegade nun.[89] And Diderot himself, who was the son of a cutler and not always well off, lived on the boundaries between "elite" and "popular" culture.

Diderot's *La Religieuse* is an example of how rumors functioned as the basis for many eighteenth-century vocation forcée novels. In many ways, novels were a nexus at which different vocation forcée genres intersected. Besides Diderot's novel, a number of other vocation forcée novels claimed to be based on actual events. One of *La Religieuse*'s most notable predecessors, Brunet de Brou's *La Religieuse malgré elle*, begins by informing its readers that "this Story is not at all make-believe, and . . . it is true."[90] Other writers followed this pattern. In her memoirs Madame de Genlis recounted the friendship she formed at the abbaye d'Origny-Sainte-Benoîte with Madame de Rochefort, whose forced vow story would be the story of Cécile in *Adèle et Théodore*.[91]

Such insistence on authenticity locates the vocation forcée novel in the larger development of the eighteenth-century novel as a genre. Authors sought to legitimate this new genre by achieving verisimilitude, so that by 1740 "the novel tends . . . to deal with ordinary people in familiar setting, to be contemporary or nearly so, to show how things really are."[92] For many novelists and contemporary literary theorists, achieving this social "reality" served a moral purpose: teaching readers about vice and virtue through concrete and emotionally compelling examples. In its review of *Rosalie, ou la vocation forcée* the *Mercure de France* acknowledged the novel's excessive melodrama but also praised it, asserting that "the lesson mothers and fathers can take from these tragedies is sufficient to prompt them to read this epistolary novel."[93] Hoping to inspire their readers to reflect on themselves and to adopt models of the loving family, novelists put forth a story about dysfunctional families in which power had torn apart the bonds of nature.

These examples of how the vocation forcée novels incorporated social realities into their narratives begs the following question: Did lawyers refer to or rely on fictional accounts of the vocation forcée?[94] Briquet de Mercy's *mémoires judiciaires* for Madame Delamarre indicate that lawyers could not ignore such stories. Since he was defending the family of the supposedly wronged nun, Briquet de Mercy needed to confront and counteract the tragic image of the nun. The lawyer appears to have done so by availing himself of the vast criticism directed at the novel. Opponents of the genre regarded the novel as dangerous precisely because it blurred the boundaries between "fiction and falsehood," challenging the differences between "real" and "imaginary."[95] They regarded novelists as tricksters who corrupted their reading public by exposing them to questionable morals and manners.[96] Novelists themselves addressed these accusations. In his prefatory remarks to *La Religieuse malgré elle* Brunet de Brou equivocated: "Although there is an extreme opposition between the Gallant and the Moral, I wanted to reconcile one with the other . . . [B]y exposing the vice with which Religion has disgraced itself, my design is not to approve of it." The novelist also apologized for the "vivacity" of his writing and to insist that despite the scandalous affair between the heroine Florence and a Franciscan, he tried to use "the most modest expressions."[97]

Taking advantage of the dilemmas faced by novelists like Brunet de Brou, Briquet de Mercy repeatedly identified Delamarre's story as a *roman* (novel) in his brief *Mémoire pour les héritiers.* As English Showalter has shown, critics of the novel had made the term *roman* a derogatory epithet, so much so that in 1762 Diderot began his *Eloge de Richardson* with the following disclaimer: "By 'novel' [*roman*] we have until now understood a tissue of fantastic and frivolous events which presented a threat to the taste and morals of its readers."[98] Although the lawyer did not explicitly charge Delamarre with borrowing from fictional narratives, one may easily surmise that his use of the term *roman* implicitly accused her of doing exactly that. For example, the lawyer discredited the stories regarding the mistreatment Delamarre received at age three as "a new nuance in her novel." When demolishing the nun's story, he characterized his own arguments as an "analysis of the novel of Sister de la Marre."[99] Through his repetitive references to the *roman,* Briquet de Mercy was implying that Delamarre had done something far worse than altering facts. His allusions to the novel warned his readers that they needed to be on their guard, for there was no difference between Delamarre's version of her affair and the seductive world of the novel. The lawyer's insinuations would lead the reader to conclude that just as Delamarre's story was disputable, she herself was morally suspect. By composing a novel, Delamarre appeared as the agent of her own fate, one who manipulated her judges—parlement and the reading public—by merging fiction and reality.

The vocation forcée leitmotif pervaded the world of Parisian theaters in forms that similarly blurred the boundaries between fantasy and fact, between textuality and orality. The 1760s witnessed the rise of the *drame,* or bourgeois drama, whose purpose was rooted in moral didacticism. As one of its early champions, Diderot envisioned the *drame* as achieving this goal by touching the audience's emotions.[100] From the 1760s onward, plays set in the convent or convent-like settings, such as Charles-Georges-Thomas Garnier's "La vocation forcée, drame," began to appear.[101] Even the anti-*philosophe* Fréron perceived that the marriage between the *drame* and the vocation forcée was a match made in heaven, because the nuns' and monks' misfortunes, "exposed with as much force as pathos, would excite our compassion and would make our tears run."[102]

Such plays not only touched their audiences' hearts but sparked their own controversies. Jean-François La Harpe's play *Mélanie, ou La Religieuse* generated a scandal in 1770, not on the stage but in the salons.[103] Dubois de Fontanelle's *Ericie, ou la Vestale* (1768) and Le Blanc de Guillet's *Les Druides* (1772), although set in ancient Rome and Gaul respectively, both precipitated conflict because of their thinly disguised critique of Catholic monastic practices.[104] *Les Druides*, written and performed at the height of the Maupeou crisis, came close to inciting riots in the theater.[105] Almost from the beginning, the play became a point of political conflict between the parterre and an irate clergy incensed over the disparaging images of ecclesiastic authority. In the case of *Les Druides*, it was said that an enthusiastic parterre "absolutely wants to create an occasion when during its session in May, the assembly of the clergy watches this play so as to edify and instruct itself on its sacerdotal duties."[106] Public opinion won the day as performances of *Les Druides* continued even after Christophe de Beaumont issued orders forbidding its performance. Such plays thus affirmed the politically explosive potential of the vocation forcée beyond the pages of *mémoires judiciaires* and fictional narratives. As Jeffrey Ravel has noted in his study of prerevolutionary theater, "live theater combines the discursive and the performative aspects of political cultures; playwrights require bodies, voices, movement, and gestures to animate their ideas, and eighteenth-century audiences responded to performance in a vivid, often visceral fashion."[107] For writers, actors, and audiences, the *drame* of the vocation forcée then not only represented the crimes of the church but became a vehicle through which they could articulate their resentment against the church and, indeed, hope to influence the church.

Sarah Maza's work on prerevolutionary causes célèbres has demonstrated that from the 1770s onward the *drame* also influenced *mémoires judiciaires* as lawyers availed themselves of the genre's hyperbolic emotions and its overt didacticism.[108] The *drame*, which became popular from the 1770s onward, did not influence the *mémoires* of the Lusignan and Delamarre affairs, which were written in the 1750s. However, in the final brief for Lusignan, the *Mémoire pour demoiselle Marie-Michelle de Couhé de Lusignan*, Thévenot d'Essaule pulled out all the stops and departed from the drier style he had used in the *Second mémoire pour la demoiselle de Couhé du Lusignan*. Describing the moment when her mother threateningly commanded Lusignan to sign the contract for her monastic dowry, the lawyer provided poignant details of Lusignan's reluctant acquiescence: "Finally terrified by the fierce looks of her mother, she responded after a quarter of an hour, in an extremely low voice, 'Yes, Mother.' "[109] Such tableaux combining the textual and the visual provided a thrilling read, one that was most likely intended for an audience who already encountered such scenes in novels if not yet on the Paris stage.

The overlap between legal and fictional narratives went well beyond form and style and extended to an exploration of familial relations and dysfunction. In his work on the family in Diderot's *La Religieuse* J. E. Fowler has argued that the "psychology of family relationships" provides the key to reading the novel.[110] Fowler limits himself to *La Religieuse*, but as the trial briefs for the Lusignan and Delamarre cases indicate, such a framework may be adopted for the reading of other eighteenth-century vocation forcée narratives that showcased the family even more than Diderot's novel. In general, the narrative in most vocation forcée novels and plays pitted the virtuous daughter against the ambitious and headstrong parents or parent. Although the unhappy woman, who is always young, has been forcibly placed in the convent, she expresses no bitterness against her parents, only sorrow. Her distress often involves the loss of a lover who, she is sometimes led to believe, has died, but as the reader predictably discovers a few pages later, is still alive. The dramatic conclusions of these narratives follow one of two paths. In one scenario, the parent experiences remorse, the family reconciles, and the estranged daughter reunites with her lost love. The second ending is devastatingly tragic: the young woman dies in the presence of her repentant parents and grieving lover.

But where Fowler has chosen to read the various familial tensions within *La Religieuse* using the Freudian theory of transference, I would situate that *La Religieuse* and other eighteenth-century vocation forcée fictional narratives in the contemporary anxieties about power and authority. In his review of *Ericie, ou la Vestale*, Fontanelle's vocation forcée *drame* situated in ancient Rome, Elie Fréron noted the various kinds of tragedies that appealed most to the public: "conjugal love, maternal love, filial love, fraternal love, the love between a lover and his mistress, friendship, honor, courage, happiness, mercy, ambition, adultery, jealousy, vengeance, the predilection and hardness of fathers, the ingratitude of children, the attachment to Religion, country, king, etc."[111] Fréron's itemized list of topics captures the inextricable link between the private world of the family and the larger public institutions of the Old Regime. As was the case in the *mémoires judiciaires* for Lusignan and Delamarre, this family did not adhere to a single model. Instead, men of letters constructed multiple models of family: the family as a social entity in which the unnatural parents are driven by ambition; the reinstated affective family; the potential family comprised of the young woman and her lover. Behind these shifting images of the family was the notion that public well-being depended on the restoration or creation of a family in which members were bound together by love.

In most fictional vocation forcée narratives the source of conflict and sorrow resulted from a father or mother's worldly ambition, revealing that his or her understanding of family was founded on prestige and power in society. The first lines uttered in La Harpe's *Mélanie* come from Mélanie's father, M. Faublas, who announces his "projects" to his wife: "One offers to your son a brilliant marriage. / The hope of a regiment and a rank at Court"—in effect, all the traits of social success in the Old Regime.[112] The key words describing such aspirations, "ambition" and "interest," are accompanied by constant reminders that the young woman is being "sacrificed or "immolated" for the sake of familial prestige.[113] Ambitious families with social pretensions were shown to be lacking civilized qualities. They were "barbaric" mothers and fathers who, by forcing children into the convent, were guilty of "inhuman abuses."[114] The unwilling vows made on behalf of selfish interest stood in stark contrast to the ideal vocation, the willing sacrifice one made for the good of society and state. In the early 1770s French subjects were given a living example of such a vocation when Madame Louise, Louis XV's youngest daughter, became a Carmelite to atone for her father's sins.[115]

However, most novels and plays condemned the society that demanded even a voluntary sacrifice. Le Blanc satirized such practices in *Les Druides,* in which Indumar, the high priest of the ancient Gauls, prepares to sacrifice his daughter Emirène to ensure success against the invading Romans! The society depicted in such plays and novels was unquestionably an elitist one in which privilege and hierarchy were the operating principles. Moreover, such works denounced a corporate society based on prerogatives that benefited the heads of families, leaving individual members at their mercy. Like the lawyers for Lusignan and Delamarre, writers of fiction argued that neither society nor families could deny an individual her rights. For example, the anonymous author of *Rosalie, ou la vocation forcée* declares that "liberty is a good that belongs to man" and that "to rob him of it is to remove the best part of his existence."[116] Even Fréron interpreted the vocation forcée as a suppression of "liberty" and "rights" and a sign of "parental despotism."[117] Thus, the family in the vocation forcée fiction became an illegitimate sociopolitical entity, a bastion of despotism.

Like Thévenot d'Essaule and Doulcet, novelists and playwrights judged social ambition, tyranny, and despotism by the normative ideal of the "natural" biological family. In *Rosalie, ou la vocation forcée* Rosalie grieves over her mother's distant and even contemptuous response: "Abandoned by nature entirely, it is she who persecutes me . . . her most sacred duties flee before my face."[118] Such words do more than suggest the ideals of the affective family derived from nature; they emphasize parental obligation. One of the reasons for the failure of parents to fulfill their responsibilities was an overriding devotion to a single child, an accusation made against Madame de Couhé. According to Brunet de Brou, "Animals whom nature's Author has refused reason are not so inhuman. They appear to love their young ones with the same equality."[119] This notion of an inherent equality between siblings was a critical element in the critique against tyrannical parents and, one may argue, against a society that reinforced a hierarchy among siblings.

The unnaturalness of parents was highlighted by the preponderance of cruel mothers, such as those found in *Rosalie, ou la vocation forcée*, "La Vocation forcée, drame," "La Mère punie," or *Les Métamorphoses de la religieuse*.[120] I would suggest that because maternal feeling was increasingly linked to biological motherhood, the image of cruel mothers further underscored the unnaturalness of parents who placed their children in convents. By the same token, writers portrayed both mothers and fathers as figures who had allowed social pressures and unnatural proclivities to obscure their true parental feelings. Mélanie mourns her father's lack of affection, just as Rosalie regrets her mother's coldness.

As Lynn Hunt has shown, eighteenth-century novels and bourgeois dramas repeatedly told the story of dysfunctional families replete with "unnatural" parents and victimized children, but the question remains: Why was the story of the *female* vocation forcée such a compelling one for eighteenth-century audiences? Both *mémoires judiciaires* and fictional narratives provide very similar answers. Isolated from the world, surrounded by potentially hostile figures, the cloistered nun was helpless, inherently a victim because she was a woman, and unable to withstand the powers arrayed against her. In Madame de Genlis's *Adèle et Théodore*, the Chevalier de Murville writes to the nun Cécile, whom he loves: "Ah! If I could have foreseen the horrible tyranny that one must have exercised against you, no, Cécile, no, you would not have been the victim, despite the cruel Father that banishes, despite the family that abandons you, despite yourself."[121] Moreover, youth further enhanced the image of the victimized nuns. In the introduction to "La Mauvaise Mère punie," the author describes a young nun, "pale, disfigured . . . chagrin has blighted the flowers of youth."[122]

Such assumptions regarding youth shaped the ways in which onlookers viewed actual vocation forcée trials. Although Doulcet never denied that Marguerite Delamarre was in her mid-thirties during the trial, onlookers were either not aware of this fact or chose to ignore the question of age. A letter in Grimm's *Correspondance littéraire* described the affair of Delamarre as "a *young* nun from Longchamp" who was attempting to renounce her vows.[123] And certainly, when Diderot appropriated Delamarre's story, he transformed Suzanne Simonin into a young woman in her late teens. The assumption that an unhappy nun was a young one also suggests that the eighteenth-century imagination envisioned a nun as ageless or, more tellingly, as someone whose growth was arrested once she entered the cloister. These portrayals of a young unhappy nun apparently made her a more sympathetic figure, one who was very obviously deserving of assistance. Furthermore, youth, combined with gender and religious status, stripped these young women of agency. With the notable exception of Suzanne, Florence (in *La Religieuse malgré elle*), and Rosalie, none of these young women take serious legal action against their families. Indeed, curés and relatives insist on helping these nuns, often against their will.[124]

In fictional narratives the figure who most actively rebels against familial authority is the lover, who represents another normative family, namely, the potential family of the young nun and her spouse. The nubile nun and her paramour may have hinted at the erotic, but I would also argue that the generational divide between young lovers and older parents symbolized the larger conflict between the new ideals of tightly knit families and the traditional and more hierarchical version of the family that emphasized parental authority. The lover, such as Osmide in *Ericie* or Monval in *Mélanie*, is a masculine figure, in effect a knight-errant who attempts not only to rescue his love but to overthrow the traditional family. He is a figure that was entirely absent from the *mémoires judiciaires*, perhaps because neither Lusignan and Delamarre would have had an opportunity to acquire such admirers.[125] Nor would their claims of abuse have been as convincing if the public thought that they had amorous liaisons. Fictional literature, however, pushed the ideal of the emotionally bonded family by demonstrating that the attraction between a young man and a woman was natural and not sinful. In Amélie Panckouke Suard's *Lettres d'un jeune lord à une religieuse italienne* the impassioned Lord Herron tells Isabelle, who is reluctant to break her vows and marry him, that "it is the vow that chains you to an eternal servitude, which separates you from the happiness that a charitable God has destined for the beings he has created."[126] Religious vows threaten to destroy a future family comprised of affectionate parents and children, one whose potential remains unfulfilled. Cécile, in *Adèle et Théodore*, expresses unhappiness and jealousy at seeing a young mother because it reveals to her "the horror of my fate . . . and the full extent of the awful sacrifice I have been forced to make."[127] Thus, a true vocation was exchanged for false vows founded on tyranny and sacrifice.

Despite their sacrifices, many of the nuns in these narratives do not harbor any bitterness toward the guilty parent but instead go so far as to seek reconciliation with the parent.[128] Both Mélanie and Ericie refer to themselves as "rebellious daughters" when describing their unhappiness in the cloistered environment.[129] Such self-denigration exonerates the parent and points to a central feature of many vocation forcée fictional narratives: the eventual redemption of the parent. In *Rosalie, ou la vocation forcée* Rosalie's mother finally comes to love her daughter when she sees a married Rosalie with her baby and, as a result, finally views her "with the eyes of nature."[130] Within other narratives, however, redemption is possible only if the sacrifice is total. The deaths of Mélanie, Ericie, and Euphémie bring about the salvation of their errant parents, whose remorse and grief enables them to see their "natural" duties.

Did such repentance erase parental authority? Just as *parlementaires* and barristers sought to temper royal authority and not destroy it, so did novelists and playwrights attempt to recast parental authority according to the newer family values of the eighteenth century. At the same time, however, the narratives' endings—in which parents are remorseful and reinstated—would suggest that we cannot assume that eighteenth-century writers and their public renounced parental authority in favor of a more "democratic" family. As a woman and as a nun, the heroine can never actually oust and replace the father figure as the patriarchal head of the family, a position that she, in fact, recognizes and, more importantly, respects. Once Ericie is aware that her father Aurèle regrets forcing her to become a vestal virgin, she defends him from her vengeful lover Osmide. "Stop," she pleads. "Remember that I owe him my life . . . respect my father . . . cherish his daughter within him, live to console him."[131] Similarly, regardless of their crimes, mothers are loved simply because they are mothers. Thus, even while her mother threatens and torments her, Rosalie yearns for her mother's love: "I notice her from the distance, I want to follow her . . . to wait for her, I want to touch her."[132] Indeed, once the rehabilitation has been completed, the nun herself, initially the central character, is effaced from the story. Either she dies or she is united with her lover and absorbed into another family where the hierarchical lines are more "natural," those of love between parent and child and between husband and wife.

The complete reform of the family and the erasure of female agency indicate that fictional narratives, unlike legal trials, could provide neat resolutions in which families remained intact and social disorder was contained. I would argue, however, that these packaged endings also evoked a certain ambivalence on the part of authors and their audiences. Contemporaries sometimes regarded the rehabilitation of fathers and mothers in most eighteenth-century fictional narratives to be unrealistic. In his review of *Rosalie, ou la vocation forcée* Grimm offered the following critique: "The events are too contrived; some of the characters perform atrocious actions without goal or profit."[133] Despite the obvious flaws of such works, the sudden transformation of fathers and mothers from demons to parents remained an integral part of most this literature. Such conversions signified an affirmation of parental preeminence.[134] But perhaps they rang false because this reintegration often had a price. If Lusignan obtained her freedom, heroines such as Mélanie, Suzanne Simonin, and Ericie found themselves trapped or facing death. In other words, they continued to be sacrificed.

For men of letters and for eighteenth-century barristers, the vocation forcée became a vehicle for condemning familial despotism and the institutions that supported such abuse, which leads us to a final question: what of the convent itself? How did the convent fare in the legal and fictional vocation forcée narratives? Not well. As Louis-Sébastien Mercier wrote in 1782, "convents are judged. Excessive curiosity, bigotry and hypocrisy, claustral prudery reign there."[135] We have already seen that lawyers in the mid-eighteenth century regarded the figures of power associated with the convent, such as archbishops and mother superiors, as representing the worst abuses of authority in the Old Regime. They were bad parents, parents whose behavior was out of step with the emerging model of the domestic, emotionally bonded family. Barristers reprimanded these mothers and fathers with the hope of reforming them, making them conform to the new ideal family, and integrating them better within the convent. However, within the vocation forcée scenario, this option appeared less viable as lawyers and especially men of letters cast the convent as an irredeemable family, fated by its very structure to fall into a constant state of disorder.

As a result of its far-flung circulation, the vocation forcée became, in many respects, synonymous with the convent itself, thanks to the various venues through which the story circulated in the Old Regime. Although they often praised a genuine religious vocation, lawyers and men of letters also depicted the convent as a sinister accomplice of the family, a secretive arm of the church and of the state. For example, the records of the Commission de Secours described nuns as "girls who condemn themselves to a perpetual prison."[136] According to Thévenot d'Essaule, "cloisters are the usual resource for fathers and mothers in such cases [when desiring to exclude children from their inheritance]," a sentiment affirmed in works such as *Mélanie, Ericie,* and *Rosalie, ou la vocation forcée.* The reasons for this complicity between the convent and the family were straightforward: the convent shared the vices of the greedy and authoritarian family.[137] By viewing the convent through the lens of the vocation forcée, writers and their public stripped the cloister of its sacred status and transformed it into a space of social control, a symbol of the cruel ways in which families and the larger society dealt with innocent individuals whose very existence was deemed disruptive or inconvenient.

By the end of the Old Regime, the public endowed the convent with characteristics associated with the Bastille, another symbol of despotism. In his study of revolutionary theater Marvin Carlson has noted that "the convent provided a simulacrum of the Bastille in the popular imagination as a symbol of oppression and tyranny."[138] Although Carlson draws this analogy in the context of the French Revolution, I would argue that the similarities predate the Revolution. Hans-Jürgen Lüsebrink and Rolf Reichardt have shown that in the decades preceding the Revolution, the Bastille already symbolized despotic rule with its dungeons and secret chambers.[139] Significantly, lawyers and men of letters also referred to the cloister as a "tomb" or a "prison."[140] Over the course of the eighteenth century, these sinister images of the convent came to dominate the public imagination. The convent thus appeared as a house of horrors, as suggested in the poem "Epître d'une religieuse à la marquise de ***, sa soeur," by Monsieur Rangier: "These cloisters, these caves, these immense porticos, / These frightening tombs, images of death, / Which recall death . . . / The bolted doors, the dungeons the hideous assembly, / All recount before my eyes infamous slavery."[141] Like the Bastille, the cloister signified not merely prison but the crimes of the Old Regime. Indeed, Thévenot d'Essaule foreshadowed this interpretation when he described how the nuns of Saint-François guarded Lusignan as if she were "a prisoner of State."[142]

This devastating critique of the convent inexorably led to a scrutiny of the institution's function. In the vocation forcée narrative, men of letters were not asking who should control convents and nuns so much as whether the convent had a place in society, especially as its religious purpose seemed to diminish. In effect, the real issue was whether the convent was necessary to society at all. This provocative question became even more charged in the context of changing views of women. A woman's virtue was no longer centered on her Christian morals, as had been the case with Jansenist nuns. The trial briefs for the mother superiors as well as elements of the forced vow narrative reveal that women were being redefined in terms of their biological capacity to reproduce. In chapters 2 and 3 we saw that corrupt individuals or a corrupt system prevented nuns from fully expressing their *chosen* role, that of humble servants of God. In this chapter the convent itself was presented as an obstacle to nuns fulfilling their *natural* role, that of wives and mothers. Instead of offering possibilities for reform by disciplining superiors or reforming the structure of the convent, the authors of vocation forcée narratives opened up a new possibility: the abolition of the convent entirely.

SCHOOL OF VIRTUE, SCHOOL OF VICE

The Debate on Convent Education, 1740–1789

THE VOCATION FORCÉE NARRATIVES OF THE EIGHTEENTH CENTURY created a strong impression among many readers that the convent was a lugubrious and sinister prison, inhabited by young women whose families had sentenced them to a life of celibacy and isolation. Novelists, playwrights, and social critics cast the cloister as a symbol of the decay rife in the Old Regime. Literate members of society placed less emphasis on salvation and the afterlife than on "society," defined not as a manifestation of God's will but as "an autonomous arena of human activity (separate from the natural and divine realms alike), and possessing knowable laws."[1] Their views were symptomatic of a society in which contempt for clerics had transformed into a disenchantment with religion, nourished by the religious controversies of the mid-eighteenth century and the anticlericalism of the Republic of Letters. Within this atmosphere men and women of letters no longer asked who had authority over the convent but whether the convent had a legitimate place in French society. Was the convent an appropriate institution to nurture the hearts and minds of women?

These questions became increasingly pressing in the context of female education, the convent's main contribution to eighteenth-century secular society. As we have seen, the centrality of the convent in female education was a relatively new phenomenon in early modern France, the product of the Catholic Reformation and Counter-Reformation. Whereas the medieval church had been suspicious of women as teachers, the early modern church, in the wake of the Reformation, viewed these pedagogical "brides of Christ" as a means of retaining its control over women and families. For the first time, women religious could teach, and communities like the Ursulines or the Filles de Notre-Dame made pedagogy a part of their vocation. These teaching orders were responsible for reshaping the female convent into an arena of female education as well as devotion, one that served the needs of a wider cross-section of elite society. Education in the convent became a mandatory stage in the life of a young girl from the elite, the first step in her transformation into a virtuous Christian woman.

But social theorists and educators began to question the validity of convent education as the theory of sensationalism and the expulsion of the Jesuits generated seismic shifts in pedagogical theory and practice. Eighteenth-century notions of sensationalism were influenced by the seventeenth-century English philosopher John Locke's monumental *Essay concerning Human Understanding* (1688). Locke argued that a child began life as a tabula rasa; a child's personality and character were molded by the experience of the senses and through observation. With the publication of Pierre Coste's translation of the *Essay* in 1700, Locke's ideas assumed an important place in French intellectual thought, particularly with respect to the debate over education. Furthermore, Voltaire's *Lettres philosophiques* (1734) firmly situated Locke at the center of the Enlightenment.[2] Sensationalism became one of the main threads in the diffuse Enlightenment project. Proponents of sensationalism, such as Etienne Bonnot, Charles Bonnet, and Claude-Adrien Helvétius, "attempted to explain the origin of knowledge even as they strove to reach an understanding of human behavior."[3] They connected theories of sensationalist philosophy to social reform and human progress, thereby adding a moral dimension to sensationalism.[4] Such treatises led to a reassessment of education and its ability to improve life on earth.[5]

Lockean sensationalism also contributed to the erosion of the Christian-based curriculum that was the basis of early modern French education.[6] Thinkers like Noël-Antoine Pluche and Louis Dumas criticized the curriculum of Jesuit schools and similar pedagogical institutions on the grounds that it did not suit the cognitive skills of young children. Dumas and others argued that instructors should not teach Latin through rote memorization without any real comprehension; they should be aware that children's mental faculties developed gradually and were better stimulated by appealing to the senses. But Lockean notions of child psychology did not just question the traditional methodology of religious education. More significantly, they undercut its spiritual foundation by repudiating original sin. Locke had argued that children were born unmarked by God, thus entering into the world empty of sin. The suppression of sin, the cornerstone of religious pedagogy, now became irrelevant. It was this element of Lockean thought that philosophes, most notably Condillac and Helvétius, exploited forcefully.[7] Their works ignored questions of salvation and focused entirely on social and personal happiness.[8] Moreover, Helvétius devised an educational program that took the responsibility of education away from clerics and gave it to the state.

The proposal of a state-controlled educational system and the overall upsurge in pedagogical writings may be attributed to two major developments in the early 1760s, the expulsion of the Jesuits in 1763 and the publication of Jean-Jacques Rousseau's *Emile* a year earlier. According to Marcel Grandière, "destroying the education of monks was the priority of the *parlementaires.*"[9] For many of the magistrates, Jesuit pedagogy represented "the barbarism of past centuries," an education ill suited for young men who were not destined for the clergy.[10] Critics of monastic-based education called for curricula and institutions with a more secular outlook; this goal was achieved beginning in February 1763 when Louis XV instigated reform by secularizing the administration of the male *collèges*.[11] The preoccupation with education and especially the attack on pedagogical monastic institutions unquestionably spilled over into the debate about female education precipitated by Rousseau.[12] In *Emile* and *La Nouvelle Héloïse* (1761) Rousseau prescribed a domestic education for women that encompassed a vision of a society divided into private and public arenas that were strictly gendered.

The distinction Rousseau made between the public and the private and between men and women echoed the larger discussions on feminine nature and sexuality found in the philosophical and medical writings of the eighteenth century.[13] Thomas Laqueur and Londa Schiebinger have advanced the theory that throughout the eighteenth century medical, philosophical, and fictional writings recast the paradigm of sexual hierarchy. According to Laqueur, "the old [Galenic] model, in which men and women were arrayed along an axis whose telos was male, gave way by the late eighteenth century to a new model of radical dimorphism, of biological divergence."[14] This notion of "sexual complementarity" asserted that the relationship between men and women was not necessarily one of superiority and inferiority but of fundamental physical, moral, and intellectual difference.[15] Critically, as Lieselotte Steinbrügge has pointed out, physiocratic theory tied woman's essential nature to her physical makeup. Where men had the capacity to reason, to transcend their corporeality, women could not; they were too capricious and unbalanced. Within early and medieval Christianity, the attribution of instability to female physiology was commonplace, a sign of women's inferiority and their tendency toward sin. In the eighteenth century, however, medical authors and philosophes proposed a more "scientific" explanation, arguing that a woman's nerves and organs, more fragile and susceptible to her environment, made her more sensitive than a man.[16] While her impressionability made a woman an intellectual lightweight, it also rendered her more *sensible,* that is, more sympathetic to others and more capable of love. This woman was a moral force whose virtue was derived from her physicality, especially her ability to reproduce. Women then were not necessarily the source of sin but the source of morality. Those women who fulfilled their "natural" roles as mothers and wives could influence men by making them morally aware and, therefore, better citizens within the public world. Thus, eighteenth-century writers theorized female social existence as inseparable from her physical being.

The question of how to manufacture the "natural" female paragon became inextricably linked to the philosophical and political debates on education. Such discussions centered not on the construction of a curriculum and pedagogical methodology that would enable women to achieve their intellectual potential, but rather on women's social roles as wives and mothers. Arguing that women had a moral edge over men as long as they remained within the home, Rousseau strongly advocated families in which mothers instructed their young daughters to be virtuous and prepared them for a domestic future.[17] By the 1770s, both followers and opponents of Rousseau, such as Madame de Montbart and Mademoiselle Espinassy respectively, regarded the involvement in a daughter's education as a key facet of maternal duty.[18] As this understanding of the "natural" woman became increasingly normative, it also became clear that the "unnatural" woman was one who did not fulfill her biological roles, who did not live in the home where her husband could keep an eye on her. Since nuns, the antithesis of the maternal ideal, had the responsibility of educating women, they inevitably came under a great deal of scrutiny and criticism.

The ensuing debate over female convent education was conducted in two seemingly disparate arenas: the mainstream world of the Republic of Letters and its seamier underside, the world of erotic literature. Pornography may not have had any influence on policies of female education, but it was nonetheless widely read. More to the point, some of the key works of erotica reacted both directly and indirectly to mainstream pedagogical treatises. In the first half of this chapter I will examine the more conventional debates on convent education, while in the second half I will analyze the ways in which pornographic novels took on the same theme.

These two different bodies of work were both influenced by the widespread impact of Lockean sensationalism in three ways.[19] First, Locke's emphasis on the senses and the environment shifted the focus of pedagogical writings away from the inherently sinful qualities of the child; instead, writers examined the surroundings that influenced that child. Second, writers who employed the Lockean paradigm posited a new female psychology that linked a woman's moral sensibility to her physicality. Third, the analytical framework that foregrounded the body provided pedagogues and social theorists with unlikely bedfellows, namely, libertine authors who also examined the impact convent education had on the female senses. A discussion of pedagogical works will necessarily be more diffuse than the close analysis of a specific Jansenist trial or court case. My methodological approach in this chapter reflects the abstract and systemic approach of my subjects, who were disengaged from the specifics of convent life. Much like an examination of the vocation forcée literature, a study of pedagogical writings and eighteenth-century erotica establishes key themes and patterns in a widespread cultural debate.

Both pedagogical authors and libertine writers sought to answer the following question: Did celibate women and the secluded environment of the convent help young girls to develop into "natural women"? I argue that in their efforts to address this question, both groups of writers judged nuns as they did all other women, as creatures defined by their bodies. For many pedagogues and social commentators, women religious were *femmes manquées*. True, both nuns and writers from the Republic of Letters aspired to bring out the virtues of a young girl and make her the pliable partner of strong and virile spouse. However, *gens de lettres* also regarded nuns as the victims of lifelong celibacy and unnatural seclusion, which also made them unfit to prepare young girls for domestic life. But if pedagogues and other authors on education denounced claustral celibacy, pornographic authors were even more subversive because they ridiculed chastity as well. Regardless of their choice of genre, all of the writers involved in the critique of convent education negated the convent's utility, suggesting instead that women religious be reconfigured as "natural women" existing within the parameters of male needs and desires.

During the second half of the eighteenth century, a broad range of writers from the Republic of Letters brought themes of social utility, secular morality, and female virtue to bear on the question of convent education. The participants in these debates were varied. In addition to male philosophes and physiocrats, female authors, such as Madame d'Epinay and Madame de Puisieux, also published their views of education. Outside of the Enlightenment salons, professional educators, most of whom were governesses, such as Madame de Genlis and Madame Le Prince de Beaumont, outlined their ideas on how to educate young girls. Former military personnel, obscure clerics, and aspiring literary writers, most of whom belonged to the aristocracy and the bourgeoisie, also contributed their opin-

ions regarding female pedagogy.[20] Formal institutions sanctioned by the
state deliberated the question of female education. At least three provincial academies—Besançon in 1778, Châlons in 1780, and Rouen in 1784
—sponsored competitions asking for essays on how best to educate young
women. Participants included novelists such as Bernardin de Saint Pierre
and Choderlos de Laclos as well as Manon Phlipon, the future Madame
Roland.[21]

In general, this diverse group of authors was critical of convent education. The works of these writers indicate that the scale had tipped toward
domestic education away from the trends of the seventeenth century,
which had witnessed the rise of female religious teaching orders and the
founding in 1686 of Saint-Cyr, a nonreligious institution, by Louis XIV's
morganatic wife Madame de Maintenon.[22] As Samia Spencer has suggested, their critique of the convent drew attention to the ignorance of
nuns, their lack of pedagogical calling, and the effect convents had on
their personalities and passions.[23] Many writers were troubled by the convent's link to elite society: was it too removed or too entangled in worldly
mores? These critics regarded convent education as part of a larger social
malaise in which elite women abandoned their homes and their true calling. The prescription, for many writers, was for nuns to serve the nation
by leaving the convent and procreating.

A number of writers attributed the overall failure of convent education
to the naiveté of nuns.[24] In *Conseils à une amie* Madeleine d'Arsant de
Puisieux, a friend of Diderot, gives an account of the education she received, not from nuns but from a "Madame de ***" who had withdrawn
from society to live in the convent. Unlike this worldly woman, the nun is
"a simple girl who had spent her life in the convent." For the nun, what
Madame de *** says is like "Greek or Algebra."[25] In other words, for a
woman whose life has been devoted to seclusion and devotion, social ban-
ter and wisdom are unfathomable and esoteric, beyond her reach. The
nun responds by sleeping through these advice sessions, thus falling short
in her responsibilities toward her young charge. In *Lettres d'une péruvienne*
the novelist Françoise de Graffigny similarly excoriates nuns "in whom intelligence might be held a crime."[26]

According to the pedagogue Anne d'Aubourg de la Bove de Miremont,
such ignorance and anti-intellectualism not only expose nuns to ridicule
but have far reaching implications for those who are under their care and
authority. Locked up in their convents, women religious regard practical
skills such as basic mathematics as "vain and frivolous"; according to Miremont, this prejudice sometimes results in the financial ruin of women,
such as widows, who are forced to fend for themselves.[27] Madame Roland,
however, provides a more nuanced account of intellectual life on the convent. In her memoirs she fondly recounts her relationship with one well-

educated nun, Sister Sainte-Sophie, who worked to ensure that the young Manon Phlipon received a good education. According to Madame Roland, "this good woman soon attached herself to me because of my taste for study; after having given a lesson to the entire class, she took me aside and made me recite grammar, pursue geography, extract bits of history."[28] Thus, although pedagogues regarded convent education as failing to prepare young women for their lives in the outside world, the experiences of boarders suggest that it was not necessarily a lost cause.

Some authors, including Miremont, attempted to offer solutions for reforming convent education. First appearing in 1749, André-Joseph Panckouke's *Les Etudes convenables aux demoiselles* was intended to supplement convent instruction, as suggested by the phrase "ouvrages destinés aux jeunes pensionnaires des communautés et des maisons religieuses" in the full title. Instead of explicitly critiquing convent education, Panckouke subtly demonstrated its limited scope by pointing out secular subjects that could be introduced into the convent's curriculum.[29] Thirty years later, the works of Madame de Miremont and the abbé Ambroise Riballier (1712–85) offered suggestions for incorporating physical exercise and hygiene into convent education.[30] For Miremont, the body required physical activity and freedom in order to develop properly, a notion that was antithetical to an institution determined to stifle the body. Although she ultimately advocated secularizing female education, Miremont provided blueprints on how to train nuns to be better instructors, including a six-year novitiate focusing on pedagogical instruction.[31] While her plans to reform the convent may have denoted respect, they also minimized the devotional elements of a religious vocation.

Other writers argued that the problems of monastic pedagogy resulted from the fact that a religious calling did not necessarily amount to a pedagogical one. In the *Lettres diverses et critiques* the governess Madame Le Prince de Beaumont trenchantly caricatures nuns: "I retired from the world . . . in order to free myself from the cares of a household and children," a nun complains, "and I am obliged to live my life with monkeys who do not interest me."[32] Le Prince de Beaumont concludes that as a result of their disinterest, nuns absent themselves whenever possible and therefore fail to supervise young children, leaving them to their own devices.[33] In the process of demonstrating that religious and pedagogical calling were not one and the same, Le Prince de Beaumont sundered the ties between religion and pedagogy that seventeenth-century women religious had worked so hard to establish. Moreover, she implicitly questioned whether nuns possessed a true *religious* vocation because they exhibited such callous and selfish behavior.

For other pedagogical authors, religious vows elicited very different but equally abhorrent behavior, a sure sign of the convent's corrupting structure. In *La Gamalogie ou de l'éducation des filles* the Chevalier de Cerfvol argues that monastic vows damage a nun emotionally and therefore represent a danger to young girls.[34] Seeking companionship or simply responding to boredom, nuns seduce unsuspecting girls with negative images of the world. In *La Gamalogie* a nun confides to her young pupil: "I have lived in the world; I know all that is false and dangerous."[35] Cerfvol informs his reader, a young wife called Sophie, that the nun's malicious spite originates from the "weight of the crushing chains that . . . [the nun] drags around in forced solitude."[36] Thus, seclusion was unnatural and warped the psyche. Cerfvol's arguments reflected how contemporaries cast monastic vows as prison sentences. Like Diderot, Cerfvol assumed that women religious suffered from hopeless despair because they were all forced to take vows of lifelong celibacy and isolation. And like Diderot, he ultimately denounced the convent itself as an unnatural environment damaging mentors and students alike.[37] The failure of convent education lay with the convent itself, an institution that appeared incompatible with human society and human nature.

But did the problem lie with a fundamental dissonance between society and cloister or was the convent, in fact, insufficiently removed from the corruption of the outside world? Despite the overall agreement among philosophes and pedagogues that convent education left much to be desired, writers did not always concur in their responses to this question. For some authors the convent was too worldly, and for others it was too removed from the societal pressures a young girl would face. Those who belonged to the latter camp emphasized the mismatch between claustral life and the expectations of the world. As Sophronie in Voltaire's *L'éducation des filles* pragmatically noted: "[My mother] did not raise me in a convent, because it was not in a convent that I was destined to live."[38] The moral and religious lessons of the convent did not translate into an education necessary for survival in the elite world of the salon and the court. Even the parlementary magistrate La Chatolais acknowledged the inappropriateness of convent education for those destined to live in the secular world when he concluded that "the silence and peace of cloisters is the opposite of the activity which comprises the merit and character of a good mother of a family."[39] At best, this deficiency resulted in the kind of confusion Helvétius depicts in *De l'homme,* in which a mother superior exhorts a girl never to look a man directly in the face, and then, only an hour later, the girl gazes into the face of her dance master.[40] Indeed, at the Abbaye-aux Bois in the 1770s, young *pensionnaires* received their education from tutors outside of the convent, chaperoned by the nuns.[41]

But while writers such as Helvétius and La Chatolais agreed that there was an unbridgeable gap between convent and society, others perceived the convent as an extension of society, replicating all its vices. Rousseau dismisses the convent as a "veritable school of coquetry . . . which produces all the eccentricities of women and makes them highly extravagant little mistresses."[42] Similarly, his devoted follower Madame de Montbart attributed female obsession with jewelry to the trivial nature of convent life.[43] Madame de Genlis, another Rousseau devotee, also faulted the convent for its superficiality and for fostering an atmosphere of intrigue among students. In *Adèle et Théodore* the boarder Mademoiselle de Céligni attempts to detach Adèle from her mother's guidance and then spreads lies about her after Adèle spurns her.[44] According to Adèle's mother, the convent's boarders possessed "all the folly that a bad education can give, that is to say, silliness, savagery, rudeness."[45] Ironically, Madame de Genlis's righteous pronouncements contradicted her conduct: as a young wife she had enjoyed the worldly atmosphere of convent life and had participated in its little intrigues, going so far as to join the "parti de l'opposition."[46]

According to some authors, the stark contrast between the secluded convent and the heady existence of society life often precipitates a young woman's moral descent. Convent education disfigures her personality by nurturing weakness and failing to instill the fortitude and wisdom to withstand temptation. The repressive conventual lifestyle only ensures that girls just out of the convent will plunge headlong into a frivolous and dissolute life. In Genlis's *Adèle et Théodore* the vicomtesse de Limours affirms "that when I left the convent . . . [it was] with a sole idea in my head, that of delivering myself entirely to my amusement and of compensating myself for a long and painful enslavement."[47] Joseph-François-Edouard Desmahis's entry on woman in Diderot and d'Alembert's *Encyclopédie* illustrates a similar point through the story of Chloé and her gradual decline into the vice-ridden existence of the aristocratic woman. Desmahis and other like-minded authors emphasized how the dizzying and seductive life of *le monde* lured women away from their "natural" calling, raising children. The story of Chloé underscores how convent education, undertaken by "women who have renounced the world before knowing it," failed to teach young girls how to survive in society and still retain their virtue.

The mediocrity of this education thus laid the groundwork for a libertine existence.[48] The most famous example of this potential outcome remains Cécile Volanges in Laclos's *Les Liaisons dangereuses*. Although Cécile possesses worldly accomplishments such as singing and playing the harp, she lacks basic drawing-room skills and, more profoundly, the ability to assess people's characters and intentions properly. As a result, the marquise de Merteuil and vicomte de Valmont find a pliant pupil and easily mold her into a libertine. The same naiveté marks the virtuous and older Madame de Tourvel, and both she and Cécile pay dearly for their lack of experience and end their lives unhappily in the convent.[49] Indeed, Laclos suggests that the nature of convent education was such that it made women unfit for both convent life and worldly society, a sentiment echoed in the final pages of *La Religieuse.* By the same token, the self-educated marquise de Merteuil threatens society in her attempt to escape enslavement.[50] In effect, the convent is part of an inescapable vicious circle for elite young women who are trapped in a corrupt society.

This critique of convent education dovetailed into a larger attack on elite society and particularly a denunciation of aristocratic women. Indeed, for many contemporaries, one could argue that the convent was an extension of the "unnatural" female, the aristocratic lady. Convents such as the Abbaye-aux-Bois and the Abbey of Penthémont certainly affirmed such impressions; in her memoirs the princesse de Ligne fondly remembers balls at the Abbaye-aux-Bois during carnival, which young married women often attended to escape their mothers-in-law.[51] As we have seen, lawyers cast superiors such as Madame de Lantilhac and Madame de Sesmaisons as aristocratic harridans, the most "unnatural" of mothers. Miremont explicitly contrasts the politics of the convent with an ideal of the private domestic arena. According to Madame de Miremont, "the internal bickering of the cloister little prepares the spirit for the gentleness and balance of temperament so precious in the general society, even more in the intimacy of the household."[52]

Such views reveal how the criticism aimed at convent education and aristocratic women came out of a specifically gendered vision of society shared by many educators and social theorists during the second half of the eighteenth century. When Le Chatolais and other writers outlined programs for male education, they considered male productivity in terms of the state and not fatherhood. Moreover, if men were to be serious participants in the public arena, then women had to dedicate themselves to the private realm. All women, whether aristocratic socialites or nuns, who turned their back on this domestic life were "unnatural" women. Nuns were the most unnatural because they lacked the emotional and moral sensitivity derived from reproduction. Viewed within the parameters of gendered spheres, reforming female education entailed nothing less than the moral regeneration of the nation as a whole.[53]

The parallels between the censure of convent education and the barbs aimed at aristocratic women point to the larger anxiety that philosophes, physiocrats, and state officials harbored regarding France's demographic and economic future. For social theorists such as Cerfvol, the concerns regarding convents, convent education, and female reproduction were tied directly to a larger concern—depopulation and the health of the nation.[54] Despite the fact that France's population grew by eight million over the course of the eighteenth century, the fear of depopulation, which began in the late years of Louis XIV's reign, continued well into the next century. According to Carol Blum, "the notion that France was losing population, uneasily endemic throughout the latter years of Louis XIV's reign, became one of the eighteenth century's most effective entrees into, and pretexts for, a widespread, sustained critique of the monarchy and its validating body, the Catholic Church."[55] For many social commentators, clerical celibacy was the culprit, and critics challenged its legitimacy and necessity. In the entry *célibat* in the *Encyclopédie*, Diderot demonstrated that the practice of celibacy "was not essential to the Christian religion."[56] One solution was to raise the age when individuals could pronounce vows, a solution that would give people an opportunity to rethink their choice or to resist being forced into the convent. During the late 1740s, a rumor circulated concerning a law that would increase the minimum age for taking vows from sixteen to twenty-two.[57] This proposal was greeted with enthusiasm by the philosophes as well as by relatively neutral observers such as the lawyer Edmond Barbier. According to Barbier, "it was a political coup on account of the diminution of people in the realm by war, and even more, by luxury, which prevents nearly all sensible people from marrying because of the expense of a household."[58] Barbier's comments illustrate just how widespread the anxiety about depopulation was. Even distant onlookers were conversant as to the possible causes of depopulation and the potential solutions. Given these conclusions, the moral high ground long associated with religious vows began to crumble as chastity and claustration were now seen as irrelevant and even dangerous.

Within the discussion of depopulation, social critics regarded nuns as women who were prevented from having children, a point of view that essentially accentuated the bodies of nuns. Jansenist rhetoric embraced women religious as citizens. Lawyers often defended their right to speak their consciences and to initiate litigation. However, Voltaire and other social theorists reconfigured female citizenship in terms of the body and reproduction. In 1750 Voltaire unleashed his animosity toward monastics in his incendiary pamphlet *La Voix du sage et du peuple*. A tirade against the church, the pamphlet roundly denounced monastic institutions as useless. Among the charges Voltaire laid at the door of monastics was the waste of money and the depopulation of the nation. According to Voltaire, celibate nuns would serve the country better by becoming wives and mothers and thereby contributing to the labor force of the country; a ruler could facilitate this situation by increasing the age for pronouncing vows to twenty-five.[59] The results, Voltaire argued, would be promising: "They [French women] will become what women are in Sweden, Denmark, Prussia, England, Holland, they will be citizens. . . . A woman who rears two children . . . provides more service to the Nation [*Patrie*] than all the Convents could ever give."[60] Voltaire's conclusions fused anti-Catholicism, demographic fears, and patriotism to delegitimize the female convent, a view echoed by other social commentators. In 1771 the Chevalier d'Eon de Beaumont remarked that "if the hundred thousands girls in convents or consecrated to celibacy had gotten married, they would have given on the average two children during the course of their lives—that makes two hundred thousand children who should have existed."[61] These standards of social utility based on fertility thus emphasized the worldly concerns nuns had abjured when taking vows.

Even writers who favored convents and women religious used the language of social utility in their arguments. One piece entitled *Moyen de rendre nos religieuses utiles* (1750) attempted to demonstrate the importance of nuns by using Enlightenment criteria. In the treatise a provincial curé asserted that "they [nuns] are not sufficiently useful to us, because they do not have any functions directed for our utility."[62] Using numeric figures in true physiocratic style, this obscure writer attempted to illustrate the ways in which convents could be reorganized so that nuns would be effective educators and consumers and thereby play a role in secular society and economy. Such service ironically debased the spiritual status of nuns even further.

Writings on female education in the decades after the release of the *Moyen de rendre nos religieuses utiles* indicate that such efforts to affirm the utility of women religious had gained little ground. A sensationalist critique of the convent as an educational institution and as a physical space rendered the cloister unacceptable to men and women of letters who believed in a society based on secular values. It was difficult to escape the fact that in the final analysis, the convent was a religious institution promoting religious ideals. In light of this unbreachable gap, a majority of *gens de lettres* answered the question of the convent's social function by proposing its elimination. Theories of sensationalism not only provided the philosophes and other social critics with ammunition for their anticlerical tirades, but they also recalibrated the standards of utility applied to women religious. The scrutiny of nuns was not restricted to the services they provided as instructors but extended to their bodies and what those bodies failed to produce. But as the erotic literature of the period indicates, this figure of the "natural woman" was an unstable ideal precisely because of her body.

The equation of eroticism and education, of sexuality and knowledge, defines the history of sexuality in the early modern era. In his monumental work on the history of sexuality Michel Foucault argues that at beginning of the seventeenth century, Western societies witnessed a "steady proliferation of discourses concerned with sex-specific discourses, different from one another both by their form and by their object: a discursive ferment that gathered momentum from the eighteenth century onward."[63] According to Foucault, this discourse manifested itself in *scientia sexualis*, the realm of "medical, hygienic, pedagogic and psychiatric discourses of sexuality."[64] In other words Foucault located the modern discourse on sexuality within Western pursuits of knowledge and epistemology. Sexual behavior was the subject of intellectual investigation and debate, to be categorized and organized. Foucault claimed, however, that such discourses on sexuality were limited to the realm of "science" and not found in literature and art. Thus, Foucault denied that Western societies produced any literary sexual discourses, any *ars erotica*. In recent years, however, contemporary scholars who have engaged with Foucauldian theory have suggested otherwise in their examination of early modern pornography. As Dorelies Kraakman has rightly pointed out, the early history of pornography was closely linked to the rise of the novel.[65] Both the novel and early pornography took their readers through a journey of expanding knowledge and increased awareness of the self and the larger world.

Early modern erotic literature was also tied to key early modern intellectual and political developments.[66] Historical studies have shown that the heyday of French pornography, between the 1740s and 1790s, not only coincided with the Enlightenment but was part of it. According to Robert Darnton, much of this erotic literature represented an underside of the Enlightenment by combining current philosophical and political trends with uninhibited eroticism. Eighteenth-century booksellers routinely classified erotic writings as *livres philosophiques*, a category that also encompassed the works of Rousseau and other philosophes.[67] This label acted as a subterfuge against censors and reflected the close connection between sexuality and intellectual inquiry found in eighteenth-century pornography. Darnton's inventories also indicate that these erotic works were bestsellers, purchased by individuals whose libraries also contained the more temperate works of Diderot, Voltaire, and other philosophes.[68] Members of literate mainstream society not only read such works but also wrote them. Although some anonymous writers may have come from the Grub Street described by Darnton, others came from more respectable backgrounds. For example, Gervaise de la Touche, generally thought to have written the *Histoire de Dom Bougre, portier des Chartreux* (1741), and Anne Gabriel Meusnier de Querlon, to whom the *Histoire de la tourière des carmélites* (1745) is attributed, were both lawyers.[69] Jean Baptiste de Boyer, the marquis d'Argens, son of a *parlementaire* family, was thought to have written *Thérèse Philosophe* (1748).[70]

This social intersection between the shady underworld of erotic literature and the polite society of the salon and the law courts suggests shared interests, including growing anxieties about power. Indeed, "between

1500 and 1800, pornography was most often a vehicle for using the shock of sex to criticize religious and political authorities."[71] Philosophes, such as Montesquieu and Diderot, were not above using erotic backdrops such as the seraglio to make their arguments against the state and the clergy. Indeed, as we saw in chapter 1, Diderot laced his critique of the convent with sexually charged innuendoes and episodes. Conversely, although writers of libertine literature made erotic activity the main focus of their works, they wove in attacks against the church, the family, and the state. Pornographers often chose the convent as a site for such assaults, in which the nun acted for the reader as she learned about problems of the Old Regime.

This fusion of philosophy and eroticism in the convent characterized what the literary critic Christopher Rivers has identified as the "libertine convent novel," a subcategory or "(sub)genre" belonging to the large body of eighteenth-century erotic/philosophical novels.[72] This (sub)genre contrasted dramatically with an older literary tradition that used the convent as background; such literary works revolved around romances between nuns and cavaliers or monks, alluding to sexual activity in the most tasteful way possible.[73] Although the highly suggestive literature of the Middle Ages was a distant ancestor of the eighteenth-century erotic convent novel, the more immediate point of origin was the Abbé Jean Barrin's *Vénus dans le cloître ou la religieuse en chemise* written in 1680.[74] In his work on the Société Typographique de Neufchâtel, Darnton has identified the enormous popularity of certain convent novels such as *Vénus dans le cloître* as well as the *Histoire de la tourière des carmélites*. Moreover, two of the most important pornographic novels from the period, *Histoire de Dom Bougre* and *Thérèse Philosophe*, also featured the convent at critical points in the plot.[75]

Vénus dans le cloître established a narrative centered on education, which would be the dominant thread in eighteenth-century libertine convent novels. Instead of romantic intrigue, these novels and other works featured nuns, novices, and *pensionnaires* simultaneously engaged in intellectual discussions and frenzied erotic activity.[76] Rivers has noted that these pieces hinged on the fusion between sexuality and knowledge as they reworked the plot of a young girl who benefits from a sexual education and Enlightenment discussions of God and human nature. The following discussion will feature some of these novels, some of which were bestsellers, and other works that fit this pattern. I have decided not to include the works of the Marquis de Sade because they are more representative of the revolutionary and postrevolutionary era. Titles to be discussed include *Vénus dans le cloître* (which reappeared as *Les Délices du cloître ou la none éclairée* in 1761), *Histoire de la tourière des carmélites* (1745), *Le Triomphe des religieuses* (1748), *Les Lettres galantes et philosophiques de deux nones* (1771) and *La Cauchoise* (1784). Although technically not a part of the (sub)genre described by Rivers, the anonymous play *Les Plaisirs du cloître* (1773) also employed a plot very similar to these novels.[77]

Both Darnton and Rivers have noted the prevalence of the convent in these titles, but they have failed to provide an adequate answer as to why the cloister provided such a compelling milieu for eighteenth-century erotic writers. Darnton has labeled the myriad of eighteenth-century nuns as stock figures, "incidental to the main business of providing sexual titillation."[78] By the same token, Rivers has dehistoricized convent novels, claiming they were "not visibly provoked in any obvious way by any one of the many important historical, cultural, political, and religious events [of the early modern period]." Rather, they contained "the most general notions of resistance to political and religious hegemony in the ancien régime."[79] In drawing such lackluster conclusions about why convents and nuns were so ubiquitous in erotic fiction, both Rivers and Darnton appear to have dismissed any possible link between libertine works and the Enlightenment debates over education and gendered spheres.

I would argue that the choice of the convent was not, as these scholars have suggested, incidental to this genre, but was instead a linchpin for the philosophical assertions central to these narratives and an extension of the pedagogical debate described earlier. It was precisely this merging of sexuality and knowledge that made the convent setting the critical link between erotic fiction and the Republic of Letters. Dorelies Kraakman has convincingly argued that libertine works implemented theories of sensationalism within their narrative, using both sensationalism and materialism to attack Cartesian "innate ideas" and dualism.[80] Like pedagogues and social theorists, libertine authors explored the ways in which the physical environment affected an individual's senses. But the "natural" woman in their writings was sexually *and* intellectually liberated. In erotic literature the female body and its capacity for experiencing pleasure was the starting point for female education.

Eighteenth-century pornography challenged the core premise of convent life and education, namely, the separation of the corrupt body and the spiritual soul. This body/soul dualism had defined the fate of women religious since the early history of Christianity.[81] As we saw in chapter 1, the cloister had evolved as a way of containing female sexuality and controlling female devotion. The denigration of the female body not only characterized cloistered life but was a principal element of early modern female convent education.[82] Having, at least in theory, mastered their own carnal nature, women religious went on to discipline the bodies and minds of their young charges, serving as models of virtue and sexual renunciation. In many respects convent education reflected the repressive characteristic of the cloister because "regulating body movement, controlling facial expressions, and composing exterior appearance" were "the essential points of their [girls'] education."[83] Although convents differed in terms of their austerity and the severity of the punishment given to offenders, they all subscribed to the view that women, as descendants of Eve, were prone to temptation.[84] Consequently, nuns enacted Christian dualism literally by controlling the bodies of their pupils while guiding their souls to God. Although they had ceased to use physical mortification by the eighteenth century, nuns carried on a constant surveillance of their pupils. Fears of lesbian activity and masturbation motivated nuns to be especially vigilant during the night as they patrolled the dormitories. Women religious also used prayer and other spiritual exercises to repress their charges' physical urges. As a result, although women religious taught their pupils the basics of reading, writing, and arithmetic, the bulk of their curriculum focused on devotional studies. The emphasis of convent education was not to create *femmes savantes* but to teach young girls to "know, love and serve God."[85] Thus, the suppression of desire was inextricably linked to the inculcation of Christian virtue—the one could not, in convent pedagogy, exist without the other.

Eighteenth-century erotic convent literature undermined the mind/body dualism of Christianity by negating these two key elements of convent education, the repression of sexual desire and the cultivation of piety. Instead, these works featured the acquisition of knowledge through physical experiences, quite literally putting theories of Lockean sensationalism into practice. The overall plot of this literature began with a young novice or *pensionnaire* whose sexual desire has been awakened through self-exploration, voyeurism, or the reading of famous erotic works such as the *Histoire de Dom Bougre* or *Thérèse Philosophe*.[86] At this stage, a female mentor, usually an older nun or a mother superior, assumes responsibility for the young woman's education. The instructor further arouses the pupil's desire by engaging her in lesbian activities, often stimulated through descriptions of heterosexual intercourse. Heady discussions of nature, philosophy, and Christianity accompany these exertions, initiating the young pupil into the realm of the "philosophical" as well as the sexual. The narrative generally concludes with the emergence of a young woman conversant in sexual and intellectual knowledge and equipped with a lover who shares this newfound wisdom. This plot—in which superiors become seducers and the body acts as a guide—undermined the dignity of the convent's instructors and countered the spiritual goals of convent education.

The erotic literature of the eighteenth century satirized traditional convent education by transforming the convent from an institution dedicated to chastity and self-sacrifice into a "school of *libertinage*."[87] In *La Cauchoise* the convent becomes a veritable laboratory in which experimentation feeds desire. The narrator of the piece, a whore, praises the wide variety of lessons she received at the hands of her mentor, Soeur Prudence. She declares: "I was a simple fucker when I entered this holy house, but I had, when leaving it, all the talents of a true whore."[88] Not only does the convent conceal activities worthy of the most eroticized space, it no longer functions as a school of virtue and purity. Instead, the cloister serves as a milieu tailored for instructing women how to experience maximum pleasures.[89] According to Soeur Gabrielle, the biological mother of Saturnin, the hero of the *Histoire de Dom Bougre*, "the convent for us [nuns] is a seraglio which becomes populated every day by new inmates whose numbers multiply only to multiply our pleasures."[90] Soeur Gabrielle thus appropriates the language of demography in the service of pleasure, seeking to expand the population of libertine monastics at the expense to society.

Women religious who had acted as moral disciplinarians now become sexual tutors, models of desire as opposed to models of chaste virtue. Authority figures in libertine works, like Soeur Gabrielle, expose and fan the urges of their young pupils, bringing desire and knowledge together in order to satisfy their own appetites. In the epistolary *Lettres galantes et philosophiques* Soeur Christine describes how the mother superior "had a little bed constructed for me next to her bed, telling me that she was taking me under her protection, that under her, I would learn the principal elements of Christianity." Taking advantage of the young woman's naiveté and her own authority, the mother superior introduces the susceptible Soeur Christine to lesbian activities by asking the young girl to alleviate her sufferings caused by an imaginary illness, "clitoral vapors." Similarly, in Diderot's *La Religieuse* the mother superior of Sainte-Eutrope requests Suzanne Simonin's "assistance" in relieving her of physical discomfort.[91] But where Suzanne chooses to ignore the sexual knowledge offered by her mentor, the characters in eighteenth-century pornography were far more receptive. In the *Lettres galantes et philosophiques* Soeur Christine reveals her complete awareness of the motive behind the mother superior's antics as she caustically notes "to what excess these female monsters carry devotion."[92]

Libertine mentors move from simple seduction to sexual instruction by using the body as an instructional "text," thereby replacing traditional catechism within an expansive erotic catechism. The body thus takes the place of the traditional canon and, in Lockean fashion, becomes the source of knowledge. Now, the pupil learns the "language" of the body in place of prayer and holy books. Soeur Agathe in *Les Plaisirs du cloître* teaches the young Marton about intercourse through a vivid description that identifies all the parts of the body contributing to sexual gratification.[93] For the young Soeur Julie in *Le Triomphe des religieuses*, her affair with the monk Frère Côme becomes a lesson in contemporary theories of anatomy and reproduction. Soeur Julie learns "that out of a man comes a certain viscous and subtle liquor which, by the spirits it exhales, forms an infant when it is received in the womb of the mother."[94] Like Soeur Gabrielle, Frère Côme ridicules the vows of chastity and virginity. Furthermore, he affirms contemporary anxieties about the threat monasticism poses to reproduction by making sure not to impregnate Soeur Julie.

What follows after this basic introduction to the body is a rapid and in-depth buildup of diverse sexual skills.[95] Moreover, since men are a scarce commodity, necessity becomes the mother of invention in convent libertine fiction. Every convent has its store of dildos, and female mentors do not fail to acquaint their young pupils with a variety of artificial phalluses

Eighteenth-century erotic fiction often featured nuns carrying dildos. Engraving from *Histoire de Dom Bougre, Portier des Chartreux*, 1741. Cliché Bibliothèque Nationale de France, Paris.

and the multiple ways in which to use them.[96] For example, the mentor in *La Cauchoise,* Soeur Prudence, commissions a metalworker to construct a dildo that may be used from both sides, thus allowing her partner and her "to have the same pleasure as if we were man and woman." According to the narrator, Prudence then "covers the object with crimson velvet, attaching at the middle as much hair as she can. One sees, from this attention, with what care Soeur Prudence studied and followed nature."[97] In defiance of the vows of celibacy, the "natural" woman depicted in libertine convent literature was one whose senses were constantly being stimulated, if not overstimulated, through sexual activity. "Nature" then implied sexual freedom and, most certainly, heterosexuality.

Part of this libertine "curriculum" involved lesbian activity, which served as an active tool of learning. According to Christopher Rivers, in the libertine convent novel, "homosexual desire, as a consequence of the repression of that natural desire, is clearly represented as a twisted if pleasant perversion, one that might well be rendered unnecessary—and thus obliterated—by the elimination of the vow of celibacy."[98] And indeed, with the exception of the narrator of *La Cauchoise,* who declares that two women can enjoy one another completely, lesbian encounters usually are accompanied with discussions of heterosexual encounters or the phallus itself. In the *Histoire de Dom Bougre* Suzon describes how Soeur Monique's account of her adventures with the servant Martin arouses them both: "The memory of Martin animated her [Monique], her words had produced the same effect on me . . . deluded by my caresses, she forgot that I was only a woman."[99] Over the course of the following days, Suzon relates, she and Monique work together to recapture the pleasure Monique enjoyed with Martin, "making me even more knowledgeable during the second encounter."[100] This comprehensive acquisition of sexual and philosophical knowledge suggests a critique of the shallow skills convent education provided. Instead of memorization, which many pedagogues regarded as yet another flaw of convent education, the curriculum in erotic literature includes hands-on experience. Thus, Suzon extracts the most she can from this learning opportunity, enough to transform her into a sexual powerhouse.

Such successful accumulation of sexual knowledge depends in large part on the female protagonist's active curiosity and her ability to reflect on her experiences, in effect to build on her skills. In her discussion of girls and sexual knowledge in erotic novels, Dorelies Kraakman has noted that the libertine education involves actively "collecting as many different experiences as possible and acquiring understanding through reflexive activities by means of discourse."[101] The dialogic styles of the epistolary *Lettres galantes et philosophiques* and *Le Triomphe des religieuses* advocate autodidactic learning through verbal and written exchange. Whereas the traditional convent pupil acquired her lessons "superficially and by rote," the student within the libertine text actively engages in her "studies," evaluating them as she progresses.[102] In other words, the pupil is no longer a passive receptacle of knowledge, and the monastic mentor is only a passing participant in the process through which a young girl achieves sexual awareness and expertise. Thus, lesbian encounters are only one experience among others including voyeurism and imitation. For example, Sainte Nitouche in the *Histoire de la tourière des carmélites* spies on her mother having intercourse and then attempts to imitate her.[103] And in the *Lettres galantes et philosophiques* Soeur Christine, having witnessed the mother superior's activities with the gardener Etienne, immediately imagines herself in the older woman's place. She works out that she and the young man "were both nearly the same age, and my scabbard consequently . . . should be in proportion to his sword."[104] This self-conscious cognitive activity thus reflected the ways in which the erotic convent literature reconstituted the cloister as a space of intellectual as well as sexual freedom.

Erotic literature featured women as the recipients of both sexual and intellectual knowledge. Moreover, the choice of a female student fitted into larger patterns found in Enlightenment works. The female pupil presented a genuine tabula rasa, more easily shaped because she was a woman. Both Bernard le Bovier de Fontenelle's *Conversations on the Plurality of Worlds* and Diderot's *D'Alembert's Dream* positioned female characters as the recipient of knowledge imparted by a male, adding a gendered dimension to the hierarchical relationship between mentor and student. The female student, such as the narrator of *La Cauchoise*, Marton in *Les Plaisirs du cloître*, or Soeur Agathe in *Lettres galantes et philosophiques*, played a role much like the marquise in *Conversations on the Plurality of Worlds*. According to Nina Gelbart, the marquise has "a mind ready to be filled, yet quickly developing the capacity to question and criticize, to evaluate and challenge in its own right. Hers is a mind unspoiled by false teaching, and thus all the more promising for proper cultivation."[105] The marquise and her counterparts in libertine fiction then represented the ideal readers of the Republic of Letters, unformed but intelligent, curious, and therefore open to new ideas.

Like many of the political texts of the Republic of Letters, erotic literature offered a scathing critique of the triad of power: the king, the family, and most resoundingly, the church. Eroticizing the convent put established authority on trial. In the *Histoire de Dom Bougre* Soeur Monique interrupts her story to enlighten the innocent Suzon about the relationship between the male and female organs. According to the more "learned" Monique, "a penis . . . is the member of a man. One calls it the member *par excellence* because it is the king of all others . . . the cunt is its domain."[106] Monique's buoyant vocabulary lesson destabilizes the notion of the body politic, the prevalent metaphor for political and social power. The equation of the king with the phallus was not too farfetched because the safety of the realm depended on the king's virility.[107] However, Monique's statement had more subversive implications. Written in 1748, Monique's words were probably a stab at the reported excesses of Louis XV. The "king" was ruled not by reason but by his desires which he cherished above all else.

Libertine authors extended this political critique of the monarchy to the family. Both *Vénus dans le cloître* and *Le Triomphe des religieuses* took on the vocation forcée and described how the victims of greedy parents had to endure the unnatural state of chastity. According to Soeur Angélique in *Vénus dans le cloître*, "politics" has conspired with the family and "invented vows with which to tie us and attach us eternally to the state we have been made to embrace. It [politics] has even made us renounce the rights nature gave us."[108] Soeur Angélique in effect interprets the cloister as a co-conspirator in the "family-state compact" of early modern France.[109] She notes that by supporting monastic celibacy, family-state politics destroys what nature gives the individual, a viewpoint echoing the opinions of lawyers and other mainstream writers.

Nonetheless, libertine authors also derided the mainstream criticism of the convent by interpreting freedom in terms of physical needs, which, ironically, the convent fulfilled. Although they may have criticized the greed of female convents, lawyers involved in vocation forcée cases questioned neither the moral value of the institution nor its demands for corporeal purity. However, for the characters in erotic convent literature, their forced vows justified and excused their libertine behavior, behavior that was more natural than the vows of monastic celibacy. Libertine convent literature thus exposed celibacy as a false virtue. Indeed, the female protagonist of *Thérèse Philosophe* finds herself physically ill after twelve years as a convent boarder, her body as a "machine that was listless, my complexion jaundiced, my lips inflamed. I resembled a living skeleton."[110] But *Thérèse Philosophe* remains the exception. Libertine works portray the convent as an acceptable and even desirable space because an individual could find the means through which to lessen "the rigors of . . . slavery."[111] According to Soeur Gabrielle in the *Histoire de Dom Bougre*: "Here [in the convent] . . . free from life's worries, we know only its charms, we take from love only its pleasures."[112] Soeur Gabrielle's remarks are subversive in several ways. She and her cohorts co-opt a sacred space and fill it with behaviors and attitudes that are directly opposed to the values of the church, the state, and the family. The convent's purpose is no longer to restrain female disorder but, in fact, to release it in the form of sexual activity. By valorizing enclosure and the convent's marginality, Gabrielle also

Erotic convent novels used erotic imagery to denounce monasticism as sadistic and hypo-
critical. Engraving from *Vénus dans la cloître ou la religieuse en chemise,* 1746. Cliché Bibliothèque Nationale de France, Paris.

suggests that true individual freedom can only be realized outside of
French society.

Through their portrayal of the convent as a sexual haven, libertine authors consistently and relentlessly attacked the church. And since the values of the Old Regime were explicitly Christian, the assault on the church
encompassed all aspects of the state and society. In keeping with the more
radical elements of the Republic of Letters, eighteenth-century convent
erotica contained pages and pages of anticlerical and antireligious

polemics.[113] Libertine works took aim at the church's hypocrisy by exposing the falseness of many of its leaders. In the *Lettres galantes et philosophiques* the libertine abbé de L—— informs the Carmelite Agathe that "often a superior does not fail to tell her young penitents to guard their virginity, while she does not blush to soil herself through lascivious acts."[114] Other works deride the religious controversies of the eighteenth century. Sainte Nitouche in the *Histoire de la tourière des carmélites* becomes involved with Jansenist convulsionaries and discovers that the movement serves as a "veil over libertinism."[115] Similarly, the Jesuits were also the targets of mockery and criticism. In *Les Plaisirs du cloître* Soeur Agathe's lover, the Jesuit, engages in sodomy, an "antiphysical taste . . . attached to the Jesuit habit."[116] The trivialization of religious strife represents an outright attack against Christianity itself.

Indeed, young initiates of libertine convent literature come to learn that sexual objects and activities, and not traditional devotional exercises, are sacred. For instance, Soeur Monique deifies the phallus, declaring that if women "would give it [the penis] the justice it deserved, it would be called god." Nuns also appeal either to the pagan god Priapus, the deity of lust and obscenity, or to Aphrodite, the goddess of love.[117] Such references indicate that the Christian god is displaced by deities more closely tied to sexual desire.

Erotic convent fiction expounded on Enlightenment ideas concerning religious relativism, human nature, and deism, all of which challenged the very basis of Christianity. Libertine authors, rejecting the notion that Christianity was a divinely revealed religion, argued instead that it was a man-made and deeply flawed creation. Perhaps the most fully realized example of such thinking was the *Lettres galantes et philosophiques,* one of the later libertine convent novels. In his instructions to the Carmelite Agathe, the Abbé de L—— identifies the contradictions inherent in the Christian depiction of God: "Sometimes one paints Him armed with his vengeful divine anger before the entire universe . . . sometimes one represents him . . . always animated by the desire to help us, loving and cherishing his poor children." According to the cynical abbé, such contradictions result from "the ineptitude and stupidity of man." Moreover, these conflicting and self-contradictory images are not restricted to Christianity but are found in the religion of Native Americans, Muslims, Mexicans, and Romans. Having consigned organized religions to the realm of mere opinion, the abbé offers Agathe a deistic alternative. He advises his pupil that it would be wiser to take the example of "an Arouet de Voltaire, a Jean-Jacques Rousseau . . . [who] no longer believe in Islam than in Catholicism . . . [since] religion, according to their system, is only a philosophical opinion." Religious dogma is not absolute but open for debate. The abbé then counsels Agathe to follow "in our hearts, little by little, nature, let us . . . love our neighbors as ourselves, *voilà la religion primitive.*"[118] Christ's commandment is thus taken outside of Christianity and is sexualized and secularized by being placed in the context of nature and history.

The *Lettres galantes et philosophiques* also questions the Christian definition of nature by contesting the notion of original sin. In one letter Soeur Christine, an Ursuline, reveals that she is the child of an abbess and archbishop. Instead of seeing herself as the product of multiple sins, she declares "I am [a follower] of Locke's system and I maintain, like this philosopher, that all are good."[119] She thus rejects the notion of a person inheriting depravity from her parents. Through this assertion of innate goodness, Soeur Christine renders the principal function of convent pedagogy—to direct the corrupt individual away from sin and toward God—unnecessary. Without the Christian notion of sin and its contempt for the body, Christian definitions of morality ring hollow.

By privileging the body over the soul, erotic convent literature suggested a moral alternative to Christian precepts.[120] Margaret Jacob has argued that materialism, which "removed the dominance of spirit and made matter and spirit essentially one," was an important component of eighteenth-century pornographic fiction.[121] According to Jacob, materialism provided a metaphysics that explained "the ceaseless desire, the random excess, the sheer exuberance of bodies released from traditional moorings and pious inhibitions."[122] It was a metaphysics tied no longer to God but to disembodied motion and desire. Again, the *Lettres galantes et philosophiques* provides an example of the "metaphysical materialism" described by Jacob. Soeur Christine declares that "all of the cloister's morality truthfully consists in the metaphysics of love."[123] Within traditional Christian metaphysics, the origin and structure of the universe are a part of God's mystery, and human beings must mold themselves to God's plans. In the *Lettres galantes et philosophiques*, however, morality and the purpose of human existence are no longer explained as God's will but are the result of physical desire. Libertine convent writing thus used sensationalism and materialism to render bankrupt the epistemological and ontological foundations of convent education. Salvation and sin, the driving forces of convent pedagogy, were replaced by a celebration of desire and immediate gratification.

Like many of the Enlightenment pedagogical treatises, the libertine treatments of convent education embraced sensationalist ideas and provided a systemic analysis that led to the rejection of convent pedagogy and to the displacement of nuns by a universal image of physically defined woman. Although libertine literature was a fictional fantasy and pedagogical treatises were steeped in an earnest desire for reform, both genres applied the same tenets to nuns as they did to all other women. The nun no longer possessed a sacred status sustained by her virginity. Instead, she, like other women, was a creature defined by her biological potential to procreate and to experience pleasure. The more mainstream pedagogical theorists sought to outline a curriculum whose final product would be the "natural" woman fully endowed with feminine sensibility.[124] Libertine writers also promoted physical qualities in their rendition of the "natural" woman. However, they were either uninterested or derisive of the virtues promoted by pedagogues and social commentators, and sought instead to construct a "pedagogical" style that would produce a woman who was completely attuned to her physical senses and desires. There was no effort to place limits on female disorderliness or to promote female virtue.

These differences between the two critiques of convent education were further amplified in their portrayals of the pupil. Although mainstream pedagogical theorists such as Madame de Miremont or Cerfvol may have considered the convent's emphasis on spiritual devotion excessive, they, like women religious, expected young girls to be submissive, an essential quality for being either a good wife or a good nun. And both social theorists and nuns aimed at cultivating modest, passive girls who would accept their subordination to men and not aspire to an existence outside the home. Those who upheld Christian virtues and those who spoke in favor of secular virtue both believed in a young woman who was, in the final analysis, the responsibility of a male authority figure. Although the husband figured in few pedagogical works, he was, nonetheless, an important presence, the other half of the domestic arena. Thus, the question of who would control nuns had shifted dramatically. In an ideal world, women religious would leave the convent and marry, thereby placing themselves under the authority of husbands.

In contrast, libertine works portrayed the brides of Christ as rejecting their intended Spouse and substituting, in His place, mates of their own choosing. Compared to her mainstream counterpart, the convent student in erotic fiction was an active creature, a sexual machine, and a veritable *savante*.[125] Either she left the convent versed in Enlightenment philosophy as well as sexually adept, or she carved out her own erotic and intellectual space within the cloister, ready to seduce the next ingénue.[126] At the same time, the female protagonist's independence cannot be understood to represent female autonomy. After all, libertine plays and novels were written by men for male audiences. Libertine authors provided these male readers with arousing images of an active partner whose quest for her own enjoyment resulted in the pleasure of others.[127]

But the male-centered nature of the eighteenth-century literary market should not obscure the ways in which the female *savante* of eighteenth-century pornography problematized the passive figure found in other pedagogical works. The sexually active *savante* was intellectually dynamic, commenting and often initiating discussion on contemporary highbrow topics. This fictional figure reminds us that no matter how prescriptive the works of Rousseau and his followers were, they could not easily exclude women from intellectual activity. The debate on education reveals this tension. As Mary Trouille has shown, women such as Madame d'Epinay voiced their opposition to the domestic vision of Rousseau. Even Madame Roland, who deliberately fashioned her life to fit Rousseauean principles, paradoxically subverted her own efforts through her intellectual pursuits and her political activities during the French Revolution.[128] The actions of these women and the representations of female pupils in erotic convent fiction *by men* would suggest that the eighteenth-century vision of domestic femininity was unstable.

The competing visions of the "natural" female and their use by various authors to critique convent education point to the absence of a crucial voice, the voice of eighteenth-century women religious. In the previous chapters we have seen women religious speaking out in varying degrees, whether out of conscience or a need to claim and protect certain rights. These efforts were often muted or manipulated by lawyers and other male supporters who represented nuns before the public. Nevertheless, nuns remained a presence that needed to be taken into account when magistrates, the monarchy, or the clergy had to make decisions and pass judgments. Whatever political or social agenda lawyers and magistrates may have brought to the table, the practicalities of handling the affairs of a religious community, such as electing a new superior or admitting a novice, necessitated the inclusion of nuns in the process. But in the case of convent education, which was theoretical and abstract, nuns did not have any public voice, nor were they invited to speak in their self-defense. Pedagogues, social theorists, and libertine writers had a free hand in mapping out an educational strategy that incorporated anticlerical sentiments and theories of feminine nature. Very rarely did writers consider the sincerity of religious vows or the fate of women religious outside of the cloister. Significantly, pedagogical works on convent education as well as the vocation forcée. literature became far more dominant than the trial briefs or Jansenist declarations. This skewed legacy would affect the relationship between proponents of the French Revolution and women religious.

6

FROM VICTIMS TO FANATICS

Nuns in the French Revolution, 1789–1794

IN 1796 THE PERIODICAL *L'ESPRIT DES JOURNAUX FRANÇAIS ET étrangers* offered the following description of the recently published *La Religieuse* by Denis Diderot: "This singular and endearing work will remain a monument to what convents formerly were, scourges born of ignorance and of delirious fanaticism, against which the philosophes had spoken out for so long and in vain, and from which the French Revolution will deliver Europe in a few years."[1] By bringing about the destruction of the cloister, the Revolution had rescued potential victims, innocent young girls "who will bless this philosophy to which they owe not having to fear a similar destiny [to Suzanne's]."[2] This review of *La Religieuse* amounted to nothing less than an obituary for the convent, an institution many contemporaries regarded as the embodiment of Catholicism's evil, an inherently corrupt remnant of the Old Regime. At the same time, the review underscored the triumph of the Enlightenment and the virtues of a revolutionary order that had rescued the institutions' inhabitants from Suzanne's miserable and tragic fate.

The reviewer's marked antipathy toward the convent implies that its demise was inevitable once the French Revolution began. The first five years of the French Revolution profoundly altered the relationship between church and state, severing the symbiotic relationship that had defined the social and political order of the Old Regime. Decades of "richerist egali-

tarianism (rights of priests vis-à-vis bishops), Jansenist *étatisme* (or Eras-
tianism), philosophe anticlericalism, rationalism and utilitarianism . . .
and resentment over the moral failures of clerics" shaped official state policy from the very beginning of the Revolution.[3] By the fall of 1789, the National Assembly had already taken a number of steps to limit the church's
power: church privileges were eliminated, church property was confiscated and sold, and monasticism was abolished. The Assembly completed
the process of making the church subservient to the state in July 1790
when it passed the Civil Constitution of the Clergy and fully nationalized
the church. Clerics were now paid servants of the state.

For France's fifty-five thousand nuns, the ramifications of these changes
were less clear, even though contemporaries appeared to be so dismissive
of the convent. When compared to their male counterparts, female convents enjoyed sympathetic relations with revolutionary officials.[4] Female
convents were exempted from article 3 of the February 13, 1790, decree
suppressing orders that required solemn vows.[5] Women religious received
this considerate treatment for a number of reasons. First, many communities provided some educational services while others worked in *hôtels-
dieu* as nurses. Second, there was the pressing question of what would hap-
pen to the large numbers of unmarried women whose families would not
necessarily receive them with open arms.[6] How would communities ab-
sorb the sudden appearance of five, fifteen, or even fifty women between
the ages of eighteen and eighty who did not have a secure social position
since they were without fathers or husbands? Third, nuns received prefer-
ential treatment because of what Olwen Hufton has identified as part of
the "intellectual baggage of the Assembly": the "model, mythical nun." According to Hufton, this nun was "young, beautiful, and distressed," the victim of her family who had prevented her from fulfilling her "natural destiny of wife and mother." She was essentially a passive figure, waiting "in
search of a man to solve her predicament."[7] Moreover, whereas monks
were held in universal contempt, nuns received compassion and respect
from many of their contemporaries, suggesting a gendered anticlericalism. Revolutionaries regarded nuns first and foremost as women, and they
were therefore unready or unable to rebuff them as parasitic clerics.

Nevertheless, nuns were not allowed to continue on with their lives
without any interference or scrutiny. A decree of March 20, 1790, ordered
all nuns to submit to an interrogation so that officials could verify their intentions of either remaining in or leaving their convents. On April 20,
1790, the Assembly expanded the sale of church property to include mov-
able goods; officials went to convents and inventoried their possessions,
such as linen and religious silver. Despite minor tensions triggered by
these decrees, nuns retained their positions and the respect of officials as
well as journalists and pamphleteers. Battle lines between nuns and offi-

cials would be drawn after April 1791 when revolutionaries could no longer ignore that an increasing number of nuns were collaborating with refractory priests. Such actions threatened to undermine the authority of constitutional priests funded by the revolutionary government.[8] Over the next two years, revolutionary radicals came to regard women religious as enemies of the nation, embodying the despotism long associated with the church, aristocrats, and the monarchy.

Between 1789 and April 1791 officials and polemicists fell back on the seemingly polar notions of the convent they had inherited from the Old Regime. Revolutionaries availed themselves of contradictory images of women religious as "victims" and "despots." Their rhetoric and actions cast the convent as a despotic site. Nuns, however, they saw as victims. In this period of open debate and dialogue, revolutionaries held on to gendered anticlerical notions that exempted nuns from responsibility and culpability, a position facilitated by the willingness of nuns to adjust to the revolutionary climate. The second part of this chapter demonstrates that explosive conflicts between nuns and revolutionaries took place more frequently between 1791 and 1794. As the Revolution began to place greater demands on patriotic citizens, women religious found themselves unwilling to compromise their consciences and engaged in antirevolutionary activities. For supporters of the Revolution, the nun was no longer a victim but a fanatic who could potentially undermine their achievements.

At the onset of the French Revolution, the treatment of nuns was the subject of debates that took place on the floor of the National Assembly and in the rapidly expanding world of public opinion. Old and new voices, male and female, humble and well established, expressed their views, many hoping to instigate change. Within the new government, men who had once been involved in provincial government became a part of national politics.[9] Jean-Baptiste Treilhard, who had once been a provincial intendant, now became the principal spokesman for the Comité Ecclésiastique.[10] *Gens de lettre*, such as Jean-Paul Marat, having failed in their aspirations to be philosophes during the Old Regime, now became celebrities.[11] Authors, ranging from pedagogues such as Madame de Genlis to obscure clergymen, also weighed in on the important issues of the day. These writers were not mere spectators but active participants in the various discussions concerning nuns, availing themselves of the pamphlet machinery that was part and parcel of the Revolution. Between 1789 and 1790, the Assembly deliberated on the Comité Ecclésiastique's policies regarding monastics, discussions which were then broadcast in pamphlets and periodicals.[12] Readers could easily turn to the *Moniteur,* which faithfully recorded the proceedings of the Assembly. Or they could peruse copies of its legislation, consider individual views such as the *Opinion de M. Treilhard sur le rapport du Comité Ecclésiastique* (1790), and learn of the committee's plans as recorded in the *Projet de réglemens pour le clergé et les religieux* (1789).

In addition to pamphlets and periodicals, the theater quickly became a popular vehicle through which literate citizens as well as aspiring playwrights participated in politics.[13] After the Comédie-Française lost its monopoly on theatrical productions on January 13, 1790, theaters sprung up, thus opening the world of the stage to a wider audience. Unlike novels, plays could reach a semi-literate audience, and one-act dramas could be composed quickly and tailored to fit the pressing issues of the day. New playwrights, such as the uneducated feminist Olympe de Gouges, broadcast their views of the Revolution and the Old Regime. Hitherto, playwrights had been forced to adopt a more circumspect strategy in their attack on monastic vows, often setting their stories in ancient Rome or Gaul. But by the end of 1790, theaters and playwrights confidently violated the Gallican church's ban on using clerical costumes on stage.[14] Plays such as *Le Mari directeur* and *Les Victimes cloîtrées* allowed audiences to see "nuns" in their "prisons" and to cheer when the Revolution saved them.[15]

In the next section of this chapter I offer a thematic overview of discussions about nuns, using a sample of pamphlets, periodicals, plays, and Assembly debates. A majority of writers attacked the convent and repeated themes concerning authority and power that had permeated prerevolutionary discussions of female religious. In highlighting the common themes that linked these different sources, I am following the lead of Antoine de Baecque and his study of revolutionary pamphlets. De Baecque has noted that "this universe created by the writing of pamphlets is like what could be called a 'world of representation' . . . the narrative, overflowing with portraits, details, atmospheres, unfolds on a conventional political canvas: conspiracy, corruption of power, revolt, purification of public morality, France regenerated."[16] Each pamphlet responded to other texts, pamphlets, plays, and printed debates, both in the public forum and within the private realm of letters. Despite their tendency toward hyperbole and outlandish fiction, pamphlets, de Baecque argues, remain important example of "political self-representation." Thus, pamphlets and periodicals, much like the debates and policies sponsored by the National Assembly, symbolized political action.[17] Opponents of convents and women religious alike engaged in "political self-representation," responding to the diffuse debate that was waged over monastic institutions.[18]

Following the same path as lawyers and men of letters from the Old Regime, revolutionary polemicists, playwrights, and others denounced claustral despotism, a despotism that was embodied by the mother superior and embedded within the very structure of the convent. Significantly, the story of the vocation forcée continued to hold sway and was at the heart of the images and stories concerning nuns. Within the cloister, nuns were victims, and they were often at the mercy of tyrannical abbesses who embodied the worst elements of aristocratic and feminine power. Both nuns and superiors were caught in the prisonlike cloister where passion and power were unchecked. Having condemned the convent, pamphleteers and journalists considered how to integrate nuns into the nation through social service or marriage. But no matter where this eclectic group of writers stood on the question of the female cloister, they often arrived at the same conclusion: revolutionary deputies were "benefactors" and "liberators." The question of who should control the nun had a new answer, the very masculine image of the revolutionary official.

As had been the case in the prerevolutionary era, nuns were women first, religious figures second. Deputies of the National Assembly, journalists, and playwrights claimed to respect the sincerity of true religious vocations. But their characterization of women religious indicates that such statements only paid lip service to the spiritual dimension of claustration. Deputies and polemicists were sympathetic to the plight of nuns, but their sympathy was directed toward the nuns' sex, not their vocation. In his December 17, 1789, report to the National Assembly, Jean-Baptiste Treilhard noted that, for the moment, he was not going to discuss nuns because the habits and occupations of their sex demanded separate deliberation. The former intendant reminded his audience that "the weakness of their sex makes them even more interesting. They [nuns] are worthy, in effect, of all your protection; and your hearts . . . will not be cold and insensible."[20] Treilhard's melodramatic appeal couched this feminine weakness in physical or "natural" terms, which reflected a pervasive skepticism about the sincerity of female religious vows. In the process, Treilhard downplayed any kind of volition, any kind of personal agency that might lead women to enter the convent.

Working under these gendered assumptions, officials and polemicists alike all regarded nuns as passive victims, vulnerable to malevolent, antirevolutionary influences.[21] In a letter to the National Assembly, deputies from the Department of Bouches-du-Rhône offered excuses for why nuns failed to leave their convents immediately. They argued that fear of their fate outside the cloister reduced nuns to silence. The deputies blamed the "odious agents of clerical despotism"—namely, priests and monks—who "are still the weapons of fanaticism which serve themselves by inspiring in these spirits [nuns], who are often so feeble and credulous."[22] Similarly, pamphleteers and playwrights fixated on traditional "despotic" figures such as confessors and spiritual directors who ruled over nuns.[23] The

anonymous Jansenist author of the *Adresse aux religieuses* invoked prerevolutionary religious quarrels by railing against the Jesuits who had symbolized despotism and political disorder for many. Within such works,
women religious were victims of despotism who, lacking a will of their
own, could not be held accountable for what they said and did.

Many authors attributed such weakness to female physiology. Jean-
Nicolas Billaud Varenne repeated contemporary views of the feminine
physique when he argued that a nun was easily overwhelmed and agitated
because of "the physical constitution of her sex, her heart so easily en-
flamed, her weakness for the marvelous."[24] Such descriptions reinforced
the erasure of female volition by emphasizing physical and emotional
frailty as an inherently feminine trait. Given their sense of the cruel severity of monastic life, such authors were convinced that claustration had
driven most nuns to despair, or even insanity.

But not all nuns were victims. Some held power, which enabled them
to control the fate of the many innocent nuns. The majority of writers focused specifically on the abbess, a noblewoman whose lifelong power
came from the king. The abbess was a potent figure because she was a
nexus in which the anxieties concerning clerical power intersected with
the growing hostility toward aristocratic despotism and female authority.
She embodied both the corrupt aristocrat and the grasping cleric. As we
have seen in earlier chapters, the aristocrat represented all the ills of the
Old Regime, abuse of power, decadence, and national degeneration. And
during the Revolution this image became doubly charged, synonymous
with conspiracy and counterrevolution.[25] An entity unto herself, this arrogant aristocratic woman established her own kingdom within the cloister,
a realm designed for her personal gratification. Even Madame de Genlis,
hardly an avid revolutionary, made a clear distinction between abbesses
and elected mother superiors. In the *Discours sur la suppression des couvens
de religieuses* Genlis described the abbess as "a kind of Queen [who] . . .
lives with ostentation . . . governing her sisters and her equals despotically." Indeed, Genlis went so far as to draw parallels between an abbey,
with its "flattery, vanity, jealousy, envy," and a royal court.[26] Given the proliferation of pornographic material on the life of Marie-Antoinette, Genlis's association of abbesses with queens and courts undoubtedly served to
invalidate abbatial authority and cast abbesses as a threat to the Revolution.[27] Léonard-Nicolas François Duquesnoy, a deputy from the Mozelle,
went further and complained that even superiors of chapter houses became "Sovereign Princes" ruling over others.[28]

As Pierre Rétat has noted, social distinctions, such as those separating
abbesses from other nuns, became a hallmark for characterizing the
"good" and "bad" citizen during the Revolution. Good citizenship denoted activism and outspoken support for freedom, while bad citizenship

signaled self-interested aristocracy. According to Rétat, "Marat, in the *Ami du peuple,* often contrasted the 'true citizens' (or 'honest' or 'good'), who were still referred to as 'good patriots,' with an 'aristocratic faction' of uncertain proportions but definitely sinister intentions."[29] Not surprisingly then, Marat also targeted abbesses, depicting them as anti-citizens, who threatened the Revolution. In the provocative *L'Ami du peuple* Marat described the plight of a desperate Sister Catherine who came to him after escaping the clutches of the abbess of Penthémont, an abbey famous for boarding the daughters of the high nobility. According to Marat, the abbess and her cabal were persecuting the nun because she favored the Revolution. Marat indignantly declared: "It is clear that Sister Catherine, given over to the mercy of these aristocratic beguines, has become (because of her patriotic sympathies), the object of their petty vengeance disguised under the veil of hypocrisy."[30] The clear distinction Marat drew between Sister Catherine and her abbess underscored his belief that it was possible to be a nun and a patriot at the same time. For Marat, Sister Catherine was a simple woman, just another victim of despotism. On the other hand, the abbess encapsulated the various anxieties of the Revolution: female power, aristocratic high-handedness, and political subversion. Moreover, Marat contrasted the unpatriotic abbess with the market women of Les Halles. He promised his readers that he would report the misdemeanors of Catherine's aristocratic persecutors to a "tribunal" of the women of Les Halles. According to Olwen Hufton, "such an approach . . . reflects the traditional beliefs that much of women's behaviour should be regulated either the husband or by the women of the community."[31] In this context, Marat endowed the market women with a judge's authority to decide who was a patriot and who was a despot.

If some authors, like Marat and Genlis, credited claustral despotism to a single individual or even a single class, other polemicists interpreted despotism to be the result of the convent's structure. Drawing from the rich political arsenal built up during the last decades of the Old Regime, these writers depicted the convent as the source of political corruption or despotism. They understood the convent to be an inherently despotic institution because of its hierarchical structure, which allowed whim to take precedence over rules and required an unfailing "obedience without limits."[32] According to Jacques-Antoine Creuzé Latouche, "monastic institutions in and of themselves favor despotism, servitude, and aristocracy."[33] Duquesnoy also denounced the hierarchical nature of convents as artificial and antithetical to the new revolutionary society, claiming that "it is necessary that in France, as in nature, there be no classes . . . the existence of chapter houses is incompatible with these principles."[34] "Classes" in this case should be construed not as modern-day classes but as corporate structures. In effect, the convent was represented as a classic Old Regime corporate entity, conferring upon certain individuals an identity and prerogatives which set them apart. Just as the abolition of the *compagnonnages,* or artisanal brotherhoods, in 1791 was designed to end the corporate privileges and any loyalties that ranked above allegiance to the nation, the elimination of convents was a necessary step toward social unity and justice.[35]

For some authors, the convent was politically suspicious because its walls hid tyrannical acts, and isolated helpless and abandoned victims. The *Journal universel* described the National Assembly's discussion on nuns as a debate on the "those buried virgins in those living sepulchers."[36] And in the play *Le Soeur Ste. Ange* a nun declares that "a father I loved was my own executioner; and his ambition, impervious to nature, in this odious cloister dug my grave."[37] Much like the vocation forcée literature of the prerevolutionary era, the analogy between the convent and the prison also represented an indictment of parental ambition. In *De la nécessité de supprimer les monastères* the anonymous author reiterated the well-worn narrative of the "these sad victims of arbitrary paternal power" who were "sacrificed, at a young age, to caprice and interest."[38] For parents, the convent was a resource, the right arm of arbitrary power.

The convent then continued to function like the Bastille, a symbol of the Old Regime's despotism, and its suppression symbolized the triumph of a principal revolutionary ideal: liberty. According to Hans-Jürgen Lüsebrink and Rolf Reichardt, "the storming of the Bastille represented the victory of a nation fighting for freedom against despotism."[39] I would argue that the convent similarly served as a symbol of the Revolution's achievements, and the direct analogies polemicists made between the convent and the Bastille reflected this fact. Much of the rhetoric surrounding the convent was about the liberation of its inhabitants, epitomized by the anonymous poem entitled "The Liberty of the Cloister." The poem referred to convents as these "Bastilles," "these towers / Where Religion masks tyranny." But as the title indicates, it was above all a celebration of the principal ideals and accomplishments of the Revolution.[40] The author of *De la nécessité de supprimer les monastères* also called upon the National Assembly to take what was in his opinion the next step after the destruction of the Bastille: the abolition of convents, which he regarded as "bastilles." He reminded members of the Assembly "that you will not allow [nuns] to be the only ones not to taste the enthusiasm of the return to liberty, which will become, under your auspices, the lot of all citizens."[41] For this author, where male monastics embodied all the crimes of the clergy, nuns freed from their prisons were representative of citizens liberated from the yoke of the Old Regime. These sentiments gave the abolition of the convent universal meaning, another manifestation of the Revolution's success in bringing freedom to all people.

Within this scenario, nuns would assume their rightful place in the nation. But how were nuns going to become citizens, and what was entailed in that citizenship? As certain radical tendencies gained ascendancy during the Revolution, the notion of a "good" citizen became invested with moral values such as social utility.[42] When revolutionary deputies and various polemicists tackled questions regarding the elimination of convents and the fate of their inhabitants, their words and ideas reflected this trend.[43] The radical editor of the *Révolutions de Paris*, Louis-Marie Prudhomme, spoke directly to monks and nuns: "Citizens, citizenesses whom we have just freed, it is time to make yourself available to the Nation and, through your caring, offer it the tribute of your utility."[44] Prudhomme's words revealed how he and many of his contemporaries had come to view the church and particularly the monastic state as parasitic, absorbing the resources of the French nation without giving anything in return. Now, however, monastics would swear allegiance and service to the state directly.

Some pamphleteers argued for making nuns more useful not by annihilating the convent but by reconfiguring it to fit the needs of secular society. They suggested that women religious who belonged to contemplative orders transfer into communities providing services to society. For example, in the *Essais sur les avantages, qui résulteroient de la sécularisation, modification et suppression des monastères des filles*, the anonymous author recommended that contemplative orders become "free congregations," helping the sick and the poor while providing them with instruction and work.[45] The author advocated that nuns take simple vows allowing them to leave the order if they grew weary of their tasks.[46] Convents were not entirely irredeemable as long as the National Assembly ensured that they were populated by those who entered and remained there of their own free will *and* provided useful services to secular society. Significantly, these plans detached nuns from any religious vocation. Praying for the poor was simply not enough. If the institution of the nunnery was to continue, it would be because it tended to the poor as well as rendering other social services. But for some writers such as Hubert du Maligny, even convent education, which many argued had potential social value, held no merit.[47] One journalist shifted the responsibility of educating the young to his readers: "Fathers, and mothers, you yourself [should] raise your children; that is the wish of nature."[48] Women religious could be useful only if they renounced their vows and became wives and mothers. The purpose of women was to procreate and thus provide the nation with future citizens. The anonymous author of the *Essais sur les avantages* argued that "woman was created in order to be the companion of man."[49]

Dismissing any pedagogical calling, playwrights, journalists, and other polemicists posited that a nun's natural vocation as a woman involved marriage and motherhood. Engravings depicted long lines of monks and nuns waiting to be married, their union blessed by a member of the Third Estate. Olympe de Gouges's *Le Couvent* also featured a priest who reunites the heroine with her lover.[50] The calls for procreation embraced the pre-revolutionary view that nuns should be taken from the convent and placed in the hands of husbands. Reconstituted purely as a woman, a nun would serve the nation solely through procreation. As Madelyn Gutwirth and Joan Landes have argued, this feminized image of domestic citizenship excluded nuns, as it did all other women, from the public arena.[51]

The arguments and exhortations about clerical marriage demonstrate the complex role of gender categories in nation building. Pamphleteers and journalists were also appealing to monks and priests to marry and to sire children. The symmetrical treatment of male clerics and nuns, with respect to procreation, was a response to the clerical rule of celibacy. One man of letters, Groubentall de Limière, argued that celibacy did not just undermine social well-being but violated a more sacred trust. Procreation, after all, was mandated by God and nature. Thus, "if . . . Nature does not make anything useless, to what purpose does the creative germ and the generative faculty in a monk or a nun serve?"[52] Revolutionary writers thus

Decree of the National Assembly suppressing the orders of monks and nuns, 1790. The engraving notes that "the names of mother and wife are indeed preferable to that of nun." Cliché Bibliothèque Nationale de France, Paris.

demanded that male clerics prove their worth as citizens in biological terms.

Vows of celibacy also separated the clergy from the laity and helped create an independent realm within the state that *parlementaires* had deplored. And at least on the level of rhetoric and ideology, the Revolution espoused a universalistic, all-encompassing message of citizenship that was also normative in nature. Whereas other men were not asked to prove their worth by having families, all clerics were expected to support the nation by forming families. The antagonism against clerical celibacy was so ingrained that contemporaries insisted that clerics prove their patriotism through demonstrations of "legitimate" sexual behavior. At the same time, this parity between male clerics and nuns was superficial. In the fantasies where monks and nuns married, male clerics were assigned to the domestic sphere, but only as part of their obligation to the nation. The outlook for nuns was different. The expectation was that they assimilate into the nation by placing themselves in the care of men. Women were, in effect, confined to the private arena, having traded in life in the cloister for a kind of domestic claustration.

While the fantasy of uniting monks and nuns in wedlock remained just that, women religious had very real male protectors, namely, the deputies of the Revolution whom polemicists heralded as the paternal or fraternal deliverers of nuns.[53] Perhaps the most dramatic example of this adulation was Fortin de Melleville's *Le Te Deum des religieux et des religieuses,* in which a chorus of monks and nuns offered thanks to the "fathers of the nation."[54] This and other references suggest that the representatives of the National Assembly had taken over—at least in the literary imagination—the paternal roles traditionally associated with kings and fathers. This transfer of authority is best understood in the context of legislative efforts to dismantle the parental prerogatives which had come to be associated with parental despotism.[55] As Lynn Hunt has shown, while republican revolutionaries would later enact explicitly anti-patriarchal policies, the rhetoric of the early Revolution still valued a father figure, one characterized by benevolence and paternal affection. Unlike prerevolutionary vocation forcée narratives which reconstituted the family by reforming the father, many revolutionary plays provided vivid demonstrations of the triumph of good "fathers" over bad parents by replacing fathers with revolutionary officials. Olympe De Gouges's *Le Couvent* and Boutet de Monvel's *Les Victimes cloîtrées* both concluded with scenes in which a revolutionary official entered the convent to rescue the unfortunate victim from the bad parent. The "parent" in question could be a cruel father, an obstinate abbess, or a devious priest.[56] Such plays provided a continuous staging of the Revolution's triumph, reminding the audiences of the concrete fruit of its efforts.

On me Raze ce Matin, Je me Marie ce Soir.

"I was shaved this morning, and I marry this evening," 1790. A monk prepares for his up-coming nuptials with a former nun. Cliché Bibliothèque Nationale de France, Paris.

However, many moderate clerics and lay writers held on to monastic tenets and attempted to negotiate between the ideals of the Revolution and traditional church institutions. Their appeals to the public demonstrate the diffuse impact of revolutionary rhetoric, confirming Suzanne Desan's assertion that lay Catholics employed the language of revolution to strengthen their religious claims.[57] Many pro-monastic speakers in the National Assembly deployed their arguments in the familiar language of social utility. For example, Philippe Samary, a curé from Carcassonne, stated that nuns served the nation as educators and caretakers of the poor and sick.[58] According to the lawyer Henri Jabineau, "female convents are resources for all the women of the canton who come there for assistance and remedies for their sicknesses. Moreover, within their communities, nuns live a Spartan existence and do not use up unnecessary resources."[59] But the abbé Lievain-Bonaventure Proyart chose a riskier approach and challenged the notion that monastic celibacy was necessarily bad. The un-married nun, he countered, enabled a brother or sister to marry because of an increased dowry.[60] Ironically, for Proyart and Jabineau celibacy was legitimate for its contributions to *lay* society and not in terms of spiritual purity, a position that inadvertently redefined women religious as just religious women.

The themes of utility and patriotism were not lost on women religious, who used them to maintain their communities and remain true to their vows. Revolutionaries thought they would find Suzanne cowering in the cloister, ready to acquiesce to all their plans. They made a major miscalculation. Like other women in the Revolution, nuns benefited from the unprecedented openness of revolutionary political culture of 1789 and 1790. In public and in private, nuns took advantage of the National Assembly's pledge to advance and safeguard the concern of citizens. Striving to ensure the survival of their communities, women religious appealed to officials, always careful to acknowledge the legitimacy of the Revolution. Thus, from 1789 to 1791, a process of compromise and cooperation took place. On the one hand, revolutionaries made a sincere attempts to help both individuals and entire communities even as they pursued a policy of secularization. And on the other, nuns diligently proclaimed their patriotism even while resisting official efforts to abolish their convents.

From the beginning of the Revolution, women religious publicly addressed to the National Assembly, defending their decision to remain in the convent while avowing loyalty to the new government. Their pamphlets illustrate that women religious understood that if they were going to preserve their claustral life, they needed set the record straight. The Carmelites assured the National Assembly that the public image of unwilling victims locked inside convents was false.[61] Such declarations received support from individuals like the abbé Proyart who contended that women religious were neither victims nor slaves; rather, they lived willingly under a rule that gave them choices such as periodically electing a superior.[62] At the same time, nuns also attempted to distance themselves from the church hierarchy. The nuns from the order of the Assumption reminded officials that "we had no part, sirs, in the errors and abuses which caused the misfortunes of France."[63]

Women religious portrayed themselves not as members of the church but of the larger nation and adopted the ubiquitous theme of social utility to affirm their status as citizens. For instance, the Benedictines from the Marais in Paris asserted that their "assiduous cares (uninterrupted since the foundation of this monastery) provided for the education of youth: it is for the legislators to judge the utility of the order in political reports." Similarly, the nuns from the Visitation Sainte-Marie claimed that "widows, the sick, persons disgraced in nature find a sure resource in an order that offers nothing overly austere for the body, and nothing onerous for society."[64] In this manner, women religious cast their activities not in spiritual terms but as services designed for the "Patrie."[65] The Benedictines de-

clared that they were "animated, like all other citizens should be, with true
patriotic sentiments." The order of the Assumption affirmed: "We will always put at the head of our titles the most honorable and cherished, that of
citizens of France."[66] Thus, women religious asked for protection by highlighting their solidarity with other members of the new political order.

Having established themselves as patriotic citizens, nuns also made it
clear that they expected legislators to consider their interests just as they
would those of other citizens. The petitions composed by nuns publicly acknowledged the legitimacy of the revolutionaries' authority. But it was
flattery with an edge. In addition to establishing their own loyalty, women
religious hinted that it was the patriotic duty of officials to uphold a nun's
right to remain in her convent. In the *adresse* they submitted to the National Assembly, the nuns from the order of the Assumption claimed: "You
have solemnly promised liberty to all of the French; we only ask you to
give us ours to be as we are." Similarly, the Benedictines nuns declared
that they had "confidence in your equity . . . with this confidence we have
come to you with our concerns.[67] One unusual pamphlet, *Adresse des religieuses qui se sont rendues aux devoirs de la société,* made a similar point from
a different angle. In the pamphlet a group of sixteen nuns who had chosen to leave the convent appealed to the Assembly for support in getting
employment. They audaciously asked the deputies for assistance against
men who "have even usurped from women nearly all the sedentary work
belonging by preference to the most delicate sex."[68] Women religious
adapted to the new world created by revolutionary legislators, but they
also fought to create a space for themselves by exploiting the amorphous
meaning of "citizen." Officials may have carefully distinguished between
"active" and "passive" citizens, but in the larger public arena, "citizen" had
more universal connotations. And it was precisely that broader interpretation of "citizen" that enabled nuns to claim rights and establish a degree
of autonomy.

On occasion nuns used the public forum created by pamphlets to lay
out their grievances against revolutionary officials. For example, Mother
Saint-Clement chose to leave the *hôtel-dieu* in Paris, but she and her fellow
sisters joined ranks when they learned of rumors claiming that she had
been mistreated by her fellow nuns. According to the pamphlet, the sur-
geon responsible for these rumors, Boulet, was "a man who, pushed by
some secret agent, and making the service to the poor an object of speculation, seems to desire that all the nuns of the *hôtel-dieu* leave one after the
other, in order that the surgeons can become absolute masters there."[69]
This pamphlet underscores that women religious understood how different officials and writers manipulated them through certain stereotypes. In
retaliation nuns exercised their rights as citizens by getting the National
Assembly to intervene on their behalf.

The potential friction between revolutionary officials and women religious is more apparent in the unpublished papers of the Comité Ecclésiastique. The correspondence and reports in the Comité Ecclésiastique's records fell into two categories: records in which nuns took a strong stance to protect their communities and vows, and those in which nuns asked the committee to intervene in their affairs. Like pamphlets, the committee's voluminous correspondence indicates that individual women religious and entire communities harnessed the rhetoric and ideology of the Revolution to serve their own needs. The more predictable cases involved nuns rescued from tyrannical families and mother superiors. The story of Anne Cibot in Tourraine, written by the town's officers, read like a lurid novel full of heartless relatives, scheming nuns, and, at its core, the unsuspecting victim betrayed by all until the Revolution rescued her. For the officials in the affair, it was "a tableau of tyranny against liberty, that of a true liberty, a word cherished by all French people."[70] Nuns themselves joined in making such accusations, readily evoking the specter of despotism. Sister Marie des Anges complained that certain members of the convent of the Cordeliers in Rue were making it difficult for her to leave the community, and she described the financial officer as governing "despotically . . . not ceasing by cabal and domination to create division."[71] The Benedictines from Saint-André in Rouen, asked for assistance, invoking their rights as citizens: "We are citizens, we belong to the Patrie. Free us from the unjust power, not to say the tyranny, to which we are subjected."[72]

The letters in the Comité Ecclésiastique's files also reveal hostility and defiance, a refusal to acknowledge the National Assembly's authority. For example, two Ursuline communities from Auch began their petition to the National Assembly by declaring "your two decrees concerning the emission of vows and ecclesiastical wealth have plunged all the religious orders into desolation . . . no, sirs, we will not suppress an empire in which religion seems to have established its most dear dwelling, the blessed retreats . . . far from the world's tumult, and the shelter from derision."[73] Nor did women religious always accept the role of victim that the National Assembly and the public almost always assigned them. In a letter to the Assembly written in December 1789, the Ursulines of Mans characterized such descriptions—"the cloister as an abode of horror and slavery, nuns as so many chained victims who did not breathe until after a successful Revolution"—as "calumnious" and "unjust."[74] Moreover, the steps women religious took to maintain their convents sometimes defied the National Assembly.

Despite the injunction against the admission of new members by religious orders, individuals pleaded for permission to take vows; communities made similar appeals on the grounds that they needed to take novices in order to sustain themselves financially.[75] And when the Benedictine nuns of Bayeux refused to admit Denise-Louise de Montigny, officials argued on behalf of Montigny. Disgusted with their treatment of Montigny, one administrator wrote to the Comité Ecclésiastique that "such animosity, such inhuman and really scandalous traits on their [the Benedictines'] part proves too well that one does not always find the practice of Christian virtue in cloisters."[76] That the Benedictines of Bayeux chose to disobey revolutionary mandates also indicates a strong desire to preserve their community's independence and not be dictated to by administrators.

The attitudes of administrators on the Comité Ecclésiastique demonstrate the continuity in prerevolutionary and early revolutionary perceptions of nuns. Officials and polemicists shifted between the contrasting images of the victimized nun and the despotic nun, reflecting a gendered anticlericalism that shaped the policies and rhetoric concerning nuns between 1789 and 1790. Moreover, the representation and discussion of nuns helped forge an identity for revolutionaries as "liberators," thereby legitimating their position and the Revolution itself. The deputies and pamphleteers were able to sustain their ideas regarding nuns so long as nuns adhered to these images. But the records show that many women religious rejected the images of the vocation forcée and the push to make them leave the convent. At this stage, however, their opinions were not statements of dissension. Nevertheless, as the Revolution itself began to change in early 1791 and ideological rifts made compromise impossible, the negotiations between nuns and revolutionaries collapsed.

During the first sixteen months of the Revolution, most women religious managed to sustain a viable existence within their communities. Objects of pity, they were allowed to remain within their communities if they chose, and legislation forbidding religious attire was not enforced until August 1792.[77] But the Revolution was hardly static, changing rapidly as ideological differences within the revolutionary government and challenges from abroad began to disrupt authority and consensus. The National Assembly's policies toward the church and an increasingly radical political climate reshaped the position of women religious. Specifically, the riots of April 1791 represented a turning point for nuns, after which revolutionary officials and polemicists began to sharpen their critique of women religious. By 1794, the contrasting images of nuns as victims and nuns as despots were almost entirely replaced by the figure of an aristocratic, monarch-loving, fanatical nun. The nun in effect acquired a new status in French political culture: the counterrevolutionary.

Just as *Unigenitus* had spurred conflict between nuns and ecclesiastical and secular authorities, the oath to the Civil Constitution of the Clergy transformed the fragile understanding between nuns and the revolutionary authorities into a more widespread and sustained struggle. Issued on July 12, 1790, the Civil Constitution "nationalized" the church, placing it completely under government control. On November 27, 1790, the government required all members of the secular clergy to swear an oath to the Civil Constitution. Timothy Tackett has demonstrated that more than the constitution itself, the oath of November 1790 effectively created two churches within France, one devoted to the Revolution and the other to Rome. According to Tackett, with the oath, "there was to be no middle ground, no room for compromise or ambiguity, or maneuvering of consciences. You could only be for or against, a patriot or a counter-revolutionary."[78] In this highly charged atmosphere, many nuns throughout France stood by their consciences and sided against the Revolution and began supporting refractory priests. Revolutionaries were forced to confront women religious as independent agents who openly defied the authority of the revolutionary government.

The position of women religious was further problematized in 1791 as the parameters defining modern citizenship became increasingly unstable. According to Darlene Gay Levy, the tension between popular sovereignty and the fears of *le peuple* intensified in 1791.[79] While the National Assembly continued to decrease the number of people eligible to be sovereign citizens, liberals and radicals stepped up their efforts to galvanize the public and to politicize it further, encouraging individuals and organizations to take action. Political communicators and organizers intensified their efforts to mobilize public opinion. During this contentious period, "women, along with other marginalized or excluded groups, continually tested and contested these meanings [of French revolutionary citizenship] in discourse and act, applying a rich variety of strategies to a struggle to widen, dissolve, newly imagine, and reconstruct the boundaries of prevailing definitions and practices of citizenship."[80] At the same time, both legislators and polemicists were faced with a series of other crises involving the clergy, the king, émigrés, and war. Women religious contributed to the national ethos of emergency by championing refractory priests. Olwen Hufton has described this transgression as going "beyond the mere refusal of women in the religious life to disband as the Assembly thought they should and involved a fervent and stolid support of the non-juring priesthood."[81] By refusing to conform to behavior that reflected unswerving loyalty to the nation, nuns chose instead to resist the new political order, making themselves adversaries of the Revolution.

In early 1791 nuns throughout France objected to the presence of constitutional priests within their convents' chapels, going so far as to deny themselves the sacraments. Parisian nuns protected refractory priests and

Eau Miraculeux arrive à Paris l'an du salut 1791, le six avril.

Dans le dortoir de cellule en cellule,
A la chapelle, à la cave, en tout lieu,
Ces ennemis des servantes de Dieu,
Flagellent tout sans honte et sans scrupule.

Du ceintre bleu de la céleste sphère,
L'abbé voyait le déplorable cas :
La palme en main il s'élance ici bas,
Et de rayons orne le saint derriere. Porte de Nesle.

A miraculous act takes place in Paris in the year of salvation 1791. The drawing satirizes the "divine" intervention that momentarily halts the beating of a nun in April 1791. Cliché Bibliothèque Nationale de France, Paris.

transformed their chapels into sanctuaries for non-jurors and their supporters. Their actions were not without repercussions. Between April 7 and April 11, 1791, the angry market women of Les Halles decided to punish the Parisian nuns. Incidents included the caning of an entire community that had punished their students for taking part in a constitutional mass. In other episodes nuns were stripped naked and flogged.[82] Nor was Paris the only site of such violence. On April 10, the deputy Chevalier reported to the Assembly that in Argenteuil a mob had stormed an Ursuline convent because they suspected the community of harboring a refractory priest.[83] While deploring the violence, the officials of Paris issued a decree on April 11 closing down all non-juring churches; convents were permitted to hold masses conducted by refractory priests, but these masses were not open to the larger public.[84]

The events of April 1791 produced a mixed response among journalists, who now regarded women religious with increasing suspicion. Radical polemicists such as Pierre-Jean Audouin and Louis-Marie Prudhomme, authors of the *Journal universel* and *Révolutions de Paris* respectively, now eviscerated nuns.[85] Prior to April 1791, both journalists accorded women religious the status of "victims" who had wrongfully been incarcerated.[86] Audouin's reporting on nuns between April 6 and 7, 1791, forcefully illustrates the degree to which his views of nuns had shifted. On April 6, Audouin referred to nuns as a "multitude of victims." The next day, however, when the violent episodes exploded in Paris, he had no qualms about describing nuns as "prostituting themselves through their incivism and their audacity at scorning the decrees of the nation that feeds them."[87] But Audouin and Jacques-René Hébert also blamed the nuns' behavior on priests who had seduced the women religious of the lower classes, the *soeurs grises*.[88] According to Loyseau, the author of a pamphlet denouncing refractory priests, nuns, those "unhappy women," remained "victims of ignorance and superstition."[89] Although ready to reproach nuns for their behavior, both Loyseau and Audoin still held on to the gendered notions that imbued nuns with passivity. Their critique of nuns represented a mixture of prerevolutionary perceptions of nuns and a new hostility spawned by revolutionary events.

Other journalists were not so quick to excuse nuns and linked the subversive behavior of women religion to gender-specific qualities. All women religious were seen as impassioned and devious, seeking to mislead and betray. According to the anonymous author of the *Liste de tous les soeurs et dévotes*, nuns were "hypocrites" who "under the impostor's mask of piety" carried on unimaginable debauchery. Their destruction was necessary because women religious represented a threat to the nation: they corrupted the young whom they educated and the sick they tended.[90] The journalist Prudhomme characterized nuns as harboring "petty resentments," implying a volatility and weakness intrinsic to their sex. Moreover, as women, they were prone to deceive the public. Prudhomme sketched a scenario in which the mother superior assured a priest that "without a doubt, our sex, and the holy habit we wear, will serve as a barrier against the people."[91] Not only did the journalist impute clerical hypocrisy to nuns, but he saw it compounded by feminine wiles. Prudhomme, Marat, and the anonymous author of the *Liste des soeurs et dévotes* thus came to see nuns not as victims subdued and seduced by the treacherous clergy but as politically subversive women. Nuns, in effect, belonged to the same category of women that included Marie-Antoinette and Madame Roland.[92]

An extraordinary illustration of this phenomenon is the female equivalent of the journal *Père Duchesne*, the *Lettres bougrement patriotiques de la Mère Duchesne*, most likely written by a former nun, Françoise Goupil, who would later marry Hébert.[93] One issue, written shortly after the April 1791 episodes, involved a confrontation between the narrator and the Parisian nuns of Sainte-Marie. The opponents engaged in a shouting match which the narrator won, crowing "Mesdames nuns, I am speaking here, and it is for you to listen to me." The narrator went on to itemize the treacherous acts of the nuns, which include hiding refractory priests, meddling in theology, hypocrisy, and seducing their young female pupils—accusations echoing both prerevolutionary and revolutionary discourses. These accusations, peppered with expletives, symbolized a confrontation between good and bad female citizens. With respect to herself, the narrator declared: "I am too good a citizeness; I will be extremely angry if I resembled those holy nuns, who in the depths of their cells, assuming fucking airs that create trouble among us." Her advice to nuns was to "lock yourself in your cells, and keep silent if you can."[94] These statements underscore how uncertain the position of women was at this stage of the Revolution. On the one hand, radical revolutionaries raged about women religious behaving in political ways and engaging in unpatriotic actions. On the other hand, the market women maintained a certain legitimacy and, indeed, political currency by storming convents.[95] While it is difficult to say how this work actually affected women who were its intended readers, it is noteworthy that the character of Mère Duchesne achieved its greatest popularity in April 1791, especially in the theaters.[96]

The increasing gulf between women religious and the Revolution was also reflected in the policies of the new Legislative Assembly, which convened on October 1, 1791. According to John McManners, as a consequence of the turmoil created by the Civil Constitution, the clergy was underrepresented, and the new deputies who joined the Legislative Assembly "had come up to Paris fresh from District or Departmental administrations, itching with anti-clerical vexation at the insults and tumults they had endured over the Civil Constitution of the Clergy."[97] Moreover, members of the National Assembly had agreed not to be a part of the new government, further emptying the Assembly of moderates and clergy sympathizers. For this new legislative body, facing tensions with the clergy and the king's attempted flight in June 1791, female convents represented another example of counterrevolutionary betrayal.[98] In early 1792 the members of the new Legislative Assembly questioned the existence of female convents more openly, beginning with challenges to communities comprised of only three or four women religious.[99] On August 4, 1792, the deputies issued a decree ordering all nuns and monks to leave their convents. Around the same time, they demanded a new oath from clergy, known as the Liberty-Equality oath. The oath required an individual to declare "I swear to be faithful to the Nation, to maintain with all my power Liberty, Equality, the security of persons and property, and to die, if need be, for the execution of the law."[100]

The Legislative Assembly reiterated the sentiments of the radical press and increasingly insisted that the government's principles of liberty could be realized only by emptying the cloister. On January 8, 1792, Léopold, the deputy from Eure-et-Loi, addressed the Legislative Assembly, demanding the complete suppression of *all* monastic houses in order to pay the national debt. According to Léopold, these "little congregations of superstitious women" were "very expensive," "very indecent and very dangerous," especially because many nuns used government pensions to hire refractory priests. By persistently relying on a priest who was "the president of an aristocratic cabal," nuns disturbed "public tranquility."[101] Similarly, deputies such as Rouyer and Claude Le Coz argued that to maintain nuns in convents was, in fact, to support a "remnant of aristocracy."[102] In his lengthy report on the secular congregations, Gaudin described female convents as "the source of fanaticism," an expression that the deputy Marant later repeated on August 4, 1792, when the Legislative Assembly completely suppressed the regular clergy without exception.[103]

Some deputies such as Crestin from the Comité des domaines, still defended the right of nuns to remain in their convents. Addressing the Legislative Assembly on July 31, 1792, Crestin declared that "morality and natural rights do not permit you to force from asylums these beings . . . who . . . find a kind of happiness that all the revenues of the State would not know how to procure for them."[104] In this argument, Crestin implied that it was a government's responsibility to protect an individual's liberty regardless of her or his personal definition. Despite Crestin's nuanced argument, nuns and their Christian zeal were commonly seen as another example of the feminine disorder that was besieging the French Republic.[105] And, by the early days of the Terror, the charge of fanaticism was tantamount to that of treason.[106]

Despite their hostility toward female convents, revolutionary deputies still maintained certain gendered assumptions that precluded them from crediting nuns with being active and independent agents of counterrevolution. They continued to render women religious as passive, susceptible to larger pernicious forces. Gaudin used pathological terms to describe how priests had corrupted the popular *soeurs grises* of the hospitals: "This is the crime of a rebellious clergy who have poisoned with their fanaticism souls who have known only works of charity."[107] Although the deputy Léopold inveighed against superstition in the convent, he still referred to these women as "sad victims of pride and prejudice." Gender thus continued to complicate the anticlerical attitudes of revolutionaries. Indeed, at the end of the July 30 debate in which Crestin had pleaded the cause of nuns, the deputy Henry declared "religious houses are monastic *bastilles* in which refractory priests are the turnkeys."[108] These references to prisons and turnkeys muted the hostility toward nuns, suggesting that even in 1792 revolutionaries found it difficult not only to accept female agency but to relinquish certain powerful gendered images closely intertwined with their vision of the convent.

Nevertheless, nuns who had hitherto been exempt from swearing oaths were now forced to acknowledge and accept the Revolution's republican ideology. Six days later, on August 10, the day the monarchy fell, all convents devoted to teaching were closed down. This left only the various *hospitalières* in their place, and over the course of 1793 the government shut down various hospitals under suspicion of counterrevolution. Some sisters disbanded and returned to their homes while others continued to pursue counterrevolutionary activities such as arranging masses led by non-juring priests.[109] And yet others continued to nurse by keeping their heads down and not wearing their habits.[110]

Others fought until the bitter end. In 1792, as the tide was turning against nuns, the abbess of the Benedictines of Montargis issued a virulent pamphlet against the officials of the district. Revolutionary administrators had been trying unsuccessfully to take over the convent's property; when they attempted to replace the abbess, her subordinates resisted them. The abbess made pronouncements that were overtly antirevolutionary, describing how "the blood of the French runs in our capital . . . the priest and the nobleman, after their sacrifices, are reviled and degraded." She refused to surrender the convent's papers and take the Liberty-Equality oath. Addressing the officials, she stated: "You can say, sirs, to those who sent you, that our feeble arms bend, no doubt, under the chains of oppression; but our consciences, stronger than death, only obey God alone . . . Ferocious souls, you drink our blood."[111] This remarkable pamphlet is perhaps one of the most direct public statements of the growing hostility many nuns felt toward the Revolution by 1791. The vampire imagery indicated that the Revolution had become for some a monster feeding on the innocent. In effect, the abbess availed herself of the same language used to discredit the clergy as a whole. Indeed, the last paragraph of the pamphlet is diatribe against the "despotism" of revolutionary officials.[112]

By 1793, officials now began to blame nuns directly, depicting them as malevolent agents of counterrevolution. And in certain instances, they were justified. On 16 Germinal, Year II, the same day that Georges Danton and Camille Desmoulins were guillotined, the revolutionary committee of the Parisian section of L'Homme armé arrested Marie-Nicole Bragelongne, former superior of the Ursulines in Argenteuil, and her sister Marie-Marguerite-Louise, the marquise de Montbrun, who were clearly guilty of treason.[113] According to the committee's report, officials had discovered a "den of fanaticism, aristocracy, and counterrevolution." The former superior was guilty of "the character and political opinions she had shown in the months of May, July, and October 1789, in August at the flight and death of the tyrant, and during the crisis of the war." Furthermore, she and her sister were caught with materials clearly revealing their sympathies.[114] Confiscated items included linens and silver from the Ursuline convent's chapel that should have been relinquished to the government in 1790. The most damning evidence against the sisters were antirevolutionary pamphlets with titles such as *Bref du pape à tous les cardinaux, archevêques, aux clergés et au peuple de France* and *Prieur pour le roi*. In the margins of the latter pamphlet Marie-Nicole Bragelongne made the following inscription: "Monday, January 21, 1793, Louis XVI has suffered martyrdom at Place Louis XV under the knife of the guillotine." Officials also discovered a brochure providing the names and genealogies of noble families in Paris.[115] Thus, the Bragelongne sisters, to whom the section committee referred to as "fanatics," were accused of attempting to subvert the Revolution in every way possible, from hoarding goods to harboring inflammatory material.

While the nuns who went to the guillotine were not all guilty of such counterrevolutionary activity, women such as the Bragelongne sisters helped fan the flames of anticlerical venom during the Terror. Republican officials and polemicists were probably even more incensed when the Sisters of Charity, who were considered nuns of the people, were revealed to be conspirators. In October 1793 deputy Jean-Baptiste Mailhe referred to these nuns, who generally came from the lower classes, as "these aristocratic women," who posed threats of counterrevolution.[116] Whereas in 1789 and 1790 such intense animosity had been limited to aristocratic figures like the abbess of Montmartre, republicans like Mailhe saw no distinction between nuns and their superiors, attributing the same crimes to both regardless of status. The "aristocratic" status of women religious was now derived from their crimes against the nation and not their social rank. According to Suzanne Desan, "out of Catholicism they [radical revolutionaries] forged a residual category of stereotyped characteristics—a type of theatrical stage onto which they projected all the cultural and political attributes of the Old Regime."[117] Within this framework, nuns symbolized all the elements—aristocrats, priests, feminine power—that were seeking to thwart the Revolution.

The hostility toward nuns paralleled the larger animosity toward women in 1794. In her discussion of Marie-Antoinette's trial Lynn Hunt has argued that "Marie-Antoinette in particular was the negative of the female icon of republican liberty, the bad mother in a republic that was supposed to be shaped by the lessons of good republican mothers."[118] Superiors such as the abbess of Montmartre, Madame de Montmorency-Laval, also appeared as a "bad" mother. Like Marie-Antoinette, the abbess of Montmartre threatened to undermine the Revolution itself. According to the public accuser Antoine-Quentin Fouquier-Tinville, the abbess insisted on retaining her feudal privileges, calling citizens "her vassals."[119] Perhaps revolutionary radicals became even more vociferous because nuns had, in fact, betrayed a Revolution that had initially been their ally. They had tried to be fathers, and, instead of obedient and grateful daughters, they found recalcitrant women. As a result of this treason, by 1794 female convents appeared to have been obliterated after being a part of French society for over one thousand years.

This dramatic transformation of nuns in the public sphere demonstrates the dynamic nature of the Revolution itself. As Lynn Hunt has shown, a new political class emerged with the advent of the Revolution, a class that sought to break with the past and create a unique revolutionary culture.[120] For these individuals, steeped in anticlericalism, nuns were a part of a Catholic and aristocratic tradition that was diametrically opposite to republican ideals of liberty and equality. And women religious were instrumental in redefining themselves in the public eyes. When the Revolution threatened their vows and their faith, many nuns did not hesitate to take a stance in opposition to officials and the larger public. Nonetheless, heated debates in the Convention as well as inflammatory pamphlets also reveal that it was difficult for revolutionaries to relinquish images of nuns as victims. Although revolutionary ideology was radicalizing at a fast pace during this period, gender assumptions about female agency persisted. In the end, however, the Republic's growing sense of crisis made it difficult for republicans to accommodate nuns, who by 1794 had moved from being victims to fanatics, a legacy that would prevail throughout the next century.

But the very same acts and qualities that earned women religious notoriety among proponents of the Revolution endowed them with a new status among opponents of the Revolution. Women religious like the abbess of Montmartre became martyrs of a besieged French Catholicism.[121] The most famous example of martyrdom during the Revolution was that of the sixteen Carmelites from Compiègne, north of Paris. Although the Carmelites had taken the Liberty-Equality oath, they were arrested on June 21, 1794, because "they are always together in a community . . . they always live in submission to the fanatic regime of their former convent."[122] Eventually the nuns were moved from their prison in Compiègne to the

Conciergerie in Paris, where the revolutionary tribunal accused them of being religious fanatics and harboring royalist sentiments. On that same day July 17, 1794, the sixteen Carmelites joyfully went to the guillotine, sure of their sacred martyrdom which had been prophesied in the early part of the century.[123] Similar behavior on the part of Jansenist nuns had pitted them against the church. But nuns were now embraced by orthodox Catholics as the emblem of true Catholics resisting the menace of revolutionary secularism.

Conclusion

THE STORY OF THE MARTYRED CARMELITES OF COMPIÈGNE HAD
political and religious significance for both revolutionaries and Catholics
in the nineteenth century. The Carmelites' death at the guillotine signified the completion of a process in which women religious went from
being sympathetic figures embraced by the nation to opponents of the
French Revolution. For republicans, nuns embodied the twin enemies of
the Revolution, religious zeal and royalist fervor. In essence, the eradica-
tion of women religious by 1794 symbolized the triumph of masculine reason over feminine fanaticism.[1] For devout Catholics, the Carmelites and
individuals such as the abbess of Montmartre were symbols of Catholic
martyrdom in the face of the bloodthirsty Revolution. Indeed, the brutal
death of these women religious encapsulated the Old Regime's "execution": the death of the king, the dissolution of the church, and the annihi-
lation of the nobility. Martyred nuns came to represent two important
components of ultra-conservative ideology. First, the fate of women religious exposed the vicious and destructive nature of the French Revolution. Second, nuns were a testament to the resilience of Catholic faith, a
sign that Catholicism was the true religion.[2] The symbolic power of nuns
was made apparent by the beginning of the nineteenth century when hagiographies began appearing about the Carmelites. By this period, nuns
marked a clear boundary between antirevolutionary conservatives, on the

one hand, and liberals and republicans wishing to preserve the Revolution, on the other.

The French Revolution represented a social as well as a discursive watershed for nuns themselves during the revolutionary epoch. By the end of the Terror, it would appear that women religious had disappeared from the landscape. However, when the abbé Grégoire helped revive the Constitutional Church in 1796, small numbers of nuns crept back into their communities. The Carmelite Camille de Soyecourt, who managed to escape the guillotine, returned to Paris and in 1797 reestablished the Carmelites on the rue Grenelle. She was also instrumental in reinstating the order in France, taking special care to restore the Carmelite community of Compiègne.[3] Under Napoleon, women religious began to reappear asking for permission to set up schools; "approximately thirty congregations received official authorization between 1810 and 1813, thus paving the way for future expansion in the decades to come."[4] While the increase of female religious communities was uneven, it was nonetheless notable, especially from the 1820s onward. No fewer than four hundred congregations and orders were established or restored after the convents' abolition in 1792, and between 1800 and 1880 two hundred thousand women became nuns.[5] Whereas women religious had represented one-third of the clergy in 1789, by 1878 they were a solid majority, constituting nearly three-fifths of the clergy.

The conclusion one may draw from these numbers is that despite their harrowing experiences during the French Revolution, women religion adapted successfully to the changing social climate of the nineteenth century. They provided a wide variety of services that included teaching, nursing, charity work, and the administration of orphanages, asylums, reformatories, and old people's homes and hospitals.[6] Four-fifths of female clergy were *congrégationistes* modeled on the seventeenth-century Filles de la Charité. Apostolic in nature, *congrégationistes* did not take solemn vows. In effect, they reflected the vision that revolutionary moderates had of how a nun could be useful to French society as caregivers and teachers.[7]

It was in the arena of teaching that *congrégationistes* had the most influence. In her study of nineteenth-century female education in France, Rebecca Rogers has demonstrated that convents effectively cornered the female education market, especially after the Falloux Law of 1850. Devised in the aftermath of the Revolution of 1848, the Falloux Law reinstated Catholic influence on education as a means of controlling social revolution; specifically, a provision that did not require female religious orders to have teaching certificates opened the door for religious education.[8] However, during the Third Republic, republican officials targeted religious orders, and the government sought to wrest schools away from religious control. Teaching nuns became a topic of national debate "which resulted first in their expulsion from public primary schools in 1886 and then from all teaching institutions in 1904."[9]

Despite this setback at the end of the nineteenth-century, the swelling ranks of women religious, their commitment to social services, and their place in national debates on education point to the "feminization" of religion in the nineteenth century.[10] As men turned away from the church over the course of the century, the growing number of women religious and their influential functions reflected how women shaped modern Catholicism. Religion formed a fundamental part of the education of middle-class girls, and its influence was felt beyond school.[11] Moreover, devotional practices were more feminized. For example, the cult of the Virgin Mary increased during this period. Indeed, the survival of the Catholic Church would not have been possible without the outpouring of female devotion and spiritual activity.[12] At the same time, the responses to the growing presence of women in religious establishments, as well as the power Catholicism had over women, provoked a great deal of discussion and anxiety on the part of male observers.

The feminization of religion in the nineteenth century was bound up with the legacy of the French Revolution. For conservatives, such Joseph de Maistre, the survival of the Catholic Church and its total reinstatement in the lives of French men and women was essential, the only means of truly turning back the clock and repudiating the Revolution. Ultra-Catholics, such as the Bishop of Viviers, regarded nuns as a critical element of this revitalization, sacrificing themselves to the larger cause of the church and educating children.[13] Liberal reformers and radical republicans, however, had a much more negative view of this larger phenomenon because they perceived it as nothing less than a threat to the Revolution's legacy. Maurice Agulhon has argued that in the aftermath of the failed republic of 1848, diehard republicans were virulently anticlerical in their outlook, seeing the Catholic Church as not only a force of social and political conservatism but the reason for the republic's demise.[14]

As Caroline Ford has observed, the feminization of religion resulted in "the perception of French women as a potential threat to the revolutionary settlement."[15] Thus, nuns became targets. They were regarded as fanatical creatures. They inculcated superstition in women, who were then ruled more by their priests than by their husbands.[16] The demonization of women religious sprung from a larger context in which the French public feared "the power the church exercised over the minds of French women."[17] Women religious in particular combined the dangers of clerical and feminine influence, which republicans viewed as undermining the rational and masculine republicanism that had finally triumphed in the 1880s.

To what degree can we trace this loathing of women religious to the Old Regime? True, abbesses evoked a visceral hatred on the part of the eighteenth-century public because they appeared to exemplify the worst of aristocratic and feminine power. But as this book has shown, the place of nuns in eighteenth-century society was a complex and fluid one. When writers pondered the question of who should control the convent, they attributed the various problems of the convent to feminine disorderliness. Such gendered unruliness encompassed despotic bishops, tyrannical superiors, independent-minded nuns, and unnatural parents. Thus, lawyers and men of letters constructed multiple representations of nuns that were closely tied to the political and cultural anxieties of the day. Legal briefs, literary texts, and polemics often portrayed nuns as the victims of disarray and of despotism, helpless citizens whose lives of devotion would be restored once certain problematic individuals were taken to task. Moreover, in their defense of nuns who were at odds with the various figures of authority, lawyers in particular articulated proto-liberal notions that conflicted with the patriarchal ideals of the Old Regime. They defended the rights of nuns and their communities, rights that included freedom of religious conscience, the choice of one's vocation, and the right to appeal for justice. In these instances, nuns and lawyers acted together as critics of the Old Regime.

However, by the 1760s men of letters came to view the convent itself as the source of disorder, symptomatic of the problems of eighteenth-century society. While lawyers most often considered how to reform the convent in order to preserve its sacred qualities, men of letters tended to see the convent as an institution with less and less relevance in a secular society. Unlike lawyers and magistrates who focused on specific cases, men and women of letters engaged in abstract discussions that excluded nuns. They regarded the nun not as an individual who had embraced a spiritual calling, but as a woman who had failed, or more often been prevented, from expressing her true nature. These changing views of the convent and the nun created the potential for conflict between nuns, many of whom took their spiritual calling seriously, and men of letters with ideological expectations grounded in new theories of female sexuality and education.

The rapidly changing nature of the French Revolution created the conditions for this collision. Revolutionaries were committed to the notion of nuns as victims and of themselves as liberators. But nuns were equally if not more committed to their spiritual choices and independence. By 1792 the possibility of negotiation between these two positions disappeared. Republican revolutionaries could not and would not accommodate nuns who had chosen to affiliate themselves with the church of the Old Regime. Their choices during the Revolution put them squarely on one side of the hardened ideological divide. Ironically, women religious came to represent the crimes and excesses which some of them had opposed in the eighteenth century.

Nuns continued to play a role in nineteenth-century gender constructions of feminine disorder. Ideologues on both the Left and the Right considered the "family as a microcosm of the state and argued that paternal authority served as a foundation for social and political order."[18] But where eighteenth-century lawyers and men of letters had portrayed nuns as victims of a patriarchal authority gone awry, nineteenth-century liberal and republican polemicists considered women religious as endangering paternal authority and social stability. Like eighteenth-century men of letters, state officials and social theorists operated within a gendered paradigm that prescribed a normative image of femininity, the "natural" woman in her equally "natural" domestic space. Politicians and journalists perceived women religious as destabilizing that paradigm by upsetting relationships between husbands and wives and between parents and children. For them, nuns were disorderly women, excessively pious and easily led by priests. Given this widespread distrust of women religious especially during the Third Republic, the government increasingly sought to control nuns and the role they played in society. Moreover, unlike their eighteenth-century counterparts, nuns were in a position of considerable influence, shaping the hearts and minds of young girls across the social spectrum. From the perspective of the Left and, indeed, centrist politicians and writers, the female convent was no longer a site of oppression exercised by clerics, superiors, parents, and kings but a space of female independence.[19] Women religious were social and political deviants who could disrupt the family, the bedrock of republican society.[20]

Compared to her eighteenth-century predecessor, the nun in the nineteenth century held an even more ambiguous position in French society. On the surface, women religious were an integrated, visible part of modern French society and culture. They had fully realized the dreams of sixteenth- and seventeenth-century nuns who had yearned for a *vita apostolica*. And nineteenth-century politicians and social commentators continued to obsess about them, attaching pressing issues of power and gender to the nineteenth-century nun as they had to her eighteenth-century counterpart. However, in the context of republican ideology and the broader revolutionary legacy, nuns were also outsiders to a society whose secular values were grounded in the Revolution, which a majority of nuns had rejected and, according to some, betrayed. Where the convent had once been a microcosm of the Old Regime, of its social hierarchy and its flaws, it had become—for proponents of republicanism—a foreign realm within France, an anachronistic but nonetheless dangerous remnant of the gendered despotism that the Revolution was supposed to have vanquished.

NOTES

INTRODUCTION

1. *De la nécessité de supprimer les monastères* (Paris: Garnery et Volland, 1790), 23, 22, 26. All translations are mine unless otherwise indicated.
2. For a similar assessment, see Jutta Gisela Sperling, *Convents and the Body Politic in late Renaissance Venice* (Chicago: University of Chicago, 1999).
3. On the theories of divine right kingship, see Nannerl O. Keohane, *Philosophy and the State in France: The Renaissance to the Enlightenment* (Princeton, N.J.: Princeton University Press, 1980); Ralph E. Giesey, "The King Imagined," in *The Political Culture of The Old Regime*, vol. 1 of *The French Revolution and the Creation of Modern Political Culture*, ed. Keith Baker (Oxford: Pergamon Press, 1987); Jeffrey Merrick, *The Desacralization of the French Monarchy in the Eighteenth Century* (Baton Rouge: Louisiana State University Press, 1990).
4. In French history Sarah Hanley and Jeffrey Merrick have demonstrated the symbiotic relationship between monarchical and familial ideology. Sarah Hanley, "Engendering the State: Family Formation and State Building in Early Modern France," *French Historical Studies* 16 (1989): 4–27; idem, "Family and State in Early Modern France: The Marriage Pact," in *Connecting Spheres: Women in the Western Worlds, 1500 to the Present*, ed. Marilyn J. Boxer and Jean H. Quataert (Oxford: Oxford University Press, 1987); Jeffrey Merrick, "Sexual Politics and Public Order in Late Eighteenth-Century France: The *Mémoires secrets* and the *Correspondance secrète*," *Journal of the History of Sexuality* 1 (1990): 68–84. See also Lynn Hunt, *The Family Romance and the French Revolution* (Berkeley: University of California, 1993).
5. Jean-Louis Flandrin, *Families in Former Times: Kinship, Household and Sexuality*, trans. Richard Southern (Cambridge: Cambridge University Press, 1979), 120.
6. Roger Chartier, *The Cultural Origins of the French Revolution*, trans. Lydia G. Cochrane (Durham, N.C.: Duke University Press, 1991), 96–97.
7. On Louis XIV's masculinity, see Abbie E. Zanger, "Lim(b)inal Images: 'Betwixt and between' Louis XIV's Martial and Marital Bodies," in *From the Royal to the Republican Body: Incorporating the Political in Seventeenth-and Eighteenth-Century France*, ed. Sara E. Melzer and Kathryn Norberg (Berkeley: University of California Press, 1998), 32–63.
8. On Louis XV, see Lisa Jane Graham, *If the King Only Knew: Seditious Speech in the Reign of Louis XV* (Charlottesville: University of Virginia Press, 2000); and Thomas E. Kaiser, "Madame de Pompadour and the Theaters of Power," *French Historical Studies* 19 (1996): 1025–1044. For the vast literature on Marie-Antoinette, see, for example, Dena Goodman, ed., *Marie-Antoinette: Writings on the Body of a Queen* (New York: Routledge, 2003); Chantal Thomas, *La Reine scélérate: Marie-Antoinette dans les pamphlets* (Paris: Seuil, 1989).
9. Gary Kates, *Monsieur d'Eon Is a Woman: A Tale of Political Intrigue and Sexual Masquerade* (New York: Basic Books, 1995), 159–165; Lynn Hunt, ed., *Eroticism and the Body Politic* (Baltimore: Johns Hopkins University Press, 1991), 2.
10. As cited in *Nouvelles ecclésiastiques, ou mémoires pour servir l'histoire de la bulle Unigenitus*, May 29, 1754, 88.
11. Gerbier de la Massillaye, *Mémoire pour Dames Geneviève Carré de St. Paul, Marie-Louis de Boiscourjon de Saint-Arsenne et Conforts, religieuses professes du couvent de Bon Secours contre la dame Rossignol, prieure de Bon-Secours et Conforts* (Paris: Simon, 1759). According to Gerbier de la Massillaye, the prioress desired to "revive the early times of monastic life: one

knew that superiors were sovereigns in their community; but the Church itself rejected this despotism," 5.

12. Bibliothèque Nationale de France, Fonds Joly de Fleury (hereafter BNF, JF), 206, f. 14.

13. Henry Cochin, *Mémoire à consulter pour les dames religieuses de l'abbaye royale de Malnoue* (Paris: Charles Osment, 1746), 20. Details on the Malnoue affair are found in the Archives Nationales (hereafter AN), G9 80, no. 13; G9 81, no. 9; G9 78, no. 185; S4590.

14. The study of political culture owes much to the revisionist historians who challenged the "social interpretation" of the French Revolution, which attributed the eruption of revolution to the class conflict between the aristocracy and the bourgeoisie. François Furet's *Penser la Révolution française* (1978) marked the decisive shift to the political. For more comprehensive discussions of the historiography, see Sarah Maza, "Politics, Culture, and the Origins of the French Revolution," *Journal of Modern History* 61 (December 1989): 704–23; Christine Adams, Jack R. Censer, and Lisa Jane Graham, eds., *Visions and Revisions of Eighteenth-Century France* (University Park: Pennsylvania State University Press, 1997), 1–18. Two definitive works on political culture are Lynn Hunt, *Politics, Culture, and Class in the French Revolution* (Berkeley: University of California Press, 1985), and Keith Michael Baker, *Inventing the French Revolution* (Cambridge: Cambridge University Press, 1990). On recent assessments of the historiography on eighteenth-century French political culture, see Vivian Gruder, "Whither Revisionism? Political Perspectives on the Ancien Régime," *French Historical Studies* 20 (1997): 245–286; Suzanne Desan, "What's after Political Culture? Recent French Revolutionary Historiography," *French Historical Studies* 23 (2000): 163–201.

15. Graham, *If the King Only Knew*, 4.

16. For examples of such studies, see Jeffrey S. Ravel, *The Contested Parterre: Public Theater and French Political Culture 1680–1791* (Ithaca, N.Y.: Cornell University Press, 1999); Thomas E. Crow, *Painters and Public Life in Eighteenth-Century Paris* (New Haven: Yale University Press, 1985); Mona Ozouf, *Festivals and the French Revolution*, trans. Alan Sheridan (Cambridge: Harvard University Press, 1988). See Adams, Censer, and Graham, *Visions and Revisions* for a range of comparable studies.

17. For example, see Arlette Farge and Jacques Revel, *The Vanishing Children of Paris: Rumor and Politics before the French Revolution*, trans. Claudia Miéville (Cambridge: Harvard University Press, 1991). Farge's work, based on extensive research in the Paris police archives, has done much to uncover the political voices of the working people of Paris; see *Subversive Words: Public Opinion in Eighteenth-Century France*, trans. Rosemary Morris (University Park: Pennsylvania State University Press, 1995). For a more recent study, see Graham, *If the King Only Knew*.

18. Dale Van Kley's pathbreaking studies of Jansenism and its importance in shaping the political landscape include *The Jansenists and the Expulsion of the Jesuits from France, 1757–1765* (New Haven: Yale University Press, 1975); *The Damien Affair and the Unraveling of the Ancien Regime, 1750–1770* (Princeton, N.J.: Princeton University Press, 1985); and *The Religious Origins of the French Revolution: From Calvin to the Civil Constitution, 1560–1791* (New Haven: Yale University Press, 1996). See also Merrick, *Desacralization of the French Monarchy;* Catherine Maire, *De la cause de Dieu à la cause de la nation: le jansénisme au XVIIIe siècle* (Paris: Gallimard, 1998).

19. On Enlightenment anticlericalism, see R. R. Palmer, *Catholics and Unbelievers in Eighteenth-Century France* (Princeton, N.J.: Princeton University Press, 1939); Peter Gay, *The Enlightenment: An Interpretation*, 2 vols. (New York: W. W. Norton, 1966).

20. Adams, Censer, and Graham, *Visions and Revisions*, 7. Joan Scott's theoretical work on gender has influenced how historians have examined gender in eighteenth-century French history. Joan Wallach Scott, *Gender and the Politics of History* (New York: Columbia University Press, 1988).

21. Landes uses gender analysis to revise Jürgen Habermas's influential theories of the public sphere. Joan B. Landes, *Women and the Public Sphere in the Age of the French Revolution* (Ithaca, N.Y.: Cornell University Press, 1988). A more recent formulation of her thesis can be found in *Visualizing the Nation: Gender, Representation, and Revolution in Eighteenth-Century France* (Ithaca, N.Y.: Cornell University Press, 2001). Other significant works in-

clude the Hunt, *Eroticism and the Body Politic;* Melzer and Norberg, *From the Royal to the Republican Body;* Hunt, *The Family Romance and the French Revolution;* Madelyn Gutwirth, *Twilight of the Goddesses: Women and Representation in the French Revolution* (New Brunswick, N.J.: Rutgers University Press, 1992).

22. *Relations des refus de sacramens sous lesquelles les religieuses du monastère de S. Charles d'Orléans, gémissent depuis de 33 ans, et celles de l'abbaye de S. Loup depuis plus de 28 ans* (La Haye: Neaulme, 1755), v.

23. [Voltaire], *La Voix du sage et du peuple* (Amsterdam: Le Sincere, 1750), 11.

24. The study of women religious in this period has been furthered considerably by the work of historians such as Elizabeth Rapley and Barbara Diefendorf. See Elizabeth Rapley, *A Social History of the Cloisters: Daily Life in the Teaching Monasteries of the Old Regime* (Montreal: McGill-Queen's University Press, 2001); idem, *The Dévotes: Women and Church in Seventeenth-Century France* (Montreal: McGill-Queen's University Press, 1990); idem, "Women and the Religious Vocation in Seventeenth-Century France," *French Historical Studies* 18 (1994): 613–631; Barbara B. Diefendorf, "Contradictions of the Century of Saints: Aristocratic Patronage and the Convents of Counter-Reformation Paris," *French Historical Studies* (2001): 469–500. See also Dominique Dinet, *Vocation et fidelité: le recrutement des réguliers dans les diocèses d'Auxerre, Langres et Dijon (XVIIe–XVIIIe)* (Paris: Economica, 1988), and Roger Devos, *L'Origine sociale des Visitandines d'Annecy aux XVIIe et XVIIIe siècle* (Annecy: Académie Salésienne, 1973). Numerous dissertations written since the mid-1980s indicate a growing interest in this field. For example, see Linda Lierheimer, "Female Eloquence and Maternal Ministry: The Apostolate of Ursuline Nuns in Seventeenth-Century France" (Ph.D. diss., Princeton University, 1994); Susan Eileen Dinan, "Gender, Class and Vocation: The Development of the Daughters of Charity in Seventeenth-Century France" (Ph.D. diss., University of Wisconsin, Madison, 1996); Daniella J. Kostroun, "Undermining Obedience in Absolutist France: The Case of the Port Royal Nuns, 1609–1709" (Ph.D. diss., Duke University, 2000); Karen Lenore Taylor, "Cher espoir de la nation sainte: The Maison Royale de Saint Louis at Saint Cyr" (Ph.D. diss., Georgetown University, 2000).

25. Dena Goodman, "Public Sphere and Private Life: Toward a Synthesis of Current Historiographical Approaches to the Old Regime," *History and Theory* 31 (1992): 1520. On an effort to expand the parameters of Landes's argument, see Lenard R. Berlanstein, *Daughters of Eve: A Culture History of French Theater Women from the Old Regime to the Fin de Siècle* (Cambridge: Harvard University Press, 2001); Jennifer Jones, "Repackaging Rousseau: Femininity and Fashion in Old Regime France," *French Historical Studies* 18 (1994): 939–967.

26. Elizabeth C. Goldsmith and Dena Goodman, *Going Public: Women and Publishing in Early Modern France* (Ithaca, N.Y.: Cornell University Press, 1995). On women and the law courts, see Sarah Hanley, "Social Sites of Political Practice in France." See also Zoë A. Schneider, "Women before the Bench: Female Litigants in Early Modern Normandy," and Mita Choudhury, "Despotic Habits: The Critique of Power and Its Abuses in an Eighteenth-Century Convent," in *French Historical Studies* 23 (2000). On guilds, see Clare Haru Crowston, *Fabricating Women: The Seamstresses of Old Regime France, 1675–1791* (Durham, N.C.: Duke University Press, 2001).

27. For theoretical discussions on public opinion in the eighteenth century, see Mona Ozouf, "Public Opinion at the End of the Old Regime," *Journal of Modern History* 60 (supplement, September 1988): S1–S21; Keith Michael Baker, "Public Opinion as Political Invention," in *Inventing the French Revolution,* 166–199. See also Dale Van Kley, "In Search of Eighteenth-Century Parisian Public Opinion," *French Historical Studies* 19 (1995): 215–226; William Doyle, *Origins of the French Revolution,* 2d ed. (Oxford: Oxford University Press, 1988), 78–95.

1. AUTHORITY IN THE EIGHTEENTH-CENTURY CONVENT

1. Jane T. Schulenberg, "The Heroics of Virginity: Brides of Christ and Sacrificial Mutilation," in *Women in the Middle Ages and the Renaissance: Literary and Historical Perspectives,* ed. Mary Beth Rose (Syracuse: Syracuse University, 1986), 31–32.

2. Jane M. H. Smith, "The Problem of Female Sanctity in Carolingian Europe *c.* 780–920," *Past and Present* 146 (February 1995): 3–37.

3. Jane T. Schulenberg, "Women's Monastic Communities, 500–1100: Patterns of Expansion and Decline," in *Sisters and Workers in the Middles Ages*, ed. Judith M. Bennett et al. (Chicago: University of Chicago Press, 1989), 217.

4. Suzanne F. Wemple, *Women in Frankish Society: Marriage and the Cloister, 500–900* (Philadelphia: University of Pennsylvania Press, 1983), 165.

5. Jane T. Schulenberg, "Female Sanctity: Public and Private Roles, ca. 500–100," in *Women and Power in the Middle Ages*, ed. Mary Erler and Maryanne Kowaleski (Athens: University of Georgia, 1988), 115. For broader discussions of French women religious, see Michel Parisse, *Les Nonnes au moyen age* (Le Puy: Christine Bonneton, 1983); Penelope D. Johnson, *Equal in Monastic Profession: Religious Women in Medieval France* (Chicago: University of Chicago Press, 1991).

6. In double monasteries, nuns and monks were a part of the same monastic community. Although they lived in separate quarters, they had access to the same schools and participated in religious services together. Abbesses sometimes had authority over both men and women. Wemple, *Women in Frankish Society*, 160.

7. Specifically, canon 968, sec. 1 stated that only men were eligible for ordination, and therefore only men could perform liturgical duties. Ida Raming, *The Exclusion of Women from the Priesthood: Divine Law or Sexual Discrimination*, trans. Norman R. Adams (Metuchen, N.J.: Scarecrow Press, 1976). Colin Morris, *The Papal Monarchy: The Western Church from 1050 to 1250* (Oxford: Clarendon Press, 1989), 98–108.

8. Elizabeth Makowski, *Canon Law and Cloistered Women: Periculoso and Its Commentators, 1298–1545* (Washington, D.C.: Catholic University of America Press, 1997), 1–8.

9. Johnson, *Equal in Monastic Profession*, 257.

10. Caroline Walker Bynum, "The Mysticism and Asceticism of Medieval Women: Some Comments of the Typologies of Max Weber and Ernst Troeltsch," in *Fragmentation and Redemption: Essays on Gender and the Human Body in Medieval Literature* (New York: Zone Books, 1992), 63.

11. Penelope Johnson has pointed out that nuns and particularly superiors from high-ranking families received greater respect. *Equal in Monastic Profession*, 266.

12. Brenda M. Bolton, "Mulieres Sanctae," in *Women in Medieval Society*, ed. Susan Mosher Stuard (Philadelphia: University of Pennsylvania Press, 1976), 141. See also Morris, *Papal Monarchy*, 462–470; Shulamith Shahar, *The Fourth Estate: A History of Women in the Middle Ages*, trans. Chaya Galai (London: Methuen, 1983), 52–56.

13. Bynum, *Holy Feast and Holy Fast*, 20–30; Morris, *Papal Monarchy*, 469.

14. Makowski, *Canon Law and Cloistered Women*, 14.

15. Geneviève Reynes, *Couvent de femmes: la vie des religieuses cloîtrées dans la France des XVIIe et XVIIIe siècles* (Paris: Fayard, 1987), 92–93, 180–181.

16. During the twenty-fifth session held in 1563, the Council of Trent called for the renewal of Boniface VIII's *Periculoso* to restore claustration, "even summoning for this purpose, if need be, aid of the secular arm." Council of Trent, sessions 25: 5, 7, 9, as quoted in H. J. Schroeder, *Canons and Decrees of the Council of Trent* (St. Louis: B. Herder, 1941), 220–224.

17. Barbara B. Diefendorf, "Contradictions of the Century of Saints: Aristocratic Patronage and the Convents of Counter-Reformation Paris," *French Historical Studies* 24 (2001): 472–475.

18. Henri Brémond, "Les Grandes Abbesses," in *L'Invasion mystique*, vol. 2 of *Histoire littéraire du sentiment religieux en France depuis la fin des guerres de religion jusqu'à nos jours* (Paris: Bloud et Gay, 1930).

19. Diefendorf, "Contradictions of the Century of Saints," 474.

20. Ibid., 488. For a discussion of seventeenth-century teaching orders, including the Ursulines, see Elizabeth Rapley, *A Social History of the Cloister: Daily Life in the Teaching Monasteries of the Old Regime* (Montreal: McGill-Queen's University Press, 2001). For a more complete history of the Ursuline order, see Anne Bertout, *Les Ursulines de Paris sous l'ancien régime* (Paris: Firmin-Didot, 1935); Marie de Chantal Gueudré, *Histoire de l'ordre des Ursulines en France*, 3 vols. (Paris: Editions St. Paul, 1957).

21. Elizabeth Rapley, *The Dévotes: Women and Church in Seventeenth-Century France* (Montreal: McGill-Queen's University Press, 1990), 50–60. The same fate awaited the Visitandines founded by François de Sales and Jeanne de Chantal. See Roger Devos, *L'Origine sociale des Visitandines d'Annecy aux XVIIe et XVIIIe siècles* (Annecy: Académie Salésienne, 1973), 27–35. The exception was Vincent de Paul's Filles de la Charité who worked in urban areas caring for the poor and sick. The Filles de la Charité were able to retain their autonomy because they did not claim to be nuns, and took simple vows and not public, solemn vows. See Rapley, *The Dévotes;* Jean de Viguerie, "Une forme nouvelle de vie consacrée: enseignantes et hospitalières en France aux XVIIe et XVIIIe siècles," in *Femmes et pouvoirs sous l'ancien régime,* ed. Danielle Haase-Dubosc and Eliane Viennot (Paris: Editions Rivages, 1991), 175–195.
22. Diefendorf, "Contradictions of the Century of Saints," 471.
23. Ibid.; Reynes, *Couvent de femmes,* 40.
24. John McManners, *The Clerical Establishment and Its Social Ramifications,* vol. 1 of *Church and Society in Eighteenth-Century France* (Oxford: Clarendon Press, 1998), 534.
25. Dominique Dinet, *Vocation et fidelité: le recrutement des réguliers dans les diocèses d'Auxerre, Langres et Dijon (XVIIe–XVIIIe)* (Paris: Economica, 1988), 36.
26. Sarah Hanley, "Social Sites of Political Practice in France: Lawsuits, Civil Rights, and the Separation of Powers in Domestic and State Government, 1500–1800," *American Historical Review* 102 (1997): 38.
27. Elisja Schulte van Kassel, "Vierges et mères entre ciel et terre," in *Histoire des femmes en occident,* ed. George Duby and Michelle Perrot, 5 vols. (Paris: Plon, 1991), 3:159.
28. François Isambert, *Recueil des anciennes lois françaises,* 29 vols. (Paris: Blin et Le Prieur), 20:178.
29. Ibid., 20:180.
30. René Pillorget, "Vocation religieuse et état en France au XVIe et XVIIe siècles," in *La Vocation religieuse et sacerdotale en France. XVI–XIX siècles,* ed. Jean Viguerie (Angers: Université d'Angers, 1979), 15.
31. Isambert, *Recueil des anciennes lois françaises,* 20:248. However, the edict remained circumspect about the episcopate's authority over the exempted masculine orders. Norman Ravitch, *Sword and Mitre: Government and Episcopate in France and England in the Age of Aristocracy* (The Hague: Mouton, 1966), 32–33.
32. Isambert, *Recueil des anciennes lois françaises,* 16:227.
33. In addition to singing in the choir, choir nuns were responsible for teaching and doing more refined work such as needlepoint. The converses performed the manual labor of the convent such as gardening and washing.
34. McManners, *Clerical Establishment and its Social Ramifications,* 544.
35. Robert Lemoine, *Le Monde des religieux: l'époque moderne, 1563–1789,* vol. 15, pt. 2 of *Histoire du droit des institutions de l'église en occident,* ed. Gabriel Le Bras (Paris: Editions Cujas, 1976), 211–212.
36. On the link between the female convent and the salon in the seventeenth century, see F. Ellen Weaver, "Cloister and Salon in Seventeenth-Century Paris: Introduction to a Study in Women's History," in *Beyond Androcentrism: New Essays on Women and Religion,* ed. Rita M. Gross (Missoula, Mont.: Scholars Press, 1977), 159–180.
37. See Devos, *L'Origine social des Visitandines,* 109–119; Dinet, *Vocation et fidelité,* 172.
38. Dinet, *Vocation et fidelité,* 255.
39. Thérèse-Jean Schmitt, *L'Organisation ecclésiastique et la pratique religieuse dans l'archidiaconé d'Autun de 1650 à 1750* (Autun: Société d'Imprimerie L. Marcelin, 1957), 58–59.
40. Dinet, *Vocation et fidelité,* 39; Jean de Viguerie, "La vocation sacerdotale et religieuse aux XVIIe et XVIIIe siècles: La théorie et la réalité," in Viguerie, *La Vocation religieuse et sacerdotale en France,* 27–39; Barbara B. Diefendorf, "Give Us Back Our Children: Patriarchal Authority and Parental Consent to Religious Vocations in Early Counter-Reformation France," *Journal of Modern History* 68 (1996): 265–307.
41. On the *appel comme d'abus,* see Moïse Cagnac, *De l'appel comme d'abus dans l'ancien droit français* (Paris: Libraire Poussielgue, 1906); Robert Génestal, *Les Origines de l'appel comme d'abus* (Paris: Presses Universitaires de France, 1951). The appeal first appeared in the

years immediately following the Pragmatic Sanction of Bourges (1438), the classic statement of Gallicanism declaring the king head of the French Church. Généstal, *Les Origines de l'appel comme d'abus*, 6–12.

42. Léon Abensour, *La Femme et le féminisme avant la Révolution* (Paris: Ernest Leroux, 1923), 280. The classic interpretations of *La Religieuse* are Georges May, *Diderot et "La Religieuse"* (New Haven: Yale University Press, 1954), and Vivienne Mylne, *Diderot: "La Religieuse"* (London: Grant and Cutler, 1981). A more theoretical approach may be found in Jay Caplan, *Framed Narratives: Diderot's Genealogy of the Beholder* (Minneapolis: University of Minnesota Press, 1985). For a recent psychoanalytic study of the novel, see J. E. Fowler, *Voicing Desire: Family and Sexuality in Diderot's Narrative* (Oxford: Voltaire Foundation, 2000).

43. English Showalter argues that the conflict between the individual and society was a major theme in a number of French novels written around the time of *La Religieuse*. English Showalter Jr., *The Evolution of the French Novel, 1641–1782* (Princeton, N.J.: Princeton University Press, 1972), 323–329.

44. Denis Diderot, *The Nun*, trans. Leonard Tancock (London: Penguin Books, 1972), 74; hereafter cited by page numbers in the text.

45. On the emotional conflict between Suzanne and her mother, see Louis W. Marvick, "Heart of Flesh, Hearts of Stone: A Reading of Diderot's *La Religieuse*," *Romanic Review* 80 (March 1989): 185–206.

46. According to Huguette Cohen, Diderot's Jansenist sympathies were the result of his theological studies between 1732 and 1736 at the University of Paris, an institution then dominated by hard-core Jansenist proponents. Diderot most likely borrowed images and events from the chronicles of the Jansenist convent Port-Royal-des-Champs. Huguette Cohen, "Jansenism in Diderot's La Religieuse," *Studies in Eighteenth-Century Culture* 11 (1982): 75–91. See also Jacques Proust, "Recherches nouvelles sur *La Religieuse*," *Diderot Studies* 6 (1964): 197–214.

47. Denis Diderot, "Sur les femmes," in *Oeuvres complètes de Diderot*, ed. J. Assézat, 20 vols. (Paris: Garnier Frères, 1875), 2:252. See also Lieselotte Steinbrügge, *The Moral Sex: Woman's Nature in the French Enlightenment*, trans. Pamela E. Selwyn (New York: Oxford University Press, 1995), 44–51.

48. Diderot, "Sur les femmes," 255.

49. Steinbrügge, *The Moral Sex*, 49.

50. Anne C. Vila, *Enlightenment and Pathology: Sensibility in the Literature and Medicine of Eighteenth-Century France* (Baltimore: Johns Hopkins University Press, 1998), 164.

51. On the importance of Diderot and human exchange, see Dena Goodman, *The Republic of Letters: A Cultural History of the Enlightenment* (Ithaca, N.Y.: Cornell University Press, 1994), 26–28. See also Daniel Gordon, *Citizens without Sovereignty: Equality and Sociability in French Thought, 1670–1789* (Princeton, N.J.: Princeton University Press, 1994).

52. Dominique Jullien, "Locus hystericus: l'image du couvent dans *La Religieuse* de Diderot," *French Forum* 5, 2 (1990): 133–148. On the language of pathology in *La Religieuse*, see Carole F. Martin, "Legacies of the Convent in Diderot's *La Religieuse*," *Studies in Eighteenth-Century Culture* 25 (1995): 117–129.

53. Armine Kotin Mortimer, "Naïve and Devious: *La Religieuse*," *Romanic Review* 88 (March 1997): 241–250; Julie C. Hayes, "Retrospection and Contradiction in Diderot's *La Religieuse*," *Romanic Review* 78 (March 1986): 233–242.

54. Vivienne Mylne, "What Suzanne Knew: Lesbianism and *La Religieuse*," *Studies on Voltaire and the Eighteenth Century* 208 (1982): 167–173.

55. On the forensic structure of *La Religieuse*, see Robert J. Ellrich, "The Rhetoric of *La Religieuse* and Eighteenth-Century Forensic Rhetoric," *Diderot Studies* 3 (1961): 129–154. For a discussion of the *La Religieuse* as a memoir novel, see William F. Edmiston, "Narrative Voice and Cognitive Privilege in Diderot's *La Religieuse*," *French Forum* 10 (May 1995): 133–144.

56. On Suzanne pleading her case as a woman, see Christine Clark-Evans, "Le Témoignage de Suzanne: séduction tragique et discours juridique dans *La Religieuse* de Diderot," *Recherches sur Diderot et l'Encyclopédie* (April 1996): 76–89.

2. MARTYRS INTO CITIZENS

1. Bibliothèque de l'Arsenal, Archives de la Bastille (hereafter BA, AB), 10189, April 22, 1747. This was the first of six such declarations made by Saint-Basile alone. Between 1743 and 1760, seven other nuns from Val-de-Gif signed similar statements.

2. Ibid., letter dated July 10, 1741.

3. Ibid. For other examples, see statements made by the following: Sister Flavie Bouloud, Bernadine of St. Cécile in Grenoble, on January 15, 1747; Sister Claude-Angélique de la Miséricorde, Carmelite of Beaune on November 10, 1742; Sister Morant from Soissons on February 13, 1743; Sister Elizabeth, who signed her retraction sixteen times between 1734 and 1753; Sister Elizabeth-Thérèse de Ste. Perpétue, Carmelite from the rue St. Jacques in Paris on January 27, 1749.

4. On Jansenism as a space of dissension within the Gallican church, see Henry Phillips, *Church and Culture in Seventeenth-Century France* (Cambridge: Cambridge University Press, 1997), 103–104.

5. For a discussion of *Unigenitus*, see Edmond Préclin, *Les Jansénistes du XVIIIe siècle et la constitution civile du clergé* (Paris: Librairie Universitaire J. Gambier, 1929);B. Robert Kreiser, *Miracles, Convulsions and Ecclesiastical Politics in Early Eighteenth-Century Paris* (Princeton, N.J.: Princeton University Press, 1978), 10–26.

6. Kreiser, *Miracles, Convulsions and Ecclesiastical Politics*, 15–26. See also William Doyle, *Jansenism: Catholic Resistance to Authority from the Reformation to the French Revolution* (London: Macmillan, 2000), 45–55.

7. Kreiser, *Miracles, Convulsions and Ecclesiastical Politics;* Catherine-Laurence Maire, *Les Convulsionnaires de Saint-Médard* (Paris: Editions Gallimard/Julliard, 1985); Shanti Marie Singham, "'A Conspiracy of Twenty Million Frenchmen': Public Opinion, Patriotism, and the Assault on Absolutism during the Maupeou Years, 1770–1775" (Ph.D. diss., Princeton University, 1991), 292–297. In his study of the Paris bourgeoisie, David Garrioch notes the influence of women in Parisian parishes such as the ultra-Jansenist Saint-Médard; *The Formation of the Parisian Bourgeoisie, 1690–1830* (Cambridge: Harvard University Press, 1996), 51–52, 97–98.

8. Dale Van Kley, "Préface," in *Mademoiselle de Joncoux: polémique janséniste à la veille de la bulle "Unigenitus,"* by F. Ellen Weaver (Paris: Editions du Cerf, 2002), 11. See also Elizabeth Rapley, *A Social History in the Cloister: Daily Life in the Teaching Monasteries of the Old Regime* (Montreal: McGill-Queen's University Press, 2001), 64–77.

9. The "Jansenist" epoch began in the 1630s when Angélique Arnauld formed an association with the abbé de Saint-Cyran, who became her spiritual director. Saint-Cyran had been a friend of Cornelius Jansenius, whose writings were the foundation of the Augustinian movement. See F. Ellen Weaver, *The Evolution of the Reform of Port-Royal: From the Rule of Cîteaux to Jansenism* (Paris: Beauchesne, 1978); Alexander Sedgwick, *Jansenism in Seventeenth-Century France: Voices in the Wilderness* (Charlottesville: University of Virginia Press, 1975), 14–46. See also Cécile Gazier, *Histoire du monastère de Port-Royal* (Paris: Perrin, 1929). On the appeal of Jansenism for women, see Elizabeth Rapley, "Life and Death of a Community: The Congrégation de Notre-dame of Troyes, 1628–1762," *Etudes d'histoire religieuse* 58 (1991): 12.

10. On Jansenism's popularity with elite women, see Cécile Gazier, *Les Belles amies de Port-Royal* (Paris: Librairie Académie Perrin, 1954);F. Ellen Weaver, "Erudition, Spirituality, and Women: The Jansenist Contribution," in *Women in Reformation and Counter-Reformation Europe*, ed. Sherrin Marshall (Bloomington: Indiana University Press, 1989), 189–206.

11. Alexander Sedgwick, *The Travails of Conscience: The Arnauld Family and the Ancien Régime* (Cambridge: Harvard University Press, 1998), 135.

12. As cited in Sedgwick, *Jansenism in Seventeenth-Century France*, 114.

13. Specifically, many nuns refused to accept a 1657 formulary drawn up by the Assembly of Clergy which called for submission to two anti-Jansenist papal bulls: *Cum occasione* (1653) and *Ad Sacram* (1656). See ibid., 68–74, 104–133.

14. Daniella J. Kostroun, "Undermining Obedience in Absolutist France: The Case of the Port Royal Nuns, 1609–1709" (Ph.D. diss., Duke University, 2000), 313–324.

15. Linda Timmermans, *L'Accès des femmes à la culture (1598–1715): un débat d'idées de Saint François de Sales à la Marquise de Lambert* (Paris: Honoré Champion, 1993), 735.
16. Ibid., 740–745.
17. Bibliothèque de Port-Royal, Fonds Fourqueveaux (hereafter BPR, FF), ms. 446, fol. 1. According to the inventory made by Tans and Schmitz du Moulin, the letter was most likely written at the end of 1709. J.A.G. Tans and H. Schmitz du Moulin, *La Correspondance de Pasquier Quesnel: inventaire et index analytique*, 2 vols. (Brussels: Revue d'Histoire Ecclésiastique, 1989), 1:249.
18. BPR, FF, ms. 446, fol. 1.
19. Ibid., fols. 1–2, 4; italics added.
20. Ibid., fol. 2.
21. As cited in Sedgwick, *Jansenism in Seventeenth-Century France*, 132.
22. Timmermans, *L'Accès des femmes à la culture*, 792–804.
23. For a detailed analysis of the political crisis of 1730–1732, see Peter R. Campbell, *Power and Politics in Old Regime France, 1720–1745* (London: Routledge, 1996), 237–258.
24. Ibid., 240.
25. Augustin Gazier, *Histoire générale du movement janséniste depuis ses origines jusqu'à nos jours*, 2 vols. (Paris: Libraire Ancienne Honoré Champion, 1924), 1:336–337.
26. BPR, FF, ms. 447. Although the date on the *relation* is November 16, 1753, it is somewhat unclear when this piece was written since most of the events in the piece took place during the 1730s. I am indebted to Valérie Guitienne-Mürger at the Bibliothèque de Port-Royal for giving me access to this handwritten *relation*. The Carmelite community of Lectoure was one of the early communities to experience upheaval in the first half of the 1730s. See *Nouvelles ecclésiastiques, ou mémoires pour servir l'histoire de la bulle Unigenitus* (hereafter *NE*), October 18, 1730, 12; November 23, 1730, 13; September 12, 1733, 147.
27. BPR, FF, ms. 447, fol. 2.
28. Ibid., fol. 4.
29. Ibid., fols. 27, 12.
30. Ibid., fols. 7–9.
31. Women religious sometimes aided the *Nouvelles* by keeping certain individuals apprised of such matters. Such was the case with the 1749 affair of the Hôpital général of Paris in which one Sister Elisabeth provided the lawyer Louis-Adrien Le Paige with the activities of the new superior Madame de Moysan. Bibliothèque de Port-Royal, Collection Le Paige (hereafter BPR, LP), ms. 516, no. 39.
32. This exchange between the bishop of Beauvais and the nuns of St. Francis was reported in *NE*, March 20, 1749, 46. Subsequent articles are found in the following issues: April 10, 1750, 57–59; April 17, 1750, 62–63. The Archives de la Bastille contain letters and declarations of the Franciscans in question, all of which indicate opposition to *Unigenitus*. See BA, AB, 10189.
33. *NE*, March 20, 1749, 46.
34. *NE*, April 10, 1750, 59; italics added. Also present were a secretary, a sub-delegate, the convent's immediate male superior, the abbé de Bragelonne, and the maréchaussée.
35. Timmermans, *L'Accès des femmes à la culture*, 740–741.
36. "Lettre des religieuses du Calvaire à son éminence monseigneur le cardinal de Fleury en lui addressant un mémoire et les consultations des avocats, où l'on fait voire les abus et les irrégularités du bref," in *Suite de recueil de pièces concernant l'affaire des religieuses du Calvaire*, 10. The letter is dated April 8, 1741.
37. *Mémoire pour les religieuses de la Congrégation du Calvaire* (n.p., n.d.) The *Nouvelles ecclésiastiques* kept close tabs of the affair. See the following issues: July 10, 17, 1741; September 11, 18, 1741; October 9, 23, 1741; opening editorial of 1742; March 18, 1742; December 1, 22, 1742.
38. "Declaration présentée M. l'archevesque de Paris. Les 11 et 12 decembre 1738, par les religieuses du Calvaire des deux maisons du marais et du Fauxbourg Saint Germain," in *Pièces concernant le bref de N.S. Père le papa Clément XII qui établit et delégue l'archevêque de Paris visiteur et commissiare apostolique des monastères de la congrégation du Calvaire établis à Paris* (n.p., 1739), 7; "Lettres des religieuses du Calvaire à son éminence monseigneur le cardinal de Fleury," 2.

39. "Très-humbles représentations que sone au roy. Les superieurs généraux, assistantes de la congrégations des religieuses du Calvaire en leur nom et au nome de toute la congréga-tion, prieures, religieuses et communautés des deux maisons de ladite congrégation établies à Paris," in *Pièces concernant le bref de N. S. Père le papa Clément XII*, 15.

40. *Mémoire pour les religieuses de la congrégation du Calvaire* (n.p., [1741]), 1.

41. Second letter [of Jean-Baptiste Gaultier], in *Lettres apologétiques pour les carmélites du fauxbourg S. Jacques de Paris* (n.p., 1748), 39.

42. Madeleine Foisil, Françoise de Noirfontaine, and Isabelle Flandrois, "Un Journal de polémique de propagande: *Les Nouvelles ecclésiastiques*," *Histoire, Economie et Société* 10, 3 (1991): 410–411.

43. Ibid., 412.

44. Ibid., 415.

45. Gazier, *Histoire générale du movement janséniste*, 1: 333. Using Gabrielle Nivelle, Do-minique Dinet, and Marie-Claude Dinet-Lecomte have concluded that between 1717 and 1728 less than 1 percent of the appellants against the bull were nuns; however, they also have noted that the sympathies of female communities were generally not ex-pressed in public appeals. Dominique Dinet and Marie-Claude Dinet-Lecomte, "Les ap-pelantes contre la bulle *Unigenitus* d'après Gabriel-Nicolas Nivelle," *Histoire, Economie et Société* 9 (1990): 367, 377.

46. The *Nouvelles ecclésiastiques* appeared between 1728 and 1803 with a better part of its life spent as a clandestine publication with a following unparalleled in the eighteenth cen-tury. François Bontoux, "Paris Janséniste au XVIIIe Siècle: Les *Nouvelles ecclésiastiques*," in *Mémoires de la féderation des sociétés historiques et archéologiques de Paris et Ile de France* (1956), 205–220. For a discussion of the periodical and the diffusion of figurism, see Dale Van Kley, *The Religious Origins of the French Revolution: From Calvin to the Civil Constitution, 1560–1791* (New Haven: Yale University Press, 1996), 92–95.

47. *Apologie sommaire des carmélites du fauxbourg S. Jacques* (n.p., 1749); *Relations des refus de sacremens sous lesquels religieuses des monastères de S. Charles d'Orléans gémissent depuis 23 ans* (La Haye: Neaulme et Compagnie, 1756); *Recueil des pièces justicatives qui n'ont pû être in-sérées dans la relation* (La Haye: Neaulme et Compagnie, 1756).

48. For examples, see BPR, LP, ms. 516, 542, 543.

49. Dale Van Kley, *The Jansenists and the Expulsion of the Jesuits from France 1757–1765* (New Haven: Yale University Press, 1975), 47.

50. Catherine Maire, *De la cause de Dieu à la cause de la nation: le jansénisme au XVIIIe siècle* (Paris: Gallimard, 1998), 182–204.

51. Pasquier Quesnel, *Correspondence de Pasquier Quesnel prêtre de l'Oratoire sur les affaires poli-tiques et religieuses de son temps*, ed. Albert Le Roy, 2 vols. (Paris: Perrin, 1900), 2:263.

52. Maire, *De la cause de Dieu*, 194–196.

53. For a more complete discussion of figurism, see ibid., 163–181; Catherine Maire, "L'église et la nation: du dépôt de la vérité au dépôt des lois, la trajéctoire janséniste au XVIIIe siècle," *Annales: économies, sociétés, civilisations* 46 (1991): 1177–1184.

54. Van Kley, *Religious Origins of the French Revolution*, 92.

55. Catherine Maire, "Port-Royal. La fracture janséniste," in *Lieux de mémoire*, ed. Pierre Nora (Paris: Gallimard), 1:488.

56. Ibid., 486; Maire, *De la cause de Dieu*, 195–196.

57. Maire, *Les Convulsionnaires de Saint-Médard*, 55, 184.

58. Maire, *De la cause de Dieu*, 220–228.

59. See, for example, *Lettres édifiantes, écrites pour la consolation de deux religieuses persécutées en France* (n.p., 1753), 3; [LeClerc], *Vies intéressantes et édifiantes des religieuses de Port-Royal et plusieurs personnes qui leur étoient attachées* (Compagnie: 1750), 8; *Histoire abrégée de la dernière persécution de Port-Royal suivie de la vie édifiante des domestiques de cette sainte maison* (Edition Royal, 1750), 2; [Pierre Guilbert], *Lettre d'un théologien célèbre à une dame re-ligieuse sur Port-Royal-des-Champs* (n.p., n.d.), 3.

60. *Lettres édifiantes*, 4.

61. Ibid., 27.

62. Located in the old priory of Notre-Dame-des-Champs, the Grand Carmel was the first Carmelite convent established in France in 1604. The convent remains famous for hous-

ing Louise de la Vallière, who retired to the cloister to repent her sins as mistress of Louis XIV. Similar to other female convents, it was closed down at the end of 1792. For a complete history of the convent, see Jean-Baptiste Eriau, *L'ancien Carmel du Faubourg Saint-Jacques, 1604–1792* (Paris: J. de Gigord, 1929). See also Paul Biver, *Abbayes, monastères, couvents de femmes à Paris, des origines à la fin du XVIIIe siècle* (Paris: Presses Universitaires de France, 1975), 254–279.

63. La Taste (1692–1754) was formerly a prior of the Blancs-Manteaux. During the 1730s he gained a reputation for his invectives against the convulsionaries. The compilation of these works appeared in 1740 under the title of *Lettres théologiques aux écrivains défenseurs des convulsions et autres miracles du tems*. After La Taste resigned his office as prior, Louis XV made him the bishop of Béthléem in 1738. Maire, *Les Convulsionnaires de Saint-Médard*, 174–176. La Taste also attacked other Jansenist Carmelite communities, such as the Carmelites of Riom in Auvergne and the two Carmelite communities of Troyes. On the former, see *NE,* July 31, 1750, 122–124; on the latter, *NE,* May 29, 1751, 85–88.

64. Mère Catherine-Dorothée de la Croix had already gained a reputation for eradicating Jansenism within Saint-Denis. Her report is contained in the Bibliothèque Nationale de France, Fonds Français (hereafter BNF, Ms. Fr.), 17719, fol. 120. The police maintained a surveillance over the Grand Carmel; their files contain various *lettres de cachet* exiling certain individuals, police lieutenant d'Argenson's correspondence with some of the community's exiled members, and retractions of signatures supporting *Unigenitus*. BA, AB, 10183, 10184.

65. BNF, Ms. Fr. 17719, fols. 101–107.

66. Another defense of the nuns of the Grand Carmel was *Apologie sommaire des carmélites*. See also *NE,* December 11, 1748, 197–199; April 17, 1749, 61–63; June 19, 1749, 97–98; September 25, 1749, 154–155; October 1, 1749, 158–159.

67. Maire, *De la cause de Dieu,* 104, 112, 119, 126, 498.

68. Second letter, in *Lettres apologétiques,* 70. The *Nouvelles ecclésiastiques* enthusiastically endorsed this argument (April 17, 1749, 63).

69. First letter, in *Lettres apologétiques,* 4, 5, 68.

70. Fifth letter, in *Lettres apologétiques,* 20.

71. Timmermans, *L'Accès des femmes à la culture,* 692–693.

72. Maire, *Les Convulsionnaires de Saint-Médard,* 37. Translation taken from David A. Bell, "The 'Public Sphere,' the State, and the World of Law in Eighteenth-Century France," *French Historical Studies* 17 (1992): 930.

73. Maire, *Les Convulsionnaires de Saint-Médard,* 88–89, 119–123, 153–154; idem, *De la cause de Dieu,* 261–263, 295–296, 311–312.

74. *La femme docteur; ou la théologie tombée en Quénouille* (Avignon: Pierre Sincère, n.d.). In his many pieces against the convulsionary movement, Dom La Taste argued that the "miracles" were the result of women's innate tendency to deceive. *Vingtième Lettre théologique aux écrivains défenseurs des convulsions, et autres prétendus miracles du tems* (n.p., n.d.), 1198.

75. [Jacques-Philippe Lallement], *Entretiens de Madame la Comtesse *** au sujet des affaires présentes, par rapport à la religion* (n.p., 1734), 68.

76. *Lettres des dames de la paroisse de saint-Louis dans l'îsle au R. P. le Fevre Jésuite* (n.p., n.d.); *Troisième Lettre des cent-une dames* (n.p., n.d.).

77. Lindsay Wilson, *Women and Medicine in the French Enlightenment: the Debate over Maladies des Femmes* (Baltimore: Johns Hopkins University Press, 1993), 18–19. For an example of a Jansenist fiercely opposed to the convulsionaries, see [Armande-Isabelle Duguet-Mol], *Journal historique des convulsions du tems* (n.p., n.d.).

78. Timmermans, *L'Accès des femmes à la culture,* 745.

79. Michel-Ange Marin, *La Parfaite religieuse: ouvrage également utile à toutes les personnes qui aspirent à la perfection* (1746; Marseilles: Jean Mossy, 1832), 5.

80. Timmermans, *L'Accès des femmes à la culture,* 740.

81. *Mémoires pour servir à l'histoire de Port-Royal par M. du Fossé* (Utrecht: Aux dépens de la Compagnie, 1739), ix; Maire, "Port-Royal," 497.

82. *Lettre d'un théologien célèbre à une dame religieuse sur Port-Royal des Champs,* 3.

83. *Refutation d'un libelle intitulé: la Voix du sage et du peuple* (n.p., 1751), 23. This pamphlet was the Jansenist response to Voltaire's incendiary *La Voix du sage* (1750) calling for the

abolition of monasteries and denouncing the church in general. See chapter 5 for a lengthier discussion.

84. *Lettres édifiantes*, 13.
85. *Vies intéressantes et édifiantes*, 1:5.
86. Third letter, in *Lettres apologétiques*, 65.
87. [Jean-Baptiste Gaultier], *Refutation de la captivité de la soeur Marie des Forges, dites des Anges, religieuse annonciade de Boulogne, morte à Paris le 11 decembre 1739* (n.p., 1741), 3.
88. Gary Kates, *Monsieur d'Eon Is a Woman: A Tale of Political Intrigue and Sexual Masquerade* (New York: Basic Books, 1995), 261.
89. [Pierre Guilbert], *Mémoires historiques et chronologiques sur l'abbaye de Port-Royal-des-Champs* (Utrecht, 1755), 15.
90. *Lettres édifiantes*, 13; *NE*, April 17, 1750, 63; first letter of *Lettres apologétiques*, 12, 40.
91. Timmermans, *L'Accès des femmes à la culture*, 736–737.
92. *NE*, May 22, 1751, 82 n.
93. "Quatrième Remonstrance des fidèles du diocèse de Troïes . . . au sujet des religieuses" (n.p., n.d.), 53, 56.
94. *Lettres édifiantes*, 12–13.
95. Sedgwick, *Jansenism in Seventeenth-Century France*, 194.
96. Jean-Pierre Chantin, *Le Jansénisme: entre hérésie imaginaire et résistance catholique (XVIIe–XVIIIe siècle)* (Paris: Editions du Cerf, 1996), 63–68.
97. Merry Wiesner, *Women and Gender in Early Modern Europe* (Cambridge: Cambridge University Press, 1993), 195–203; R. Po-Shia Hsia, *The World of Catholic Renewal* (Cambridge: Cambridge University Press, 1998), 33–41.
98. Caroline Walker Bynum, "'And Woman His Humanity': Female Imagery in the Religious Writing of the Later Middle Ages," in *Fragmentation and Redemption: Essays on Gender and the Human Body in Medieval Religion* (New York: Zone Books, 1992), 157–166; the quotation is taken from 166.
99. Second letter, *in Lettres apologétiques*, 22. See also *Apologie sommaire*, 71; *Relations des refus de sacremens*, v; *Lettre d'un théologien*, 6.
100. Maire points out that in general, Jansenist curés taught figurist principles to girls who attended schools in certain Parisian parishes, such as Saint-Jacques-du-Haut-Pas. Moreover, certain convents in Paris served as "offices" for the *Nouvelles ecclésiastiques*. *De la cause de Dieu*, 119, 158.
101. Sister Saint-Louis to Saint-Hilaire, n.d., BPR, LP, ms. 542. On Sister Saint-Louis, see Augustin Gazier, *Une Suite à l'histoire de Port-Royal* (Paris: Société Française d'Imprimerie et de Libraire, 1906), 15–20.
102. NE, May 22, 1751, 82; Lallement's emphasis.
103. Maire, *De la cause de Dieu;* Campbell, *Power and Politics in Old Regime France;* Van Kley, *Religious Origins of the French Revolution;* idem, *The Damiens Affair and the Unraveling of the Ancien Régime, 1750–1770* (Princeton, N.J.: Princeton University Press, 1984); idem, *Jansenists and the Expulsion of the Jesuits;* David A. Bell, *Lawyers and Citizens: The Making of a Political Elite in Old Regime France* (New York: Oxford University Press, 1994); Jeffrey Merrick, *The Desacralization of the French Monarchy in the Eighteenth Century* (Baton Rouge: Louisiana University Press, 1990).
104. Much of this discussion is taken from Van Kley, *Religious Origins of the French Revolution*, chap. 2; Merrick, *Desacralization of the French Monarchy*, chap. 3.
105. Merrick, *Desacralization of the French Monarchy*, 64.
106. Monique Cottret, *Jansénisme et lumières: pour un autre XVIIIe siècle* (Paris: Albin Michel, 1998), 280–281. François A. Isambert, ed., *Recueil des anciennes lois françaises*, 29 vols. (Paris: Blin et Le Prieur, 1821–25), 20:249.
107. Jules Flammermont, *Remontrances du Parlement de Paris au XVIIIe siècle*, vol. 60, pt. 1, *Collection de documents inédits sur l'histoire de France* (Paris: Imprimerie Nationale, 1888), 267.
108. Cottret, *Jansénisme et lumières*, 282.
109. Van Kley, *Religious Origins of the French Revolution*, 135
110. Edmond J. F. Barbier, *Journal historique et anecdotique du règne de Louis XV*, 4 vols. (Paris: Jules Renouard, 1847), 3:417. For a very brief history of Ste. Agathe, see Biver, *Abbayes, monastères, couvents de femmes*, 328.

111. Maire, *De la cause de Dieu,* 158; Kreiser, *Miracles, Convulsions and Ecclesiastical Politics,* 250–251.
112. "Mémoire de ce qui s'est passé a St. Médard à l'occasion de la maladie de la soeur du Pays fille de sa communauté de Ste. Agathe," BA, AB, 10183.
113. Ibid. In addition to Hardy de Lavaré's *mémoire* noted above, see also correspondence between Hardy de Lavaré and the archbishop of Paris, October 24, 1742, and from Hardy de Lavaré to d'Argenson, November 2, 1742, BA, AB, 10183.
114. Garrioch, *Formation of the Parisian Bourgeoisie,* 33–41.
115. See also a letter from d'Argenson to Berryer dated December 24, 1752, BA, AB, 10183.
116. Eight days earlier, Hardy de Lavaré had demanded that Sister Thècle provide a *billet de confession* with the name of her confessor, a request the ailing nun rejected; as a result, Sister Thècle died on December 5 without having received the sacraments. Bibliothèque du Sénat, Registres de la première Chambre des Enquêtes (1752–1754) (hereafter BS, RCE), ms. 722, fol. 99, 106; *NE,* March 6, 1753, 38; Bibliothèque Nationale de France, Fonds Joly de Fleury (hereafter BNF, JF), ms. 1569, fol. 1–141; BPR, LP, ms. 512, "Journal du Parlement 1740–1756," fols. 198–287. Archives Nationales (hereafter AN), U 1098, no. 4. The *Nouvelles ecclésiastiques* (February 28, 1753, 35) identified the individual who denounced Hardy de Lavaré as the abbé Baurry, counselor.
117. Garrioch, *Formation of the Parisian Bourgeoisie,* 37ff.
118. According to the nineteenth-century institutional historian Marcel Marion, Sister Perpétue was not ill, and the whole affair was a setup designed to draw out Beaumont. "La Rédaction des Grandes Remontrances de 1753," *Annales de la faculté des lettres de Bordeaux* (1893): 136.
119. Barbier, *Journal historique,* 3:418; Marquis d'Argenson, *Journal et mémoires du marquis D'Argenson,* ed. E. J. B. Rathery, 9 vols. (Paris: Jules Renouard, 1859), 7:356.
120. NE, March 6, 1753, 37.
121. Barbier, *Journal historique,* 3:417–429; d'Argenson, *Journal et mémoires,* 7:355–381.
122. In letters dated December 23 and 24, 1752, police lieutenant d'Argenson wrote that the removal of Sister Perpétue was delayed because it might provoke "a new uproar." BA, AB, 10183.
123. *Supplément à la Gazette d'Utrecht,* January 9, 1753, 2.
124. Ibid., January 3, 1753, 1–2. In a letter of February 15, 1753, to d'Argenson, Boyer stated that the *Gazette,* in fact, had lied, and he described the paper as a "public nuisance" that confused facts. BA, AB, 10183.
125. AN, G9 80, fol. 37
126. Jacques Parguez, *La Bulle "Unigenitus" et la jansénisme politique* (Paris: Les Presses Modernes, 1936), 137.
127. For more detailed discussions, see Bell, *Lawyers and Citizens,* 115–116; Van Kley, *Religious Origins of the French Revolution,* 137–144.
128. On Beaumont, see Pierre Chaunu, Madeleine Foisil, and Françoise de Noirfontaine, *Le Basculement religieux de Paris au XVIIIe siècle* (Paris: Fayard, 1998), 243–251.
129. On the controversies over taxation at the end of the 1740s, see Merrick, *Desacralization of the French Monarchy,* 72–77. Bibliothèque de la Ville de Paris (hereafter BHVP), ms. 650, fol. 403.
130. Maire, *De la cause de Dieu,* 373.
131. Van Kley, *Jansenists and the Expulsion of the Jesuits,* 57–60; Maire, *De la cause de Dieu,* 414–415.
132. Bell, *Lawyers and Citizens,* 72. On the Parlement of Paris, see Lucien Goldmann, *Le Dieu caché: étude sur la vision tragique dans les pensées de Pascal et dans le théâtre de Racine* (Paris, 1955); Van Kley, *Jansenists and the Expulsion of the Jesuits,* 42–57.
133. "Chanson sur le Parlement sur l'air 'Du cap de bonne espérance,'" BHVP, ms. 651, fol. 76.
134. Maire, *De la cause de Dieu,* 418.
135. BPR, LP, ms. 627, fols. 61–62.
136. Le Paige to Saint-Hilaire, April 12, 1758, BPR, LP, ms. 542. The affair of the Religieuses Hospitalières centered around Christophe de Beaumont's refusal to allow the nuns to elect a new mother superior.

137. Elie Carcassonne, *Montesquieu et le problème de la constitution française au XVIIIe siècle* (1927; reprint, Geneva: Slaktine Reprints, 1970), 382–383.
138. Lisa Jane Graham, *If the King Only Knew: Seditious Speech in the Reign of Louis XV* (Charlottesville: University of Virginia Press, 2000).
139. Thomas Kaiser, "Madame de Pompadour and the Theaters of Power," *French Historical Studies* 14 (1996): 1025–1044; idem, "Louis *le Bien-Aimé* and the Rhetoric of the Royal Body," in *From the Royal to the Republican Body: Incorporating the Political in Seventeenth- and Eighteenth-Century France*, ed. Sara E. Melzer and Kathryn Norberg (Berkeley: University of California Press, 1998), 131–162
140. D'Argenson, *Journal et mémoires*, 6:342.
141. Graham, *If the King Only Knew*, 82. See also Sarah Maza, *Private Lives and Public Affairs: The Causes Célèbres of Prerevolutionary France* (Berkeley: University of California, 1993), 169–170, 210–211.
142. According to one police report, the superior and rector protected Jansenism "openly." BA, AB, 10171.
143. A more detailed account is contained in Henri Legier Desgranges, *Madame de Moysan et l'extravagante affaire de l'Hôpital-Général (1749–1758)* (Paris: Hachette, 1958).
144. D'Argenson, *Journal et mémoires*, 6:23.
145. The full title of the poem is "Epitre à très haute tous puissant et maintenant tous vertueuse Dame Urbine Robin veuve et nouvelle supérieure de la Salpetrière, Bicêtre, la Pitié, Scipion et autres lieux," in [Nicolas Jouin], *Le Vrai recueil des sarcelles, mémoires, notes et anecdotes intéressantes sur la conduite de l'archevêque de Paris et de quelques prélats françois*, 2 vols. (Amsterdam: Aux dépens de la Compagnie, 1766), 2:196–202. For the article in question, see *NE*, March 20, 1750, 45.
146. "Vers sur M. l'archevêque de Paris (Beaumont) à l'occasion de l'affaire entre luy, et le Parlement sur l'administration des hôpitaux," BNF, Ms. Fr., 15155, fols. 99–100.
147. BPR, LP, ms. 512, fol. 234. See also *NE*, March 6, 1753, 40. The report in the *Nouvelles* leaves out the word "caprice."
148. *NE*, March 6, 1753, 38. The *Nouvelles* reported the debates in these meetings in great detail, which were likely provided by Adrien Le Paige. See BPR, LP, ms. 512, fols. 216, 218–219.
149. Flammermont, *Remonstrances du Parlement*, 531.
150. Ibid., 596.
151. Ibid., 550–551, 568, 596.
152. Ibid., 596–597. A comparable assertion was made in the April 15, 1752, remonstrance about "the pious girls who, solely occupied with God and their salvation in the depths of their retreat, lived through the most rigorous acts of penitence, [are] treated like refractors." Ibid., 496.
153. Ibid., 596–597.
154. J. Michael Haydon has noted that while gender was an important component of ecclesiastical policies of the seventeenth-century Gallican church, the French early modern laity did not make gender distinctions, considering women religious and male clerics all to be members of the First Order. However, I would suggest that the early modern laity was indeed sensitive to gender differences as indicated in the "Great Remonstrances." J. Michael Haydon, "States, Estates and Orders: The *Qualité* of Female Clergy in Early Modern France," *French History* 8 (1994): 51–76. See also J. Michael Haydon and Malcolm R. Greenshields, "The Clergy of Early Seventeenth-Century France: Self-Perception and Society's Perception," *French Historical Studies* 18 (1993): 157.
155. BPR, LP, ms. 512, fol. 287.
156. Flammermont, *Remonstrances du Parlement*, 601. A similar comment had been made earlier about "their entire submission [of women religious] to the Church and the innocence of their morals." Ibid., 597.
157. Ibid., 602.
158. Ibid., 597.
159. Much of Thomas Kaiser's work has examined the growing critique of Louis XV. See also Arlette Farge, *Subversive Words: Public Opinion in Eighteenth-Century France*, trans. Rosemary Morris (University Park: Pennsylvania State University Press, 1995), 125–199; Lisa

Jane Graham, "Crimes of Opinion: Policing the Public in Eighteenth-Century Paris," in *Visions and Revisions of Eighteenth-Century France*, ed. Christine Adams, Jack R. Censer and Lisa Jane Graham (University Park: Pennsylvania State University Press, 1997), 79–103.

160. Flammermont, *Remonstrances du Parlement*, 587, 589.

161. BHVP, ms. 651, fol. 234. The translated title of the piece is "Lettre de cachet from the public to the king, in response to those His Majesty addressed to the officers of the Parlement of Paris the night of 8 or 9 May 1753"; it refers specifically to the exile of the magistrates.

162. This statement was made December 15, 1752. BS, RCE, ms. 722, fol. 113; BPR, LP, ms. 512, fol. 235.

163. BS, RCE, ms. 722, fol. 128; BPR, LP, ms. 512, fols. 269–270.

164. Merrick, *Desacralization of the French Monarchy*, 33.

165. Ibid., 95–96; idem, "Conscience and Citizenship in Eighteenth-Century France," *Eighteenth-Century Studies* 21 (1987): 48–71.

166. *Pièces concernant le bref de N. S. Père le pape Clément XII*, 13.

167. Gail Bossenga, "Rights and Citizens in the Old Regime," *French Historical Studies* 20 (1997): 217–218.

168. Dale Van Kley, ed., *The French Idea of Freedom: The Old Regime and the Declaration of Rights of 1789* (Stanford: Stanford University Press, 1994).

169. David A. Bell, *The Cult of the Nation in France: Inventing Nationalism, 1680–1800* (Cambridge: Harvard University Press, 2001); Van Kley, *Religious Origins of the French Revolution*.

170. Bell, "The 'Public Sphere,'" 930.

171. BNF, JF, ms. 1569, fols. 8–9.

172. NE, April 3, 1753, 53.

173. Jeffrey Merrick, "Subjects and Citizens in the Remonstrances of the Parlement of Paris in the Eighteenth Century," *Journal of the History of Ideas* 51 (1990): 459.

174. Ibid., 455–456.

175. Flammermont, *Remonstrances du Parlement*, 609.

176. On the Religieuses Hospitalières, see BPR, LP, ms. 542, 543; BNF, JF, ms. 367, fols. 99–104; AN, U1106, fols. 98–101; Gazier, *Une Suite à l'histoire de Port-Royal*. On the Ursuline affair at Saint-Cloud, see BPR, LP, ms. 540; BNF, JF, ms. 1545; *NE*, May 2, 1766, 73–76; May 8, 1766, 77–80. On the conflict in the Hôtel-Dieu, see BNF, JF, ms. 455; *NE*, July 18, 1769, 115–116; November 28, 1769, 189–192; December 5, 13, 1769, 197–200. On the Ursulines of Mans, see *Mémoire à consulter pour les religieuses Ursulines de la ville du Mans* (n.p., n.d.). The brief was signed by anti-Maupeou lawyers such as Gabriel-Nicolas Maultrot and André Blonde.

3. Despotic Habits

1. *Nouvelles ecclésiastiques, ou mémoires pour servir l'histoire de la bulle Unigenitus* (hereafter NE), October 16, 1777, 167.

2. See Sara Chapman, "Patronage as Family Economy: The Role of Women in the Patron-Client Network of the Phélypeaux de Pontchatrain Family, 1670–1715," *French Historical Studies* 24 (2001): 11–35; Natalie Zemon Davis, *Society and Culture in Early Modern France: Eight Essays* (Stanford: Stanford University Press, 1975), 70–71.

3. Gillet, Cellier, De Lambon, D'Outrement, Aubry, Mey, Vulpian, and Leon, *Mémoire à consulter* (Paris: Simon, 1769), 11–12. This *mémoire* was written sometime after August 27, 1770, and it pertains to a high-profile case involving the priory of Bon Secours. In the late 1760s Madame de Saillant became prioress through a papal bull. Her appointment became controversial because it violated the terms of Louis XIV's 1695 Edict of Blois which stated that an individual could not take possession of a benefice without presenting herself before the diocesan bishop or archbishop. See Bibliothèque Nationale de France, Fonds Joly de Fleury (hereafter BNF, JF), ms. 469, fols. 259–304; BNF, JF, ms. 1604, fols. 9–60; Archives Nationales (hereafter AN), S 4590.

4. Geneviève Reynes, *Couvents de femmes: la vie des religieuses cloîtrées dans la France des XVIIe et XVIIIe siècles* (Paris: Fayard, 1987), 77–78.

5. On the various attacks against Pompadour, see Thomas Kaiser, "Madame de Pom-

padour and the Theaters of Power," *French Historical Studies* 14 (1996): 1025–1044; Madelyn Gutwirth, *The Twilight of the Goddesses: Women and Representations in the French Revolutionary Era* (New Brunswick, N.J.: Rutgers University Press, 1992), 79–84.

6. Lisa Jane Graham, *If the King Only Knew: Seditious Speech in the Reign of Louis XV* (Charlottesville: University of Virginia Press, 2000), 58.

7. As cited in Dale Van Kley, *The Jansenists and the Expulsion of the Jesuits from France, 1757–1765* (New Haven: Yale University Press, 1975), 110. This statement, referring to the superior general (the head of the Jesuits), was made by the abbé Chauvelin, who delivered an address on the Jesuits before the Parlement of Paris on April 17, 1761.

8. As cited in ibid., 218. A lengthy discussion of D'Alembert's piece and the Jansenist responses may be found in ibid., 208–228.

9. One of the most famous incidents, which never involved a trial, was the Jansenist attack in 1749 on Madame de Moysan, the new superior of the Hôpital général (see chapter 2). Another superior, Madame de Rossignol, was the source of conflict for over a decade starting in the mid-1740s. First, as abbess of Malnoue, she precipitated the abbey's suppression and subsequent reunion with the priory of Bon Secours, which the nuns of Malnoue opposed. See AN, G9 80, no. 13; G9 81, no. 9; G9 78, no. 185; BNF, JF, ms. 469, fols. 257–259; Henry Cochin, *Memoire à consulter pour les dames religieuses de l'abbaye royale de Malnoue, opposantes à l'enregistrement des lettres patentes obtenues sur le decret d'union* (Paris, 1746). In 1759 the nuns of Bon Secours again quarreled with Madame Rossignol over the admission of a novice. See Gerbière de la Massillaye, *Mémoire pour dames Genevieve Carré de St. Paul, Marie-Louise de Boiscourjon de Saint-Arsenne et conforts, religieuses professes du couvent de Bon Secours* (Paris: Simon 1759).

10. Duclosel, *Requête présentée à monsieur l'official par les dames ALBANEL, BRUNEL et GASCHIER, religieuses de l'abbaye royale de Beaumont contre LA dame de LANTILLAC leur abbesse, et la dame de SEDIERES* (Clermont-Ferrand: Viallaner 1764), 14. On the Saint-Cloud affair, see Bibliothèque de Port-Royal, Collection Le Paige, ms. 540; BNF, JF, ms. 1545; *NE,* May 2, 1766, 73–76; May 8, 1766, 77–80. The lawyers also referred to the 1720s conflict between the abbess of Maubuisson and her community; Henry Cochin, *Oeuvres de feu M. Cochin, écuyer, avocat au Parlement, contenant le recueil de ses mémoires et consultations,* 6 vols. (Paris: De Nully, 1751–57), 6:493–501; A. Marsy, *Les Abbesses de Maubuisson* (Paris: J.B. Dumoulin, 1868), 10.

11. BNF, JF, ms. 1849, fol. 206.

12. My account of this trial is taken from the records found in BNF, JF, ms. 1849, fols. 174–360.

13. For a copy of the bishop's *règlement,* see BNF, JF, ms. 1849, fols. 207, 217.

14. Jean-Prosper Duvert d'Emalleville, *Mémoire pour Marie-Thérèse de Lantilhac, abbesse de l'abbaye royale de Saint-Pierre de Beaumont-des-Clermont, Auvergne, appellante* (Paris: Veuve Quillau, 1764), 98.

15. *Arrest de la cour du parlement du 21 Juillet 1764* (Paris: Louis Cellot, 1764).

16. Correspondences contained in the Joly de Fleury collection and within the *mémoires judiciaires* indicate that the scandal achieved a great deal of notoriety in Clermont-Ferrand and throughout Auvergne. While Louis Petit de Bachaumont's *Mémoires secrets* and newspapers such as the *Courrier d'Avignon* and the *Gazette de Leyde* did not carry the story, internal evidence from the legal briefs, as well as a revolutionary pamphlet titled *La Chemise levée,* suggest otherwise. See BNF, JF, ms. 1849, fols. 229, 239; Duclosel, *Requête présentée à monsieur l'official,* 1–2, 18; Pierre-Daniel-Jean Le Roy de Fontenelle, *Mémoire aux chambres assemblées, pour les dames Albanel, Brunel et Gaschier, religieuses professes de l'abbaye royale de Beaumont contre dame Marie-Thérèse, abbesse de ladite abbaye* (Paris: Louis Cellot, 1764), 7, 10; *La Chemise levée, ou visites faites à l'abbaye de Montmartre, dans plusieurs maisons religieuses, et avec une idée sur la nécessité, si l'on veut extirper le despotisme* (n.p., 1789), 1.

17. Joly de Fleury's papers note that Le Gouvé was representing the nuns Albanel, Gaschier, Brunel, the Veisset sisters, Grandpré, Martinet, Maisson, and Gras before the Parlement of Paris; BNF, JF, ms. 1849, fols. 175, 207. On Jean-Baptiste Le Gouvé (1730–82), see Van Kley, *Jansenists and the Expulsion of the Jesuits,* 100, 102, 109; idem, *The Damiens Affair and the Unraveling of the "Ancien Régime," 1750–1757* (Princeton, N.J.: Princeton University Press, 1984), 91–92.

18. For an inventory of French literature on nuns from the early Middle Ages through the first half of the twentieth century, see Jeanne Ponton, *La Religieuse dans la littérature française* (Québec: Presses de l'Université Laval, 1969), 364–424. An even more exhaustive list of eighteenth-century novels may be found in Daniel R. Dupêcher, "L'Image du couvent dans le roman français du XVIIIe siècle" (Ph.D. diss., Princeton University, 1973), 399–414.

19. The police kept a file on the *pensionnaires* of Longchamp. Bibliothèque Galante, *Notes secrètes pour l'abbaie de Longchamp en 1768* (Paris: Emile Voitelaire, 1870).

20. Sarah Maza, "Luxury, Morality, and Social Change: Why There Was No Middle-Class Consciousness in Prerevolutionary France," *Journal of Modern History* 69 (1997): 216–221.

21. *A monsieur le lieutenant-général en la sénéchaussée d'Auvergne à Clermont* (n.p., n.d.), 2. The authorship is unclear, although it was commissioned by the nuns and signed by *procureur* Boyer. The references to royal and ecclesiastical decrees indicate the author's familiarity with the legal world, a familiarity most likely possessed by Monsieur Béraud, the brother-in-law of one of the nuns, Madame de Grandpré; the abbess accused Béraud and his wife of influencing the nuns against her.

22. The only known rank is that of Madame de Grandpré, whose grandfather was a general and whose brother-in-law, Monsieur Béraud, was attached to the Cour des Aides. Le Roy de Fontenelle, *Mémoire aux chambres assemblées*, 13. BNF, JF, ms. 1849, fol. 211.

23. On luxury in the eighteenth century, see Maza, "Luxury, Morality, and Social Change," 216–221; Pierre Rétat, "Luxe," *Dix-Huitième Siècle* 26 (1994): 79–88. On the association with libertine behavior and aristocracy, see Jeffrey Merrick, "Sexual Politics in Late Eighteenth-Century France: The *Mémoires secrets* and the *Correspondance secrète*," *Journal of the History of Sexuality* 1 (1990): 68–84.

24. *A monsieur le lieutenant-général*, 2.

25. Maza, "Luxury, Morality, and Social Change," 217.

26. Le Roy de Fontenelle, *Mémoire aux chambres assemblées*, 5. See also *A monsieur le lieutenant-général*, 2; Duclosel, *Requête présentée à monsieur l'official*, 3–7.

27. Le Roy de Fontenelle, *Mémoire aux chambres assemblées*, 7.

28. Duclosel, *Requête présentée à monsieur l'official*, 3, 8, 30.

29. Jean-Jacques Rousseau, *Lettre à M. d'Alembert sur son article "Genève"* (Paris, 1967), 116–117.

30. Ibid. On the negative image of actresses and their powers, see Lenard R. Berlanstein, "Women and Power in Eighteenth-Century France: Actresses at the Comédie-Française," in *Visions and Revisions of Eighteenth-Century France*, ed. Christine Adams, Jack R. Censor, and Lisa Jane Graham (University Park: Pennsylvania State University Press, 1997), 155–190; idem, *Daughters of Eve: A Cultural History of French Theater Women from the Old Regime to the Fin de Siècle* (Cambridge: Harvard University Press, 2001), 33–83. See also Jeffrey Ravel, "Actress to Activist: Mlle Clairon in the Public Sphere of the 1760s," *Theatre Survey* 35 (1994): 73–86.

31. Sarah Maza, *Private Lives and Public Affairs: The Causes Célèbres of Prerevolutionary France* (Berkeley: University of California, 1993), 169. See also John Shovlin, "The Cultural Politics of Luxury in Eighteenth-Century France," *French Historical Studies* 23 (2000): 577–606.

32. Thomas Brennan has suggested that in general, early modern French elites linked excessive alcohol consumption to the lower classes and tavern life. See Brennan, *Public Drinking and Popular Culture in Eighteenth-Century Paris* (Princeton, N.J.: Princeton University Press, 1988); idem, "Social Drinking in Old Regime France," in *Drinking: Behavior and Belief in Modern History*, ed. Susanna Barrows (Berkeley: University of California Press, 1991), 61–86. However, accusations of drinking were not always restricted to non-elites. In the 1730s there was also much public anxiety about Louis XV's drinking. Thomas E. Kaiser, "Louis *le Bien-Aimé* and the Rhetoric of the Royal Body," in *From the Royal to the Republican Body: Incorporating the Political in Seventeenth- and Eighteenth-Century France*, ed. Sara E. Melzer and Kathryn Norberg (Berkeley: University of California Press, 1998), 142.

33. Le Roy de Fontenelle, *Mémoire aux chambres assemblées*, 7; Duclosel, *Requête présentée à monsieur l'official*, 4.

34. Duclosel, *Requête présentée à monsieur l'official*, 10.
35. Le Roy de Fontenelle, *Mémoire aux chambres assemblées*, 7–8.
36. For a historically grounded discussion of oriental despotism, see Thomas Kaiser, "The Evil Empire? The Debate on Turkish Despotism in Eighteenth-Century French Political Culture," *Journal of Modern History* 72 (2000): 6–34. Alain Grosrichard, *Structure du sérail: la fiction du despotisme asiatique dans l'occident classique* (Paris: Seuil, 1979), 96.
37. René-Louis de Voyer de Paulmy, marquis d'Argenson, *Journal et mémoires du marquis d'Argenson*, ed. E. J. B. Rathery, 9 vols. (Paris, 1857–67), 6:342; 7:400.
38. Thomas Kaiser has noted that this "perception of Pompadour as the seducer and usurper of sovereign authority" was rampant within the Parisian populace. Kaiser, "Madame de Pompadour," 1040.
39. *A monsieur le lieutenant-général*, 2
40. Ibid., 3.
41. Duclosel, *Requête présentée à monsieur l'official*, 3.
42. Ibid., 19. There were also accusations that the abbess and her sister seduced other nuns to support them. Ibid., 33
43. Ibid., 31.
44. The full text from the *mémoire judiciaire* written for the abbess states the following: "A nun belongs to her abbess as does a daughter to her mother. A mother would be acting very reasonably to forbid a daughter under her power all conversation, even with the closest relatives, if the effect of these conversations [on the nun] was to sour tempers, corrupt the heart, or to engage in a conspiracy against her own mother." Duvert d'E-malleville, *Mémoire pour Marie-Thérèse de Lantilhac*, 70; Le Roy de Fontenelle, *Mémoire aux chambres assemblées*, 33.
45. *A monsieur le lieutenant-général*, 2.
46. Duclosel, *Requête présentée à monsieur l'official*, 4; Le Roy de Fontenelle, *Mémoire aux chambres assemblées*, 9.
47. Cissie Fairchilds, "Women and Family," in *French Women and the Age of Enlightenment*, ed. Samia I. Spencer (Bloomington: University of Indiana Press, 1984), 103.
48. During his childhood, Louis XV received instruction from his tutor, the future Cardinal Fleury, on the values of being a paternalistic monarch, loved and not feared by his subjects. Kaiser, "Louis *le Bien-Aimé*," 137–138.
49. Jeffrey Merrick, "Patriarchalism and Constitutionalism in Eighteenth-Century Parlementary Discourse," *Studies in Eighteenth-Century Culture* 20 (1990): 317–330.
50. Ibid., 321.
51. Antoine-Gabriel Gravière du Rauloy, *Mémoire à consulter; et consultation sur l'excommunication des Religieuses Hospitalières du faubourg Saint-Marcel* [Paris, 1756], 18. For a more detailed analysis of the *mémoire*, see Sumita Choudhury, "School of Virtue, School of Vice: Convents and Nuns in French Thought and Culture, 1740–1794" (Ph.D. diss., Northwestern University, 1997), 119–145.
52. Lieselotte Steinbrügge, *The Moral Sex: Woman's Nature in the French Enlightenment*, trans. Pamela E. Selwyn (New York: Oxford University Press, 1995), 30–34; Gutwirth, *Twilight of the Goddesses*, 51–66.
53. A few months before the Beaumont affair, the Parlement of Paris was hearing the vocation forcée trial of René Lelievre, a monk from the Abbey of Sainte-Geneviève. Claude-Christophe Courtin, *Mémoire pour René Le Lievre, prétendu chanoine-regulier de la congrégation de France, appellant comme d'abus et demandeur* (Paris, [1764]), 44. The sovereign courts ruled against Lelievre. *Arrest de la Cour de Parlement dans cause entre René LE LIEVRE, et les supérieurs de la congrégation des chanoines réguliers de France du 16 Avril 1764* (Paris, 1764).
54. Le Roy de Fontenelle, *Mémoire aux chambres assemblées*, 10. He also evoked the infamous *lettre de cachet*.
55. Jeffrey Merrick, *The Desacralization of the French Monarchy in the Eighteenth Century* (Baton Rouge: Louisiana State University Press, 1990), 83.
56. Duclosel applauded his clients for correctly construing this right to the sacraments as "a law of the church, but [also] a law authorized by the prince, a law on which one could not infringe." Duclosel, *Requête présentée à monsieur l'official*, 21–22. Le Roy de Fontenelle

presented similar arguments regarding the freedom to choose a confessor (*Mémoires aux chambres assemblées*, 51).

57. Duclosel, *Requête présentée à monsieur l'official*, 12.

58. On the *mort civile*, see Elizabeth Rapley, *The Dévotes: Women and Church in Seventeenth-Century France* (Montreal: McGill-Queen's University Press, 1990), 39.

59. Le Roy de Fontenelle, *Mémoire aux chambres assemblées*, 10.

60. Duclosel, *Requête présentée à monsieur l'official*, 12.

61. Duvert d'Emalleville, *Mémoire pour Marie-Thérèse de Lantilhac*, 75; Le Roy de Fontenelle, *Mémoire aux chambres assemblées*, 38.

62. Le Roy de Fontenelle, *Mémoire aux chambres assemblées*, 38.

63. Ibid., 25; Duclosel, *Requête présentée à monsieur l'official*, 2, 16, 23.

64. Scholars such as Carole Pateman have suggested that the world of contractual theory and by extension the law itself was essentially masculinist. Carole Pateman, *The Sexual Contract* (Stanford: Stanford University Press, 1989), chap. 1. As Sarah Maza has suggested, from the 1760s to the 1790s "feminine Nature, characterized by deceit, seduction, and the selfish pursuit of private interest, was construed as the extreme antithesis of the abstract principles of reason made law that were to govern the public sphere." *Private Lives and Public Affairs*, 209, 211. See also Joan Landes, *Women in the Public Sphere in the Age of the French Revolution* (Ithaca, N.Y.: Cornell University Press, 1988), 67.

65. Duclosel, *Requête présentée à monsieur l'official*, 34.

66. Ibid., 24.

67. *A monsieur le lieutenant-général*, 5.

68. Le Roy de Fontenelle, *Mémoire aux chambres assemblées*, 9. Relatives included a nephew whose education was completed with an eighteen-month residence in the convent where "he had free access to all the dormitories, and where he renewed his infantile courses with the novices."

69. BNF, JF, ms. 1849, fol. 206.

70. Le Roy de Fontenelle, *Mémoire aux chambres assemblées*, 3; Duclosel, *Requête présentée à monsieur l'official*, 1.

71. Duclosel, *Requête présentée à monsieur l'official*, 14. Le Roy de Fontenelle, *Mémoire aux chambres assemblées*, 10.

72. Duclosel, *Requête présentée à monsieur l'official*, 34

73. Le Roy de Fontenelle, *Mémoire aux chambres assemblées*, 37.

74. Nadine Bérenguier, "Victorious Victims: Women and Publicity in *Mémoires Judiciaires*," in *Going Public: Women and Publishing in Early Modern France*, ed. Elizabeth C. Goldsmith and Dena Goodman (Ithaca, N.Y.: Cornell University Press, 1995), 62, 77. Bérenguier has argued that lawyers persistently shied at making grandiose demands calling for changes in marriage because it would upset the foundation of masculine power within the home. For a different perspective, see Sarah Hanley, "Social Sites of Political Practices in France: Lawsuits, Civil Rights, and the Separation of Powers in Domestic and State Government, 1500–1800," *American Historical Review* 102 (1997): 27–52.

75. Le Roy de Fontenelle, *Mémoire aux chambres assemblées*, 17–18.

76. There is a strong likelihood the nuns did compose the letters. In the *procureur-général*'s papers regarding the case there is a handwritten note by the nuns sent immediately after the parlement had issued its judgment regarding the case. BNF, JF, ms. 1849, fols. 232–233.

77. On the association of masculinity and the legal profession in Victorian America, see Michael Grossberg, "Institutionalizing Masculinity: The Law as a Masculine Profession," in *Meanings of Manhood: Constructions of Masculinity in Victorian America*, ed. Mark C. Carnes and Clyde Griffen (Chicago: University of Chicago Press, 1990), 133–151.

78. Le Roy de Fontenelle, *Mémoire aux chambres assemblées*, i.

79. Translation taken from Alan E. Astin, *Cato the Censor* (Oxford: Oxford University Press, 1978), 154.

80. Alan Brinton, "Quintilian, Plato, and the *Vir Bonus*," *Philosophy and Rhetoric* 16 (1983): 167–184.

81. David A. Bell, "The 'Public Sphere,' the State, and the World of Law in Eighteenth-Century France," *French Historical Studies* 17 (1992): 928. On the importance of this expres-

sion and the appeal of Cato in the early modern French legal milieu, see Marc Fumaroli, *L'Age de l'éloquence: rhétorique et "res literaria" de la Renaissance au seuil de l'époque classique* (Geneva: Droz, 1980), 320, 444, 465–66, 485, 557, 622.

82. Le Roy de Fontenelle, *Mémoire aux chambres assemblées*, i. On Portail (1674–1736), see Peter R. Campbell, *Power and Politics in Old Regime France, 1720–1745* (London: Routledge, 1996), 250–258.

83. Le Roy de Fontenelle, *Mémoire aux chambres assemblées*, i.

84. Ibid., 54.

85. Duclosel, "Mémoire de M. Duclosel pour Mademoiselle Duclosel sa fille, religieuse novice du Monastère de Montmartre," in AN, DXIX 25, no. 389. He signed off as an "active citizen of Auvergne." See also Marie-Françoise-Catherine Barbat Duclosel, *Mémoire présenté par Mlle. Duclozel novice prébendée du monastère du Montmartre* (Clermont-Ferrand, 1791).

86. The account of this trial is taken from BNF, JF, ms. 602, 159. The *Nouvelles ecclésiastiques* also included detailed accounts of the affair, printing articles on December 6, 1768; February 14, 1769; and July 18, 1769. At the very same time as the Parlement was hearing the Le Coq affair, it was also involved in the case of Madame de Saillant, prioress of Bon Secours. The bookseller Siméon-Prosper Hardy's journal contains several entries noting both trials. Bibliothèque Nationale de France, Fonds français, ms. 6680, April 14–15, 1768; April 21–22, 1768; and April 29, 1768.

87. Le Coq did not return to Saint-Nicolas without some resistance from Sesmaisons. See *NE*, July 18, 1769, 113–115. Sesmaisons also complained to Joly de Fleury that the nuns continued to disobey her. BNF, JF, ms. 1597, fols. 289–290.

88. Maza, *Private Lives and Public Affairs*, 281.

89. Jean-Baptiste Faré, *Plaidoyer pour le sieur Lecoq, marchand à Paris, Marie Louise Wantin, son épouse, et Marie-Anne Lecoq, leur fille* (n.p.: Knapen et Delaguette, 1769), 45.

90. For example, in the same year as the Pontoise affair, the sisters of the Hôtel-dieu in Paris were locked in combat over the election of a new superior. Sixty-seven nuns opposed the presence of two clerical onlookers, the abbés Luker and Lucas. The lawyers for the sixty-seven proposed changing the constitutions so that the new nuns would not have to submit to "an arbitrary government." Texier, Piet Duplessis, Maultrot, Le Paige, Aubry, Viard, Vanquetin, Mey, Piales, Camus, Jabineau, and de Santer, *A messieurs les doyens, chanoines et chapître* (Paris: Simon, 1769), 6. Many of the lawyers were prominent Jansenists, most of whom sided with the parlements during the Maupeou crisis. David A. Bell, *Lawyers and Citizens: The Making of a Political Elite in Old Regime France* (New York: Oxford University Press, 1994), 146. Documents relevant to the case may be found in BNF, JF, ms. 455, 602, 1216.

91. *Lettres concernant Madame de Sesmaisons, prieure de l'Hostel-Dieu de Pontoise* (n.p., 1769), 14.

92. Ibid., 11.

93. Henri Racine, *Mémoire pour la dame de Sesmaisons, ancienne abbesse de Bival, et prieuré de Saint-Nicolas de Pontoise et la mère de Saint-Clement, religieuse au même prieuré* (Paris: P. G. Simon, n.d.), 18.

94. Faré, *Plaidoyer pour le sieur Lecoq*, 25.

95. Ibid., 5, 2.

96. *NE*, February 14, 1769, 27.

97. Jean-Baptiste Faré, *Mémoire pour le sieur le Cocq, marchand à Paris, Marie-Louise Vantin, son épouse, et Marie-Anne Le Cocq, leur fille* (n.p.: Knapen et Delaguette, 1769), 4.

98. Keith Michael Baker, *Inventing the French Revolution: Essays on French Political Culture in the Eighteenth Century* (Cambridge: Cambridge University Press, 1990), 33–37. See also Dale Van Kley, *The Religious Origins of the French Revolution: From Calvin to the Civil Constitution* (New Haven: Yale University Press, 1996), 191–218.

99. As quoted in Van Kley, *Religious Origins of the French Revolution*, 204. According to Le Paige, the clerical efforts to weed out so-called Jansenism were the result of "fantasies" and "chimera." Louis-Adrien Le Paige, *Lettres historiques sur les fonctions essentielles du parlement, sur le droit des pairs, et sur les lois fondamentales du royaume*, 2 vols. (Amsterdam: Aux dépens de la Compagnie, 1753), 1:375.

100. Le Paige, *Lettres historiques*, 1: 34, 172.

101. Van Kley, *Jansenism and the Expulsion of the Jesuits*, 110.
102. Ibid., 35.
103. Indeed, the *Nouvelles ecclésiastiques* also recounted an incident in which Sesmaisons or-dered the nuns to read the works of the Spanish Jesuit Rodriguez instead of scripture. *NE*, February 14, 1769. Hardy also noted this fact in his journal. Bibliothèque Na-tionale de France, Fonds français, ms. 6680, 10 March 1769.
104. *NE*, December 6, 1769, 194–196; Faré, *Plaidoyer pour le sieur Lecoq*, 34.
105. Faré, *Plaidoyer pour le sieur Lecoq*, 13.
106. If there was any doubt as to who these monks were, Faré included a footnote stating Ses-maisons's familial connection to the Jesuits. Ibid., 34.
107. Faré, *Mémoire pour le sieur le Cocq*, 4, 10, 6, 11.
108. Ibid., 5.
109. Faré, *Plaidoyer pour le sieur Lecoq*, 20–21.
110. Ibid., 24.
111. Ibid., 43.
112. Faré, *Mémoire pour le sieur le Cocq*, 11.
113. Ibid., 48.
114. Faré, *Plaidoyer pour le sieur Lecoq*, 42, 43.
115. Ibid., 3.
116. Ibid., 2.
117. Faré, *Mémoire pour le sieur le Cocq*, 10.
118. Graham, *If the King Only Knew*, 164.
119. *Plaidoyer pour le sieur Lecoq*, 3.
120. François A. Isambert, ed., *Recueil des anciennes lois françaises*, 29 vols. (Paris: Blin et Le Prieur, 1821–1825), 22:476–482.
121. Suzanne Lemaire, *La Commission des réguliers, 1766–1780* (Paris: Société Anonyme de Receuil Sirey, 1926), 5.
122. *Arrêt du conseil d'état du roi, qui décharge les sieurs commissaires nommés pour l'exécution de l'arrêt du 19 avril 1727* (Paris: Imprimerie Royale, 1788). On the Commissions de Sec-ours, see the introduction.
123. BNF, JF, ms. 1849, fol. 234. This letter was a response to one by the nuns.
124. *La Chemise levée*, 1.
125. Huguette Cohen, "Jansenism in Diderot's *La Religieuse*," *Studies in Eighteenth-Century Culture* 11 (1982): 75–91.
126. On Maubuisson, see A. Dutilleux and J. Depoin, *L'Abbaye de Maubuisson (Notre Dame La Royale)* (Pontoise: Typographie de Amédée Paris, 1882). See also *NE*, June 12, 1783, 93–96.
127. Taking Jürgen Habermas's model concerning the emergence of the public sphere, Maza has argued "that the 'intimate' or 'particular' stories recounted in the causes célèbres briefs brought French readers together in a common concern with issues per-taining to private life." Maza, *Private Lives and Public Affairs*, 14.
128. Faré, *Plaidoyer pour le sieur Lecoq*, 47–49.

4. THE VOCATION FORCÉE IN FRENCH POLITICAL AND LITERARY CULTURE

1. Jean-Baptiste Faré, *Plaidoyer pour le sieur Lecoq, marchand à Paris, Marie Louise Wantin, son épouse, et Marie-Anne Lecoq, leur fille* (n.p.: Knapen et Delaguette, 1769), 1–2.
2. Claude Thévenot d'Essaule, *Mémoire pour demoiselle Marie-Michelle de Couhé de Lusignan, appelante comme d'abus, contre Dame Elisabeth de Couhé, intimée* (Paris: Paulus-du-Mesnil, 1752).
3. Brunet de Brou's *La Religieuse malgré elle*, first published in 1720, was reprinted in 1740 and again in 1751. Angus A. Martin and Vivienne Mylne, *Bibliographie du genre ro-manesque français, 1751–1800* (London: Mansell, 1977).
4. *Le Courrier du mardi*, July 10, 1764, 223; *Supplément aux nouvelles extraordinaires de divers endroits*, July 13, 1764, 4. Louis XV issued a *lettre de cachet* imprisoning the nun for the rest of her life.
5. Archives Nationales (hereafter AN), Z10, 220.

6. Elizabeth Rapley, "Women and the Religious Vocation in Seventeenth-Century France," *French Historical Studies* 18 (1994): 613–631. Jean de Viguerie, "La Vocation sacerdotale et religieuse aux XVIIe et XVIIIe siècles: la théorie et la réalité," in *La Vocation religieuse et sacerdotale en France: actes de la deuxième rencontre d'histoire religieuse de Fontevraud*, ed. Jean de Viguerie (Angers: Université d'Angers, 1979), 27–39. Barbara Diefendorf, "Give Us Back Our Children: Patriarchal Authority and Parental Consent to Religious Vocations in Early Counter-Reformation France," *Journal of Modern History* 68 (June 1996): 265–307.

7. Lucien Perey, ed., *Memoirs of the princesse de Ligne*, trans. Laura Ensor, 2 vols. (London: Richard Bentley and Son, 1887), 1:176.

8. Louis-Sébastien Mercier, *Tableau de Paris*, 12 vols. (Amsterdam, 1783–88), 7:98. Dominique Dinet, *Vocation et fidelité: le recrutement des réguliers dans les diocèses d'Auxerre, Langres et Dijon (XVIIe–XVIIIe)* (Paris: Economica, 1988), 219.

9. English Showalter Jr., *The Evolution of the French Novel, 1641–1782* (Princeton, N.J.: Princeton University Press, 1972), 303.

10. Sarah Maza, *Private Lives and Public Affairs: The Causes Célèbres of Prerevolutionary France* (Berkeley: University of California Press, 1993); Jeffrey Merrick, "The Family Politics of the Marquis de Bombelles," *Journal of Family History* 21 (1996): 503–518; Lynn Hunt, *The Family Romance of the French Revolution* (Berkeley: University of California, 1992).

11. Quotation taken from Sarah Maza, "Only Connect: Family Values in the Age of Sentiment: Introduction," *Eighteenth-Century Studies* 30 (1997): 208. The literature on the family in the early modern period is vast. The "classics" that have spawned research and debate include the following: Philippe Ariès, *L'Enfant et la vie familiale sous l'ancien régime* (Paris: Plon, 1960); Jean-Louis Flandrin, *Families in Former Times: Kinship, Household and Sexuality*, trans. Richard Southern (Cambridge: Cambridge University Press, 1979); Lawrence Stone, *The Family, Sex, and Marriage in England, 1500–1800* (New York: Harper and Row, 1977). For the different areas touched by familial issues in the eighteenth century, see the spring 1997 issue of *Eighteenth-Century Studies* titled "Family Values in the Age of Sentiment." For a study on how new ideals of the domestic family played out in actual families, see Christine Adams, *A Taste for Comfort and Status: A Bourgeois Family in Eighteenth-Century France* (University Park: Pennsylvania State University Press, 2000).

12. James F. Traer, *Marriage and the Family in Eighteenth-Century France* (Ithaca, N.Y.: Cornell University Press, 1980), 70–78; Carol Blum, *Strength in Numbers: Population, Reproduction, and Power in Eighteenth-Century France* (Baltimore: Johns Hopkins University Press, 2002), 61–76.

13. On the incarceration of wives, see Georg'Ann Cattelona, "The Regulation of Female Sexuality: The Hôpital du Réfuge in Marseille, 1640–1789" (Ph.D. diss., Indiana University, 1991).

14. Diefendorf, "Give Us Back Our Children," 274.

15. Bossuet touched on this theme in his funeral oration for Anne of Gonzagua in 1685. Jacques Bossuet, "Oration funèbre de Madame Anne de Gonzague de Clèves, princesse Palatine," *Oeuvres complètes de Bossuet, Evêque de Meaux*, 11 vols. (Paris: J. P. Migne, 1857), 7:1266.

16. Georges May, *Diderot et "La Religieuse"* (New Haven: Yale University Press, 1954), 169–178.

17. Jacques Bossuet, *Théologique sociale-politique tirée des propres paroles de l'écriture sainte*, in *Oeuvres complètes de Bossuet*, 11:507. For a brief discussion of Bossuet and patriarchalism, see Jeffrey Merrick, "The Body Politics of French Absolutism," in Sara E. Melzer and Kathryn Norberg, eds., *From the Royal to the Republican Body: Incorporating the Political in Seventeenth- and Eighteenth-Century France* (Berkeley: University of California Press, 1998), 11–31.

18. Sarah Hanley, "Engendering the State: Family Formation and State Building in Early Modern France," *French Historical Studies* 16 (1989): 4–27; idem, "Family and State in Early Modern France: The Marriage Pact," in *Connecting Spheres: Women in the Western Worlds, 1500 to the Present*, ed. Marilyn J. Boxer and Jean H. Quataert (Oxford: Oxford University Press, 1987).

19. Sarah Hanley, "A Juridical Formula for State Sovereignty: The French Marital Law Compact, 1550–1650," in *Le Second Ordre: l'idéal nobiliaire: hommage à Ellery Schalk*, ed. Chantal

Grell and Arnaud Ramière de Fortanier (Paris: Presses de l'Université de Paris–Sorbonne, 1999), 189–195; see also Traer, *Marriage and the Family in Eighteenth-Century France,* 32–34.

20. Julie Hardwick, *The Practice of Patriarchy: Gender and the Politics of Household Authority in Early Modern France* (University Park: Pennsylvania State University Press, 1998), 226

21. Rapley, "Women and the Religious Vocation in Seventeenth-Century France," 629; Viguerie, "La Vocation sacerdotale et religieuse," 27–39.

22. The family was known as Couhé, but the nun claimed that their full title was de Lusignan. In the following discussion, Couhé will be used for the mother and Lusignan for the daughter. The proceedings of this trial, including the various testimonials as well as the *mémoires judiciaires,* can be found at the Bibliothèque Nationale de France, Fonds Joly de Fleury (Hereafter BNF, JF), ms. 1814.

23. In 1731, four years after pronouncing her vows, Lusignan had attempted to discuss her case with a *procureur* from Poitiers. When the convent's superior learned about Lusignan's attempt to get legal assistance, she refused to allow her visitors. Thévenot d'Essaule, *Mémoire pour demoiselle Marie-Michelle de Couhé de Lusignan,* 13.

24. At this time, she was residing in the convent of the Petites-Cordelières in Paris, and therefore under the jurisdiction of the diocese of Paris.

25. The Gallican church stipulated that an individual wishing to reclaim his or her vows had the right to do so within the first five years after pronouncing those vows.

26. Lusignan's defense also proved that the letter was in fact a forgery. BNF, JF, ms. 1814, fol. 255.

27. An important consequence of becoming a nun was the renunciation of rights such as those of succession. "Civil death" (*la mort civile*) was the legal term used to describe this state.

28. Marguerite Delamarre had also been a boarder at the Ursuline convent at Chartres and again in Paris, at the convent of Dames de Sainte-Marie. Before going to Longchamp in 1734, Delamarre had been a postulant at the royal abbey of Val-de-Grace which had rejected her application to pronounce vows. For a chronology of Delamarre's activities up until her attempts to revoke her vows, see BNF, JF, ms. 1827, fols. 1–8.

29. Ibid., fols. 7–8.

30. A more detailed version of Marguerite Delamarre's story can be found in May, *Diderot et "La Religieuse,"* 47–76. For a follow-up of Delamarre's life after the trial, see Annie Flandreau, "Du Nouveau sur Marguerite Delamarre et "La Religieuse" de Diderot," *Dix-Huitième Siècle* 24 (1992): 410–419.

31. BNF, JF, ms. 1827, fol. 39. The remarks were dated September 11, 1755.

32. *Le Courrier d'Avignon,* March 28, 1758, 103; italics added. In his exhaustive 1954 study of *La Religieuse* Georges May noted that there was a surprising omission of the Delamarre trial in personal memoirs and periodicals. While May's assertions regarding Delamarre were inaccurate, his general conclusion that news of the Delamarre affair spread orally was most likely valid for the Lusignan case as well. The *mémoires judiciaires* for the Lusignan trial were printed, and the barristers of the Delamarre affair made constant reference to it. May, *Diderot et "La Religieuse,"* 72.

33. Louis Doulcet was an elderly lawyer who had been a member of the Ordre des Avocats since 1703 and who died in 1764.

34. Thévenot d'Essaule, *Mémoire pour demoiselle Marie-Michelle de Couhé de Lusignan,* 27. Louis Doulcet, *Mémoire pour la demoiselle Delamarre, appelante comme d'abus. Contre la dame Delamarre, sa mère* (Paris: Bernard Brunet, 1758), 7.

35. Thévenot d'Essaule, *Mémoire pour demoiselle Marie-Michelle de Couhé de Lusignan,* 27.

36. Ibid.

37. Louis D'Héricourt and Mallard, *Mémoire à consulter pour demoiselle Marie-Michelle de Couhé contre la dame de Saint-Georges* (n.p.: Paulus-du-Mesnil, 1751), 3. This was the first *mémoire judiciaire* for Lusignan. One of the lawyers, Louis D'Héricourt du Vatier (1687–1752), was best known for writing *Les Lois ecclésiastiques de France dans leur ordre naturel* (1719) which was reprinted several times. Doulcet, *Mémoire pour la demoiselle Delamarre,* 7.

38. Claude-Christophe Courtin, *Mémoire pour René Le Lievre, prétendue chanoine-régulier de la*

congrégation de France, appellant comme d'abus et demandeur (Paris: Guillaume Despress, [1764]), 53.

39. Thévenot d'Essaule, *Second mémoire pour la demoiselle de Couhé du Lusignan contre la Dame de Saint-Georges et les supérieures et religieuses du couvent de Saint-François de Poitiers* (n.p.: Paulus-du-Mesnil, 1751), 1.

40. Thévenot d'Essaule, *Mémoire pour demoiselle Marie-Michelle de Couhé de Lusignan*, 3–4, 7.

41. Doulcet, *Mémoire pour la demoiselle Delamarre*, 2–3.

42. Thévenot d'Essaule, *Mémoire pour demoiselle Marie-Michelle de Couhé de Lusignan*, 30.

43. Ibid., 16, 36, 45.

44. Doulcet, *Mémoire pour la demoiselle Delamarre*, 1, 7.

45. Thévenot d'Essaule, *Mémoire pour demoiselle Marie-Michelle de Couhé de Lusignan*, 2, 23, 10, 1, 61–62; italics in original.

46. Thévenot d'Essaule, *Second mémoire pour la demoiselle de Couhé*, 12.

47. Doulcet, *Mémoire pour la demoiselle Delamarre*, 1; italics added.

48. Ibid., 11.

49. Elie Carcassonne, *Montesquieu et la problème de la constitution française au XVIIIe siècle* (1927; reprint, Geneva: Slaktine Reprints, 1970), 383.

50. Thévenot d'Essaule, *Mémoire pour demoiselle Marie-Michelle de Couhé de Lusignan*, 61–62.

51. Hanley, "Engendering the State."

52. Pierre-Jean Georges de Caillère de l'Estang, *Précis pour dame Elisabeth de Couhé, Veuve de Messire Louis de Saint-Georges* (n.p.: Veuve Lamesle, n.d.), 6; See Odot Briquet de Mercy, *Mémoire pour les héritiers et la dame veuve du sieur Claude de la Marre, écuyer, sécretaire du Roy, intimées. Contre la Soeur de la Marre, religieuse professe de l'abbaye royale de Longchamp* (n.p.: Paulus-du-Mesnil, 1758), 1.

53. Briquet de Mercy, *Mémoire pour les héritiers*, 67; Caillère de l'Estang, *Précis pour dame Elisabeth de Couhé*, 5.

54. Pierre-Jean Georges de Caillère de l'Estang, *Mémoire pour dame Elisabeth de Couhé, veuve de Messire Louis de Saint-Georges, Chevalier de Regnier et de Perissé* (n.p.: Veuve Lamesle, n.d.), 13, 29.

55. Briquet de Mercy, *Mémoire pour dame Marguerite Roussin, veuve de Claude de la Marre, écuyer, sécretaire du Roy, appelante comme d'abus. Contre Soeur Marguerite de la Marre, religieuse professe de l'abbaye de Longchamp intimée* (n.p.: Paulus-du-Mesnil, 1755), 27–28; idem, *Mémoire pour les héritiers*, 67. However, the *Mémoire pour la demoiselle Delamarre* contains no sustained discussion or reference to these "natural laws" and rights. Briquet de Mercy may have been responding to claims that were being put forth in salons, treatises, and novels.

56. On the importance of merit to the seventeenth-century nobility, see Jay Smith, *The Culture of Merit: Nobility, Royal Service, and the Making of Absolute Monarchy in France, 1600–1789* (Ann Arbor: University of Michigan Press, 1996).

57. Caillère de l'Estang, *Mémoire pour dame Elizabeth de Couhé*, 5–6.

58. Ibid.

59. Briquet de Mercy, *Mémoire pour les héritiers*, 2–4, 10–11, 19–23; idem, *Mémoire pour dame Marguerite Roussin*, 3–6, 43–44.

60. Briquet de Mercy, *Mémoire pour dame Marguerite Roussin*, 5.

61. Briquet de Mercy, *Mémoire pour les héritiers*, 11.

62. Ibid., 50–51; idem, *Mémoire pour dame Marguerite Roussin*, 10.

63. Thévenot d'Essaule, *Second mémoire pour la demoiselle de Couhé*, 1 n.

64. Caillère de l'Estang, *Mémoire pour dame Elizabeth de Couhé*, 3–4.

65. Briquet de Mercy, *Mémoire pour les héritiers*, 19.

66. Delamarre had incurred so many debts that at one point her mother requested that she economize. Ibid., 16, 46.

67. Briquet de Mercy, *Mémoire pour dame Marguerite Roussin*, 10.

68. Natalie Zemon Davis, *The Return of Martin Guerre* (Cambridge: Harvard University Press, 1983).

69. Caillère de l'Estang, *Mémoire pour dame Elisabeth de Couhé*, 2; Briquet de Mercy, *Mémoire pour les héritiers*, 2.

70. Liselotte Steinbrügge, *The Moral Sex: Woman's Nature in the French Enlightenment*, trans. Pamela E. Selwyn (Oxford: Oxford University Press, 1995), 18–24.

71. Caillère de l'Estang, *Mémoire pour dame Elisabeth de Couhé*, 11; idem, *Précis pour dame Elisabeth de Couhé*, 17.

72. The man in question was the engineer Jacques Vaucanson, whose invention of a silk-throwing machine had brought him to Longchamp in 1751. The nuns of Longchamp earned money through sewing. Briquet de Mercy, *Mémoire pour dame Marguerite Roussin*, 9; idem, *Mémoire pour les héritiers*, 6. On the Vaucanson episode, see May, *Diderot et "La Religieuse,"* 64–66.

73. Thévenot d'Essaule, *Memoire pour demoiselle Marie-Michelle de Couhé de Lusignan*, 2.

74. Paul Friedland, *Political Actors: Representative Bodies and Theatricality in the Age of the French Revolution* (Ithaca, N.Y.: Cornell University Press, 2002), 60.

75. Caillère de l'Estang, *Mémoire pour dame Elisabeth de Couhé*, 25.

76. On public opinion, see Keith Baker, "Public Opinion as Political Invention," in *The French Revolution in Social and Political Perspective*, ed. Peter Jones (London: Arnold, 1996, 131–66.

77. Briquet de Mercy, *Mémoire pour les héritiers*, 1.

78. Sarah Maza, "Le Tribunal de la nation: les mémoires judiciares et l'opinion publique à la fin de l'ancien régime," *Annales: économies, sociétés, civilisations* 42 (1987): 73–90.

79. Jeffrey Merrick, "Patriarchalism and Constitutionalism in Eighteenth-Century Parlementary Discourse," *Studies in Eighteenth-Century Culture* 20 (1990): 326.

80. On social dramas see Victor Turner, "Social Dramas and Stories about Them," *Critical Inquiry* (1980): 141–168.

81. Elie Fréron, "*Mélanie*, Drame en trois Actes et en vers, par M. de La Harpe," *L'Année littéraire* 1 (1770): 149.

82. Turner, "Social Dramas," 158.

83. Sarah Maza, "Stories in History: Cultural Narratives in Recent Works in European History," *American Historical Review* 101 (1996): 1514.

84. See, for example, Thomas Laqueur, "The Queen Caroline Affair: Politics as Art in the Reign of George IV," *Journal of Modern History* 54 (1982): 417–466.

85. Gabrielle Spiegel, *Romancing the Past: The Rise of Vernacular Prose Historiography in Thirteenth-Century France* (Berkeley: University of California Press, 1993), 10.

86. Louis de Rouvroy, duc de Saint-Simon, *Mémoires; additions au journal de Dangeau*, 8 vols. (Paris: Gallimard, 1987), 7:508–509. On Madame de Tencin, see Jean Sareil, *Les Tencins: histoire d'une famille au dix-huitième siècle d'après de nombreux documents inédits* (Geneva: Libraire Droz, 1969).

87. Hans-Jürgen Lüsebrink, "L'Espace public semi-royal dans les *Mémoires secrets*," in *The "Mémoires secrets" and the Culture of Publicity in Eighteenth-Century France*, ed. Jeremy D. Popkin and Bernadette Fort (Oxford: Voltaire Foundation, 1998), 82.

88. Thévenot d'Essaule, *Mémoire pour demoiselle Marie-Michelle de Couhé de Lusignan*, 11.

89. Despite the absence of vocation forcée episodes, Ménétra's memoirs indicate that as a glazier he did have access to convents, where, according to his account, the nuns flirted with him. Jacques-Louis Ménétra, *Journal of My Life*, trans. Arthur Goldhammer (New York: Columbia University Press, 1986), 36, 54. Denis Diderot, *The Nun*, trans. Leonard Tancock (London: Penguin Books, 1972), 187–189.

90. [Brunet de Brou], *La Religieuse malgré elle: histoire galante, morale et tragique* (Amsterdam: Claude Joradan, 1740), viii. See note 3 above. Although not technically a vocation forcée piece, Pierre de Longchamp's *Mémoires d'une religieuse écrits par elle-même* used similar themes. Pierre de Longchamps, *Mémoires d'une religieuse écrits par elle-même et recueillis par M. de l**** (Amsterdam, 1766), xi.

91. Caroline Stéphanie-Félicité du Crest, countess of Genlis, *Mémoires inédits de Madame la comtesse de Genlis pour servir à l'histoire des dix-huitème et dix-neuvième siècles*, 2 vols. (Paris: Colburn, 1825), 1:143–145.

92. Showalter, *Evolution of the French Novel*, 3. Other works consulted include the following: Vivienne Mylne, *The Eighteenth-Century French Novel: Techniques of Illusion* (New York: Manchester University Press, 1963); Philip Stewart, *Imitation and Illusion in the French Memoir-Novel, 1700–1750* (New Haven: Yale University Press, 1969); Georges May, *Le Dilemme du roman au XVIIIe siècle* (New Haven: Yale University Press, 1951); Françoise Barguillet, *Le Roman au XVIIIe siècle* (Paris: Presses Universitaires de France, 1994).

93. *Mercure de France,* January 1774, 88.
94. In her collection of the cases pertaining to women that are in the lawyer Nicolas-Toussaint Des Essarts's compilation of court cases, Isabelle Vissière has noted that Des Essarts's description of a vocation forcée trial involving a bourgeois family named Revel in Cahors in 1779 strongly resembled the meta-narrative of the vocation forcée that was so popular. Isabelle Vissière, ed. *Procès de femmes au temps des philosophes ou la violence masculine au XVIIIe siècle* (Paris: Des femmes, 1985), 48–49.
95. Mylne, *The Eighteenth-Century French Novel,* 12.
96. Barguillet, *Le Roman au XVIIIe Siècle,* 23.
97. Brunet de Brou, *La Religieuse malgré elle,* x–xii.
98. Showalter, *Evolution of the French Novel,* 19. The translation of Diderot's "Eloge à Richardson" was taken from http://www.engl.virginia.edu/enec981/dictionary/25diderotC1.html.
99. Briquet de Mercy, *Mémoire pour les héritiers,* 24, 27, 37.
100. For a brief discussion on the *drame* and Diderot, see Maza, *Private Lives and Public Affairs,* 61–65. See also Félix Gaiffe, *Le Drame en France au XVIIIe siècle* (Paris: Armand Colin, 1910).
101. Charles-Georges-Thomas Garnier, "La Vocation forcée, drame, en un acte," in *Nouveaux Proverbes dramatiques, ou receuil de comédies de société, pour servir de suite aux théâtres de société et d'éducation* (Paris: Cailleau, 1784), 211–230.
102. *L'Année littéraire* 7 (1770): 7.
103. Based on the circulating rumors of a "young girl, forced by her unjust parents to become a nun," who subsequently hanged herself, *Mélanie* was a blazing success, first in the salon circles in which the play was read to avid audiences. La Harpe sold two thousand copies of *Mélanie* in three days. Melchior Grimm et al., *Correspondance littéraire, philosophique, et critique,* 16 vols. (Paris: Garnier, 1877–1882), 8:458. See also [Louis Petit de Bachaumont], *Mémoires secrets pour servir à l'histoire de la république des lettres en France, depuis M.DCC.LXII jusqu'à nos jours; ou journal d'un observateur,* 36 vols. (London: John Adamson, 1777–1787), 5:85–86, 108–110; Dena Goodman, *The Republic of Letters: A Cultural History of the French Enlightenment* (Ithaca, N.Y.: Cornell University Press, 1994), 146–147.
104. In the case of the vocation forcée play *Ericie,* although the Comédie-Française "received it with approbation" fully intending to perform the play, the archbishop of Paris censored it and made it difficult for *colporteurs* to sell it clandestinely; the play was relegated to the provinces. The *Mémoires secrets* criticized *Ericie* for lacking "the style necessary to paint all the horror of monastic life." *Mémoires secrets,* 3:381; Grimm et al., *Correspondance littéraire,* 7:42–43, 8:471; *L'Année littéraire* 7 (1770): 5–37.
105. While critiquing the quality of *Les Druides,* the *Mémoires secrets* also praised its goal of fighting "superstition and fanaticism, to abolish a cult of horrors and abomination." *Mémoires secrets,* 6:127. *Les Druides* also formed part of the *patriote* literature of the Maupeou years. Durand Echevarria, *The Maupeou Revolution: A Study in the History of Libertarianism, France, 1770–1774* (Baton Rouge: Louisiana State University Press, 1985), 59–60.
106. Quotation taken from Grimm et al., *Correspondance littéraire,* 9:479–480. For a full account, see 9:479, 465–481, 492, 508; *Mémoires secrets,* 6:104–108, 112, 128. [Le Blanc], *Les Druides, tragédie* (Petersbourg, 1783).
107. Jeffrey S. Ravel, *The Contested Parterre: Public Theater and French Political Culture, 1680–1791* (Ithaca, N.Y.: Cornell University Press, 1999), 6.
108. Maza, *Private Lives and Public Affairs,* 60–67.
109. Thévenot d'Essaule, *Mémoire pour demoiselle Marie-Michelle de Couhé de Lusignan,* 11.
110. J. E. Fowler, "Competing Causalities: Family and Convent in Diderot's *La Religieuse,*" *The Eighteenth Century* 37 (1996): 76.
111. "*Ericie, ou la Vestale,* drame en trois Actes en vers; par M. de Fontanelle," *L'Année littéraire* 7 (1770): 6.
112. Jean-François La Harpe, *Mélanie,* in *Théâtre du XVIIIe Siècle,* ed. Jacques Truchet (Paris: Gallimard, 1974), 837. See also *Rosalie, ou la vocation forcée; mémoires de la comtesse d'Hes* (Amsterdam, 1773), pt. 1, 1–4.
113. La Harpe, *Mélanie,* 843, 850, 853; Brunet de Brou, *La Religieuse malgré elle,* 2; Dubois de

Fontanelle, *Ericie, ou la Vestale, drame en trois actes* (London, 1768), 10, 34; "La Mauvaise Mère punie. Conte moral," *Mercure de France,* November 1776, 16. In *Euphémie, ou le triompe de la religion,* Baculard d'Arnaud describes Euphémie's mother, the comtesse d'Orcé, as blinded by "rank and opulence." *Euphémie, ou le triomphe de la religion,* 3d ed. (Paris: Le Jay, 1768), 32.

114. "La Mauvaise Mère," 15; "*Euphémie*," *L'Année littéraire* 6 (1769), 159; Brunet de Brou, *La Religieuse malgré elle,* 95. On the accusations of being inhuman, see La Harpe, *Mélanie,* 848, 859.

115. On Princess Louise, see for example the following pamphlets: [P. Richard], *Dissertation sur les voeux en général, et sur les voeux solomnels des religieux et des religieuses en particulier; avec les lettres de N. S. le pape Clément XIV, touchant la prise d'habit de Madame Louise-Marie de France* (Paris: Butard, 1771); [Poncet de la Rivière], *Discours pour la prise d'habit de Madame Louise-Marie de France* (n.p., n.d.).

116. *Rosalie,* pt. 2, 197. The curé in *Mélanie* rebukes Mélanie's father, Faublas, with the language of "rights," declaring, "No man, whoever he is, has this right [to decide a person's unhappiness] over another." La Harpe, *Mélanie,* 870.

117. "*Mélanie*," *L'Année littéraire* 7 (1770), 176; Stéphanie-Félicité du Crest, countess of Genlis, *Adèle et Théodore ou lettres sur l'éducation consultant tous les principes relatifs aux trois différens plans d'éducation des princes et de jeunes personnes de l'un et de l'autre sexe,* 3 vols. (Paris: M. Lambert, 1782), 1:146. Brunet de Brou, *La Religieuse malgré elle,* 93.

118. *Rosalie,* pt. 2, 28. La Harpe, *Mélanie,* 867.

119. Brunet de Brou, *La Religieuse malgré elle,* 90. See also La Harpe, *Mélanie,* 838; Fontanelle, *Ericie,* 14.

120. *Les Métamorphoses de la religieuse. Lettres d'une dame à son amie* (Amsterdam: Schreuder, 1768).

121. Genlis, *Adèle et Théodore,* 1:146.

122. "La Mauvaise Mère," 16. Some authors took the opportunity to suggest that all women, and not just female religious, were victims of society's restrictions and prejudices against their sex. La Harpe, *Mélanie,* 851; Fontanelle, *Ericie,* 12.

123. Cited in Denis Diderot, *La Religieuse* (Paris: Flammarion, 1968), 209; italics added.

124. See La Harpe's *Mélanie* and *La Vocation forcée, drame.*

125. There was a hint that in 1748, instead of being with nuns of Saint-Thomas, Lusignan spent eight months with a carpenter named Bonneau. However, these allegations were not substantiated. Caillère de l'Estang, *Précis pour dame Elisabeth de Couhé,* 14.

126. Amélie Panckouke Suard, *Lettres d'un jeune lord à une religieuse italienne. Imitiées de l'Anglois* (Paris: Marchands le Nouveautés, 1788), 88.

127. Genlis, *Adèle et Théodore,* 1:271.

128. In addition to Diderot's *La Religieuse,* a notable exception is Brunet de Brou's *La Religieuse malgré elle* in which the author declared "that it is difficult to cherish the people who persecute us" (104–105).

129. La Harpe, *Mélanie,* 852; Fontanelle, *Ericie,* 34.

130. *Rosalie,* pt. 2, 200–202.

131. Fontanelle, *Ericie,* 36–37.

132. *Rosalie,* pt. 2, 28. The mother in "La Mauvaise Mère," Madame de Prévalle, is the only character to be ostracized. Not only does her younger daughter, Sophie, die in the convent, unreconciled with her mother, but her favorite, the elder daughter, also dies of illness. In the aftermath of these tragedies, the relatives of her deceased husband punish Madame de Prévalle socially and financially because of her cruelty toward Sophie. "La Mauvaise Mère," 41.

133. The review does not provide the full title of the novel, only calling it "*La Vocation forcée.*" However, the date and description of a two-volume novel fit the description of *Rosalie, ou la vocation forcée.* Grimm et al., *Correspondance littéraire,* 10:280. Comments on other vocation forcée narratives found in the *Correspondance littéraire,* the *Mémoires secrets,* and *L'Année littéraire* similarly pointed out plot and character discrepancies but separated these faults from the moral aims of the pieces. See especially the reviews of La Harpe's *Mélanie* in *Mémoires secrets,* 19:195–199, and in Grimm et al., *Correspondance littéraire,* 8:459–460.

134. One example of this affirmation of authority, particularly male authority, may be found in the changes made to La Harpe's *Mélanie*. Both the *Correspondance littéraire* and the *Mémoires secrets* regarded Mélanie, her mother, and her lover as the weakest characters and, indeed, called for more sustained conflict between them and M. Faublas. However, in his revisions of 1778, La Harpe chose to make adjustments in the characters and speeches of M. Faublas, rendering his conversion more understandable; the curé's protest against Mélanie's profession is more vociferous. La Harpe may have undertaken the alterations that would be the most effective dramatically and the least likely to cause heavy revisions. But it is significant that the two male authority figures are made sympathetic while those characters who challenged the father figure were left intact. Thus, while the authoritarian relationships are renegotiated, the patriarchal family structure remains. La Harpe, *Mélanie*, 234; Grimm et al., *Correspondance littéraire*, 8:466, 475–476.
135. Louis-Sébasien Mercier, *Tableau de Paris*, chap. 55,
136. The author Nouet was arguing that many young girls were seduced into entering the convent, usually by the members of the convent. BNF, JF, ms. 206, fol. 26.
137. Thévenot d'Essaule, *Mémoire pour demoiselle Marie-Michelle de Couhé de Lusignan*, 1, 7, 10. For a fictional equivalent, see *Rosalie*, pt. 1, 196.
138. Marvin Carlson, "The Citizen in the Theater," in *The French Revolution and the Meaning of Citizenship*, ed. Renée Waldinger, Philip Dawson and Isser Woloch (Westport, Conn.: Greenwood, 1993), 83.
139. Hans-Jürgen Lüsebrink and Rolf Reichardt, *The Bastille: A History of a Symbol of Despotism and Freedom*, trans. Norbert Schürer (Durham, N.C.: Duke University Press, 1997), chap. 1.
140. "La Mère mauvaise," 32; La Harpe, *Mélanie*, 842; *Les Métamorphoses de la religieuse*, 18.
141. M. Rangier, "Epître d'une religieuse à la marquise de ***, sa soeur," *Mercure de France*, June 1775, 11.
142. Thévenot d'Essaule, *Mémoire pour demoiselle Marie-Michelle de Couhé de Lusignan*, 12.

5. SCHOOL OF VIRTUE, SCHOOL OF VICE

1. David A. Bell, "Culture and Religion," in *Old Regime France, 1648–1788*, ed. William Doyle (Oxford: Oxford University Press, 2001), 90.
2. On the impact of Locke in France, see John C. O'Neal, *Authority of Experience: Sensationist Theory in the French Enlightenment* (University Park: Pennsylvania State University Press, 1996); John W. Yolton, *Locke and French Materialism* (Oxford: Clarendon, 1991); Jørn Schøsler, *John Locke et les philosophes français: la critique de idées innées en France au dix-huitième siècle* (Oxford: Voltaire Foundation, 1997).
3. O'Neal, *Authority of Experience*, 1.
4. Anne C. Vila has explored the connection between morality and sensationalism in her study of sensibility in eighteenth-century French thought. According to Vila, "Sensibility . . . was seen as the root of all human perceptions and reflections, as the innate and active principle of sociability that gave rise to human society, as a kind of sixth sense whose special affective energy was essential both to virtue and to art." Anne C. Vila, *Enlightenment and Pathology: Sensibility in the Literature and Medicine of Eighteenth-Century France* (Baltimore: Johns Hopkins University Press, 1998), 2.
5. O'Neal, *Authority of Experience*, 173–195.
6. The following discussion of Locke's influence on French pedagogy during this period is taken from Marcel Grandière, *L'Idéal pédagogique en France au dix-huitième siècle* (Oxford: Voltaire Foundation, 1998), 77–110.
7. Grandière has noted that the focus on earthly happiness could be seen in pedagogical works written after 1725. Earlier examples include Anne-Thérèse de Marquemont de Courcelles, marquise de Lambert, whose ideas on female education possessed a decidedly secular and worldly dimension. Ibid., 69–70, 113.
8. Ibid., 113–128. See also O'Neal, *Authority of Experience*, 173–182.
9. Grandière, *L'Idéal pédagogique en France*, 216.
10. As cited in ibid., 219. The treatise *Plan général d'instruction particulièrement destiné pour la jeunesse du ressort du Parlement de Bourgogne* (Dijon: Carsse, 1763), by the *procureur-général*

of the Parlement of Brittany, Louis-René de Cardeuc de La Chatolais (1701–85), remains one of the best-known works from the period.

11. Other examples, most of which are anonymous, include *Mémoire de l'université sur les moyens de pourvoir à l'instruction de la jeunesse, et de la perfectionner;* [J. B. Daragon], *Lettre de M ** à M. l'Abbé ** sur la nécessité et la manière de faire entrer les cours de morale dans l'éducation publique* (Paris: Durand, 1772). On the impact of the Jesuit departure on educational theories, see Grandière, *L'Idéal pédagogique en France*, 216–247; Yves La Grée, "La Chatolais (1701–1785). Un magistrat pédagogue au siècle des lumières," in *Education et pédagogies au siècle des lumières*, Actes du Colloque 1983 de l'Institut des Sciences de l'Education Université Catholique de l'Ouest (Angers: Presses de l'Université Catholique de l'Ouest, 1983), 189–203; R. R. Palmer, *The Improvement of Humanity: Education and the French Revolution* (Princeton, N.J.: Princeton University Press, 1985), 48–78; Roger Chartier, Dominique Julia, and Marie-Madeleine Compère, *L'Education en France du XVIe au XVIIIe siècle* (Paris: SEDES, 1976), 207–217.

12. Samia I. Spencer, "Women and Education," in *French Women and the Age of Enlightenment*, ed. Samia I. Spencer (Bloomington: Indiana University Press, 1984), 84.

13. The following discussion of Rousseau is based on Lieselotte Steinbrügge, *The Moral Sex: Woman's Nature in the French Enlightenment*, trans. Pamela E. Selwyn (Oxford: Oxford University Press, 1992), 25–34; and Gilbert Py, *Rousseau et les éducateurs: étude sur la fortune des idées pédagogiques de Jean-Jacques Rousseau en France et en Europe au XVIIIe siècle* (Oxford: Voltaire Foundation, 1997), 338–405. See also Mary Trouille, *Sexual Politics in the Enlightenment: Women Writers Read Rousseau* (Albany: State University of New York Press, 1997), 13–38.

14. Thomas Laqueur, *Making Sex: Body and Gender from the Greeks to Freud* (Cambridge: Harvard University Press, 1990), 5–6; Vila, *Enlightenment and Pathology*, 225–257.

15. Londa Schiebinger, *The Mind Has No Sex? Women in the Origins of Modern Science* (Cambridge: Harvard University Press, 1989), 216–217.

16. Steinbrügge, *The Moral Sex*, 106–107. For a discussion of the connections between sentimentality and the female body, see chapter 7.

17. For examples, see M. Morelly, *Essai sur l'esprit humain, ou principes naturels de l'éducation* (Paris: Delespine, 1743); Caroline-Stéphanie-Félicité du Crest, countess of Genlis, *Adèle et Théodore ou lettres sur l'éducation contenant tous les principes relatifs aux trois différens plans d'éducation des princes et de jeunes personnes de l'un et de l'autre sexe*, 3 vols. (Paris: M. Lambert, 1782); Jean-Jacques Rousseau, *Emile ou de l'éducation* (Paris: Garnier-Flammarion, 1966), bk. 5; M. Bachelier, *Mémoire sur l'éducation des filles* (Paris: Imprimerie Royale, 1789); Mademoiselle Espinassy, *Essai sur l'éducation des demoiselles* (Paris: Barthelemi Hochereau, 1764); Marie Le Prince de Beaumont, *Lettres diverses et critiques* (Nancy: Thomas, 1750); Cerfvol, *La Gamalogie ou de l'éducation des filles destinées au mariage* (Paris: Duchesne, 1772).

18. Little is known about the woman Mademoiselle Espinassy who authored the *Essai sur l'éducation des demoiselles*. Like Madame d'Epinay and Madame de Genlis, she complained that Rousseau's ideas were not practical and were prejudiced against women.

19. On Locke's impact on pedagogy, see Marcel Grandière, "Regard sur l'enfant au siècle des lumières," in *Education et pédagogies au siècle des lumières*, 29–30.

20. Jean Bloch, "Knowledge as a Source of Virtue: Changes and Contrasts in Ideas concerning the Education of Boys and Girls in Eighteenth-Century France," *British Journal for Eighteenth-Century Studies* 8 (1985): 86.

21. Laurent Versini, *Laclos et la tradition: essai sur les sources et la technique des "Liaisons dangereuses"* (Paris: Klincksieck, 1968), 541. For a discussion of Laclos's pedagogical treatises, see Jean Bloch, "Laclos and Women's Education," *French Studies* 38 (1984): 144–157.

22. A counterexample to Maintenon was Fénélon, the bishop of Cambrai and tutor to the Sun King's grandson, who published *L'Education des filles* advocating domestic education. On Fénélon's influence, see Albert Cerel, *Fénélon au XVIIIe siècle en France (1715–1800): son prestige et son influence* (Geneva: Slaktine Reprints, 1970). Carolyn C. Lougee provides a discussion of both Fénélon and Maintenon in *Le Paradis des Femmes: Women, Salons and Social Stratification in Seventeenth-Century France* (Princeton, N.J.: Princeton University Press, 1976), chaps. 11, 12.

23. Spencer, "Women and Education," 89–90. On the discourse on eighteenth-century female education, see P. L.-M. Fein, "The Convent Education as Depicted through the Characters of Certain French Eighteenth-Century Novels," *Studies on Voltaire and the Eighteenth Century* 264 (1989): 737–774; Bloch, "Knowledge as a Source of Virtue," 83–92; idem, "Women and the Reform of the Nation," in *Woman and Society in Eighteenth-Century France: Essays in Honour of John Stephenson Spink*, ed. Eva Jacobs et al. (London: Athlone, 1979), 3–18; Chartier et al., *L'Education en France*, chap. 8; Versini, *Laclos et la tradition*, 521–580; Albert de Luppé, *Les Jeunes Filles dans l'aristocracie et la bourgeoisie à la fin du XVIIIe siècle* (Paris: Edouard Champion, 1924); Paul Rousselot, *Histoire de l'éducation des femmes en France*, 2 vols. (Paris: Didier, 1883).

24. For another brief discussion of why nuns were considered to be unsatisfactory teachers, see Versini, *Laclos et la tradition*, 555–556. Gary Kates has described convents as "centers of genuine learning and piety that provided important intellectual opportunities for young women." He does, however, note that they functioned more as finishing schools. Gary Kates, *Monsieur d'Eon is a Woman: A Tale of Political Intrigue and Sexual Masquerade* (New York: Basic Books, 1995), 259.

25. Madeleine d'Arsant Puisieux, *Conseils à une amie* (n.p., 1749), ix–x. Madame de Puisieux (1720–95) was the wife of a lawyer, who also devoted himself to literary pursuits.

26. Françoise de Graffigny, *Letters from a Peruvian Woman*, trans. David Kornacker (New York: Modern Language Association of America, 1993), 143.

27. [Anne d'Aubourg de la Bove de Miremont], *Traité de l'éducation des femmes, et cours complet d'instruction*, 7 vols. (Paris: Ph.-D. Pierres, 1779), 1:68. Not much is known about Miremont (1735–1811) beyond her lengthy contribution to the eighteenth-century debate on female education. For a brief discussion of her opus, see Py, *Rousseau et les éducateurs*, 365–368.

28. Marie-Jeanne Phlipon Roland de la Platière, *Mémoires de Madame Roland*, ed. Berville and Barrière, 2 vols. (Paris: Baudoin Frères, 1820), 1:38.

29. [Antoine-Joseph Panckoucke], *Les Etudes convenables aux demoiselles, contenant la grammaire, la poésie, la rhétorique . . . ouvrages destinés aux jeunes pensionnaires des communautés et des maisons religieuses*, 2 vols. (Paris: Libraires Associés, 1782), 1:vi.

30. Py, *Rousseau et les éducateurs*, 365.

31. Rousselot, *Histoire de l'éducation des femmes*, 144–145. Ambroise Riballier and Charlotte-Catherine Cosson de la Cressonière, *L'Education physique et moral des femmes* (Brussels: Frères Estienne, 1779).

32. Le Prince de Beaumont, *Lettres diverses et critiques*, 89. Once a governess to an English family, Le Prince de Beaumont (1711–1810) is best known for writing children's books, including publications like *Le Magasin des enfants*. According to the files of police inspector Joseph de Hémery, Le Prince de Beaumont led a dissolute life in her younger years. Bibliothèque Nationale de France, Nouvelles Acquisitions Françaises, 10783, fol. 47.

33. Another criticism of the neglect children encountered in the convent is found in Genlis, *Adèle et Théodore*, 3:206.

34. Cerfvol, *La Gamalogie*, 5–10. Although a prolific writer especially with respect to the question of divorce, "Cerfvol" remains an allusive figure. Carol Blum has suggested that he was, in fact, not a real person. Either Cerfvol was a "political conspiracy" involving Madame du Barry, the abbé Terry, and the Duc d'Aiguillon, or he was the writer Charles Palissot de Montenoy, who used this nom de plume to voice his despair in an unhappy marriage. Blum, *Strength in Numbers: Population, Reproduction, and Power in France* (Baltimore: Johns Hopkins University Press, 2002), 69–70.

35. Cerfvol, *La Gamalogie*, 8. See also Jean-François Dumas, *Discours sur cette question: "Quels sont les moyens de perfectionner l'éducation des jeunes demoiselles?" proposé et couronné en 1783 par l'Académie des sciences, arts et belles lettres de Châlons-sur-Marne* (Neuchâtel-Fauche, 1783), 57.

36. Cerfvol, *La Gamalogie*, 5.

37. See [Anne d'Aubourg de la Bove de Miremont], *Mémoires de Madame de la marquise de Crémy, écrits par elle-même*, vol. 1 (Lyon: Pierre Duplair, 1766).

38. Voltaire, *L'Education des filles*, in *Oeuvres complètes de Voltaire*, 52 vols. (Paris: Garnier Frères, 1879), 24:286. Translation taken from Spencer, "Women and Education," 91.

39. Chatolais, *Plan général*, 35; for a similar conclusion, see also the anonymous "Suite de l'Analyse de *L'Histoire des ecclésiastiques en France*," in *Pièces détachées relatives au clergé séculier et régulier*, 3 vols. (Amsterdam: Marc Michel Rey, 1771), 2:52.

40. C. A. Helvétius, *De l'homme, de ses facultés intellectuelles et de son éducation*, 2 vols. (London: Société Typographique, 1773), 1:38.

41. Lucien Perey, ed., *Memoirs of the Princesse de Ligne*, trans. Laura Ensor, 2 vols. (London: Richard Bentley and Son, 1887), 1:18.

42. Rousseau, *Emile*, 509.

43. Marie-Joséphine de Lescun de Monbart, *Sophie ou de l'éducation des filles* (Berlin: G. J. Decker, 1777), 118–119.

44. Genlis, *Adèle et Théodore*, 3:209–210.

45. Ibid., 206.

46. Because of her husband's military career, the newly married Stéphanie spent some months at the Abbaye d'Origny. Caroline-Stéphanie-Félicité du Crest, countess of Genlis *Mémoires inédits de Madame la comtesse de Genlis pour servir à l'histoire des dix-huitième et dix-neuvième siècles*, 2 vols. (Paris: Colburn, 1825), 1:140–154.

47. Genlis, *Adèle et Théodore*, 1:21.

48. Denis Diderot and Jean Le Rond d'Alembert, eds., *Encyclopédie ou dictionnaire raisonné des sciences, des arts et des métiers, par une société des gens de lettre*, 17 vols. (Paris: Briasson, 1751–63), 6:472. For a discussion of this entry, see Steinbrügge, *The Moral Sex*, 30–34. Joseph-François Edouard Desmahis (1722–61), the son of a magistrate, was an *homme de lettres* known for his poetry and plays.

49. Choderlos de Laclos, *Les Liaisons dangereuses* (Paris: Gallimard, 1970), 37–38.

50. Bloch, "Laclos and Women's Education," 148.

51. Perey, *Memoirs of the Princesse de Ligne*, 121–126.

52. Miremont, *Traité de l'éducation*, 1:67–68.

53. Bloch, "Women and the Reform of the Nation," 7–11; idem, "Knowledge as a Source of Virtue," 86. For a brief discussion of citizenship and education, see C. A. Ottevanger, "From Subject to Citizen: The Evolution of French Educational Theory in the Eighteenth Century," *Studies on Voltaire and the Eighteenth Century* 264 (1989): 714–717.

54. Carol Blum, "The Literature of Depopulation Delusion in Eighteenth-Century France," in *Transactions of the Eighth International Congress on the Enlightenment*, vol. 3 (Oxford: Voltaire Foundation, 1992), 1692–1695; idem, "Demographics, Divorce, and the Male Imagination in Eighteenth-Century France," in *The Past as Prologue: Essays to Celebrate the Twenty-Fifth Anniversary of ASECS*, ed. Carla H. Hay (New York: AMS, 1995), 233–234.

55. Blum, *Strength in Numbers*, 2.

56. "Célibat," *Encyclopédie*, 2:801–806.

57. This was not the first time that the government considered raising the age. Many of the discussions surrounding the Commission des Secours in the early 1730s included concerns about the age for admission into the monastery. Bibliothèque Nationale de France, Fond Joly de Fleury, ms. 206, fols. 25–27.

58. Edmond J. F. Barbier, *Journal historique et anecdotique du règne de Louis XV*, 4 vols. (Paris: Jules Renouard, 1847), 3:102. See also Marquis d'Argenson, *Journal et Mémoires du Marquis D'Argenson*, ed. E. J. B. Rathery, 9 vols. (Paris: Jules Renouard, 1859), 6:31.

59. Three decades later Louis-Sébastien Mercier would continue the call for increasing the age to twenty-five. Louis-Sébastien Mercier, *Tableau de Paris*, 12 vols. (Amsterdam, 1783–88), 7:95.

60. [Voltaire], *La Voix du sage et du peuple* (Amsterdam: Le Sincere, 1750).

61. As cited in Blum, *Strength in Numbers*, 35.

62. Monsieur Huel [Curé de Rouceux], *Moyen de rendre nos religieuses utiles et de nous exempter des dots qu'elles exigent* (n.p., 1750).

63. Michel Foucault, *The History of Sexuality*, trans. Robert Hurley, 2 vols. (New York: Random House, 1978), 1:18.

64. Dorelies Kraakman, "Pornography in Western European Culture," in *Sexual Cultures in Europe: Themes in Sexuality*, ed. Franz X. Eder, Lesley A. Hall, and Gert Hekma (Manchester: Manchester University Press, 1999), 113.

65. Ibid., 112. Another challenge to Foucault's dismissal of any western *ars erotica* may be

found in Peter Cryle, *Geometry in the Boudoir: Configurations of French Erotic Narrative* (Ithaca, N.Y.: Cornell University Press, 1994), 7–8.

66. Lynn Hunt, "Introduction: Obscenity and the Origins of Modernity, 1500–1800," in *The Invention of Pornography: Obscenity and Origins of Modernity, 1500–1800*, ed. Lynn Hunt (New York: Zone Books, 1993), 11. See also Jean Marie Goulemot, *Forbidden Texts: Erotic Literature and Its Readers in Eighteenth-Century France*, trans. James Simpson (Philadelphia: University of Pennsylvania Press, 1994); Peter Wagner, ed. *Erotica and the Enlightenment* (Frankfurt am Main: Peter Lang, 1991).

67. Darnton's well-known thesis may be found in *The Literary Underground of the Old Regime* (Cambridge: Harvard University Press, 1982). Other relevant works by Darnton include *Edition et Sédition* (Paris: Gallimard, 1991) and *The Forbidden Best-Sellers of Pre-Revolutionary France* (New York: W. W. Norton, 1995).

68. Diderot's *Les Bijoux indiscrets* ranks among the better-known erotic pieces in the period.

69. Not much is known about Gervaise de la Touche (1715–82) beyond his occupation. In addition to his legal background, Meusnier de Querlon (1702–80) was the librarian of the Bibliothèque du Roy and an editor of the *Gazette de France*.

70. Among the writers suspected of having authored *Thérèse Philosophe* was Denis Diderot, who was arrested in July 1749 as a suspect. Barbier, *Journal historique*, 3:89–90. The marquis d'Argens (1704–71) was a contemporary of Diderot's.

71. Hunt, "Introduction," 10.

72. Rivers argues that the libertine convent novels were a separate and definable category because of the "striking intertextual similarities." Christopher Rivers, "Safe Sex: The Prophylactic Walls of the Cloister in the French Libertine Convent Novel of the Eighteenth Century," *Journal of the History of Sexuality* 5 (1995): 383.

73. Since at least the twelfth century, convents and nuns had been significant components of ribald literature; one category of popular medieval literature was called the *chanson de nonne*. See Graciela S. Daichman, *Wayward Nuns in Medieval Literature* (Syracuse: Syracuse University Press, 1986), chap. 3. Notable works of this tradition included Bocaccio's *Decameron* and Marguerite de Navarre's *The Heptameron*. Pieces imitating these works appeared well into the eighteenth century with works such as [Jean-Baptiste Boyer d'Argens], *Les Nones galantes ou l'amour embéguiné* (La Haye: Jean van Es, 1740); P. Perere, *Amours, galanteries, intrigues, ruses et crimes des capucins et des religieuses depuis les temps les plus reculés jusqu'à nos jours*, 3 vols. (Amsterdam, Paris, 1788); and the anonymous *Vie voluptueuse des capucins et des nonnes, tirée de la confession d'un frère de cet ordre* (Cologne: Pierre le Sincere, 1775).

74. There have been some scholarly disagreements as to whether *Vénus dans le cloître* was written in the 1680s or as late as 1719. Despite this dispute, the novel was undoubtedly the first of its kind. *Vénus dans le cloître* was reprinted in 1700, 1702, 1719, 1737, 1739, 1740, and 1746. Rivers, "Safe Sex," 383 n. 4.

75. Darnton, *Edition et Sédition*, 219–245; idem, *Forbidden Best-Sellers*, chap. 2.

76. This mixture of intellectual dialogue with sexual gymnastics makes the classification of eighteenth-century erotic literature difficult. In *Forbidden Texts*, Jean Goulemot uses "pornographic," "erotic," and "licentious" interchangeably (1–9).

77. [Jean Barrin], *Vénus dans le cloître ou la religieuse en chemise*, in *Oeuvres érotiques du XVIIe siècle*, L'Enfer de la Bibliothèque Nationale, vol. 7, ed. Jean-Pierre Dubost (Paris: Fayard, 1988). Apart from the older novice's name changing from Agnès to Dorothy, the dialogues in *Les Délices du cloître* are identical to the ones found in *Le Triomphe des religieuses*. *Les Délices du cloître ou la nonne eclairée avec un discours préliminaire* (n.p., 1761). One notable work that will not be discussed, despite its convent setting at the beginning and end of the novel, is Mirabeau's *Le Rideau levé, ou l'éducation de Laure*. Honoré-Gabriel de Riquetti de Mirabeau, *Oeuvres érotiques*, L'Enfer de la Bibliothèque Nationale, vol. 1, ed. Michel Camus (Paris: Fayard, 1984), 309–446.

78. Darnton, *Forbidden Best-Sellers*, 72.

79. Rivers, "Safe Sex," 385.

80. Dorelies Kraakman, "Reading Pornography Anew: A Critical History of Sexual Knowledge for Girls in French Erotic Fiction, 1750–1840," *Journal of the History of Sexuality* 4 (1994): 517–548.

81. For a complete discussion of attitudes toward the body, see Peter Brown, *The Body and Society: Men, Women, and Sexual Renunciation in Early Christianity* (New York: Columbia University, 1988); Shulamith Shahar, *The Fourth Estate: A History of Women in the Middle Ages*, trans. Chaya Galai (London: Methuen, 1983), 22–37.

82. The following discussion is taken from Martine Sonnet, *L'Education des filles au temps des lumières* (Paris: Edition du Cerfs, 1987), chaps. 3, 5; and Geneviève Reynes, *Couvents de femmes: la vie des religieuses cloîtrées dans la France des XVIIe et XVIIIe siècles* (Paris: Fayard, 1987), chaps. 13, 14.

83. Graffigny, *Letters from a Peruvian Woman*, 144.

84. Sonnet, *Education des filles*, 150–154, 164.

85. *Mémoire instructif pour faire connoître l'utilité des écoles charitables du Saint-Enfant-Jésus*, 1; quoted in Sonnet, *Education des filles*, 235.

86. Some of the outline of this plot is taken from Rivers, "Safe Sex," 388–391.

87. Fein, "Convent Education," 739.

88. *La Cauchoise ou mémoires d'une courtisane célèbre*, in *Oeuvres anonymes du XVIIIe siècle*, L'Enfer de la Bibliothèque, vol. 1, ed. Michel Camus (Paris: Fayard, 1984), 1:407. For other examples, see Rivers, "Safe Sex," 388–389.

89. In the *Histoire de la tourière des carmélites*, Sainte Nitouche also receives her "training" in the convent. [Meusnier de Querlon], *Histoire de la tourière des carmélites d'après l'original de l'auteur* (La Haye: Pierre Marteu, 1745).

90. [Gervaise de la Touche], *Histoire de Dom Bougre*, in *Oeuvres anonymes du XVIIIe siècle*, 1:190.

91. Denis Diderot, *The Nun*, trans. Leonard Tancock (London: Penguin Books, 1972), 148–151.

92. *Lettres galantes et philosophiques de deux nones, purlieus par un apothem du libertinage*, in *Oeuvres anonymes du XVIIIe siècle*, 3:248–249.

93. *Les Plaisirs du cloître, comédie en trois actes, en vers par M.D.L.C.A.P.*, in *Théâtre critique français au XVIIIe siècle* (Paris: Jean-Jacques Pervert, 1993), 250–251.

94. *Le Triomphe des religieuses ou les nones capillaries*, in *Oeuvres anonymes du XVIIIe siècle*, 3:223.

95. Sonnet, *Education des filles*, 150–161. For a discussion of how the individual's sense of the body is the "building block" of knowledge, see Peter Brooks, *Body Work: Objects of Desire in Modern Narrative* (Cambridge: Harvard University Press, 1993), 7–8.

96. *Histoire de Dom Bougre*, 63; *Le Triomphe des religieuses*, 212; *Lettres galantes et philosophiques*, 237, 279, 285; *La Cauchoise*, 411–413.

97. *La Cauchoise*, 411.

98. Rivers, "Safe Sex," 595–596.

99. *Histoire de Dom Bougre*, 86; for other examples, see *La Cauchoise*, 410; *Lettres galantes et philosophiques*, 277–278.

100. *Histoire de Dom Bougre*, 88.

101. Kraakman, "Reading Pornography Anew," 538–540.

102. Graffigny, *Letters from a Peruvian Woman*, 143.

103. *Histoire de la tourière des carmélites*, 20; other examples are found in *Lettres galantes et philosophiques*, 253–262.

104. *Lettres galantes et philosophiques*, 254.

105. Nina Rattner Gelbart, introduction to Bernard le Bovier de Fontenelle, *Conversations on the Plurality of Worlds*, trans. H. A. Hargreaves (Berkeley: University of California, 1990), xxvii.

106. *Histoire de Dom Bougre*, 63.

107. See Abby Zanger, "Lim(b)inal Images: 'Betwixt and between' Louis XIV's Martial and Marital Bodies," in *From the Royal to the Republic Body: Incorporating the Political in Seventeenth-and Eighteenth-Century France*, ed. Sara E. Melzer and Kathryn Norberg (Berkeley: University of California, 1998), 32–63.

108. *Vénus dans le cloître*, 325; *Le Triomphe des religieuses*, 219–220; *Les Délices du cloître*, 9–10. While the characters of *Vénus dans le cloître* and *Le Triomphe des religieuses* repudiate monastic vows as unnatural in favor of sexual activities, the "Discours préliminaire" of *Les Délices du cloître* links the misery of unwilling nuns to an excessive preoccupation with sex and their self-abandonment to "a violent and uncontrolled passion which plunges them into an abyss of impurity and terrible crimes." *Les Délices du cloître*, 10.

109. On the "family-state compact," see Sarah Hanley, "Engendering the State: Family Formation and State Building in Early Modern France," *French Historical Studies* 16 (1989): 4–27.
110. [d'Argens], *Thérèse Philosophe*, in *Oeuvres anonymes du XVIIIe siècle*, 3:54. Translation taken from Darnton, *Forbidden Best-Sellers*, 253.
111. *Les Plaisirs du cloître*, 244.
112. *Histoire de Dom Bougre*, 190.
113. *Vénus dans le cloître*, 318; *Lettres galantes et philosophiques*, 265. A brief discussion of the fictional depictions of conventual hypocrisy may be found in Jacques Rustin, *Le Vice à la mode: étude sur le roman français du XVIIIe siècle de "Manon Lescaut" à l'apparition de "La Nouvelle Héloïse" (1731–1761)* (Paris: Ophrys), 175–178.
114. *Histoire de Dom Bougre*, 83. Soeur Christine writes about having seen a sexagenarian nun having intercourse with a gardener, *Lettres galantes et philosophiques*, 236–237. Another diatribe against monastic hypocrisy is found in the "Discours préliminaire" of *Les Délices du cloître*.
115. *Histoire de la tourière des carmélites*, 82–83.
116. *Les Plaisirs du cloître*, 282. Other anti-Jesuitical observations are found in *Mémoires de Monsieur le Marquis de St*** ou les amours fugitifs du cloître*, vol. 1 (Amsterdam: Aux depens de la Compagne, 1749), 111. In the *Vie voluptueuse des Capucins*, Capuchin monks are considered the worst of all monks, 8–9.
117. *Histoire de Dom Bougre*, 63; *Lettres galantes et philosophiques*, 236; *Les Plaisirs du cloître*, 284.
118. *Lettres galantes et philosophiques*, 267, 269, 270.
119. Ibid., 247. The themes found in the *Lettres galantes et philosophiques* stand in sharp contrast with those found in the "Discours préliminaire" of *Les Délices du cloître*. The author of the latter asserts that "human nature is so corrupt that it tends toward vice; it regards virtue as a tyrant" (13).
120. G. S. Rousseau and Roy Porter, "Introduction: Toward a Natural History of Mind and Body," in *The Languages of Psyche: Mind and Body in Enlightenment Thought: Clark Library Lectures, 1985–1986*, edited by G. S. Rousseau (Berkeley: University of Berkeley, 1990), 3–44.
121. Margaret C. Jacob, "The Materialist World of Pornography," in Hunt, *Invention of Pornography*, 162.
122. Ibid., 158.
123. *Lettres galantes et philosophiques*, 286.
124. On the link between sensibility and education, see Steinbrügge, *The Moral Sex*, 99–104.
125. Jacob, "The Materialist World of Pornography," 164–175; Kraakman, "Reading Pornography Anew," 535.
126. Soeur Monique, Suzon, and the prostitute in *La Cauchoise* belong to the former category while the characters in *Le Triomphe des religieuses*, *Lettres galantes et philosophiques*, and *Les Plaisirs du cloître* find satisfaction within the convent.
127. Manuela Mourao has argued that early modern pornography was potentially empowering for women in "The Representations of Female Desire in Early Modern Pornographic Texts, 1660–175," *Signs* 24 (1999): 573–596.
128. Trouille, *Sexual Politics in the Enlightenment;* idem, "Revolution in the Boudoir: Madame Roland's Subversion of Rousseau's Feminine Ideals," *Eighteenth-Century Life* 13, no. 2 (1989): 65–86. Jean Bloch, *Rousseau and Education in Eighteenth-Century France* (Oxford: Voltaire Foundation, 1995), 19–66; Jeanne Kathryn Hageman, *"Les Conversations d'Emilie*: The Education of Women by Women in Eighteenth-Century France" (Ph.D. diss., University of Wisconsin, Madison, 1991).

6. From Victims to Fanatics

1. *L'Esprit des journaux français et étrangers* 7 (1796): 206–207, cited in Georges May, *Diderot et "La Religieuse": étude historique et littéraire* (New Haven: Yale University Press, 1954), 22.
2. *Reimpression de l'Ancien Moniteur seule authentique et inaltérée de la révolution française* (hereafter *Moniteur*), December 11, 1796, 234, cited in May, *Diderot et "La Religieuse,"* 22–23.

3. Emmet Kennedy, *A Cultural History of the French Revolution* (New Haven: Yale University Press, 1989), 145.
4. The most complete history of the revolutionary government's treatment of nuns in Paris is Jean Boussoulade, *Moniales et hospitalières dans la tourmente révolutionnaire: les communautés de religieuses de l'ancien diocèse de Paris de 1789 à 1801* (Paris: Letouzey et Ané, 1962). See also Augustin Sicard, *Le Clergé de France pendant la révolution*, vol. 1 (Paris: Victor Lecoffre, 1912), chaps. 7–10; Elizabeth Rapley, "'Pieuses Contre-Révolutionnaires': The Experience of the Ursulines of Northern France, 1789–1792," *French History* 2 (1988): 453–473; Françoise Kermina, "Quand on forçait les religieuses à choisir la liberté," *Historama* (1985): 50–54.
5. Like male monastics who departed from the monastery, the minority of nuns who chose to leave the cloister received pensions based on the decree of October 8, 1790, effective January 1, 1791. The terms of the decree stated that a sister of the choir received 700 livres per annum while a converse received 350. Abbesses received larger pensions of 1,000, 1,500, or 2,000 livres depending on the wealth of their individual abbeys.
6. John McManners, *The French Revolution and the Church* (New York: Torchbook Library, 1970), 33.
7. Olwen H. Hufton, *Women and the Limits of Citizenship in the French Revolution: The Donald G. Creighton Lectures 1989* (Toronto: University of Toronto Press 1992), 55–56.
8. Ibid., 72.
9. For an in-depth study of the revolutionary officials of 1790, see Timothy Tackett, *Becoming a Revolutionary: The Deputies of the French National Assembly and the Emergence of a Revolutionary Culture* (Princeton, N.J.: Princeton University Press, 1996).
10. Jean-Baptiste Treilhard (1742–1810) was a lawyer who stood against Maupeou and worked for the Prince de Condé; in addition to being the voice of the committee, Treilhard was briefly involved with the Directory in 1798. Ibid., 37. The Comité Ecclésiastique, created by the National Assembly in August 1789, was in charge of all ecclesiastic affairs. Similar to the Commission des Réguliers created in the 1760s, its members included a mixture of lay and ecclesiastic persons, titled and untitled. Alphonse Aulard, *La Révolution française et les congrégations: exposé historique et documents* (Paris: Edouard Conrely, 1903), 53.
11. Robert Darnton, *The Literary Underground of the Old Regime* (Cambridge: Harvard University Press, 1982).
12. For a discussion of revolutionary periodicals, see Jack Richard Censer, *Prelude to Power: The Parisian Radical Press, 1789–1791* (Baltimore: Johns Hopkins University Press, 1976); and Jeremy D. Popkin, *Revolutionary News: The Press in France, 1789–1799* (Durham, N.C.: Duke University Press, 1990). See also Carla Hesse, *Publishing and Cultural Politics in Revolutionary Paris, 1789–1810* (Berkeley: University of California Press, 1991).
13. New theaters in Paris included the Louvois, the Théâtre de Marais, and the Théâtre National de Molière. Marvin Carlson, *The Theater of the French Revolution* (Ithaca, N.Y.: Cornell University Press, 1966), chap. 3; a complete list of the new theaters and their "genealogies" may be found on 289–291. See also Kennedy, *Cultural History of the Revolution*, 168–185.
14. This trend of using clerical clothes on stage had started earlier in 1790. Carlson, *Theater of the French Revolution*, 40, 75–76.
15. Jacques-Marie Boutet de Monvel, *Les Victimes cloîtrées, drame en quatre actes et en prose* (Paris: Le Petit, 1792). The play was presented for the first time in March 1791 at the Théâtre National. Carbon de Flins des Oliviers, *Le Mari directeur, ou le deménagement du couvent, comédie en un acte* (Paris: Brunet, 1790). For reviews of *Le Mari directeur* and *Les Victimes cloîtrées*, see *Moniteur*, March 7, 1791, 560; April 1, 1791, 7. A poet and playwright, Carbon de Flins des Oliviers (1757–1806) was associated with the *Almanach des Muses*. Jacques-Marie Boutet Monvel (1745–1811?) was an associate of the Comédie-Française from 1772 to 1780, after which he spent time in Sweden working in the theater. One of the most popular "convent plays" was Louis-Picard Benoît, *Les Visitandines*, which was performed at the Feydeau between 1792 and 1794. Kennedy, *Cultural History of the French Revolution*, 274.
16. Antoine de Baecque, *The Body Politic: Corporeal Metaphor in Revolutionary France, 1770–1800*, trans. Charlotte Mandell (Stanford: Stanford University Press, 1993), 13.

17. Ibid., 15.
18. The abolition of monastic orders was not the first time female religious felt compelled to speak. A few communities had submitted *cahiers de doléances* that mostly spoke to financial needs and grievances. *1789: Cahiers de doléances des femmes et autres textes* (Paris: Des femmes, 1989), 59–69.
19. Hufton, *Women and the Limits of Citizenship*, 55–56. "La Soeur Sainte-Ange ou la victime du cloître, opéra," Bibliothèque Nationale de France, Fonds Français, ms. 9273, fols. 181–202. In addition to Boutet de Monvel's *Les Victimes cloîtrées* and Olympe de Gouges's *Le Couvent ou les voeux forcés*, other plays used the vocation forcée theme: Joseph Fiévée, *Les Rigeurs du cloître, comédie* ([Paris]: De l'Imprimerie de l'Auteur, 1790); and Marie-Joseph Chenier, *Fénélon ou ses religieuses de Cambrai, tragédie en cinq actes* (Paris: Moutard, 1793). References in pamphlets are found in the following: *Adresse aux religieuses ou dialogue entre une religieuse sortie d'un couvent, son frère, et son directeur* (n.p., 1791), 20; *Essais sur les avantages, qui résulteroient de la sécularisation, modification et suppression des monastères des filles religieuses* (London; Paris, 1789), 66; *La Chemise levée, ou visites faites à l'abbaye de Montmartre dans plusieurs maisons religieuses* (n.p., n.d.), 5; Jacques-Antoine Creuzé Latouche, *Lettre de M. Creuzé de La Touche, membre de l'Assemblée Nationale à Madame ***, ci-devant religieuse sortie de la communauté de *** ([Paris]: Imprimerie de Cusac, n.d.), 10; [Desmoutiers], *La Liberté du cloître, poème* (n.p., n.d.). Periodical references included *Moniteur,* November 29, 1789, 263; *Journal universel ou révolutions des royaumes,* September 4, 1790, 2288; September 23, 1790, 2435; *Révolutions de Paris,* February 13, 1790, 7.
20. J. M. Mavidal and M. E. Laurent, *Archives Parlementaires de 1787 à 1860: recueil complet des débats legislatives et politiques des chambres françaises,* 99 vols. (Paris: Librairie Administrative du Paul Dupont, 1879), 10:623.
21. Rapley, " 'Pieuses Contre-Révolutionnaires,' " 472–473.
22. Archives Nationales (hereafter AN), DXIX, 69, fol. 444. The letter is dated August 20, 1790. For a similar response see *Journal universel,* January–April 1791, 3528.
23. *Adresse aux religieuses,* 7; see also *Journal universel,* September 4, 1790, 2288; November 24, 1790, 2933.
24. Jean-Nicolas Billaud Varenne, *Le Dernier coup porté aux préjugés et à la superstition* (London, 1789), 23. A radical belonging to the left wing of the Jacobin club, Jean-Nicolas Billaud Varenne (1756–1819), was associated with the overthrow of the monarchy as well as the Hébertists and the sans-culottes. He was instrumental in the downfall of both Georges Danton and Maximillien Robespierre.
25. Antoine de Baecque, "The Citizen in Caricature: Past and Present," in *The French Revolution and the Meaning of Citizenship,* ed. Renée Waldinger, Philip Dawson, and Isser Woloch (Westport, Conn.: Greenwood, 1993), 63–70; idem, *Body Politic,* 157–182.
26. Caroline-Stéphanie-Félicité du Crest, countess of Genlis, *Discours sur la suppression des couvens de religieuses et sur l'éducation publique de femmes* (Paris: Onfroy, 1790), 2, 3. In her play *Le Couvent ou les Voeux Forcés,* the royalist Olympe de Gouges also made the evil mother superior an abbess. Thus, even sympathizers of the monarchy denounced the powers enjoyed by abbesses, powers the king had bestowed. Olympe de Gouges, *Oeuvres,* ed. Benoîte Groult (Paris: Mercure de France, 1989), 180–211. The play was performed unsuccessfully in October 1790 at the Théâtre Français et Lyrique. Carlson, *Theater of the Revolution,* 148.
27. Lynn Hunt, "The Many Bodies of Marie-Antoinette: Political Pornography and the Problem of the Feminine in the French Revolution," in *Eroticism and the Body Politic,* ed. Lynn Hunt (Baltimore: Johns Hopkins University Press, 1991), 119.
28. Léonard-Nicolas François Duquesnoy, *Suppression des chapîtres de femmes* (Paris: Imprimerie Nationale, n.d.), 6. A lawyer during the prerevolutionary era, Duquesnoy (1760–1794?) spoke out against the nobility and clergy at the Estates General. As a republican, Duquesnoy was a member of the Convention. But his loyalty to the Girondins resulted in his arrest. Although he escaped imprisonment, he died in exile.
29. Pierre Rétat, "The Evolution of the Citizen from the Ancien Régime to the Revolution," in *The French Revolution and the Meaning of Citizenship,* ed. Waldinger, Dawson, and Woloch, 8.

30. Jean-Paul Marat, *Oeuvres de J. P. Marat l'Ami du peuple*, ed. A. Vermorel (Paris: Décembre-Alonnier, 1869), 84. This story appeared in *L'Ami du peuple ou le publiciste Parisien*, January 5, 1790, 3–7.

31. Hufton, *Women and the Limits of Citizenship*, 73.

32. *Le clergé dévoilé pour être presenté aux Etats-généraux par un citoyen patriote* (n.p., 1789), 39. This pamphlet emphasized the male clergy but argued that all monastic institutions suffered from the same problems.

33. Creuzé Latouche, *Lettre de M. Creuzé*, 6.

34. Duquesnoy, *Suppression des chapîtres de femmes*, 2.

35. William H. Sewell Jr., *Work and Revolution in France: The Language of Labor from the Old Regime to 1848* (Cambridge: Cambridge University Press, 1980), 86–91. Cynthia Maria Truant, *The Rites of Labor: Brotherhoods of Compagnonnage in Old and New Regime France* (Ithaca, N.Y.: Cornell University Press, 1994), 195.

36. *Journal universel*, September 23, 1790, 2434. The *Journal universel* was produced single-handedly by Pierre-Jean Audouin (1764–1808), who came from the ranks of Robert Darnton's Grub Street. Although an active Jacobin and a supporter of radical revolutionaries, Audouin's own words were, according to Jack Censer, moderate. Censer, *Prelude to Power*, 17–19; Robert Darnton cites the police records on Audouin in "The High-Enlightenment and the Low-Life of Literature," in *The Literary Underground*, 26

37. *Le Soeur Ste. Ange*, Bibliothèque Nationale de France, Fonds Français, ms. 9273, fol. 185. See also Olympe de Gouges, *Le Couvent, ou les voeux forcés* in *Olympe de Gouges, Théâtre* (Cocagne: Centre National de Lettres, 1993), 215. For examples of journalistic diatribes against parents, see *Révolutions de Paris*, February 13, 1790, 7; *Journal universel*, April 6, 1791, 3996–3997; *Le Toneau de Diogène, ou les révolutions du clergé* (Paris: Brune, 1790), n. 29, 226–229.

38. *De la nécessité de supprimer les monastères* (Paris: Garnery et Volland, 1790), 27.

39. Hans-Jürgen Lüsebrink and Rolf Reichardt, *The Bastille: A History of a Symbol of Despotism and Freedom*, trans. Norbert Schürer (Durham, N.C.: Duke University Press, 1997),79

40. [Desmoutiers], "La Liberté du cloître, poème," 23.

41. *De la nécessité de supprimer les monastères*, 27.

42. Rétat, "Evolution of the Citizen," 13.

43. Ibid., 3.

44. *Révolutions de Paris*, February 13, 1790, 8.

45. *Essais sur les avantages*, 5.

46. Ibid., 6; [Groubentall de Limière], *L'Anti-Moine ou considerations politiques, sur les moyens et la nécessité d'abolir les ordres monastiques en France* (n.p., 1790), 68. Groubentall (1739–1815) was an *homme de lettres* associated with writers such Dulaurens. Although he was not active during the Revolution, he was imprisoned in the Bastille briefly in 1762.

47. On the discussion of female education see Hubert du Maligny, *Traité philosophique, théologique et politique de la loi de divorce demandé aux Etats par S. A. S. Monseigneur Louis-Philippe Joseph d'Orléans* (n.p., 1789), 67; *Révolutions de Paris*, September 17, 1790, 474–475.

48. *Le Toneau de Diogène*, n. 12, 91.

49. *Journal universel*, August 8, 1790, 2498; *Essais sur les avantages*, 66–67.

50. Marvin Carlson has noted that a recurrent theme in the theater was the reunion of a nun with her "republican" lover. In the case of Julie's lover, the Chevalier, while not a "republican," is certainly in favor of the Revolution. Carlson, "The Citizen in the Theater," 83.

51. Madelyn Gutwirth, "*Citoyens, Citoyennes*: Cultural Regression and the Subversion of Female Citizenship in the French Revolution," in *French Revolution and the Meaning of Citizenship*, ed. Waldinger, Dawson, and Woloch, 22–26.

52. [Groubentall de Limière], *L'Anti-Moine*, 25.

53. *Journal universel*, September 4, 1790, 2288.

54. Fortin de Melleville, *Le Te Deum des religieux et des religieuses, en actions de grâces des décrets bienfaisans de l'Assemblée Nationale* (n.p, n.d.), 1.

55. Lynn Hunt, *The Family Romance of the French Revolution* (Berkeley: University of California Press, 1992), 40–43.

56. De Gouges, *Le Couvent*, 209–211; Fiévée, *Les Rigeurs du cloître*, 40; Boutet de Monvel, *Les Victimes cloîtrées*, 55–56.

57. Suzanne Desan, *Reclaiming the Sacred: Lay Religion and Popular Politics in Revolutionary France* (Ithaca, N.Y.: Cornell University Press, 1990), 122–164.

58. Ibid., 643. Samary's speech was also circulated in a pamphlet titled *Reclamation en faveur des ordres religieux* (Paris: Imprimerie Nationale, n.d.), 7–8. In addition to being a well-known curé in Carcassonne, Samary (1731–1803) was an *homme de lettres* who dabbled in poetry. A deputy for the First Estate, he refused the oath and went into exile in Rome.

59. Henri Jabineau, *Lettres d'un ami de province, sur les destructions des ordres* (n.p., 1790?), 4, 24. Henri Jabineau (d. 1792) was a religious lawyer involved in the prerevolutionary parlementary quarrels.

60. Lievain-Bonaventure Proyart, *Considérations sur l'existence des religieuses en France* (Paris, Brussels, 1790), 16. Proyart (1743–1808) was an ecclesiastic devoted to pedagogy. Because of his pro-monarchical sentiments, he was deported to the Low Countries in the later years of the Revolution.

61. *Adresse à l'Assemblée Nationale de la part des carmélites de France, de la reforme de Sainte-Thérèse* (Marseilles: P. A. Faret, 1790), 3.

62. Proyart, *Considérations sur l'existence des religieuses en France*, 10.

63. *Adresse à l'Assemblée Nationale de la part des religieuses du monastère de l'Assomption* (n.p., n.d.), 4.

64. *Requête à l'Assemblée Nationale de la part des religieuses de la Visitation Sainte-Marie de France* (Paris, [1789]), 2.

65. *Adresse de la part des carmélites*, 2; *Adresse à l'Assemblée Nationale de la part des religieuses Bénédictines de l'Adoration pérpetuelle du très-saint sacrement de l'autel, du second monastère de Paris; établie rue Saint Louis au Marais* (n.p., n.d.), 2; *Adresse de la part des religieuses de l'Assomption*, 3.

66. *Adresse de la part des religieuses Bénédictines*, 1; *Adresse de la part des religieuses de l'Assomption*, 6.

67. *Adresse de la part des religieuses de l'Assomption*, 4; *Adresse de la part des religieuses Bénédictines*, 1.

68. The nuns represented four different convents. *Adresse des religieuses à l'Assemblée Nationale qui se sont rendues aux devoirs de la société* (Paris: Moutart, [1789]), 3.

69. *Plainte de la mère Saint-Clément, religieuse de l'hôtel-dieu, et plainte de toute sa communauté; contre le sieur Boulet, chirugien dudit hôtel-dieu* (Paris: Herissant, 1790), 3.

70. AN, DXIX, 13, no. 203, fol. 1. For a similar example, see the letter by Catherine Grelet from Cognac, AN, DXI, 62, no. 6.

71. AN, DXIX, 66, no. 89.

72. AN, DXIX, 25, no. 389, no. 18.

73. AN, DXIX, 79, no. 20.

74. AN, DXIX, 63, no. 33.

75. For an example of the former, see a letter, dated August 9, 1790, by Séraphine, novice of the Religieuses Concéptionistes of Béthune, AN, DXIX, 66, no. 58. An example of the latter request was made by the community of Saint-Nicolas in Lorraine in a letter dated May 12, 1790, AN, DXIX, 58, no. 248.

76. AN, DXIX, 79, no. 2, fol. 592.

77. Boussoulade, *Moniales et Hospitalières*, 67.

78. Timothy Tackett, *Religion, Revolution, and Regional Culture in Eighteenth-Century France: The Ecclesiastical Oath of 1791* (Princeton, N.J.: Princeton University Press, 1986), 25.

79. The following discussion is taken from Darlene Gay Levy, "Women's Revolutionary Citizenship in Action, 1791: Setting the Boundaries," in *French Revolution and the Meaning of Citizenship*, ed. Waldinger, Dawson, and Woloch, 169–184.

80. Ibid., 182–183.

81. Hufton, *Women and the Limits of Citizenship*, 71.

82. Joan Landes, *Visualizing the Nation: Gender, Representation, and Revolution in Eighteenth-Century France* (Ithaca, N.Y.: Cornell University Press, 2001), 49–52; William Doyle, *The Oxford History of the French Revolution* (Oxford: Oxford University, 1990), 48; H. M. Delasart,

La Dernière abbesse de Montmartre Marie-Louise de Montmorency-Laval, 1723–1794 (Paris: Lethielleux, 1921), 76–77.

83. *Journal universel,* April 10, 1791, 4027–4029.

84. AN, FN 612/3, "Section de la Croix Rouge." Hufton, *Women and the Limits of Citizenship,* 73; Boussoulade, *Moniales et Hospitalières,* 74–83. *Moniteur,* April 10, 1791, 87; April 12, 1790, 101. An undated letter from the director of the Department of Paris to the Ministry of the Interior indicates that officials did not welcome the attacks on women religious. According to the author, "the reign of liberty is only the reign of law." AN, F19, 209.

85. An example of this equivocation is a letter written in May 31, 1791, by the minister of the interior, de Lessart, to the directors of all departments. Responding to a printed appeal written by the Sisters of Charity, the letter, also printed, defended the right of the sisters to continue their duties. AN, F19, 470. Other moderates released similar statements. For example, in a consultation for nuns from the diocese of Tours, the lawyer T. J. A. Cottereau argued that nuns, like all other citizens, "were entitled to their individual religious opinions and freedom of conscience," rights protected by decrees issued on April 13, 1790. [T. J. A. Cottereau], *Consultation pour les religieuses du diocèse de Tours au sujet de l'evêque élu dans le département de l'Indre et Loire* (Paris: Guerbart, 1791), 1, 5.

86. *Journal universel,* September 23, 1790, 2434; *Révolutions de Paris,* February 13, 1790, 8n.

87. *Journal universel,* April 6, 1791, 3995; April 7, 1791, 4007.

88. Ibid., February 16, 1791, 3607; April 7, 1791, 4007; Jacques-René Hébert, "Grand Complot du père Duchesne de foutre le fouet aux dévots et dévotés . . . ," in *Le Père Duchesne, 1790–1794,* ed. Albert Soboul, 10 vols. (Paris: EDHIS, 1969), 2–3, 5.

89. Loyseau, *Coup d'oeil sur les tentatives, aussi ridicules que sédietieuses, des prêtres refractoires au serment préscrit par la constitution civil du clergé* (n.p, 1791), 12–13.

90. *Liste de tous les soeurs et dévotes qui ont été fouetées par le dames des marchés des différens quartiers de Paris* (Paris: Tremblay, n.d.), 2.

91. *Révolutions de Paris,* June 11, 1791, 510–511.

92. On the women of Paris during the French Revolution, see Dominique Godineau, *The Women of Paris and Their French Revolution,* trans. Katherine Streip (Berkeley: University of California Press, 1998). For a broader discussion of the fate of women during the Revolution see Joan B. Landes, *Women and the Public Sphere in the Age of the French Revolution* (Ithaca, N.Y.: Cornell University Press, 1988), 93–151; Hunt, *Family Romance,* chap. 4.

93. The *Lettres bougrement patriotiques de la mère Duchesne* received its inspiration from the *Lettres bougrement patriotiques du Père Duchesne* of Antoine Lemaire, one of a number of journals entitled *Père Duchesne* that purported to be the voice of the sans-culottes. The former appeared between February and April of 1791. Ouzi Elyada, "Préface: La presse patriotique pour les femmes du Paris," in *Lettres bougrement patriotiques de la mère Duchesne suivi de "Journal des Femmes 1791,"* ed. Elyada (Paris: Editions de Paris/EDHIS, 1989), 8–9.

94. *Lettres bougrement patriotiques de la mère Duchesne,* 124, 127, 125.

95. According to Olwen Hufton, "feminine *sans-culotterie* embodied a notion of citizenship for women which was not passive and which called upon them to be vigilant in the elimination of the internal enemy whilst their sons fought at the front." *Women and the Limits of Citizenship,* 22.

96. Elyada, "Préface," 11.

97. In the Legislative Assembly, there were only twenty clergy, all of whom had taken the oath.

98. Rapley, "'Pieuses Contre-révolutionnaires,'" 467.

99. *Archives Parlementaires,* 37:155–156.

100. As cited in McManners, *French Revolution and the Church,* 65.

101. *Archives Parlementaires,* 37:156.

102. Aulard, *La Révolution française et les congrégations,* 189.

103. Ibid., 224, 195.

104. Ibid., 186–187. Deputy Laureau concurred and argued that to "free" nuns from the cloister would place them in "true captivity." Ibid., 188.

105. Hufton, *Women and the Limits of Citizenship,* 142.

106. Rapley, "'Pieuses Contre-Révolutionnaires,'" 467.

107. Gaudin specifically mentions the Filles de la Sagesse, Filles Saint-Thomas, Soeurs de la

Providence, and Filles de l'Union. Aulard, *La Révolution française et les congrégations*, 225–226.

108. Ibid., 190; italics added. Aulard states that there was no such deputy attached to the Legislative Assembly. The Henry in question may have been Pierre-Paul Henry from Cantal or François-Joseph Henry from the Haute-Marne.

109. When nuns were forced to abandon their convents in September 1792, many of them chose to live in small groups in the town where their convent was located. As a result, nuns were able to maintain their rules and thereby live as a religious community. Boussoulade, *Moniales et hospitalières*, 127–134.

110. Hufton, *Women and the Limits of Citizenship*, 73–81.

111. *Discours de Madame de Lévi de Mirepoix, abbesse des religieuses bénédictines de Montargis, âgée de vingt-sept ans; en réponse aux officiers du district de cette ville, entrant par force dans sa maison* (n.p., n.d.), 1, 4.

112. During 1792 and 1793, the Benedictines of Montargis left France for England in small groups; the abbess herself barely managed to escape the guillotine.

113. The documents pertaining to the arrest are found in AN, F7, 4615, no. 15 and AN, W, 354 12, no. 1854. The statement is found in the "bulletin du 21 Germinal." The two sisters were executed 9 Floréal, Year II.

114. Document of arrest in AN, F7, 4617, no. 15.

115. AN, W, 354 12, no. 1854.

116. *Archives Parlementaires*, 75:497. As the chairman of the National Convention's legislative committee, Jean-Baptiste Mailhe worked against the king, eventually casting the first vote in favor of the king's execution. See David P. Jordan, *The King's Trial: The French Revolution vs. Louis XVI* (Berkeley: University of California Press, 1979), 63–65, 183–185.

117. Desan, *Reclaiming the Sacred*, 227.

118. Hunt, *Family Romance*, 122.

119. AN, W, 431, fols. 969–971. She was executed on 6 Thermidor, Year II.

120. Lynn Hunt, *Politics, Culture, and Class in the French Revolution* (Berkeley: University of California Press, 1984).

121. For examples of Parisian communities, see Boussoulade, *Moniales et hospitalières*, 154–160.

122. As quoted in Marie André, *La véridique histoire des carmélites de Compiègne* (Paris: Editions Saint-Paul, 1962), 31. Once in prison, the Compiègne Carmelites repudiated their oath.

123. Ibid., 21.

CONCLUSION

1. Olwen H. Hufton, *Women and the Limits of Citizenship in the French Revolution: The Donald G. Creighton Lectures 1989* (Toronto: University of Toronto Press, 1992), 99.

2. The Bishop of Metz published the first account of the sixteen Carmelites, which was followed by other works including one by a survivor of the community, Sister Marie de l'Incarnation. Twentieth-century histories, many of which are written by clerics, all approach the subject with reverence. For examples, see Victor Pierre, *Les Seize Carmélites de Compiègne* (Paris: Librairie Victor Lecoffre, 1905); Dom Louis David, *Les Seize Carmélites de Compiègne: leur martyre et leur béatification 17 juillet 1794–27 mai 1906* (Paris: H. Oudin, 1906); Bruno de J.-M., *Le Sang du Carmel, ou la véritable passion des seize carmélites de Compiègne* (Paris: Editions de Cerfs, 1992); William Bush, ed., *La Relation du martyre des seize carmélites de Compiègne aux sources de Bernanos et de Gertrud von Le Fort* (Paris: Editions de Cerfs, 1993).

3. On Camille de Seycourt (1757–1849), see Jean Boussoulade, *Moniales et hospitalières dans la tourmente révolutionnaire: les communautés de religieuses de l'ancien diocèse de Paris de 1789 à 1801* (Paris: Letouzey et Ané, 1962), 132–133; John McManners, *The French Revolution and the Church* (New York: Torchbook Library, 1970), 129. Thanks to friends, Camille de Seyecourt was released from prison on May 11, 1793.

4. Rebecca Rogers, "Competing Visions of Girls' Secondary Education in Post-Revolutionary France," *History of Education Quarterly* 34 (1994): 167.

5. Caroline Ford, "Private Lives and Public Order in Restoration France: The Seduction of

Emily Loveday," *American Historical Review* 99 (1994): 41; Susan O'Brien, "French Nuns in Nineteenth-Century England," *Past and Present* 154 (1997): 142.

6. O'Brien, "French Nuns in Nineteenth-Century England," 143; Ralph Gibson, *A Social History of French Catholicism, 1789–1914* (London: Routledge, 1989), 105–106.

7. Gibson, *Social History of French Catholicism*, 106–107.

8. Ibid., 124.

9. Rebecca Rogers, "Retrograde or Modern? Unveiling the Teaching Nun in Nineteenth-Century France," *Social History* 23 (May 1998): 149. See also idem, "Boarding Schools, Women Teachers, and Domesticity: Reforming Girls' Secondary Education in the First Half of the Nineteenth Century," *French Historical Studies* 19 (1995): 153–181; idem, "Reconsidering the Role of Religious Orders in Modern French Women's Education," *Vitae Scholasticae* 10 (1991): 43–51. For a brief summary of the Third Republic's action against religious orders, see Gibson, *Social History of French Catholicism*, 128. Two critical pieces of legislation were the 1886 Goblet Law which installed lay personnel in the place of *congrégationistes*, and the July 7, 1904, law which shut down religious teaching orders entirely.

10. On the importance of women to nineteenth-century Catholicism, see, for example, Olwen Hufton, "The Reconstruction of a Church, 1796–1801," in *Beyond Terror: Essays in French Regional and Social History, 1794–1815*, ed. Gwynne Lewis and Colin Lucas (Cambridge: Cambridge University Press, 1983), 21–52; Claude Langlois, *Le Catholicisme au féminin: les congrégations françaises à supérieure générale au XIXe siècle* (Paris: Cerf, 1984); Odile Arnold, *Le Corps et l'âme: la vie des religieuses au XIXe siècle* (Paris: Seuil, 1984); Ralph Gibson, "Le Catholicisme et les femmes en France au XIXe siècle," *Revue d'histoire de l'Eglise de France* 79 (1993): 63–93.

11. Rogers, "Retrograde or Modern?" 148.

12. Nigel Aston, *Religion and Revolution in France, 1780–1804* (Washington, D.C.: Catholic University Press, 2000), 348–349.

13. Rogers, "Retrograde or Modern?" 149.

14. Maurice Agulhon, *The Republican Experiment, 1848–1852*, trans. Janet Lloyd (Cambridge: Cambridge University Press, 1983), 189.

15. Ford, "Private Lives and Public Order," 41.

16. Rogers, "Retrograde or Modern?" 149.

17. Ford, "Private Lives and Public Order," 41.

18. Ibid., 23.

19. Rogers, "Reconsidering the Role of Religious Orders," 50.

20. Ford, "Private Lives and Public Order," 42–43; Rogers, "Competing Visions of Girls' Secondary Education," 169.

INDEX

Italic page numbers refer to illustrations.